Wilfried Raussert, Olaf Kaltmeier (eds.)

InterAmerican Perspectives in the 21st Century

Festschrift in Honor of Josef Raab

INTER-AMERICAN STUDIES
Cultures – Societies – History

ESTUDIOS INTERAMERICANOS
Culturas – Sociedades – Historia

Volume 23

Wilfried Raussert, Olaf Kaltmeier (eds.)

InterAmerican Perspectives in the 21st Century

Festschrift in Honor of Josef Raab

WVT Wissenschaftlicher Verlag Trier

Copublished by

UNO University of New Orleans Press

InterAmerican Perspectives in the 21st Century.
Festschrift in Honor of Josef Raab /
Wilfried Raussert, Olaf Kaltmeier (eds.). –
(Inter-American Studies | Estudios Interamericanos; 23)
Trier: WVT Wissenschaftlicher Verlag Trier, 2021
ISBN 978-3-86821-803-9
New Orleans, LA: University of New Orleans Press, 2021
ISBN 978-1-60801-211-4

Cover Image: Luis Quintero

Cover Design: Brigitta Disseldorf

Library of Congress Cataloging-in-Publication Data

Names: Raussert, Wilfried, editor. | Kaltmeier, Olaf, 1970- editor. | Raab, Josef, honouree.
Title: Interamerican perspectives in the 21st century : Festschrift in honor of Josef Raab / ed. Wilfried Raussert and Olaf Kaltmeier.
Description: [New Orleans] : Wissenschaftlicher Verlag Trier ; copublished by University of New Orleans Press, [2021] | Series: Interamerican studies ; 23 | Includes bibliographical references. | Summary: "This collection of scholarly essays presents recent lines of research and results in the field of hemispheric InterAmerican Studies. The book also opens new perspectives for future research. The collection of essays is interdisciplinary and brings together historical, film, literary and cultural studies approaches to the Americas. Renowned scholars and young researchers make this book a cross-disciplinary anthology highly suitable for scholars and students"-- Provided by publisher.
Identifiers: LCCN 2021009124 | ISBN 9781608012114 (paperback)
Subjects: LCSH: America--Civilization. | America--History. | America--Literatures. | Performing arts--America. | Cross-cultural studies--America.
Classification: LCC E20 .I5757 2021 | DDC 970--dc23
LC record available at https://lccn.loc.gov/2021009124

Publisher: WVT Wissenschaftlicher Verlag Trier, Postfach 4005, D-54230 Trier, Bergstraße 27, D-54295 Trier, Tel. 0049 651 41503, Fax 41504, www.wvttrier.de, wvt@wvttrier.de

Copublisher: University of New Orleans Press, 2000 Lakeshore Drive, Earl K. Long Library, Room 221, New Orleans, LA 70148, United States, 504-280-7457, unopress.org

Table of Content

Introduction

WILFRIED RAUSSERT

This book is in honor and memory of Josef Raab, a dedicated scholar, an academic leader, an intellectual with a clear vision, a mentor with a warm-hearted personality, and a good friend to many of us. Sadly, Josef Raab left us on November 10th 2019 after a long struggle with severe health issues. This book includes his own inspiring writing and extends his academic vision of InterAmerican Studies by bringing together new scholarly work in the field. Most of the contributors are close companions who worked intensively with him during his academic career.

Josef Raab was among the first in German American Studies to recognize the need to think North America, Latin America, and the Caribbean in relation and dialogue. His academic career in a way predestined his hemispheric approach to the Americas. After a solid German academic education at the Catholic University of Eichstätt with several stays abroad in England, Spain, and France, he completed MA and PhD programs at the University of Southern California in Los Angeles. His California experience with additional teaching stints in Texas brought him into close contact with Chicanx literature and cultures and paved the way for a deep interest in interAmerican border studies. Together with his mentor Roland Hagenbüchle and in collaboration with Marietta Messmer, he edited the two volume project *Negotiations of America's National Identity* in 2000 and, around the same time, completed his postdoctoral study *Borderlands of Identity in Mexican American Literature* with his habilitation at the Catholic University of Eichstätt-Ingolstadt.

He brought his intercultural competence into the fabric of Bielefeld University during his professorship from 2000 until 2004 and nourished the vision of future InterAmerican Studies in collaboration with Sebastian Thies and other colleagues at Bielefeld University. The MA program InterAmerican Studies at Bielefeld University started in the fall of 2006 when Josef was already chair of American Studies at the University of Duisburg-Essen (2004–2019). He returned to Bielefeld for several interdisciplinary and bilingual conferences at the Center for Interdisciplinary Research (ZiF): "E Pluribus Unum: Ethnic Identities in Transnational Integration Processes in the Americas" (2005), "Of Fatherlands and Motherlands: Gender and Nation in the Americas/De Patrias y Matrias: Género y nación en las Américas" (2006), and "ImagiNations/ImagiNaciones: Documentaries and the Narration of Nation in the Americas: El cine documental y la narración de la nación en las Américas" (2008). With the ZiF group "E Pluribus Unum" (coordinated by him, Olaf Kaltmeier, and Sebastian Thies), he continued his dialogue with the growing field of InterAmerican Studies at Bielefeld University and advanced the cause of hemispheric American Studies. As the Founding President of the International Association of Inter-American Studies (2009), he welcomed *forum for inter-american research (fiar)*, the online journal founded by Wilfried Raussert, his successor as chair of American Studies at Bielefeld University, as the official bilingual journal of the International Association of Inter-American Studies. In 2011, he attended the opening conference of the Center for InterAmerican Studies (CIAS) that was co-founded by Olaf Kaltmeier and Wilfried Raussert, and continued working closely with the CIAS and the members of the Advisory Board of the International Association of Inter-American Studies. Together, they have expanded a network of scholars around the globe that would develop new paradigms, concepts, and visions for InterAmerican Studies and turn them into a prospering field of scholarship and dialogue.

From 2008 until 2019, Josef Raab was chief editor (with Olaf Kaltmeier and Sebastian Thies) of the series *Inter-American Studies/Estudios interamericanos* at WVT/ Bilingual Press (now WVT/UNO Press) which has brought forth more than 30 volumes dedicated to inter-American scholarship since 2008. He also joined the editorial group of the Routledge series *InterAmerican Research: Contact, Communication, Conflict* launched by Olaf Kaltmeier and Wilfried Raussert in 2015. He continued working with colleagues from Bielefeld and international scholars in the project Entangled Americas that was funded by the Federal Ministry of Research and Education (BMBF) from 2013–2019. As co-editor, in spite of his severe illness and with great spirit, he managed to complete *The Routledge Handbook to the History and Society of the Americas* that was published in the spring of 2019 as part of the Entangled Americas project.

Josef Raab was among the key figures in the hemispheric turn within the discipline of American Studies in Germany that has led to the founding of a number of new research centers, including, among others, the Center for InterAmerican Studies at Bielefeld University (Germany), the Center for the Americas at the University of Groningen (The Netherlands), the Center for the Americas at the University of Graz (Austria), and the Center for Inter-American Studies at the University of Innsbruck (Austria). In addition, France has established a nation-wide research institute called Institut des Amériques in 2007, and, on a global scale, this approach has found its most visible representation in the founding of the International Association of Inter-American Studies in 2009.

In one of our last personal conversations with Josef Raab, when we visited him in his home in April 2019, we addressed pending issues and future challenges for Inter-American Studies. The field faces new tests in contemporary times of crisis that manifest themselves throughout the Americas. The United States of America have turned into a deeply divided and conflicted society, not only between Republicans and Democrats. Mexico is struggling hard to overcome the ongoing violence and corruption of the drug war and narcopolitics. Protests in Chile, Columbia, Ecuador, Argentina, and Brazil reflect deep economic crisis, political shifts from left to right, and demonstrate that the whole continent faces turmoil, violence, and increasing inequality. U.S. interventionism once more appears on the rise as Latin American governments face tough challenges and often seem to fail in times of crisis. These recent developments underscore the importance of interAmerican research and inquiry. Josef Raab would certainly agree that we need to continue this dialogic interAmerican project to better grasp how these locally and globally motivated changes and processes are embedded within a strong interconnectedness between the South and the North. The essays included address various dimensions of the field and directly and indirectly express our gratefulness in memory of a dedicated and passionate scholar.

Abstracts

Josef Raab's "Neither Same nor Separate: Hemispheric Horizons of American Studies" appears as a republication in a slightly revised version here and addresses the hemispheric turn in American Studies that will uncover what Euro-American Studies may have overlooked, namely the ways in which U.S. power monopoly and other power inequalities in the Americas have affected individuals, communities, and nations in the hemisphere. Raab considered this essay his most important contribution to rethinking American Studies in a hemispheric perspective. He argues that in exploring the inter-American contexts of [U.S.] American power, a hemispherically informed American Studies will not try to see the rest of the Americas through the lens of the U.S.A., its culture, and academic practices, but will be open to testing the findings of Canadian, Caribbean, and Latin American Studies.

Stefan Rinke, in his essay "The Power of Perceptions: Theodore Roosevelt, Latin America, and the European Powers, 1898–1909," explores changes in the balance of power for politics in the Americas. After victory in the Spanish-American war, the United States emerged as a great power on the scene of international politics. The balance of power in the world system changed profoundly and so did the perceptions that global players maintained of each other. While a lot of research has been done on the history of international relations during these years, we still know little about perceptions and even less about their impact on foreign policy. It is Rinke's hypothesis that perceptions and images of the other and of oneself played an important role in international politics in the era of imperialism. Between 1898 and 1908, the incarnation of the youthful and exuberant United States was Theodore Roosevelt. In a way, he personified the self-image of a large proportion of Americans and many identified with him. Roosevelt's views of leading powers like Germany, France, and Great Britain and European images of Roosevelt thus serve as a case study to approach the complex reality of perceptions.

In "Breaking the Vicious Circle of Gang-Related Violence: Central American Minors and the Current U.S. Refugee Regime," Marietta Messmer analyzes the current U.S. refugee practice through the lens of unaccompanied Central American minors, arguing that (1) the U.S.'s current refugee practice tends to be overdetermined by its immigration policy priorities (focused on enforcement), in this way contributing to the escalation of the vicious circle of gang-related transnational violence; and that (2) children have repeatedly been reconceptualized in U.S. legal refugee discourse since the 1990s but have never been conceived of as agents in their own right. In this way, the (still too strongly) adult-centered U.S. refugee regime systematically disenfranchises minors by denying them the capacity for agency. Drawing on M. Aryah Somers, Pedro Herrera, and Lucia Rodriguez's survey of legal constructions of childhood, Messmer demonstrates how the U.S. refugee regime has shifted from conceptualizing child refugees as dependent upon special protection during the 1990s, towards a more ambivalent framing of them as both vulnerable and potentially threatening after 9/11, while the administration under President Donald Trump has practically reduced unaccompanied Central American minors almost entirely to a national security risk. Messmer contends that the current U.S. refugee practice needs to return to a more balanced framing of Central American minors that acknowledges their complex situation, but most importantly, it also needs to recognize these adolescents' capacity for autonomous agency in the context of resisting gang-recruitment. Such a reconceptualization of unaccompanied Central American minors within the current U.S. regime's refugee policy could arguably contribute substantially to a reduction of the gang-related transnational violence that is currently spiraling out of control throughout the northern triangle countries.

Olaf Kaltmeier, in his essay "From Color to Whiteness: Thinking the Transfiguration of the Political Body in the Americas from Evo Morales and Barack Obama to Jair Bolsonaro and Donald Trump," analyzes the transformation of the representation of the political body taking the examples of Barack Obama and Evo Morales from 2004 to the end of the 2010s. It draws on Josef Raab's approach to analyze the field of identity politics through the visual representation of political leaders and the seminal works of Ernst Kantorowicz and Claude Lefort on political representation. It focuses first on political representation in Bolivia in the context of the election of Evo Morales, using two film posters as points of reference; second, on the transformation of the patterns of political representation with the recent turn to the right. This essay concludes with a discussion of the political impact of the dramatically changing mechanism of political representation for those segments of the political community who have benefitted most from the democratic opening of the 1990s/2002s, namely ethnic and indigenous groups, popular/impoverished sectors of society, and women.

In the chapter "Cecilia Absatz's *Los años pares* or the Challenge of Reevaluating Autochthonous Latinamericanism," Luz Angélica Kirschner studies Absatz's novel *Los años pares* [The Even-Numbered Years] (1985) to explore the limitations of dichotomous approaches, whether Eurocentric or autochthonous, to national identity formation that seek to redefine collective Latin American identity discourses. Kirschner's analysis reveals how Absatz's anti-essentialist and feminist critique of Latin American identity discourses eventually fails to resolve the dialectical tension between the Western "center" and the Latin American "periphery," thereby bringing her project close to the very oppositional, conservative, and essentialist versions of Latinamericanism that her work endeavors to challenge.

Isabel Caldeira, in her essay "Reclaiming Voices and Bodies of the Nobodies: The Transformation of Silence into Language and Action," offers rereadings of writings on the Middle Passage. Along with a continued inequality in access to civil rights and discrimination in all the societies with a colonial past, Afro-descendants are also marked by invisibility and silencing in the historical records. Besides the fact that much of the experience related to the lives of slaves was never registered or was erased, many lives were lost in the Atlantic Ocean during the slave traffic, buried in eternal silence. In this chapter, Caldeira analyzes several literary texts from the context of the Americas that break that silence and claim the bodies that never received a proper burial. Herman Melville, Robert Hayden, Édouard Glissant, NourbeSe Philip offer the examples of representations of the Middle Passage that Caldeira chooses to reread, finding in them different ways of tying together aesthetics and ethics in an attempt to humanize those dehumanized bodies, furnish the gaps of memory through the imagination, and in the process retell the history of colonial violence.

In "Saint or Scoundrel? Remembering and Representing Padre Martínez in Early (Auto)Biography and Fiction," Astrid Haas explores selected (auto)biographical and fictional representations of the eminent priest and politician Padre Antonio José Martínez of Taos who is known primarily for his antagonism to the bishop of New Mexico. He is held in high esteem among Latina/o New Mexicans to this day as a community activist and educator and has become the subject of several scholarly biographies since the mid-twentieth century. The present essay addresses the complexity of written representations of the padre preceding these scholarly assessments. It studies selected (auto)biographical and fictional representations of Martínez's life and work from his lifetime to the interwar years. Discussing these works against the backdrop of the changing historical contexts, Haas argues that they paint a contradictory picture of this historical figure in line with their respective poetic-political agendas for distinct target audiences.

In "Of Love Songs, Open Wounds, and (Almost) Everything In-Between: Borderlands and InterAmerican Literature," Saskia Hertlein engages with Josef Raab's contributions on borderlands, especially – but not exclusively – concerning the U.S.-Mexican border. She argues that despite the many challenges and obstacles that an interAmerican approach to literature possibly entails (issues as diverse as linguistic and disciplinary training as well as questions of foci or the prioritizing of specific perspectives, backgrounds, or materials), this endeavor is promising both as a truly interdisciplinary approach and as a means to continuously expand the schemas – as in Paula L.M. Moya's *Social Imperative* linking schema theory and close reading. The approach may thereby relate to both materials which involve border crossings, or to a border-crossing approach to materials, along with a continuous reconsideration of what an "interAmerican" approach entails. Either way, the dictum "Let us think differently!" and Josef Raab's transfer of the original quote from Chang Rae Lee's *Native Speaker* to his own work concerning Mexican American/Chicano literature is used as a continuous reminder challenging us to (re-)consider our potential blind spots in our engagement with both "interAmerican" literature and literature in our respective fields, thereby emphasizing the reciprocal contribution such a mode of thinking may provide both to the emerging field and the fields in which the individual scholars originated. Overall, the (examples of) "love songs," "open wounds," and "(almost) everything in-between" therefore do not only provide us with a diverse range of materials and issues with which to engage, but also provide incentives to further expand our schemas, and to recognize the inherent – and noteworthy – diversity of materials and approaches, beyond potential stereotypical or oversimplifying modes of thinking.

The central objective of Francisco A. Lomelí's "Political Organization at the Grass-Roots Level in Oscar Zeta Acosta's *The Revolt of the Cockroach People*" is to analyze the novel in order to better understand how the text depicts grass-roots political organization within the Chicano Movement. Although at times enigmatic because of the contradictory protagonist, the work nonetheless unveils the revolutionary spirit of the times between the end of the 1960s and early 1970s. Zeta Brown leads efforts to challenge the police, the church, and political officials because of their unfair way of ignoring the Chicano community. He attempts to empower various sectors of the community, mainly students, but then we discover the internal turmoil of the protagonist and the inner contradictions of his actions. He speaks one way but rarely acts consistently with what he professes. The novel, then, focuses on his personal flaws while unveiling the inner workings of political action in an urban setting (Los Angeles). The work offers a good example for Chicanos of the difficulties of achieving complete decolonialization within a system that they had upheld for so long.

In her contribution "The Politics of Remembering in Carmen Aguirre's *The Refugee Hotel*," Gabriele Pisarz-Ramirez discusses the politics of remembering in Aguirre's play. "It takes courage to remember, it takes courage to forget. It takes a hero to do both," the sentences that open Canadian-Latina playwright Aguirre's *The Refugee Hotel* emphasize the difficulties of remembering and forgetting both on a personal level and in the public sphere. Nearly 30 years after General Augusto Pinochet seized power in Chile, Aguirre in her comedic drama revisits the history of Chilean exiles who fled in the wake of the September 1973 military coup that overturned the government of Salvador Allende. Written in 2000, *The Refugee Hotel* was produced by Marilo Nuñez and the Alameda Theater Company in Toronto where it premiered at Theatre Passe Muraille in October 2009. It received a nomination for the prestigious Dora Mavor Moore Award, an important Canadian theater prize, for Outstanding New Play in 2010. Set in Vancouver, the play dramatizes the agony, concerns, and survival strategies of a group of Chileans who come to Canada after their escape from the military regime and who are sheltered in a residential hotel. Aguirre explores the individual forms and public politics of remembrance and interrogates the trauma of exile, while her play and its production history also address questions of (in)visibility with respect to the Latina/o community in Canada and within the field of Latino/a and InterAmerican Studies.

Juliana Fillies Testa Muñoz's essay "Silence and Voice in Villanueva's *Scene from the Movie GIANT*" addresses Tino Villanueva as one of the most important contemporary Chicano writers. His collection of poems *Scene from the Movie GIANT* received the American Book Award in 1994 and is considered one of his most important works. The scholars Juan Bruce-Novoa, Maher A. Mahdi, and Julián Olivares have observed that silence and voice are essential aspects of Villanueva's poetry. This essay raises the hypothesis that this dichotomy is particularly manifested in the poetic collection *Scene from the Movie GIANT*, in which, we propose, the poet gradually breaks silences and conquers his voice. The studies of the mentioned scholars, as well as the concept of memory proposed by Walter Benjamin, shall serve in this article as theoretical basis for the analysis of the collection. The purpose of this essay is to demonstrate how the process of breaking the silence and taking ownership of the word takes place in *Scene from the Movie GIANT*.

In "*Piedra Rodante*: The Memory of the Musical Consumption of a Generation of Mexican Youth in the Seventies," Yolanda Minerva Campos García explores Mexican music and counterculture in an interAmerican dimension. At the dawn of the sixties, the magazine *Piedra Rodante* emerged in Mexico, a publication that had the seal of being a franchise of the prestigious and long-standing American magazine *Rolling Stone* launched in San Francisco in 1967. With only eight numbers, the magazine stood at the center of attention of some youth sectors that professed a special interest in and taste for rock music, the central concern of *Piedra Rodante*. The magazine was a good showcase for contemporary countercultural manifestations in Mexico. It was not limited to publishing Spanish translations of articles originally published in English in *Rolling Stone* but also encouraged a musical journalism that promoted rock groups from the U.S. and England as well as Mexican rock groups identified as the *Onda Chicana*. This chapter offers a contextualized reading of the eight issues of the *Piedra Rodante* magazine and tells the history of a generational music consumption. By looking at selected magazine contributions, the chapter reflects on the type of information and channels of communication to which young people had access. As the chapter shows, *Piedra Rodante*, despite its brief existence, revealed the presence of a youthful, underground, and irreverent culture.

In "Sonic America(s): Politics of Recognition and Recent Trends in Music Documentary," Wilfried Raussert argues that from songs of enslaved African Americans to murals of Mexican modernists, from hip hop sounds to street art, sound- and imagescapes from the Americas have shaped and performed the social in the Americas. These scapes at times supersede language as mediators and commentators of the social. In the late twentieth century, MTV music/video culture established musical sound and image as interconnected and almost inseparable expressions of youth cultures (Edgar, Fairclough-Isaacs, and Halligan). The music documentary and its growing presence in TV programs, film festivals, cinema programs, and museums of popular culture point toward the genre's increasingly important role in endorsing celebrity culture and rewriting music history. The music documentary provides a new matrix to rethink music historiography in narrative forms where image, sound, and word interact intensely. It also lends itself to relocating music in history and at the intersection of entertainment, commerce, and booming heritage politics in the Americas.

In "Noir Aesthetics, Institutional Racism, and Social Critique: Anthony Mann's *Devil's Doorway* and the Denial of Legal Rights to First Americans," Chris Lippard analyzes *Devil's Doorway*, Anthony Mann's 1950 western, as highly unusual in the explicitness of its critique of settler colonialism in the American West. Set in 1870 Wyoming, the film has previously been identified as a noir western. Lippard argues that *Devil's Doorway* uses a cinematography associated with noir in order to register its social critique. Although the film employs some common Hollywood strategies to reify and appropriate indigenous culture – most markedly perhaps in the casting of Robert Taylor as the native protagonist – Lippard looks at both the extant film and the development of the narrative and of racial and gender dynamics from the original story treatment to the final script in order to suggest how more progressive elements are also prominent. To further this point, Lippard contrasts *Broken Arrow*, the better-known, supposedly pro-Indian western released the same year, with *Devil's Doorway*, and finally ties the significance of confrontations over native land and water rights to contemporary disputes in the United States.

The article by Annette L. Rukwied "Border Crossings, Memory, and Performativity in Juan Carlos Zaldívar's *90 Miles* (2001)" explores the ways film may provide an arena for counter-memories, the bridging of difference, and for reconciliation and healing, using the example of Juan Carlos Zaldívar's performative documentary, *90 Miles* (U.S.A. 2001). The film traces the story of Zaldívar's family, who had left Cuba for the U.S. by way of the 1980 Mariel Boatlift, exploring the tremendous impact of this life-changing decision on all of its members. Special attention is devoted to Zaldívar's father, Pachuco, whose traumatic experience of exile has left him disillusioned and withdrawn, also casting a shadow over the relationship with his son. *90 Miles* combines home video, family photos, archive footage, and interviews conducted with family and friends in Miami, New York City, and Holguín, Cuba.

With the steadily growing presence and influence of Latinos in all parts of U.S. society, Clara E. Rodríguez, in "Latinos on U.S. Primetime Entertainment Television," maintains that one might expect to find more Latina/o characters on television than has been the case in the past. Are (or were) the highly visible Latina/o characters in such hit shows as *Ugly Betty* and *Dora, the Explorer* representative of greater *Latinidad* across the primetime programming board? This chapter investigates that issue, reviewing the settings and the opening credit casts of the most watched (according to Nielsen ratings) primetime dramatic programs during the spring 2006 and spring 2007 seasons. Despite some notable improvements, it finds that Latina/os continue to be underrepresented in lead roles, even in shows set in cities and areas where Latina/os make up substantial proportions of the populations. It also finds Latino actors and characters tend to be concentrated in certain programs, with other programs having no Latina/os in lead or supporting roles. Finally, it finds a number of ambiguously drawn Latina/o characters.

María Herrera-Sobek's "Prickly Politics in Borderlands Art: Aesthetic Activism and the Barbed Wire Motif in Consuelo Jimenez Underwood's Artwork" employs artivism not only to discuss the works of visual artists but a wider scope of artistic production such as literary works, sculpture, artistic installations, music, film, photography, comic strips, textile weavings, as well as other types of artistic expressions. The border has generated a substantial work of artistic production due to the suffering and deaths of immigrants trying to cross the U.S.-Mexican border. The political climate extant in the United States continues to elicit anti-immigrant discourse and policies; these factors in turn motivate artists to articulate their aesthetic activism through their works. Visual artists have incorporated the icon of barbed wire or the devil's rope, as it is also known in popular usage, to convey an image representing extreme pain and suffering. The focus in the essay lies on the artwork of Consuelo Jimenez Underwood.

Neither Same nor Separate: Hemispheric Horizons of American Studies[1]

JOSEF RAAB

"Relations stop nowhere."
– Henry James, *Roderick Hudson*

Looking beyond the nation

In an essay on "American Studies as Mobility Studies" (2011), Rüdiger Kunow proposed that "over long periods and in different historical contexts, a powerful link has existed between mobility and 'America,' a link which has allowed the signifier 'America' to operate as a potent designator for the telos of individual and collective, real and imagined mobility" ("American" 247). The seasonal movements of indigenous tribes in pre-Columbian North America, the settlement of the continent by Europeans, the shifting sites of slavery, the westward expansion of the United States of America throughout the nineteenth century, and the relocations of businesses and industries in the twentieth and twenty-first century are just some of the features that illustrate Kunow's point and that have received significant critical attention in American Studies since the 1950s. "The development since the 1990s of a new or transnational American studies," Kunow continues,

> can be read as perhaps the most recent grounding of our understanding of 'America' in practices of mobility, except that this time it does not operate as the telos of worldwide mobility but as its origin and center: ... American studies has one more time 'mobilized' the signifier 'America,' tracing its multiple new deployments and redeployments all over the world. (247)

Indeed, there is much to be said for designating "America" as both a "telos" and an "origin" of mobility. However, Kunow's unease with the term "America" can be felt through its use in quotation marks and in a phrase like "'America,' – however that term might be specifically defined" ("American" 247). This unease may stem from a reluctance to equate the current United States of America with "America" and from a

1 It was Josef Raab's wish to have a slightly revised version of "Neither Same nor Separate: Hemispheric Horizons of American Studies" included in this book. The original essay was published in *Crossroads in American Studies: Transnational and Biocultural Encounters. Essays in Honor of Rüdiger Kunow.* Ed. Frederike Offizier, Marc Priewe, and Ariane Schröder. Heidelberg: Universitätsverlag Winter, 2016. 215–242.

The editors thank Frederike Offizier, Marc Priewe, and Ariane Schröder and the Winter Verlag for the permission to reprint the article.

sense that positioning "America" as the telos and origin of mobility reflects an exceptionalist view of the nation that would contradict our experience of the "web of connections" (Greenblatt qtd. in Kunow, "American" 247) that we observe in so many arenas and our need for "rethinking … the national in the light of … additional dimensions of relationships" (Dirlik qtd. in Kunow, "American" 251). Wilfried Raussert underscores this necessity when he points toward "inter-American webs and networks that manifest mutual entanglements between locations, regions, and nations beyond a North-South divide" (60).

Rather than remaining immured in what John Carlos Rowe has termed "the prison-house of the nation" ("Music" 38) or dwelling on the unease associated with "America," I would like to propose refashioning the term in the light of the incipient hemispheric turn in American Studies. While the role of North America and the United States as both telos and origin of mobility has been amply explored in global and especially in transatlantic contexts, scholarly attention to interAmerican connections and transfers remains the exception. The hemispheric horizons of American Studies are shunned by some ("Do you want me to learn Spanish, or what?"), acknowledged by others (as in Shelley Fisher Fishkin's 2004 presidential address to the American Studies Association), but researched by few. Yet, a closer look at the examples mentioned in the opening paragraph of this essay (from nomadic indigenous practices to the profit-oriented relocation of production sites and those working in them) reveals that all of them have not only a U.S. American or North American, but also an interAmerican dimension, which is well worth exploring: migratory patterns of indigenous populations throughout the Americas past and present, similarities and differences in modes of European settlements in the New World (e.g. a comparison of nineteenth-century German settlements in Saskatchewan, Wisconsin, Texas, Yucatán, Bahia, and Valdivia), the impact of the Caribbean on the institution of slavery in the United States, the clash of a westward U.S. expansion from the East Coast with a northward Spanish/Mexican expansion from Mexico City in 1830s and 1840s Texas, or the establishment of maquiladoras south of the U.S.-Mexican border as a consequence of the North American Free Trade Agreement. Such hemispheric horizons may benefit American Studies in identifying sites and situations for comparisons (like German settlements in a myriad of locations in the Americas) and in understanding the wider ramifications of issues (like slavery) that affect the United States as well as other regions/nations/cultures in the Western Hemisphere.

Rather than foregrounding the nation and "a national culture" the way American Studies of the myth-and-symbol school has done, a hemispherically conscious American Studies recognizes national borders in the Americas as "historically produced political constructs" (Levander and Levine 7), within and across which there are numerous other markers of distinction (like gender, ethnicity, class, age, language, religion, ideology, education, experience, sexual orientation, taste, etc.) that shift and that underlie continual encounters of sameness and difference in intercultural scenarios. In these encounters site-specific, national, and transnational factors interact, which may produce local, national, and transnational ramifications. Sites, encounters, constellations, and issues will not emerge as uniform throughout the Americas, but neither will they emerge as entirely separate from one another. While New York City, Miami, and Buenos Aires are in no way exchangeable cities, they all feature a strong reggae scene with links to Jamaica and to each other. The reggae cultures of New York City, Miami, Kingston, and Buenos Aires are not the same, but neither are they completely separate from one another. Failing to see that the nation is "just one category in a broader interpretive field" (Levander and Levine 9) might limit a (U.S.-centered) comparative analysis to the reggae scenes of New York City and Miami, while turning a blind eye to their hemispheric and transnational horizons.

I would therefore like to suggest that there are good reasons for complementing the national(ist) perspectives of American Studies with considerations of transnational and global interconnections generally and of interAmerican contexts specifically. What will be particularly useful are (a) comparative hemispheric approaches (for example, to the development of a German community in Braunfels, TX and in Blumenau in the Brazilian state of Santa Catarina), (b) the analysis of transfers and flows (like that of reggae from Jamaica to the United States, Venezuela, and Argentina), and (c) a recognition of interconnections and impacts (for example, the mutual influences of magical realism à la Jorge Luis Borges and Gabriel García Márquez and U.S. postmodern writing à la Donald Barthelme and John Barth).[2] Rather than suggesting a vague kind of sameness, exploring some of the hemispheric horizons of what we study in American Studies helps to pinpoint difference and reasons behind this difference – reasons which an isolated analysis is unable to reveal. Agendas, issues, developments, and encounters throughout the Americas are more interconnected than they might appear at first sight. While establishing hemispheric horizons will limit the degree of exceptionalism with which we can invest the United States in our academic practice, it will also reveal a truer, more complete, and more complex picture.[3]

---

2 Focusing on transnational American Studies rather than hemispheric studies, Shelley Fisher Fishkin has proposed three similar categories of transnational scholarship, which she labels "*broadening the frame*," "exploring the *cross-fertilization* of cultures," and "*renewed attention to travel and to how texts travel*" ("Mapping" 31; emphasis original).

3 While a general acknowledgment that transnational "American Studies" cannot exclude the Americas from its research focus seems to be taking hold, many endeavors go little beyond a cursory mention. Udo J. Hebel's preface to *Transnational American Studies* is a case in point. While he writes that "[t]he extension of traditional perspectives on the United States or on North America to include the larger spaces and issues of, among other, even more complex trajectories, Atlantic Studies, Hemispheric Studies, Studies of the Americas, and Pacific Studies has generated fundamental questions with regard to the contents and concepts of 'American Studies'" (1), his deliberation on transnational American Studies remains all too limited to the European dimension.

Some historical foundations of hemispheric horizons

Before Christopher Columbus's voyage in 1492 and the subsequent European conquest of the New World, numerous indigenous peoples and tribes lived in the Americas – all with their own language or linguistic variety, cultural traditions, and territories. Hardly any of them were separate groups or nations cut off from one another; instead, a manifold exchange of beliefs, practices, and goods forged interdependencies. Tribal areas kept shifting and some of them transcended present-day international borders: Territories of the Sioux and Blackfeet, for example, covered areas in present-day U.S.A. as well as Canada; while the Papago (Tohono O'odham) and the Diegueño lived in territories that are now both north and south of the U.S.-Mexican border. Indigenous American civilizations were dynamic: they moved around, their cultural traditions changed as they came into contact with other groups, and their territories were not always confined to sites that American Studies considers as its domain.

In the time of colonization the area that is now the United States became an arena in which various European powers – especially France, England, Spain, and the Netherlands – vied for territories and resources, allied themselves with indigenous groups, and kept shifting their spheres of influence. All too often, however, American Studies has approached the European presence in early colonial North America with a narrow focus on English-speaking settlements. While we usually hear of Jamestown, VA (founded in 1607) and of Plymouth Plantation, MA (founded in 1620) and of the contrasting economies and social structures of these colonies, the founding of St. Augustine in Florida in 1565 gets hardly ever mentioned in American Studies (with a tacit understanding that this settlement is the domain of Latin American history). Likewise, comparative analyses, say of French colonial rule in North America, may traditionally look at Québec and Louisiana, while they will often fail to include French colonialism in Haiti. A hemispheric turn in American Studies, on the other hand, considers the interconnections between a French colonial presence in Québec, Louisiana, and Haiti and French colonies in Acadia, the West Indies, Brazil, and Guiana. Moreover, it does not limit its attention to rivalries between French and English colonizers but relates those to rivalries between French, Spanish, and Portuguese colonizers in order to gain a fuller understanding of the situation's complexity. A hemispherically conscious American Studies both differentiates between the types of colonialism and the parameters of an ensuing condition of coloniality in sites that would later become part of the United States and seeks to understand how the colonial aspirations of a particular European nation played out in different parts of the Americas – neither in the same ways nor totally separate from one another. For example, Dutch colonialism along the Hudson River could and should be related to the Dutch colonial presence in the West Indies and Brazil. Commonalities other than national origin remain equally pertinent. Consider, for example, the role of gender and literacy in the establishment of American literary traditions with authors like Anne Bradstreet and Sor Juana Inés de la Cruz. Also, a hemispheric turn might suggest that a research topic like ideas on indigeneity penned in and around the twenty-one Franciscan missions in California from the southernmost Mission San Diego de Alcalá in San Diego to the northernmost Mission San Francisco Solano in Sonoma needs to put the situation in Alta California in the larger context of Spanish missions elsewhere in the Americas, especially of Franciscan, Jesuit, and Dominican missions in Baja California. Where does "America" end and where do "the Americas" start? Can we really exclude the latter from "American Studies" because Alta California became a U.S. territory in 1848 and Baja California remained Mexican?

Subsequently, in the history of the New World, within the half century following 1776 most European colonies in the Americas became nations. Again, the differences are significant. But while the independence struggles and early nationalisms are not the same throughout the Americas, they are nonetheless interrelated, as many colonies were looking toward the United States as a model. While a Europe-oriented transnational American Studies might, in this context, focus on the impact of European Enlightenment thinkers on the driving forces behind the U.S. Declaration of Independence, a hemispheric turn complements this transnational outlook by considering how developments and ideologies in North America propelled rebellions in Spain's and France's American colonies from 1808 onward. That the popular Spanish translation of Thomas Paine's *Common Sense* did much for the independence movements elsewhere in the Americas (Sexton n. pag.) is not usually explored in a nation-centered American Studies or in a transnational American Studies that privileges Europe.

In the early nineteenth century, the power elites in the Americas felt that the Western Hemisphere ought to be separate from Europe yet interconnected. Thomas Jefferson was one of the first to proclaim the idea of the Western Hemisphere as a separate entity. In 1813, he declared "that the unity of the American peoples extended to all their 'modes of existence'" (Jefferson qtd. in Whitaker 2). Two years earlier, Jefferson had written to Alexander von Humboldt, who was, among other things, an expert on Spanish America,

> [t]he European nations constitute a separate division of the globe; their localities make them part of a distinct system; they have a set of interests of their own in which it is our business never to engage ourselves. America has a hemisphere to itself. It must have a separate system of interest which must not be subordinated to those of Europe. (qtd. in Whitaker 29)

The view of the interconnectedness of the Americas and of their separateness from Europe remained in constant competition with a U.S. exceptionalism defining the United States as separate from the rest of the world and with the lingering conception of the United States and the Americas as extensions of European civilization that suffered from a colonial complex of cultural inferiority. The focus on the special situation of the United States and the privileging of Europe in international U.S. relations also shaped academic engagement with North America, which for a long time failed to heed Jefferson's prescient remarks on a hemispheric connection and neglected departures from U.S. models, such as José Vasconcelos's theory of a "raza cosmica."

A century after Jefferson's presidency, U.S. dominance in the Western Hemisphere had been firmly established. The Americas continued to be important to the United States in many areas from territorial expansion to the practice of slavery and from the U.S. war against Mexico to the U.S. war with Spain. The latter was triggered less by a U.S. need to assist other Western Hemisphere peoples and more by a desire to protect U.S. economic and political interests. The Big Stick policy of Theodore Roosevelt followed, which proved right those in Latin America who had long warned against the imperialist tendencies of the new superpower. Roosevelt's corollary to the Monroe Doctrine, which he proclaimed in a speech to Congress in 1904, states that

> [a]ll that this country desires is to see the neighboring countries stable, orderly, and prosperous. Any country whose people conduct themselves well can count upon our hearty friendship. If a nation shows that it knows how to act with reasonable efficiency and decency in social and political matters, if it keeps order and pays its obligations, it need fear no interference from the United States. Chronic wrongdoing, or an impotence which results in a general loosening of the ties of civilized society, may in America, as elsewhere, ultimately require intervention by some civilized nation, and in the Western Hemisphere the adherence of the United States to the Monroe Doctrine may force the United States, however reluctantly, in flagrant cases of such wrongdoing or impotence, to the exercise of an international police power. (Roosevelt n. pag.)

This attitude confirms the rejection of U.S. interventionism that José Martí had voiced in "Our America" and it presents a rich field of research for InterAmerican Studies.

So is Nicaraguan poet Rubén Darío's response to Roosevelt's Big Stick policy, which came in his poem "A Roosevelt" (1904). Roosevelt had become president in 1901 and had acquired the Panama Canal area in 1903, an act that Darío recognized as a potential preliminary to further U.S. expansion: "[m]añana podremos ser yanquis (y es lo más probable)" [Tomorrow we might be Yankees (that is most likely)], he feared (*Cantos* 626). While Darío had criticized Walt Whitman in an earlier sonnet (composed in 1889), he presents him as one of the few positive aspects of the U.S. in "A Roosevelt." Both poems use the image of iron (of a "país de hierro") to depict the United States as cold and warmongering. In the later text, Darío calls the U.S. President a "Hunter," whereas Whitman is seen as a potential defender of the weaker parts of Pan-America: "[t]he voice that would reach you, Hunter, must speak/in Biblical tones, or in the poetry of Walt Whitman" (Darío, *Selected* 69).

What unites Darío's (Spanish) America is its common heritage and its threatened position. The poet tells Roosevelt:

> Eres los Estados Unidos,
> eres el futuro invasor
> de la América ingenua que tiene sangre indígena,
> que aún reza a Jesucristo y aún habla en español.
> ...
> Crees que la vida es incendio
> que el progreso es erupción;

en donde pones la bala
el porvenir pones.

No.

[You are the United States,
future invader of our naive America
with its Indian blood, an America
that still prays to Christ and still speaks Spanish.
...

You think that life is a fire,
that progress is an eruption,
that the future is wherever
your bullet strikes.

No.] (Darío, *Selected* 69)

Darío uses Roosevelt as a metonym for the powerful United States. The invocation of his subject in the poem's first section is studded with attributes of might and aggression, which dominate this view of Roosevelt and of his nation. The U.S. belief in "progress" through attack and invasion is answered by Darío's simple "No." Less directly, the poet uses the alleged U.S. position "that life is a fire" [Crees que la vida es incendio]: this reference alludes to the liberty torch, which appears later in the poem. Darío employs this emblem to illustrate Roosevelt's betrayal of the ideal of liberty: while the torch should light the path for freedom throughout the Western Hemisphere, in Roosevelt's "iron claws" it only lights the path for conquest. Roosevelt is charged with turning the torch's fire into a destructive force: "y alumbrando el camino de la fácil conquista,/la Libertad levanta su antorcha en Nueva-York" [Liberty, lighting the path/to easy conquest, raises her torch in New York]. U.S. territorial expansion in the name of liberty and progress, says Darío, is actually carried out for economic and financial profit. Darío opposes "la América nuestra," a Catholic Spanish America with a proud indigenous heritage, to the U.S. devotion to the cults of Hercules and of Mammon.

The unity in the Western Hemisphere, which "A Roosevelt" limits to "Spanish America," is extended in Darío's later poem "Salutación al Aguila" to include also the United States. The original Spanish poem has an English subtitle, namely "May this grand Union have no end!" The U.S. American eagle and the Latin American condor, writes Darío, "puedan ambos juntarse en plenitud, concordia y esfuerzo" [can both unite in plenty, concord, and force]. So Darío wavers between rejecting U.S. imperialism and threats and envisioning a harmonious Western Hemisphere of partners.[4]

Darío's poem "A Roosevelt" raises the question of the subject of transnational American Studies. Written neither in English nor by an author living in the United

---

4 In his later "Dilcidaciones," Darío would revise his judgment of Roosevelt and declare that "el terrible cazador es un varón sensato" [the terrible hunter is a reasonable and good man] (qtd. in Balseiro 136).

States, this text has been the domain of Latin American Studies. On the other hand, it shows that U.S. imperialism cannot adequately be studied with a national focus (e.g., on Roosevelt's "Corollary" and debates in the U.S. surrounding it) or with only a transatlantic outlook (on the U.S. rivalry with Spain about Spain's remaining colonies in the Americas). U.S. imperialism at the beginning of the "American Century" is a research topic that invites a hemispheric turn in order to complement the national and transatlantic approaches to this topic. Under the rubric "interconnections and impacts" that I mentioned in the introduction (in addition to "comparative hemispheric approaches" and "transfers and flows"), Darío's literary response to Roosevelt's policies merits scholarly attention in an American Studies that is not confined by national and transatlantic perspectives, as does the larger context of the Pan-American movement.

As an outgrowth of this movement Franklin Delano Roosevelt's "Good Neighbor Policy" of the 1930s acknowledged interAmerican ties much more in the sense of a partnership than had Theodore Roosevelt's "Corollary." As a consequence, the consciousness of hemispheric relations rebounded among politicians and intellectuals. According to Arthur P. Whitaker, "by 1940 the underlying Western Hemisphere idea was more popular throughout the Americas and apparently closer to realization than at any previous period in its history" (132). These developments, along with the inter-American alliance during the Second World War, contributed to the founding of the Organization of American States in 1948 and to its coordinating role in the Western Hemisphere. Economic free-trade agreements like MERCOSUR in 1991, NAFTA in 1994 and plans for a Free Trade Area of the Americas followed. An InterAmerican Democratic Charter is adopted in 2001, and non-governmental organizations dedicate themselves to supporting citizens' movements, securing human rights, and promoting economic well-being in the Western Hemisphere. The twentieth and twenty-first century also see a myriad of revolutions, civil rights movements, ethnic conflict, human rights issues, migration patterns, ideological ties, transnational media, and cultural exchange in the Americas. All these developments certainly have their local and national specificities, but a large number of them can and should also be studied from a hemispheric point of view that establishes comparisons, traces transfers and flows, and uncovers interconnections and impacts.[5]

Intensifying migration, international markets, transnational culture industries, and the Internet have made interAmerican border crossings by people, goods, services, cultural practices, and ideas the norm, rather than the exception. The venues and manners of these border crossings may be new and ever changing, but the phenomenon is not. It has been a Western Hemisphere phenomenon all along. The United States of America plays an important role in this web of interconnections and flows and its cultures should be studied with a consciousness of these hemispheric horizons. Considering the contexts and continuities of "America" will reveal aspects that a U.S.-fo-

5 A good example for the innovative potential that a hemispheric consciousness can open up is the collection *Mutual Impressions: Writers from the Americas Reading One Another* (1999), edited by Ilan Stavans.

cused approach leaves unexplored. Viewing "America" as mobile and dynamic rather than as static and nation-centered opens up important venues for American Studies. As Rüdiger Kunow states, "[i]f we accept the proposition that mobilities constitute cultural relations in our time, then mobility must in a systematic fashion become part also of our critical lexicon, especially so in an American studies that defines itself as cross-cultural, comparatist, and transnational" ("American" 245).

Yet, when the Ethnogeographic Board that the U.S. government had set up in 1942 devised a model of world areas, "North America" and "Latin America" were identified as separate spheres, a decision that, as John Carlos Rowe states, "continues to shape area studies to this day" ("Areas" 323). It has contributed to a sense of hemispheric separateness, which InterAmerican Studies needs to help revise. Rowe therefore joins Walter D. Mignolo in his call for a "double consciousness" ("Areas" 334; derived from W.E.B. Du Bois) that allows us to explore the differences between areas like "North America" and "Latin America" as well as challenging their designation as distinct areas by focusing on the heterogeneity of each as well as the interdependencies between them.

The limits of "America"

In a programmatic essay published in *PMLA* in 2003, Djelal Kadir cautioned against a nationalist, reductionist U.S. American Studies that would reflect "the continuity of America's ongoing national and nationalist project" (12). He deemed the knowledge landscapes used by many American Studies scholars to be confined by national outlooks and national boundaries: "[h]istorically, the field of American studies has served as the ideological and discursive locus of national mythographies, and its constructs were reiteratively consolidated by a number of stentorian voices during the twentieth century" (Kadir 12). A year earlier, John Carlos Rowe had similarly questioned a practice of American Studies that is governed by the notion of American exceptionalism. He wrote in *The New American Studies*: "[i]f a single nationalist mythology of the United States no longer prevails, our understanding of just what constitutes the cultural border of the United States is no longer clear" (Rowe, *New* 52). Where are the limits of the "America" that American Studies should be concerned with? Rowe explains that

> the dominance of the United States according to the nationalist paradigm has often led to the neglect of other nations of the western hemisphere, each of which has its own complex multicultural and multilingual history, as well as its own interactions with other nationalities of the region. The new American Studies tries to work as a genuinely comparatist discipline that will respect the many different social systems and cultural affiliations of the "Americas." Rather than treating such cultural differences as discrete entities, however, this new comparative approach stresses the ways different cultures are transformed by their contact and interaction with each other. (53)

Comparisons and the study of encounters are central to the "new American Studies" that Rowe has devised. A hemispheric turn in American Studies will complement those with a questioning of the limits of "America" and will also look at the interAmerican flows and transfers that occasion encounters as well as at the transborder implications, interconnections, and impacts of the phenomena, scenarios, texts, and ideas that American Studies scholars examine with reference to the United States. Often their limits do not coincide with the geographical borders of the nation.

The de-centering of American Studies has also been the basis of various presidential addresses to the American Studies Association from Janice Radway's to Shelley Fisher Fishkin's; and it infuses a project like *A New Literary History of America* (2012), edited by Greil Marcus and Werner Sollors, who have long argued for an understanding of American literature as polylingual and multicultural. In the same vein, Djelal Kadir speaks of the "myriad plurality" of the United States (13), which, he states, has revealed "the unassimilability of difference" (14). What is crucial is the manner in which we deal with this difference and in which we expand its scope beyond national boundaries. We must neither project a sameness onto U.S. issues and their interAmerican contexts nor try to establish a separateness by focusing exclusively on "national mythographies" (Kadir 12). Consciousness of the hemispheric horizons of American Studies should reveal, on the contrary, that the "American" issues we are dealing with are neither same nor separate.

This lack of sameness also has methodological consequences. While different scenarios in different "American" contexts often require a differentiated methodology and critical vocabulary, there is a danger of falsifying transfers. As John Carlos Rowe points out, "[i]n its claim to encompass the many cultures and political organizations in the western hemisphere, the new American Studies threatens to impose its own kind of cultural imperialism" (*New* 55). Rüdiger Kunow agrees that we need "to deal with difference [both inside the United States and between the United States and elsewhere] without negating or submerging it" ("American" 262). Donald Pease concurs that a transnationally-oriented American Studies establishes no sameness where there is none; instead, it analyzes "transit," "translation," and "displacement," which can sharpen the contours of both national specificities and "non-national formations" ("Re-Mapping" 5).

A hemispheric turn orients the transnational toward the interAmerican, well aware that while the interAmerican is more central than much traditional American Studies scholarship has made it out to be, this is only one angle in the larger global framework.

What is needed is both an awareness of intra-U.S. and interAmerican difference and a recognition that American Studies cannot be confined by the borders of the United States. Sandhya Shukla and Heidi Tinsman speak in this context of an "Americas paradigm," explaining that

> an Americas paradigm challenges both the myth of U.S. exceptionalism and the idea of categorical Latin American otherness. It offers a much-needed critique of the old, but still very much alive, cold war categories of Latin American and U.S. American area studies, categories that have tended to emphasize essential political, cultural, and economic difference, juxtaposing a "developed" United States to a "developing" Latin America. (2–3)

Seeing the United States and the Americas in new ways of interrelatedness will open up what Paula Moya and Ramón Saldívar have called a "trans-American imaginary":

> [t]he trans-American imaginary is "imaginary" to the extent that it figures a very real but fundamentally different syntax of codes, images, and icons, as well as the tacit assumptions, convictions, and beliefs that seek to bind together the varieties of American national discourses. The transnational imaginary is thus to be understood as a chronotope, a contact zone, that is both historical and geographical and that is populated by transnational persons whose lives form an experiential region within which singularly delineated notions of political, social, and cultural identity do not suffice. (2)

Such a contestation of singular identity has been identified by Marc Priewe in contemporary Chicana/o texts, which, as he writes oscillate "between resistance and co-optation, between opposition to and partial complicity with U.S. American culture.... In doing so, these narratives provide insights into nondualistic notions of resistance and are thus indicative of how cultural spaces of opposition to the dominant society have become more complex and flexible" (275–276).[6]

The bigger framework of the Americas plays into this complexity, as do categories like gender, ethnicity, class, or age.[7]

In view of the Americas' cultural plurality and interconnectedness, a hemispheric turn in American Studies also promotes what Günter H. Lenz has called "a *transnational and transcultural theory of democracy*" (401; emphasis original). Such a theory transgresses old colonial hierarchies and takes into account "changing parameters and dynamics of transcultural practices, perspectives on transnational migrations, governance, justice, citizenship, and reconfigurations of 'culture(s)'" (401). Lenz therefore pleads for a dialogic American Transcultural Studies, in which "'American' ... refers to the United States as a force field of heterogeneous and hybrid cultures, set in their multiple and contested hemispheric contexts and explored in their multivoiced and multidirectional transnational and transcultural dynamics" (420). An American Studies thus conceived will embrace a hemispheric turn and will allow us to "move beyond the time-honored 'methodological nationalism' (Sassen 5) of American Studies" (Kunow, "American" 261).[8]

---

6 Priewe refers to texts by Gloria Anzaldúa, Cherríe Moraga, El Vez, and Guillermo Gómez-Peña as "Chicana/o narratives in which the project of claiming the nation is not altogether discarded but rather readjusted to serve certain cultural needs or political actions," thus underlining the plurality of identity markers (270).

7 Recent work by Laura Bieger and other scholars on belonging is therefore also a branch that requires an interAmerican awareness in exploring how belonging, as Bieger writes, "affects the construction of social realities and how it works as a social and cultural practice" (219). Various approaches to belonging referring to different sites in the Americas are taken by the essays in Josef Raab, ed. *New World Colors: Ethnicity, Belonging, and Difference in the Americas*.

8 For a discussion of the limits of national(ist) approaches in studying the Western Hemisphere, see my essay "Thinking Beyond the Nation: The Project of Inter-American Studies."

Hemispheric horizons

Not every topic, text, or tendency analyzed in American Studies invites an equal measure of hemispheric horizons to be taken into account in its analysis, of course. While a transnational approach to Henry James's *The Portrait of a Lady* (1881) will surely benefit from a discussion of the transatlantic dimension of the novel, a transnational approach to María Amparo Ruiz de Burton's *The Squatter and the Don* (1885) requires a hemispheric consciousness. A transnational approach to a text like Mark Twain's *Adventures of Huckleberry Finn* (1884) needs both: a transatlantic consciousness of the literary conventions against which Twain rebelled and an interAmerican consciousness of race, slavery, "civilization," and wilderness.

All three works mentioned above include mobility and the resulting encounters. As Rüdiger Kunow states,

> mobility produces *encounters*, and in our descriptions of these encounters we have a choice: we may show how the differences between the cultural parties involved are sublated into a Homi Bhabha-inspired "hybridity," or we may focus instead on the semantics of conflict and incompatibility as they unfold in these encounters. In the former view, mobility is that which lies always already behind us; in the latter, mobility becomes an instance of *reflexivity*, cultures acting on themselves. ("American" 262; emphasis original)

Mobility studies thus constitutes an important aspect of transnational American Studies – both before and after a hemispheric turn. Ideally, it will aid in reflecting on comparative hemispheric contexts, transfers, and flows, as well as interconnections and impacts.

A paradigmatic case in American Studies that requires a hemispheric consciousness is the 2006 debate on immigration restriction under HR 4437 – along with the resulting protests, and their texts. One of those texts is "Nuestro Himno," a Spanish-language rendition of the U.S. national anthem by an interAmerican group of performers that started airing on Spanish-language radio stations across the United States on April 28, 2006 in preparation for the May Day demonstrations against the criminalization of unauthorized immigration. John Carlos Rowe explains:

> [c]onceived by British music executive Adam Kidron, performed by Haitian-American singer Wyclef Jean (currently running for the Presidency of Haiti), Cuban-American rapper Pitbull, and Puerto Rican singers Carlos Once and Olga Tañón, "Nuestro Himno" is a genuinely transnational work that calls attention to the increasingly limited horizons of the nation-state for understanding and governing our economic, political, cultural, and human relations. ("Music" 37)

"Nuestro Himno" sets lyrics in Spanish that proclaim anti-imperialism and an interAmerican connectedness across nationalities to the tune of "The Star-Spangled Banner": "somos iguales./Somos hermanos, es nuestro himno" [we are equal./We are brothers, this is our anthem.]. As Rowe points out, the song is also in the tradition of the *corrido*, a type of ballad which expressed the heroic Mexican American resistance to Anglo oppression. This anthem presents a stance against U.S. isolationism and monolingualism, against the privileging of whiteness and against nativism. Rather than relying on a master narrative told by one voice of authority, "Nuestro Himno" is multivocal. It uses concurrent voices, sometimes singing in a chorus, at other times following one another, intoning one set of lyrics while a different set of lyrics is being sung by another performer, or echoing one another. This multivocality is complemented by a multiplicity of musical styles ranging from the melodious tune of "The Star-Spangled Banner" to rhythm and blues, and spoken lyrics. There is, however, a unity in this diversity, a readiness to stand together for liberty, equality, and victory:

> Sus estrellas, sus franjas, la libertad,
> eh, somos iguales.
> Somos hermanos, es nuestro himno.
> En el fiero combate, en señal de victoria,
> fulgor de lucha (Mi gente,¡sigue luchando!)
> al paso de la libertad (¡Ya es tiempo de romper las cadenas!)
>
> [Its stars, its stripes, liberty,
> hey, we are equal.
> We are brothers, this is our anthem.
> In the fierce combat, to signal victory,
> the brilliance of battle (My people, keep fighting!)
> in step with liberty (The time has come to break the chains!)].[9]

The fight against British imperialism that Francis Scott Key commemorated in his lyrics to "The Star-Spangled Banner" is echoed in "Nuestro Himno"'s "fierce combat" against immigration restriction in the United States and against elitist or reductionist definitions of "America." The performers appropriate the "tierra de libres" ["land of the free"] as a place that is also the land of Latinas/os and Caribbean Americans, a place of their "hermanos y hermanas" [brothers and sisters]. By postulating that "The time has come/to break the chains" they also link their discourse of unity to the slogan derived from the Communist Manifesto, "Workers of the world, unite! You have nothing to lose but your chains!"

The CD on which "Nuestro Himno" is contained is fittingly entitled *Somos Americanos* [We Are American] – another marker of protest against exclusion. Commenting on charges that this revised anthem is allegedly un-American, John Carlos Rowe has suggested that "[w]hat threatens many Americans in 'Nuestro Himno' is the reality that the fiction of the U.S. national border can no longer be maintained" ("Music" 38).

Because of the transfers and flows it illustrates as well as the interconnections that it foregrounds, a text like "Nuestro Himno" requires a consciousness of its hemispheric horizons. While this text is centrally concerned with the U.S. nation, its ideals, and its anthem, it is transnational in terms of production and contents, a song whose analysis benefits from a hemispheric turn in American Studies that recognizes the na-

9 https://lyricsondemand.com/miscellaneouslyrics/nationalanthemslyrics/nuestrohimno lyrics.html (verso 2).

tion but is not confined by it. As Levander and Levine have stated: "Moving beyond the nation does not mean abandoning the idea of nation altogether but rather recognizing its dynamic elements and fluid, ever-changing, essentially contingent nature" (9). While the transnational turn in American Studies has led to a stronger consideration of international flows and global processes, what often gets neglected is a recognition of the rest of the Americas. The long history of unequal relations between the United States and other parts of the Western Hemisphere has resulted in all too many American Studies scholars turning a blind eye to interAmerican contexts.

It has also led to undue divisions in cross-border phenomena. For example, numerous North American indigenous tribes inhabited areas that were later divided up between the United States and Canada. Different narratives, ideologies, and imaginaries developed in reference to the same tribes. As Barbara Buchenau points out, "common parlance speaks of First Nations in Canada and Native Americans in the U.S.A. and even literary representations of North American Indians have acquired different short-hands: Berkhofer coined the term 'white man's Indian' for the U.S.A.; Francis speaks of the 'imaginary Indian' in Canada" (n. pag.). Such notions fostered a practice of "counterdistinction" that implies a separateness of one and the same people. What a consciousness of the hemispheric horizons will reveal is that there are superimposed markers of difference and that among them the marker of (modern-day) nationality often takes undue precedence. Nation-centered approaches and discourses, however, for the sake of "counterdistinction," may tend to introduce or construct differences where there are none and may overlook the many layers of transnational interconnection.

Prospects and challenges of a hemispheric turn

Not every issue or text worth examining in American Studies has the kind of hemispheric context and reach of "Nuestro Himno." In numerous cases, it might be more fitting for a transnational approach to foreground African, Asian, or European contexts and intertexts rather than hemispheric horizons. Nonetheless, from literature to popular music, from television to social movements, and from precolonial times to the present, countless research topics in American Studies will benefit from the wider perspective that a hemispheric turn opens up. Can a topic like slavery in the United States really be adequately researched with a focus exclusively on the American South or on the U.S.A.? Is it not necessary to explore in this context the inclusion of Canada in the underground railroad, of the Caribbean as part of the middle passage and a center of the slave trade, and of Mexico as a territory where some escaped slaves took refuge after the abolition of slavery in Mexico (which then included Texas) in 1829 by President Vicente Guerrero, who was of Spanish, African, and indigenous descent?

Like cultural mobility studies, InterAmerican Studies needs to focus on concrete encounters, locally grounded individual experiences and interactions, impacts of the other onto the self and vice versa. Encounters relating to U.S. slavery can certainly be locally grounded in Canada, the Caribbean or Mexico. Those encounters outside the U.S. borders should not escape the American Studies scholar. As Rüdiger Kunow points out, there needs to be

> *a move from area to site*, or, more precisely, from the vastness of the trans to a number of local, concrete, constellational sites where the inside and the outside of "America" and other cultural domains are intertwined, where more than one location, tradition, or practice are coming into play. [Our research needs to examine] moments in the process of transnational mobility in which this "here" and "there," or "them" and "us," intersect and interact in processes of mediation and negotiation, or adaptation/acculturation or rejection/expulsion, whatever the case may be. ("American" 260; emphasis original)

"Intertwined," "intersect," and "interact" are keywords here that should make us question any (nationally defined) container models of cultural analysis; they alert us to the need to explore "the inside and the outside of 'America,'" their mutual impacts, the flows between them, and the differently grounded contexts in which they are embedded.

If we look at another topic, say, twenty-first-century urban transformations in the U.S.A., a hemispheric approach will likewise open up prospects that a nationally confined approach might not be able to explore to the full. When we think of urban interculturalism, we will need to take into account its link to demographic changes, and those show clearly the steady rise of the percentage of U.S. residents who (or whose parents) were born in the Americas, but outside the United States. InterAmerican migration has drastically altered U.S. cities not only in the Southwest, Florida, and along the East coast. The twenty-first-century narratives, discourses, and imaginaries of U.S. cities therefore often have a hemispheric component; they are also increasingly authored by interAmerican immigrants and their descendants. Kunow has aptly used Mary Louise Pratt's concept of the "contact zone" for "city spaces where one encounters, sometimes with alarming frequency, unfamiliar people who bring with them materials visible and invisible and which may or may not transform both residents and newcomers" ("City" 172). The communicable diseases transmitted in such urban encounters, writes Kunow, "possess great representational significance" because they lead to representations of an urban community in crisis and to discourses about who is to blame: "[w]hat matters is the vocabulary used in this process of fashioning an imaginary community, the stories told about the how, why, wherefore, and especially wherefrom of the communicable disease" (172–173). With increasing numbers of migrants arriving from Latin America and the Caribbean there are increasing numbers of U.S. urban narratives, discourses, and imaginaries that rely on and create interAmerican alterity.

Slavery and urban transformations are but two topics in which a hemispheric turn in American Studies may open up areas of research located beyond the confines of a nationally focused approach. As Earl E. Fitz remarked in an essay published in 2004 and reprinted in 2008:

> InterAmerican Studies is an exciting and fast developing new field, one that has the potential to revolutionize not only how we think about the Americas (including their relationships with Europe and Africa and their pre-Columbian worlds) but about the various

> disciplines – from literature to economics, from politics to law, and from anthropology to music – that link them together. (32)

Among concrete challenges to InterAmerican Studies, Fitz mentions "the language problem," the absence of InterAmerican Studies departments, the tendency to privilege breadth over depth (with rudimentary knowledge in many areas at the expense of specializations), as well as the absence of standard courses and curricula in InterAmerican Studies. Also, many academic disciplines tend to be nationally defined (e.g. "U.S. History"), and this impedes the transnational outlook of InterAmerican Studies.

The broad perspective that a hemispheric turn requires also runs the risk of obscuring or neglecting differences resulting from local, regional, or national specificities, from different academic traditions, or from different languages. For example, George Yúdice has warned against equating North American *cultural studies* with Latin American *estudios culturales*. Daniel Mato cautions that when we look at an issue like ethnicity at an interAmerican level, we might fall into the trap of trying to create categories that are too murky to be useful and that overlook specificities. He gives the example of constructing a pan-Latina/o identity, which, in his view, lumps together heterogeneous communities: "[c]urrent representations of a US Latina/o identity as well as of a 'Latin' American identity and of an all-encompassing transnational US Latina/o-'Latin' American identity entail images that, according to several social actors' representations, obscure differences that are significant" (Mato 598). Elsewhere, Mato has complained about the application of U.S.-based assumptions and terminology to non-U.S. subject matters, which, to him, is yet another form of U.S. imperialism. For example, the InterAmericanist needs to keep in mind that "race" concepts that have been developed to analyze the situation and discourses in the United States cannot clarify "race" issues in Brazil or in the Dominican Republic.[10] Yet, a hemispheric turn in American Studies will mean that the analysis of "race" issues in the United States may benefit from knowledge of "race" discourses in Brazil and the Dominican Republic – especially in cases when migrants from those countries are involved in the U.S. "race" issues that are being explored.

An American Studies that is not guided by U.S. exceptionalism will be open to exploring interAmerican comparative contexts, transfers, and flows, as well as interconnections and impacts. When Winfried Fluck complains that "in the U.S., … American Studies has progressively dissolved into programs for the study of particular ethnic or gendered groups, a development that would be further intensified in hemispheric or similar studies" (75), he fails to recognize the integrative function and the transdisciplinary *modus operandi* of InterAmerican Studies.[11] Fluck is right to point out,

10 For a differentiation of the significance of race and ethnicity in different parts of the Western Hemisphere, see my essay "Difference Matters: Toward an Inter-American Approach to 'Race,' Difference, and Belonging."

11 Fluck's own practice tends to equate transnational American Studies with transatlantic American Studies. For a research topic like U.S. literary realism, privileging European contexts (the way Fluck has done very insightfully in his own work on the topic) is ap-

though, that also in the age of globalization "it is still a major issue for the rest of the world whether, how and to what extent it is subjected to, or affected by, [U.S.] American power. In this situation, the original goal of the American Studies movement – the analysis of the cultural sources of [U.S.] American power – continues to be as urgent as ever" (73). This is exactly where a hemispheric turn in American Studies will uncover what "Euro-American Studies" may have overlooked, namely the ways in which this power has affected individuals, communities, and nations elsewhere in the hemisphere.

In exploring the interAmerican contexts of "[U.S.] American power," a hemispherically informed American Studies will not try to see the rest of the Americas through the lens of the U.S.A., its culture and academic practices, but will be open to testing the findings of Canadian, Caribbean, and Latin American Studies and the work of writers, intellectuals, and cultural agents throughout the Western Hemisphere against the U.S. phenomena it examines. While a number of leading Latin American academics have accepted positions at prestigious U.S. universities and while the work of others has been translated into English, their positions have mainly been influential in Latin American Studies and in the social sciences, often failing to be acknowledged (or implemented) in North American Studies. But it is time to open up the knowledge production in North American Studies to interAmerican contexts and concepts. Notions like José Vasconcelos' "mestizaje," Aimé Césaire's "négritude," Patrick Chamoiseau's "créolité," Néstor García Canclini's "hybrid cultures," Aníbal Quijano's "coloniality of power," Nelson Maldonado-Torres's "decolonial turn" or Walter D. Mignolo's "border thinking" – while bearing the danger of misappropriation – also offer us new ways of approaching North America in our scholarly practice and of uncovering what an exceptionalist perspective had previously obscured. While the obstacles to an interAmerican approach are numerous, the opportunities are even more so.

Conclusion

The interconnectedness of the Western Hemisphere is nothing new: Alexander von Humboldt, Thomas Jefferson, and Simón Bolívar stressed it more than two centuries ago. But when American Studies developed as an academic discipline and when it was propelled forward by the myth-and-symbol school, there was a concentration on a national literature, culture, and imaginary. As a consequence, the rest of the hemisphere tended to be ignored in the exploration of "America." This approach of the fledgling discipline led to a tunnel vision and misconceptions. For example, as Herbert Eugene Bolton pointed out in his 1932 presidential address to the American Historical Association, speaking of the "original thirteen" colonies of England in America is a sign of a rather limited view. Bolton writes: "England alone had not thirteen but nearly thirty col-

---

propriate, while for a research topic like the folk ballad in the U.S. during the times of literary realism, such a Euro-American focus would overlook the *corrido* traditon.

onies in the islands and on the Atlantic seaboard, strung all the way from Guiana to Hudson Bay. As commonly used, the phrase 'Original Thirteen' has been very misleading and even pernicious" (451). The tendency of thinking only of those English colonies that later became the original states of the U.S.A. demonstrates the mindset that the notion of U.S. American exceptionalism has fostered, which sees developments related to the United States as separate from the rest of the hemisphere and from the rest of the world.

With the increasing mobility of people and ideas, economic goods and cultural products, political ideologies and social movements that the twentieth and the twenty-first century have seen and with the growing density of connecting networks from flight paths to digital routes, holding on to parochial positions in American Studies becomes increasingly problematic. Olaf Kaltmeier remarks: "[w]e must consider the multiple dimensions of interAmerican integration. Therefore, an interAmerican approach involves understanding cultural and political elements not bounded by a closed national space but instead situated in a space of entanglements" (3). Speaking also of "the integration of the Américas," José David Saldívar has coined the term "Trans-Americanity."[12] Again, integration does not mean sameness; yet neither does it mean separateness. It means participation in the same transnational processes. A hemispheric turn in American Studies, by engaging in comparative analyses, reflects the idea that situations and issues are not the same throughout the Western Hemisphere; by exploring transfers and flows, interconnections and impacts, it contests notions of separateness. In the analysis of imaginaries in American Studies (driven by the work of Winfried Fluck), which recognizes that "the transnational and imaginary interact in bringing forth uncharted worlds" (Bieger, Saldívar, and Voelz xxvi), the element of the hemispheric needs to be part of the research agenda.

The time is ripe to take a new look at the so-called New World – a look that allows for a transdisciplinary consideration of the wider interAmerican contexts as much as for a continuing focus on national, regional, and local specificities. The "global flow" and the "global phenomena" of which Shelley Fisher Fishkin spoke in her presidential address to the American Studies Association in 2004 ("Crossroads" 24) have long been researched in American Studies as they pertain to Europe, and those transnational studies have in later decades branched out to include Africa, the Black Atlantic, and Asia. Pertaining to the Americas, this research may have addressed Canada and, more recently, the Caribbean. But it has rarely considered Spanish America and Brazil. The contexts of what Bolton called "greater America" tend to be neglected. What Rüdiger Kunow has formulated as a research agenda for cultural mobility studies

12 Saldívar remarks that "[t]he key historical and structural difference between Latin America and the United States in the nineteenth century and today, in the twenty-first century, however, is that Latin America and the United States of America (through globalization) are now part of what Quijano and Wallerstein presciently called a *single world order*, for the Americanization of the Américas is coming into 'full bloom'" (*Trans-Americanity* xiv; emphasis original).

therefore also applies to InterAmerican Studies: we need, writes Kunow, "a sustained attention toward the transversal relations, the various flows of people, money, images, and other objects, all of which make up the significatory outreach of the object 'America'" ("American" 261).

Works cited

Balseiro, José Agustín. *Seis estudios sobre Rubén Darío*. Madrid: Editorial Gredos, 1967. Print.

Bieger, Laura. "Belonging and Transnational American Studies: Reflections on a Critical Approach and a Reading of Richard Powers's *The Echo Maker*." *Re-Framing the Transnational Turn in American Studies*. Ed. Winfried Fluck, Donald E. Pease, and John Carlos Rowe. Hanover, NH: Dartmouth UP, 2011. 219–264. Print.

Bieger, Laura, Ramón Saldívar, and Johannes Voelz. "The Imaginary and its Worlds: An Introduction." *The Imaginary and its Worlds: American Studies after the Transnational Turn*. Ed. Laura Bieger, Ramón Saldívar, and Johannes Voelz. Hanover, NH: Dartmouth UP, 2013. vii–xxviii. Print.

Bolton, Herbert Eugene. "The Epic of Greater America." *American Historical Review* 38.3 (1933): 448–474. Print.

Buchenau, Barbara. "Inventing Iroquoia? Migrating Tropes of Similarity and Heritage in Francophone Narratives of Colonial Possession." *FIAR: Forum for Inter-American Research* 4.2 (2011).

Darío, Rubén. *Cantos de vida y esperanza*. 1904. Ed. Alfonso Méndez Plancarte. Madrid: Aguilar, 1967. Print.

———. *Selected Poems of Rubén Darío*. Trans. Lysander Kemp. Austin: U of Texas P, 1965. Print.

Dirlik, Arif. "American Studies in the Time of Empire." *Comparative American Studies* 2.3 (2004): 287–302. Print.

Fishkin, Shelley Fisher. "Crossroads of Cultures: The Transnational Turn in American Studies: Presidential Address to the American Studies Association, November 12, 2004." *American Quarterly* 51.1 (2005): 17–57. Print.

———. "Mapping Transnational American Studies." *Transnational American Studies*. Ed. Udo J. Hebel. Heidelberg: Winter, 2012. 31–74. Print.

Fitz, Earl E. "Inter-American Studies as an Emerging Field: The Future of a Discipline." *Review of International American Studies* 3.1–2 (2008): 32–44. Web. 10 Jul. 2015.

Fluck, Winfried. "Theories of American Culture (and the Transnational Turn in American Studies)." *REAL: Yearbook of Research in English and American Literature* 23 (2007): 59–77. Print.

Greenblatt, Stephen. "Cultural Mobility: An Introduction." *Cultural Mobility: A Manifesto*. Ed. Stephen Greenblatt, Ines Županov, Reinhard Meyer-Kalkus, Heike

Paul, Pál Nyíri, and Friederike Pannewick. Cambridge: Cambridge UP, 2009. 1–23. Print.

Hebel, Udo J. "Preface." *Transnational American Studies*. Ed. Udo J. Hebel. Heidelberg: Winter, 2012. 1–9. Print.

Kadir, Djelal. "America and its Studies." *PMLA* 118.1 (2003): 9–24. Print.

Kaltmeier, Olaf. "Transnational Americas: Envisioning Inter-American Area Studies in Globalization Processes." *Transnational Americas: Envisioning Inter-American Area Studies in Globalization Processes*. Ed. Olaf Kaltmeier. Trier: WVT; Tempe, AZ: Bilingual Press, 2013. 1–14. Print.

Kunow, Rüdiger. "American Studies as Mobility Studies: Some Terms and Constellations." *Re-Framing the Transnational Turn in American Studies*. Ed. Winfried Fluck, Donald E. Pease, and John Carlos Rowe. Hanover, NH: Dartmouth UP, 2011. 245–264. Print.

———. "City of Germs: Biological Identities and Ethnic Cultures in the Metropolis." *EthniCities: Metropolitan Cultures and Ethnic Identities in the Americas*. Ed. Martin Butler, Jens Martin Gurr, and Olaf Kaltmeier. Trier: WVT; Tempe, AZ: Bilingual Press, 2011. 171–189. Print.

Lenz, Günter H. "Toward a Politics of American Transcultural Studies: Discourses of Diaspora and Cosmopolitanism." *Re-Framing the Transnational Turn in American Studies*. Ed. Winfried Fluck, Donald E. Pease, and John Carlos Rowe. Hanover, NH: Dartmouth UP, 2011. 391–425. Print.

Levander, Caroline F., and Robert S. Levine. "Introduction. Essays Beyond the Nation." *Hemispheric American Studies*. Ed. Caroline F. Levander and Robert S. Levine. New Brunswick: Rutgers UP, 2008. 1-17. Print.

Marcus, Greil, and Werner Sollors, eds. *A New Literary History of America*. Cambridge, MA: Harvard UP, 2012. Print.

Mato, Daniel. "On the Making of Transnational Identities in the Age of Globalization: The U.S. Latina/o-'Latin' American Case." *Cultural Studies* 12.4 (1998): 598–620. Print.

Moya, Paula, and Ramón Saldívar. "Fictions of the Trans-American Imaginary." *Modern Fiction Studies* 49.1 (2003): 1–18. Print.

Pease, Donald E. "Introduction: Re-Mapping the Transnational Turn." *Re-Framing the Transnational Turn in American Studies*. Ed. Winfried Fluck, Donald E. Pease, and John Carlos Rowe. Hanover, NH: Dartmouth UP, 2011. 1–46. Print.

———. *The New American Exceptionalism*. Minneapolis: U of Minnesota P, 2009. Print.

Priewe, Marc. "Resistance without Borders: Shifting Cultural Politics in Chicana/o Narratives." *Re-Framing the Transnational Turn in American Studies*. Ed. Winfried Fluck, Donald E. Pease, and John Carlos Rowe. Hanover, NH: Dartmouth UP, 2011. 265–279. Print.

Raab, Josef. "Difference Matters: Toward an Inter-American Approach to 'Race,' Difference, and Belonging." *The International Turn in American Studies*. Ed. Marietta Messmer. Frankfurt: Peter Lang, 2015. 129–171. Print.

———. "Thinking Beyond the Nation: The Project of Inter-American Studies." *Crossing Boundaries in the Americas: Dynamics of Change in Politics, Culture, and Media/ Cruzando fronteras en las Américas: Las dinámicas des cambio en la política, la cultura y los medios*. Ed. Yolanda Campos García and Graciela Martínez-Zalce, 2015. 21–51. Print.

———, ed. *New World Colors: Ethnicity, Belonging, and Difference in the Americas*. Trier: WVT; Tempe, AZ: Bilingual Press, 2014. Print.

Raussert, Wilfried. "Mobilizing America/América: Toward Entangled Americas and a Blueprint for Inter-American 'Area Studies.'" *FIAR: Forum for Inter-American Research* 7.3 (2014): 59–97. Web. 10 July 2015.

Roosevelt, Theodore. "Corollary to the Monroe Doctrine." *Our Documents*. Our Documents Initiative. N.d. Web.

Rowe, John Carlos. "Areas of Concern: Area Studies and the New American Studies." *Re-Framing the Transnational Turn in American Studies*. Ed. Winfried Fluck, Donald E. Pease, and John Carlos Rowe. Hanover, NH: Dartmouth College UP, 2011. 321–336. Print.

———. "Music and the New American Studies." *Cornbread and Cuchifritos: Ethnic Identity Politics, Transnationalization, and Transculturation in American Urban Popular Music*. Ed. Wilfried Raussert and Michelle Habell-Pallán. Trier: WVT; Tempe, AZ: Bilingual Press, 2011. 27–39. Print.

———. *The New American Studies*. Minneapolis: U of Minnesota P, 2002. Print.

Saldívar, José David. *Trans-Americanity: Subaltern Modernities, Global Coloniality, and the Cultures of Greater Mexico*. Durham: Duke UP, 2012. Print.

Sassen, Saskia. "Globalization or Denationalization?" *Review of International Political Economy* 10.1 (2003): 1–22. Print.

Sexton, Jay. "The US and Spanish American Revolutions." *The Gilder Lehrman Institute of American History*. The Gilder Lehrman Institute of American History. N.d. Web.

Shukla, Sandhya, and Heidi Tinsman. "Editor's Introduction." *Our Americas: Political and Cultural Imaginings*. Ed. Sandhya Shukla and Heidi Tinsman. Spec. issue of *Radical History Review* 89 (2004): 1–10. Print.

Stavans, Ilan, ed. *Mutual Impressions: Writers from the Americas Reading One Another*. Durham: Duke UP, 1999. Print.

Whitaker, Arthur P. *The Western Hemisphere Idea: Its Rise and Decline*. Ithaca: Cornell UP, 1954. Print.

Yúdice, George. "Los estudios culturales en la encrucijada de la incertidumbre." *Revista Iberoamericana* LXIX.203 (2003): 449–464. Print.

The Power of Perceptions: Theodore Roosevelt, Latin America, and the European Powers, 1898–1909

STEFAN RINKE

"He is American in every corpuscle of his blood, in every fiber of his brain.
He is American by nature, and not by legend … Everything is strenuous in him,
the idea as well as the expression, the form as well as the substance,
because everything is natural, as in ancient nations, whom we call barbarian;
but everything is also pure, like the heart of the earth,
which no one has ever touched."
La Tribuna (Rome), quoted in Louis E. Van Norman (304).

After victory in the Spanish-American war, the United States emerged as a great power on the scene of international politics. During the presidencies of William McKinley and Theodore Roosevelt, the U.S. acquired colonies, emphasized its exclusive claim to the Western Hemisphere by expanding the Monroe Doctrine, and for the first time actively intervened in European diplomatic tangles. Not only in terms of political power but also in terms of economic growth, the U.S. seemed to symbolize incessant progress and expansion. European contemporaries were fascinated by this phenomenon but they also feared the "Americanization of the World" in the twentieth century (Stead 1). Developments on the other side of the Atlantic were simply amazing and stood in sharp contrast to what many felt was the slow but inevitable and obvious decay of old Europe.

At the turn of the century, then, the balance of power in the world system changed profoundly and so did the perceptions that global players maintained of each other. While a lot of research has been done on the history of international relations during these years we still know little about perceptions and even less about their impact on foreign policy. In this context, perceptions shall be defined as a system of images and stereotypes that allows us to understand, and interpret a distinct part of objective reality. They are instruments which enable us to structure the numerous information we receive e.g. of a foreign country into a meaningful whole by relating it to patterns of interpretation about ourselves and our view of the world that are already existing. The images are like a filter that determines not only what we see but also the way we see it (König and Rinke 10–12).

At this point a methodological caveat is in order. The analysis of perceptions or images and stereotypes on an international scale is problematic. The more so when we are dealing with a distant past. Much of what people at a given time thought about one another has to be read between the lines of a great variety of sources ranging from written to graphic and sound materials. Even if a historian makes ingenuine use of these sources she or he will still not be able to grasp the perception in all its dimensions. Because in order to do that a historian of national stereotypes, for example, would face the impossible task of scrutinizing the minds of all inhabitants of a given nation at a given point in time. For some the whole study of perceptions is thus futile or even ahistorical because its result will remain a construction (Barth 188–192). Modern historical discourse has taught us to bid farewell to the certainties of empirical scholarship of past epochs. All terms and forms of narration we use in order to explain some processes of the past are in itself constructions and can at best claim to get close to some aspects of that reality.

Moreover, perceptions research might even be a possible innovative way out of the methodological deadlock that historians of foreign relations have faced for such a long time (Ziebura 80). It is my hypothesis that perceptions and images of the other and of oneself played an important role in international politics in the era of imperialism. They were a basic framework and to a certain degree determined what was possible in terms of changes in the international constellation. My paper will focus on the interaction of power and perceptions. I am interested in the transition and influence of stereotypes, images, and prejudices on a transnational scale in a time of crucial alterations and crises. Hence, my guiding questions are: What did representatives of one given country think about other countries and in deduction of themselves? Under what circumstances and in how far did these perceptions change? To what degree did they affect international relations?

Between 1898 and 1908, the incarnation of the youthful and exuberant United States was Theodore Roosevelt – "American in every corpuscle of his blood, in every fiber of his brain" as the Roman newspaper *La Tribuna* once described it.[1] As politician, book author, and chief executive, he had a profound influence on the outlook and on the fate of the nation at the beginning of the twentieth century. To be sure, Roosevelt should not be confounded with American public opinion as such. But, in a way, he personified the self-image of a large proportion of Americans and many identified with him. In addition, as historian Lewis Gould has put it, Roosevelt was the "first modern celebrity president" ("Theodore Roosevelt" 43) combining effective leadership with an urban, aristocratic, and cosmopolitan style that was new to the White House. Roosevelt's celebrity status was known far beyond U.S. borders and contributed to European fascination (Collin 65). For these reasons, Roosevelt's views of leading powers like Germany, France, and Great Britain and European images of Roosevelt were chosen as a case study to approach the complex reality of perceptions. I will discuss them in two consecutive steps. In a third step, I will concentrate on the effects of this set of images on international relations.

1 For the German case, Gerhards states: "the whole German image of America in the decade prior to the First World War is decisively influenced by the evaluation of Theodore Roosevelt" (2).

I

In order to gain an understanding of Roosevelt's perceptions of Europe, it is important to recapitulate some of the basic facets of his worldview. Roosevelt was a firm believer in a way of life that he had termed the "strenuous life" (Roosevelt, *The Strenuous Life* 1). That implied a cult of physical fitness, masculine strength, and individualism which went hand in hand with contempt for everything weak. Being a rather typical child of his time, Roosevelt's belief in strenuousness was complemented by his ideas on nationalism and race. He represented the type of ardent nationalist who lived in the belief that his country could never do wrong (Beale 23–26). In addition, he was convinced of the superiority of some "races" over others. According to his views, the United States clearly belonged to those superior "races." The United States had reached the highest possible stage of civilization which reflected in its power to dominate weaker nations e.g. in the Western Hemisphere. There was no reason to rest on the laurels, however, because of the dangers inherent in decadence and decline. The virtues of civilization had to be counterbalanced by a healthy mixture with the barbarian heritage as expressed in martial qualities and expansionism (Dyer 23). To a man of his mind-set, international rivalries seemed to be a natural result of the eternal struggle for the survival of the fittest. War was the ultimate competition, a romantic adventure, and Roosevelt gladly accepted the opportunity to actively participate in the Spanish-American conflict of 1898/1899.

In how far did Roosevelt's worldview influence his perceptions of the European powers? Following his own priorities, we first have to talk about Great Britain. An important part of Roosevelt's set of ideas on race was his Anglo-Saxonism. There existed a strong bond of ethnic or cultural kinship between what he called the "English speaking race" (Beale 26–28). He admired the British for their ability to rule their vast empire. Indeed, Roosevelt was convinced that Great Britain and the United States shared a quasi-religious mission to expand and thus spread civilization. Being in close contact with a great number of English friends and correspondents, his image of the British was based on personal experiences. He attributed qualities like chivalry, bravery, honesty, and a strong sense of practical-mindedness to the Britons. Being birds of a feather, the British qualities reflected those of the United States.

There was a difference, though. The deterministic topos of the rise and fall of powers loomed large in the thought of many contemporaries and for some it was a dogma, a matter of faith (Kennedy, *The Rise and Fall* 195–197). It certainly had a strong influence on Roosevelt's perceptions. The British "race" was older and more civilized but also more senile and prone to decadence. While the British were endangered to lose their preponderance, their younger American brothers were still on the rise. Statistics of industrial and agricultural output and population growth proved this beyond doubt. Although Roosevelt detected signs of decay in his own country, e.g. in the anti-imperialist thought of his days, that was nothing in comparison to the rapid decline the British seemed to experience at the turn of the century. The Boer War and other problems of the empire made him answer a letter from his German diplomat-friend Hermann Speck von Sternburg as follows: "What you tell me about England's decay makes me feel rather sad, but is in exact accord with my own observations and with what I hear from other sources."[2] Nevertheless, Roosevelt upheld his belief in a providential Anglo-American community of interest.

As to the Germans themselves, the president's image was not as positive as that which he held of the British. On the one hand, he at times included Germany into a "teutonic race" which he thought was chosen to rule the world. Roosevelt who had been to Germany in his youth had a strong predilection for German culture and especially for the Nibelungenlied where he found the tales of adventure and bravery that thrilled his imagination. Indirectly, he claimed that epic as a remote part of the American heritage comparing it to the experiences on the American frontier (Roosevelt, *Autobiography* 23). In the German empire of his own times, Roosevelt detected many traces of the admirable ancient heroes: efficiency, courage, military strength. Indeed, Germany seemed to be a young, sound, dynamically growing and expanding nation still on its rise and thus comparable to the United States.

However, Roosevelt's perceptions of Germany also included a notion of dangerous militarism and war-mongering. While he wished his fellow Americans would be more willing to adopt some of the military spirit, the degree of militarization of German society simply went too far. The more so because Germany remained an autocracy. A hierarchically structured society that cherished values of deference and philosophical idealism could hardly appeal to U.S. republicanism and materialism (Kennedy, "British and German Reactions" 18). Prussian military stiffness gave Roosevelt cause for derision and ridicule as even the relationship to Sternburg, his closest German acquaintance, shows (Rinke, "The German Ambassador" 5). There was a fundamental ambivalence in Roosevelt's perception of the modern German empire. An ambivalence that reflected the inner-German contradiction of a modern industrial complex and an archaic social system.

France did not hold a very high place in Roosevelt's sympathies. In his racial thought, the Latin race was clearly on the losing side. France had once been strong but overcivilization and decadence had become obvious in the war of 1870/71. Like many Americans, Roosevelt appreciated French culture and refinement. But he was also unequivocal about what to him was a tendency to "race suicide." To him the declining birth rate in France was a clear sign of the ruin of morals and decency by sexual promiscuity. Despite this negative predisposition, Roosevelt was flexible enough to modify his views. The close personal relationship to French ambassador Jean Jules Jusserand made him reevaluate some of his extreme judgments. The conviction of a great difference between French and American national character and the latter's superiority, however, remained.

2 Roosevelt to Sternburg, October 11, 1901 (Morison and Blum 173).

II

A prolific writer and celebrity, Roosevelt was quite outspoken as to his views on other nations. We will now have to ask how Europeans reacted to and perceived the U.S. president. The perception of Roosevelt that emerges will by inference also allow some results about the European image of the United States at large.

Early after Roosevelt's accession to office the British *St. James Gazette* rhymed:

> Smack of Lord Cromer,
> Jeff Davis, a touch of him;
> A little of Lincoln,
> But not very much of him;
> Kitchener, Bismarck, and Germany's Will,
> Jupiter, Chamberlain, Buffalo Bill. (Van Norman 299)

Although not very significant in its aesthetic quality, this little doggerel to a considerable extent reflects popular imagination on the American President in Europe. According to the anonymous poet, Roosevelt resembled European politicians like Lord Cromer, Kitchener, Bismarck or the Kaiser. The common ground of this heterogeneous set of officials lay in their intense nationalism and – apart from Bismarck – their advocacy of imperialism. In addition, Roosevelt's power and his struggle against crime, corruption, and vice gave him the mythological aura of a Jupiter. What, then, was American about him? A little of a Jefferson Davis or a Lincoln, but not very much, as the poet makes clear; much more, however, of a Buffalo Bill, an American cowboy, simple, uncivilized, but courageous, strong, and trustworthy.

The rhyme in the *St. James Gazette* reflected the admiration many Britons – and Europeans at large – felt for an American who seemed to unify qualities commonly related to Old World leaders with those character traits that had developed in the New. His family background and upbringing made Roosevelt an urban American aristocrat who could easily stand his ground in the international arena. Europeans sensed this. They were aware that Roosevelt had spent several years in England, Germany, and France and that he had moved in the highest social circles. From these years stemmed the many friendships especially with British officials and intellectuals who had risen to influence when he became president and who strongly influenced the way Roosevelt was perceived in Great Britain. After many decades, here again was a president Europeans could accept as socially equal to their own leaders. A cosmopolitan who knew Europe first hand and who probably understood more of the workings in the European power system than any of his predecessors since the days of a Monroe or an Adams. For some, however, Roosevelt's sense of aristocracy went too far.

Figure 1: "Die Entdemokratisierung der Vereinigten Staaten."[3]

This strip cartoon of the German *Kladderadatsch* depicts the "De-democratization of the United States" by Roosevelt's rule. The subtitle reads:

> Where are the nice times gone when one could negotiate shirtsleeved in the White House and blow one's nose without a hanky. – Today "Teddy's" head is in such a high stand-up collar that he cannot even look down during audiences anymore. Secretly, when all the doors of the White House are shut, the President has an imported poet laureate from Berlin sing his praise as "Teddy, the first" or "the Great."

According to this and related publications, Roosevelt was more royal than the king. And as such he was typically American, a parvenu with an arrogance Europeans found hard to bear.

But on the whole, most Europeans agreed that Roosevelt fulfilled the necessary preconditions for an important statesman. There was more than a vein of this notion when *The Times* remarked in 1904 that Roosevelt possesses

> the elements that make a great man, and he will leave a strong impress for good or for ill on the history of his country. His advantages are his transparent honesty of purpose, his "Bismarckian" frankness, his keen insight into the heart of things, his impatience of irrelevant and insignificant details, and his generosity in acknowledging mistakes …. Since he became President not a rash or provocative word has fallen from his lips. (Van Norman 301)

3 *Kladderadatsch* 25 (21st Jun. 1908): 2. Beiblatt.

"Since he became President ..."! But what was before Roosevelt's presidency? This question directly leads us to the other and from a European perspective even more conspicuous and captivating side of Roosevelt. Indeed, Roosevelt was also admired and sometimes feared for "his other qualities, – his breezy and invigorating self-confidence, his great political courage, his buoyant, eager, somewhat slapdash temperament ..." (Van Norman 300) as the editor of the English *Saturday Review* and Roosevelt intimate, Sidney Brooks, put it in 1904.

Roosevelt's exuberance caught great public attention. Europeans perceived and admired this father of six children, Colonel of the Rough Riders, hunter, rider, and sportsman for his vigor, his masculinity, and virility.[4] His sheer strength and impressive physical appearance, his self-confidence, his temperament, and the power of his personality simply could not be bypassed. These were important elements in European perceptions of Roosevelt. Analyzing the many cartoons and sketches of Roosevelt, it is easily discernible how the artists were attracted by his outward appearance. They had a particular predilection for his pince-nez glasses, his vivid eyes, his angular skull, and big nose. More important, though, was his mouth with its big teeth and its typical broad grin as well as his massive body (Albala 554). The cartoonist of the leading German journal *Kladderadatsch* grasped Roosevelt's physical exuberance convincingly in his sketch, subtitled "Roosevelt, the voice of imperialism."

Figure 2: "Roosevelt der Überseeredner."[5]

4 In Germany, popular magazines like *Die Woche* or *Über Land und Meer* contained numerous human interest stories about TR and his family (Gerhards 17–18).

5 *Kladderadatsch* 29 (19 Jul. 1903), Beilage. The German review *Die Zukunft* wrote in October 1900: "He always looks like he wants to eat somebody" (Gerhards 25).

This and many similar visual depictions of Roosevelt transported an aura of violence and aggressiveness which troubled European commentators. Thus, *Le Temps* of Paris wrote: "His friends cannot forget his constant jingo dithyrambs. No one since General Jackson has more complacently given free rein to the American eagle – that is to say, indulged in the spreadeagleism which the more sober tradition of Washington, Jefferson, and Lincoln had systematically avoided" (Van Norman 300–301). The London *Speaker* went a step further and stated that Roosevelt "in his ardent expansiveness, his dogmatic impatience, and the violent aggressiveness of his militarism, represents in all its nakedness the extreme type of the reaction against many of the soundest and most genuinely conservative tendencies of the American character" (301–302). The unease about growing American power on the world scene was reflected in a German cartoon on Roosevelt's role during the First Moroccan Crisis and the Algeciras Conference:

Figure 3: "Amerika auf der Marokko-Konferenz."[6]

6 *Kladderadatsch* 59 (21 Jan. 1906): 13.

The subtitle reads: "Just like old Munchausen Teddy manages to ride upon a coffee table without damaging the high horse of the Monroe Doctrine in the slightest way."

In this type of commentaries and cartoons Roosevelt was the incarnated American threat to European dominance (Lamprecht 77–78).

In an age that discovered youth as a new and independent way of life, Roosevelt's age was another important factor of fascination and mystique. At around the turn of the century, in Europe and foremost in Germany with its *Jugendbewegung*, youth was commonly associated with vitalism and rebellion against the given social order. There were hopes for a regeneration of society by some action of the young. They were to lead into a bright future of progress free of decadence and materialism. Youthful strength and health were to be guarantors for the conservation of the race. Roosevelt was 42 years old when he became President in 1901 and thus by far younger than the average top politician in Europe. The *Westminster Gazette* remarked that he was: "a remarkable example of a man who has reached the highest place without losing any of his youthful enthusiasms" (Van Norman 300). In many a press commentary the President's youth was cited as further proof of the youthful energies of the United States.

The following cartoon from the French illustrated journal *Le Rire* demonstrates exactly the antagonism of the youthful and strong United States as symbolized by Roosevelt and Old Europe looking worried over his shoulder.

Figure 4: "E pluribus unum" (Shaw 86).

Roosevelt's youthful revolutionary approach to politics was reflected foremost in his fight against corruption and the trusts during his first term as President. The big corporations were still a new phenomenon at the turn of the century. They were an outgrowth of capitalism that seemed to be uncontrollable and to endanger the whole sociopolitical system in the United States where they had acquired enormous proportions (Gould, *The Presidency* 27). But not only in the U.S. the trusts stirred fears of social unrest and the loss of economic opportunities especially in the middle class. The modern industrial agglomerations brought with them a new degree in corruption and vice which muckraking journalism so vividly exposed in these years. Consequently, the reputation of the whole political system had suffered.

To many Europeans who sensed similar problems in their own societies, the progressivist conservative Roosevelt who had obviously taken up the task of cleaning up the Augean stable appealed as a "New Hercules" like in this Swiss cartoon of *Der Nebelspalter* (Zurich):

Figure 5: "Der Neue Hercules" (Van Norman 301).

Or as (more or less) fearless tamer of wild and dangerous crocodiles like in this one from the English *Punch*:

Figure 6: "A strenuous performance" (Shaw 123).

Many European contemporaries perceived Roosevelt as the ideal type of a straightforward and honest politician who lived true to his beliefs and whose words – as reflected in his numerous translated publications – were in harmony with his actions. A Polish newspaper praised him for "the idealism of his views on life" and "the deep ethical meaning of his suggestions" and the English *Spectator* added:

> He is the inaugurator of a new era in American public life, a revolutionary who has dared to face the apathy of the cultivated classes and the ingrained corruption of party politics, and by the sheer force of a masterful personality has compelled the majority of his countrymen … to think with him. … America's eyes have been opened to the chances in her destiny, old catchwords have been discredited, old abuses exposed. A thrill of electric energy has gone through classes which at one time saw in the political life only a sordid career without honor or ideals. (Van Norman 301, 305)

Who could ask for more? But, then again, the cartoonist of *Punch* had clearly understood that Roosevelt knew how to gain that public interest, how to create this ideal image. If we look again at the top right corner of the cartoon we see a crowd of people watching Roosevelt's crocodile stunt. Indeed, a good deal of Roosevelt's positive image rested on the fact that he knew how to use publicity effectively to serve his own purposes. As President he took great pains to make sure that there was an extensive news coverage of his person and politics. He cooperated with a corps of journalists which he brought into line with stick and carrot (Gould 9). While Europeans admired his unquestionable qualities they also asked themselves at times if there was more show than substance to him and noted his "joy in splendour and in showing off his own personality" (Voechting 66). After all, this was a period when the concept of public relations had not yet come of age.

Puzzled *Le Temps* once called Roosevelt "a somewhat spectacular person" (Van Norman 301). This spectacular aspect of Roosevelt's personality was the one thing that all European commentators whether critical or enthusiastic could agree upon. But on the whole, the balance of European public opinion was certainly strongly in favor of the American President. For most, the reconciliation of the American cowboy with the European statesman had succeeded in the very person of Theodore Roosevelt. As the *Spectator* pointed out: "That he speaks in loud and firm tones, nay, shouts – that he holds on like a bulldog, is doubtless true; but he does not hold on to extreme things, but to the sensible and moderate things" (301). Usually, Europeans could forgive Roosevelt his more obtrusive character traits because he possessed something that they had only rarely associated with Americans, and that was charisma.

III

In this third part we will ask for the basic significance of these perceptions on the international system. Roosevelt's perceptions of the major European powers and European images of the President were reflected in profound changes in bilateral relations. Most important was the rapprochement with Great Britain which was in the offing ever since the Spanish-American War when the British had adopted a position of benevolent neutrality. From the American perspective it seemed that Great Britain was the only European power not openly against the United States (Beale 92). Certainly, there were many myths about the intensity of Anglo-American cooperation during this conflict. But they were made possible by a set of mutually positive perceptions. Moreover, they were reciprocated by a grateful American public during the Boer War, when Great Britain's policy and warfare caused almost unanimous international criticism (Anderson 137). Roosevelt and many other Americans who shared his views justified the British actions. Although they sympathized with the Boers, they left no doubt that Great Britain fought a just war for the cause of civilization (Noer 69).

Immediately prior and during Roosevelt's presidency, the British themselves created the basis for an even closer understanding with the United States. In the negotiations for a new Isthmian Canal treaty, Great Britain went a long way to satisfy American demands for complete control of that strategically important waterway. Roosevelt had made it clear that he could not accept the United States tolerating any restriction to its sovereignty in the future canal. The second version of the Hay-Pauncefote Treaty signed in 1901 reflected the British willingness to comply with U.S. demands. While British participation in the blockade of Venezuela a year later caused frictions, this did not contribute to a worsening of relations because American top politicians and public opinion held Germany responsible for this massive threat to the Monroe Doctrine (Rinke, *Weltpolitik* 73). Further proof of English compliance gave the Alaskan-boundary question that was settled in autumn 1903 to the great satisfaction of Roosevelt (Gould, *The Presidency* 81).

British interest in an Anglo-American understanding was more than obvious by 1903. It certainly reflected foreign policy considerations like the growing disputes with Germany or the problems within the empire. Moreover, the complimentary character of the English and American economies was understood. But, in addition, there was a third and perhaps even more solid pillar to rapprochement, that is the underlying British perception "that the American people are good boys – as nations go" (Van Norman 300). Americans like Theodore Roosevelt held similar views of the British. They developed the idea of a natural Anglo-American partnership based upon ideological and cultural factors such as a common heritage, language, and world view. This cross-identification resulted from positive images of the Briton or the Yankee that both parties held of each other.

Anglo-American relations stood in marked contrast to developments in the relationship between the United States and Germany. At the turn of the century, it was overshadowed by numerous frictions which could not be settled without leaving a bad aftertaste. The diplomatic incidents during the Spanish-American War when German foreign policy and public opinion favored Spain though officially remaining neutral have to be mentioned in this context. More important was the German role during the Venezuelan crisis of 1902/1903. In order to collect outstanding debts, an alliance of European powers had sent warships off the Venezuelan coast. In U.S. public opinion, the ensuing blockade was interpreted as a threat to the Monroe Doctrine. President Roosevelt exerted diplomatic pressure and firmly made his government's attitude known. The crisis was a decisive turning point in German-American relations because Germany was seen as ringleader (Rinke, *Weltpolitik* 91). And certainly what one scholar has termed Roosevelt's "Germanophobia" reached its peak between 1898 and 1903 (Coogan 63).

After the Venezuelan crisis, the empire tried to mend the damage done by sending Roosevelt's friend Sternburg as ambassador to Washington. In addition, Germans actively sought to harmonize the relationship by cultural measures. With the European situation worsening after the creation of the *entente cordiale* in 1904, the United States was ever more important as a potential German partner in the Far East and during the First Moroccan crisis (Rinke, *Weltpolitik* 109, 163). However, the nationalist right criticized the policy of German-American reconciliation. The negative image of the ambitious and aggressive American upstart who had no business in European or world affairs played an important role and was played upon in the interested parts of the German public.

On the other side of the Atlantic, the seed of mistrust sown at the turn of the century was not easily uprooted either. On the contrary, the Kaiser's escapades and bombastic speeches in combination with the zigzag of German foreign policy made Germany a major threat to European stability. In March 1901, Roosevelt had confided to his friend Henry Cabot Lodge: "the only power which may be a menace to us in anything like the immediate future is Germany."[7] He and many Americans continued to regard Germany as a constant source of trouble not only in the Western Hemisphere. Hence, five years later the President wrote: "Now I like and respect Germany, but I am not blind to the fact that she does not reciprocate the feeling. I want us to do everything we can to stay on good terms with Germany, but I would be a fool to be blind to the fact that Germany will not stay in with us if we betray weakness."[8] The deeply ingrained stereotype of a militaristic Germany can easily be detected in such a statement.

Roosevelt's sympathies for Great Britain and his mistrust for Germany went so far that when Britain concluded the Entente in 1904 the status of France was automatically enhanced. A reevaluation of Franco-American relations had been discernible ever since ambassador Jean Jules Jusserand had started to serve in Washington. Jusserand befriended Roosevelt and convinced him to modify his views about the French role in the international system. During the First Moroccan Crisis of 1905 and the Algeciras Conference of 1906, Roosevelt went to great lengths to strengthen the Entente, that is the French position against Germany (Forsberg 330). However, cooperation with France never was an aim in itself. Notions of an inferior Latin "race" on the one hand and of a breed of "uncultivated" American cowboys on the other continued to influence the relations between the two countries.

Theodore Roosevelt's perceptions of European powers and European images of the American President did not fit into clear-cut dichotomies of good or bad, right or wrong. Positive and negative ingredients freely intermingled. They were based on a variety of ideas that dominated the contemporary Zeitgeist, for example ideas on nationalism and race. Roosevelt had built his worldview accordingly. His predilection for the Anglo-Saxons but also his criticism of the decadence of old England stemmed from his belief in a racially structured world. His images of the British, Germans or French fed on these convictions. On the other side, European perceptions of Roosevelt reflected admiration for this aristocratic and youthful American. In addition, they proved the respect for the new great power United States. However, the images also showed European mistrust, envy, and fear of the American parvenu. The typical ambivalence in European views on America as such were reproduced on the level of an outstanding personality.

Perceptions are part of what people think about the world at large, part of their worldview. They are part of what they carry around with them each day. Hence, they are not easily nor rapidly changed. However, at around the turn of the century, a basic transformation in international perceptions took place in transatlantic relations. The

7 Roosevelt to Lodge (27 Mar. 1901 [Roosevelt, *Selections* 485]).

8 Roosevelt to Oscar S. Straus (27 Feb. 1906 [Morison and Blum 168]).

traditional Anglo-American antagonism of the nineteenth century was substituted by the conviction that the Briton or the Yankee respectively were good boys, after all. Britons and Americans discovered that they shared a common heritage and bonds of language etc. With a wise policy of compliance to U.S. desires in the Western Hemisphere, the British created the preconditions for a "partnership for civilization" that both nations were to undergo.

Britain's rival Germany could not keep pace. The empire's new role as international troubleshooter fitted to the stereotype of a militaristic nation that many Americans held. The differences in national interest between the United States and Germany were real during the decade from 1898 to 1908. But they were not such that they alone would explain the lasting negative effect of diplomatic frictions. There was also the sense for a fundamental difference in political cultures that gave German-American frictions a new dimension. Old stereotypes were reinforced along this line until finally in 1917 to be German meant to be the very opposite of a "real" American – an equation that worked both ways.

The perceptions, the images, and stereotypes that the actors held of each other contributed decisively to Anglo-American rapprochement as well as to the rise of the German-American antagonism. The very fact that Europeans accepted the United States – a country which did not even possess a respectable army – as a great power, that they were willing to include the U.S.A. in their diplomatic and strategic schemes can only be explained by their perception of a rising, young country. In addition, the way Americans accepted their new role and chose their partners and opponents cannot be understood by looking at the allegedly objective element of national interest. Beyond doubt, perceptions were powerful factors in the changing international system at the turn of the century.

Works cited

Albala, Monica T. "Theodore Roosevelt: The Man and the Image in Popular Culture." *Theodore Roosevelt: Many-Sided American*. Ed. Natalie A. Naylor, Douglas Brinkley, and John Allen Gable. Interlaken: Heart of the Lakes Press, 1992. 549–571. Print.

Anderson, Stuart. *Race and Rapprochement: Anglo-Saxonism and Anglo-American Relations, 1895–1904*. London/Toronto: Fairleigh Dickson UP, 1981. Print.

Barth, Boris. "Das Land der unbegrenzten Möglichkeiten: Die USA im Blick deutscher liberaler Finanzexperten vor 1914." *Transatlantische Perzeptionen: Lateinamerika – USA – Europa in Geschichte und Gegenwart*. Ed. Hans-Joachim König and Stefan Rinke. Stuttgart: Akademischer Verlag, 1998. 187–212. Print.

Beale, Howard K. *Theodore Roosevelt and the Rise of America to World Power*. Baltimore: Johns Hopkins UP, 1984. Print.

Collin, Richard H. *Theodore Roosevelt, Culture, Diplomacy, and Expansion: A New View of American Imperialism*. Baton Rouge: Louisiana State UP, 1985. Print.

Coogan, John W. *The End of Neutrality: The United States, Britain, and Maritime Rights, 1899–1915*. Ithaca: Cornell UP, 1981. Print.

Dyer, Thomas G. *Theodore Roosevelt and the Idea of Race*. Baton Rouge: LSU Press, 1980. Print.

Forsberg, Aaron P. "Ambassador J.J. Jusserand and Theodore Roosevelt." *Theodore Roosevelt: Many-Sided American*. Ed. Natalie A. Naylor, Douglas Brinkley, and John Allen Gable. Interlaken: Heart of the Lakes Press, 1992. 329–340. Print.

Gerhards, Josef Werner. *Theodore Roosevelt im Urteil der deutschen öffentlichen Meinung, 1901–1919*. PhD. Diss., Johannes-Gutenberg-Universität Mainz, 1962. Print.

Gould, Lewis L. "Theodore Roosevelt, Woodrow Wilson, and the Emergence of the Modern Presidency: An Introductory Essay." *Presidential Studies Quarterly* 19.1 (1989): 39–57. Print.

———. *The Presidency of Theodore Roosevelt*. Lawrence: UP of Kansas, 1991. Print.

Kennedy, Paul M. *The Rise and Fall of the Great Powers: Economic Change and Military Conflict from 1500 to 2000*. New York: Random House, 1987. Print.

———. "British and German Reactions to the Rise of American Power." *Ideas into Politics: Aspects of European History, 1880–1950*. Ed. Roger J. Bullen, Hartmut Pogge von Strandmann, and Antony B. Polonsky. London: Barnes & Noble, 1984. 15–34. Print.

König, Hans-Joachim, and Stefan Rinke. "Einleitung." *Transatlantische Perzeptionen: Lateinamerika – USA – Europa in Geschichte und Gegenwart*. Ed. Hans-Joachim König and Stefan Rinke. Stuttgart: Akademischer Verlag, 1998. 7–22. Print.

Lamprecht, Karl. *Americana: Reiseeindrücke, Betrachtungen, Geschichtliche Gesamtsicht*. Freiburg: Heyfelder, 1906. Print.

Morison, Elting E., and John M. Blum, eds. *The Letters of Theodore Roosevelt*. Vol. 5. Cambridge, MA: Harvard UP, 1952. Print.

Noer, Thomas J. *Briton, Boer, and Yankee: The United States and South Africa, 1870–1914*. Kent: Kent State UP, 1978. Print.

Rinke, Stefan. "The German Ambassador Hermann Speck von Sternburg and Theodore Roosevelt, 1889–1908." *Theodore Roosevelt Association Journal* 27.1 (1991): 2–12. Print.

———. *Zwischen Weltpolitik und Monroe-Doktrin: Botschafter Speck von Sternburg und die deutsch-amerikanischen Beziehungen, 1898–1908*. Stuttgart: Akademischer Verlag, 1992. Print.

Roosevelt, Theodore. *The Strenuous Life. Essays and Addresses*. London: Nelson, 1911. Print.

———. *The Autobiography*. New York: Scribner's Sons, 1929. Print.

———. *Selections from the Correspondence of Theodore Roosevelt and Henry Cabot Lodge, 1884–1918*. Vol. 1. New York: Scribner's Sons, 1925. Print.

Shaw, Albert. *A Cartoon History of Roosevelt's Career*. New York: The Review of Reviews, 1910. Print.

Stead, William T. *The Americanization of the World; or the Trend of the Twentieth Century*. London: The Review of Reviews, 1902. Print.
Van Norman, Louis E. "President Roosevelt as Europe Sees Him." *The American Monthly Review of Reviews* 30.7 (1904): 298–306. Print.
Voechting, Fritz. *Über den amerikanischen Frauenkult*. Jena: Diederichs, 1913. Print.
Ziebura, Gilbert. "Die Rolle der Sozialwissenschaften in der westdeutschen Historiographie der internationalen Beziehungen." *Geschichte und Gesellschaft* 16.1 (1990): 79–103. Print.

Breaking the Vicious Circle of Gang-Related Violence: Central American Minors and the Current U.S. Refugee Regime

MARIETTA MESSMER

Introduction

As early as fall 2011, an unprecedented number of families and unaccompanied minors coming primarily from the Central American countries of Guatemala, El Salvador, and Honduras began to make their way to the United States (Women's Refugee Commission, [WRC] 1).[1] The majority of these people, according to interviews conducted by the Women's Refugee Commission, "said that their flight northward had been necessitated by the dramatic and recent increases in violence and poverty in their home countries"; they cited "rising crime, systematic state corruption and entrenched economic inequality" (1) as the three most important reasons for coming to the U.S. For unaccompanied minors alone, however, the primary reason for leaving their home countries was "the growing influence of youth gangs and drug cartels .... Not only are they [children and adolescents] subject to violent attacks by the gangs, they explained, they are also targeted by police, who assume out of hand that all children are gang-affiliated" (1). The WRC thus concludes that gang-related violence in Central America "is generating 'lost' children" (1).

During recent years, approximately 6,000–8,000 of these children were taken into U.S. custody each year. While this number also includes infants, most of them (approximately 70 percent) are between the ages of 15 and 17 (WRC 3). Many of these young people have fled to the U.S. in the hopes of being granted protection against persecution by gangs. Yet, the U.S.'s current emphasis on securitization, which includes the management of migrant and refugee populations by means of deterrence, detention and deportation (cf. Messmer), has resulted in the rejection of most of their asylum claims. As a consequence, the vast majority of these minors faces deportation back to their home countries, which in effect delivers them back into the hands of the gangs or *maras* they had tried to escape from.

This essay proposes to analyze the current U.S. refugee practice through the lens of unaccompanied Central American minors. To date, the complexity of under-age migration and refugee movements is just beginning to be explored; for far too long child migrants and refugees were often just seen as "appendages" to migrating adults (Bhabha 2). Yet, child migration raises a lot of questions that differ from the issues raised by adult migrants and refugees due to the former's heightened vulnerability, as

1 Ca. 35% came from Guatemala, 27% from El Salvador, and 25% from Honduras (WRC 1).

well as their ambivalent legal position with regards to their capacity for agency. Not acknowledging these differences will lead to unsatisfactory or even oppressive migration and refugee policies. In other words, looking at the U.S.'s current refugee regime through the lens of Central American minors can reveal some fundamental inconsistencies, interrogate facile binaries, and challenge us to rethink seemingly easy categorizations. In *Means Without End*, Giorgio Agamben argues that the refugee "brings a radical crisis to the principles of the nation-state and clears the way for a renewal of categories that can no longer be delayed" (22). In analogy to this, one can argue that Central American under-age refugees bring a radical crisis to the U.S.'s current refugee regime (1) by highlighting the extent to which the U.S.'s current refugee practice tends to be overdetermined by its immigration policy priorities (focused on enforcement), in this way contributing to the escalation of the vicious circle of gang-related violence; and (2) by throwing into relief the extent to which children have repeatedly been reconceptualized in U.S. legal refugee discourse since the 1990s but have never been conceived of as agents in their own right. In this way, the (still too strongly) adult-centered U.S. refugee regime systematically disenfranchises minors by denying them the capacity for agency. Drawing on M. Aryah Somers, Pedro Herrera, and Lucia Rodriguez's survey of legal constructions of childhood, I will demonstrate how the U.S. refugee regime has shifted from conceptualizing child refugees as dependent upon special protection during the 1990s, towards a more ambivalent framing of them as both vulnerable and potentially threatening after 9/11, while the current administration under President Donald Trump has practically reduced unaccompanied Central American minors almost entirely to a national security risk. My contention will be that the current U.S. refugee practice needs to return to a more balanced framing of Central American minors that acknowledges their complex situation, but most importantly, it also needs to recognize these adolescents' capacity for autonomous agency in the context of resisting gang-recruitment. Such a reconceptualization of unaccompanied Central American minors by the current U.S. refugee regime could arguably contribute substantially to a reduction of the gang-related violence that is currently spiraling out of control throughout the northern triangle.

The *Maras* in Central America: U.S. origins and transnational activities

Many observers agree that currently, "[t]he problem of gang violence has reached epidemic proportions in Central America" (Corsetti 407). Because local and national governments are frequently unable to control them, "the gangs, or *maras*, operate as the de facto government within their zones of control" (407). The two most influential gangs across the northern triangle (El Salvador, Guatemala, and Honduras) are the Mara Salvatrucha ("MS-13"), and the 18th Street Gang ("Barrio 18"), both of which originated as Latino street gangs in the U.S. (Franco 1). MS-13 was first formed in Los Angeles during the 1980s by former Salvadoran guerrilla fighters and government soldiers (3). Their rival, the 18th Street Gang, was first established by Mexican migrants during the 1960s (3) because a local gang "rejected all youths who could not prove 100% Mexican ancestry" (Howell and Moore 14). Today, both *maras* "have an established presence in Washington DC; Northern Virginia; certain cities in Maryland; Nashville, Tennessee; New York, New York; Houston, Texas; and other rural and urban areas" in the U.S. (Franco 2).

When, due to changes in U.S. immigration law during the 1990s, many members of these gangs were deported back to their countries of origin, these deportees started to regroup in various parts of Central America.[2] While today MS-13 are still largely Salvadoran and Barrio 18 largely Mexican, "both gangs have established gang cliques in El Salvador, Honduras, Guatemala, and Mexico" (Franco 2). Because of this history, "some experts suggest that U.S. deportation policies have effectively transported U.S.-style gang culture to parts of Central America and Mexico" (n. pag.) while others insist that these deportations merely aggravated an already existing gang problem in the region (Howell and Moore 14). Yet, all observers agree that the U.S.'s deportation practice during the 1990s has had a significant impact on the growth of gang activities in the northern triangle as the deportees helped already existing Mexican and Central American gangs to adopt more sophisticated methods (15).

In addition, these gangs increasingly also began to establish connections to their gang affiliates in the U.S., which facilitated "cross-border communication, organization, and growth among gang members in the U.S., Central America, and Mexico" (USAID 18). Now, all cliques of MS-13 and Barrio 18 "conduct business internationally," including "the trafficking of illegal substances and people, kidnapping, robbery, extortion, assassinations, and other illicit profit-generating activities" (6, 16). Moreover, "[o]n Mexico's northern border, gangs are reportedly hired by international drug cartels for various services such as drug distribution and assassinations" (19). As USAID observes: "While gangs in each country have singular characteristics, gang members and their activities are intricately linked across borders. International borders in Central America and Mexico offer minimal obstacles to illegal crossings" (16). In addition, the so-called "revolving door" phenomenon also encourages transnational contact and cooperation:

> [W]hen gang members in Central America commit crimes in their own countries, they often flee the crime scene and hide out in the United States with acquaintances or family members – thus the door swings from the south to the north. Once in the U.S., deportation proceedings may eventually result in gang members being returned to their home countries (door swings from the north to the south). (USAID 19–20)

The Council on Foreign Relations estimates that more than 85,000 gang members currently operate throughout Guatemala, Honduras, El Salvador, and Mexico (Labrador

2 "In 1996, changes to U.S. immigration laws dramatically expanded the crime-related deportability grounds for non-citizens, including lawful permanent residents," which "resulted in the deportation of thousands of Salvadorans who had lived in the U.S. for many years" (IHRC 21–22).

and Renwick). Additionally, ca. 19,000 members of MS-13 and Barrio 18 are active along the U.S.-Mexican border (USAID 16). According to many reports, "Guatemala and El Salvador are internationally among the most violent countries today" (Howell and Moore 16), and "[t]he Government of El Salvador claims that 60 percent of the homicides are related to gang violence" (21). In the U.S., gang activity seems less dramatic, but still on the increase: According to 2009 FBI statistics (which are the most recent official data available), the United States has 8,000 to 10,000 MS-13 members (Correa-Cabrera, Lopez-Santana, and Pardo), yet, *The Daily Mail* claims that an estimated 30,000-50,000 Barrio 18 members currently reside throughout 20 U.S. states (Griffith).

Recent governmental responses to gang activity: the detrimental effects of the *Mano Dura* policy on children and youth

It is fair to say that at this point in time, "[g]ang activity has … evolved into a transnational concern that demands a coordinated, multi-national response to effectively combat increasingly sophisticated gang networks" (USAID 5). However, the various countries affected by these networks have not yet managed to fully coordinate their responses. Since 2007, the U.S. government closely cooperates with Mexico on a political, military, and economic level to fight the war on drugs, and it also assists the governments of Honduras and El Salvador (Franco 12), but the latter two efforts are less integrated. USAID regards the actions undertaken so far as "fragmented [and] disjointed" (6) and emphasizes that "[s]tructural weaknesses in the central American and Mexican judicial, law enforcement, criminal justice, and penitentiary systems" (7) often impede effective cooperation.

The report also criticizes that to date, those efforts that have been undertaken, have primarily focused on increasing law enforcement, with a special emphasis on "the arrest, detention, prosecution, and incarceration of criminals" (USAID 16). Most importantly, El Salvador, Honduras, the U.S., and to a lesser extent also Mexico and Guatemala, have prioritized passing harsher anti-gang laws as part of the so-called enforcement first or *mano dura* [firm hand] policy, while only the latter two countries also emphasize the need for prevention measures (6–7).[3] In USAID's view, however, the *mano dura* approach is too one-sided: "Gang and youth violence problems are complex and … a coordinated response that incorporates prevention, intervention, and law enforcement approaches is needed in order to achieve sustainable results" (21). One of the central goals of their report is to highlight the problematic effects of an anti-gang policy that is primarily based on stricter law enforcement.

3 Franco notes that the U.S. has implemented various measures: the FBI launched the MS-13 National Gang Task Force (2004); the Safe Streets and Violent Crimes Initiative; the National Gang Intelligence Center (2005); and the Gang Targeting Enforcement Coordinating Center (Franco 9–11).

Honduras and El Salvador, the two countries with the harshest anti-gang laws, can serve as good illustrations here. In the context of its *mano dura* policy, Honduras has started to militarize its civilian security forces. "In 2010, a law was passed to enable joint military/police action to combat organized crime, a move that Honduran Defense Minister Marlon Pascua has called 'positive and significant'" (WRC 10). Moreover, the U.S. Drug Enforcement Administration "has established military-style operating bases in the country and conducted commando-style anti-trafficking raids alongside Honduran troops under a policy known as 'Operation Anvil'" (9). This, however, has done nothing to curb the level of violence. According to the Women's Refugee Commission, "[o]ver the past few years, Honduras has become one of the most dangerous countries in the world. In 2011, Honduras earned the dubious distinction of having the highest murder rate in the world, with 86 people killed for every 100,000, up from 82 in 2010" (9). This violence particularly affects children and youth: Mexican drug cartels have started to recruit Honduran children

> to carry out kidnappings, extortion and murder. Collaboration between the drug cartels and the *maras* has led to a significant increase in both inter-gang and generalized violence, with children and teens being the primary targets. According to statistics from the University of Democracy, Peace and Security, 920 Honduran children were murdered between January and March of 2012. (WRC 9)

As the WRC report concludes: "[I]nstead of curbing corruption, which remains rampant at all levels of the police force, the intervention of the military under this so-called *mano dura* [iron fist] policy has done little apart from ramping up the state's use of force against children suspected of gang involvement" (10).

The International Human Rights Clinic (IHRC) confirms similar developments for El Salvador: "The primary governmental response to the gang phenomenon [in El Salvador] … relies heavily on repressive law enforcement-military tactics, mass arrests, and profiling of youth and alleged gang members" (ii).[4] At the same time, the report concludes, these measures have been "ineffective and even counter-productive …. Homicide rates have soared since 2003, when former President Francisco Flores launched the Mano Dura [Iron Fist] crackdown" (ii), and even more so, when in August 2004 former President Antonio Saca announced the Súper *Mano Dura* [Super Firm Hand] plan (43),[5] which was strengthened even further by the anti-terrorism

---

4 "[W]ith the exception of the underfunded [and therefore largely ineffective] Mano Amiga and Mano Extendida plans …, the Salvadoran government has failed to develop any alternative to the Mano Dura-style strategies for addressing the gang phenomenon" (IHRC 45).

5 "Súper Mano Dura included permanent reforms to the penal code, the penal process code, and the juvenile law. The penal code reforms made membership in an illicit association an aggravating circumstance in a crime. The law amended Article 345 of the penal code, relating to illicit associations to increase the punishment for membership in such an association to three to five years in prison and for leadership in such an association to six to nine years in prison. Under the pre-existing Article 345, only committing or planning to commit crimes was punished. The definition of illicit associations was

measures of 2007. "In 2011, El Salvador had a homicide rate that was only marginally lower than that of Honduras, with 66 people killed for every 100,000 inhabitants" (WRC 10).[6] Moreover, "[v]iolence against women and gender-based murders ("femicides") are on the rise in Honduras, with over 2,000 women murdered between 2006 and 2011. Gender-based violence is now the second highest cause of death for women of reproductive age in the country" (10). Today, "most experts attribute the organizational evolution and consolidation of the two major gangs [MS-13 and Barrio 18] largely to the Salvadoran …. '*Mano Dura*' [Firm Hand] and 'Súper Mano Dura' [Super Firm Hand] anti-gang policies" (26). According to the IHRC report, these policies

> have catalyzed the development of more sophisticated organizational structures within Salvadoran gangs. These policies, for instance, have led to the arrest and detention of high-level gang leaders (as well as many other gang members) and to efforts to segregate the resultant high number of prisoners by gang affiliation. In practice, such efforts have led to the extended congregation of gang leaders in single locations, giving these leaders the opportunity to enhance their level of organization. (26)

In other words, "the prisons became breeding grounds for [new levels of] gang violence" (Harris and Weibel 6).

> One illustration of this new dynamic is the increasingly widespread practice of extortion carried out against businesses and individuals, commonly referred to as "collecting *renta*," which includes charging bus operators or taxi drivers a daily fee of $1 per vehicle, or charging residents who happen to live in a specific neighborhood controlled by gangs. (IHRC 28–29)

Those who do not comply with these "requests" routinely receive death threats (29). Yet, despite its harsh law-enforcement measures, the Salvadoran government seems unable to control corruption, which leaves the vast majority of homicides unsanctioned (IHRC ii):

> Beyond the failure to investigate death squad killings of gang members, there is evidence of complicity on the part of state authorities in the actual execution of these crimes. One NGO director working in a poor neighborhood on the outskirts of San Salvador notes that death squad killings of gang members in his area "coincide with weapons going missing from the police station." (93)

Moreover, "[g]angs continue to have influence over prison guards, security forces, and even the judiciary, which boasts a criminal conviction rate of less than 5 percent" (WRC 10).[7]

---

amended to include any group that carries out violent acts or that uses violent means to initiate, retain, or mark the exit of its members. Since President Saca's announcement of the Súper Mano Dura Plan, the homicide rate in El Salvador has risen markedly" (IHRC 44).

6 "In late spring of 2012, however, the murder rate in El Salvador dropped off sharply as a result of a peace pact between the feuding Mara Salvatrucha and Barrio 18" (WRC 10).

7 Corsetti confirms similarly widespread levels of corruption for Guatemala: "civilians risk their lives whenever they assist authorities in the identification of gang members" because the latter may be released right away by courts (410, 412).

> In sum, the current resurgence of death squad activities in El Salvador indicates that the Salvadoran government has yet to build public institutions capable of providing for public security in accordance with the rule of law. In the absence of such institutions, centuries-old patterns of clandestine violence aimed at social control persist in their most brutal forms today. (IHRC 18–19)

The people who are most victimized by these conditions in Honduras and El Salvador, but also in Guatemala and Mexico, are children and adolescents: "A demographic youth bulge has created a cohort of youth without jobs, decent education, or realistic expectations of employment. The four Central American countries have a combined total population of nearly 30 million people and approximately 60 percent are under 25 years old" (USAID 17). Many of these youth are at risk of joining or being recruited by a gang. As the WRC report observes, "[g]angs have increasingly begun targeting children at their schools, resulting in El Salvador having one of the lowest school attendance rates in Latin America" (10).[8] In Honduras, too, gangs dominate state-run schools (5). They also seem to target increasingly younger children: "Researcher and IUDOP Director Jeannette Aguilar told our team that her research had uncovered evidence that gangs were targeting children as young as eight or nine years old for recruitment" (31).

The recruitment process is usually shaped by high levels of violence: "[T]he initiation rites associated with becoming a full-fledged member of one of the two major gangs have become much more extreme in recent years" and include rituals such as "sending new recruits on 'missions' [*misiones*] to kill rival gang members or others" (IHRC 31).[9] Female recruits are frequently subjected to "the notorious practice of the 'train' [tren]" during which they "are forced to have sex successively with several gang members as a means of initiation" (32). All observers unanimously agree that to oppose a gang by resisting recruitment is tantamount to a death sentence: "To publicly oppose the gangs, through refusal to join them or open confrontation, is to risk death, not only for oneself, but also for one's loved ones" (Corsetti 407). As Corsetti continues, "[t]he gangs often make no distinction between the actual recruit and their families for purposes of persecution" (422). "Previously, youth gangs used a variety of tactics to put pressure on children to join; now, the gangs operate under a ruthless 'join or die' policy" (WRC 7–8).

Numerous interviewees confirm the life-threatening dangers faced by those who refuse to join: "It's like being in a war and being the only one without a weapon," a 30-year-old former Salvadoran gang member said, referring to daily life for non-gang-members in El Salvador (IHRC 76). "Today if you're not part of the gang, they kill you; joining a gang is the only way of surviving in the environment. Before the gang

8 However, as the report also notes, "the government … has consistently denied evidence that gangs are targeting children at schools" (WRC 10).

9 "Numerous sources with whom we spoke in El Salvador referred to the conflict between the MS-13 and the Mara 18 as a war in which members of each side were obligated by internal codes to kill anyone thought to belong to the enemy" (IHRC 33).

was like your family; now you have to join or they kill you," he continued (76–77). IHRC also reports an incident "in which gang members attacked and killed a man who lived in gang territory but had failed to join the gang, as well as multiple incidents in which gang members murdered youths who rejected the members' explicit invitations to join them" (77–78). Another former gang member who left his gang seven years prior to the interview explains the procedure: "We would tell the young people to join …. We recruited four or five at a time. We killed several [people in the neighborhood] for not wanting to join us …. Ever since I was eleven, I was always with them. We killed about six guys around thirteen or fourteen years old" (78). And the desperate story of a 17-year-old youth illustrates how the constant pressure to join a gang can ultimately result in reverse killing:

> The ones from Mara 18 were always harassing me [for not joining the gang]. They wanted to rob things from me and my family. This was happening for like two years before I killed that guy Tiny. Tiny did this to a lot of people in our area. Whenever a kid was twelve or thirteen years old, he'd want that kid to do what he said. The ones in 18 would always bother me in the streets. If they saw that I had money, they'd take it away from me. If I rode a bike, they'd take that away from me. They had a strong presence in my neighborhood. And I couldn't go to another neighborhood, because that neighborhood was MS, and they thought that I was in the 18, just because of my neighborhood. They said that I hung out with the 18 and they threatened me. I didn't want to get involved with any gang, because I didn't like how they are. The gang members are always in the streets harassing people. At night, they were being loud, shooting guns, throwing stones at whatever. They charge renta; they wanted to do this to my family. They started to bother my family when we didn't do what they said. (IHRC 78–79)

Yet, it is not only gang resisters who face death; those who try to leave a gang are equally at risk. Prior to the implementation of the *mano dura* policies, leaving a gang was possible in rare cases:

> Occasionally gangs will allow people to leave who have become parents or who have undergone a religious conversion. Lorena Cuerno Clavel, a social anthropologist who has worked with gangs for over ten years, explains that in practice, a gang member never ceases being part of a gang but may, in certain rare circumstances, become inactive. She also suggested that there are three ways of becoming inactive in a gang: embracing evangelical Christianity, forming a family, and migrating. (IHRC 79)

Currently, however, leaving a gang alive has become well-nigh impossible: "There is overwhelming evidence of extreme brutality and persecution within gangs, particularly against those who decide to leave them or reject membership in the first place" (Bhabha 234). As the IHCR confirms: "Those who were once part of gang life and decide to change their life paths face severe consequences; gangs consider abandoning the gang as a betrayal that justifies a death sentence" (76).[10] This is corroborated by

10 Tim Mc Conville, Coordinator of Equipo Nahual, explains: "Before [the] *mano dura* [plan], it was possible to leave the gang. Difficult, but possible. Now it's no longer possible" (IHRC 79). "Active and former gang members report that it is increasingly difficult, if not impossible, for young people to escape the pressure of gang recruitment or to

the experience of ex-gang members: "Right now the only way to leave a gang is to die. They tell you that if you find God you can leave, but even then they still kill you" (IHRC 80). Another former gang member explains that "killing people who left the gang was part of the initiation for new gang members" (80).[11] According to the IHRC,

> [y]oung people with gang tattoos are particularly at risk when they attempt to leave behind gang life. A staff person of a health clinic outside San Salvador, which offers a tattoo removal program sought by many former gang members, told our researchers that she has received threats and that she has heard that current gang members keep watch on the clinic, presumably to threaten those who seek help there. (34)

What is arguably even worse is that, at this moment, the governments of the northern triangle countries are not only unable to protect the children and youth who try to resist gang recruitment or want to leave a gang, but, as a result of their *mano dura* approach, they frequently even contribute to their persecution as suspected gang members. As the WRC report observes, "in certain neighborhoods in El Salvador, the simple facts of being young, male, and in a public space were sufficient to trigger frequent police suspicion and arrest" (IHRC 47). And in such cases, "the Salvadoran security forces have employed increasingly punitive measures against children suspected of gang involvement" (WRC 10). IHRC cites

> [a]n eighteen-year-old boy who became a street child in San Salvador at the age of thirteen [and who] reported that when he lived on the streets, he was repeatedly subjected to physical abuse by police: I had a lot of problems with police on the streets. Sometimes they grabbed me and beat me up hard, sometimes because they saw me rob something. They would hit me really hard, they would take me to dark areas … they would hit me with guns and sticks … sometimes when I was asleep in the street they would wake me up to beat me up … sometimes they beat me up and just left, sometimes they brought me into the police station. (53)

For this reason, children and youth throughout the northern triangle can be said to have become the targets of violence from two sides: the gangs, as well as the (frequently corrupt) police and government officials, with no government institution able or willing to protect them. At the same time, due to the gangs' transnational contacts, those who attempt to escape their violent neighborhoods "literally have nowhere to run and hide" (Corsetti 410), which is why more and more youth at risk seek refuge in the U.S. in order to escape the gangs, their corrupt government officials, as well as the militarized state police. These young people unanimously affirm that leaving for the U.S. is their only chance of survival because "staying in their country would guarantee death" (WRC 7). As Carlos, a WRC interviewee, confirms: "In El Salvador, there is a wrong – it's being young. You're stalked by gangs, authorities beat and follow kids because

---

leave a gang" (IHRC ii) because "gang leaders have intensified the system of internal obedience" and therefore "[g]ang members seeking to withdraw from active gang life face the same threat of fatal retribution from their fellow members" (33, 34).

11 "If people tried to leave the gang, we would kill them. This happened maybe six times during my time, always guys. This was a 'mission' for new gang members" (IHRC 80).

they don't trust them; they think they're gang members. There are no jobs for young people because employers don't trust the kids either …. It is better to be old" (qtd. in WRC 7). And another under-age WRC interviewee adds: "If you stay you will die, if you leave, you might … either way it's better to try" (9). Yet, when these minors arrive in the U.S., they frequently do not get the protection they are hoping for.

The current challenges faced by unaccompanied Central American minors seeking refuge in the U.S.

Jacqueline Bhabha has observed that, even though "children constitute almost half of the world's refugees, they amount to less than a third of asylum seekers in developed states" (209). She continues to note that in the U.S.,

> [f]or much of the 1980s and 1990s child asylum seekers and refugee children were in effect invisible to policy makers and enforcers, ignored in broader contemporary debates about migrant protection. The needs of accompanied children were subsumed under the general eligibilities of their families" while unaccompanied children were treated "on an ad hoc basis. (205–206)

"Not considered 'real' refugees in their own right, the best these unaccompanied or separated children could hope for was a compassionate or humanitarian status allowing them to remain on a discretionary basis … outside the formal system of refugee adjudication" (206). At the time, "no one pressed the case that children had an entitlement to refugee protection independent of related adults" (206).

This changed substantially during the 1990s when child refugees began to occupy a more prominent place in U.S. legal discourse. While this increased visibility has remained constant ever since and has led to a number of child-specific refugee laws and provisions, the nature of these provisions has changed quite dramatically since the 1990s. This can be attributed to major policy shifts, which, I would argue, are at least in part shaped by divergent conceptualizations of childhood. M. Aryah Somers, Pedro Herrera, and Lucia Rodriguez distinguish between five different constructions of childhood in legal discourses: developmental construction, dependency construction, privacy construction, autonomous construction, and threatening construction. The developmental construction, which according to Somers et al. is the most dominant one in legal discourse, "presents childhood as a progression of cognitive and psychosocial development toward adulthood" (Somers, Herrera, and Rodriguez 325). In other words, under this framework, children are perceived as gradually progressing towards understanding and reasoning (326). The dependency framework presents children as having "limited agency and depend[ing] upon adults to determine their objectives, make decisions for them, and represent their interests" (327). According to Somers et al., this construction is "often combined with a romanticized view of children as pure, innocent, in need of protection" (326). This view, however, results in denying children political agency; children are seen as passive and dependent victims rather than as agents or rights holders. In a similar way, the privacy construction "presents childhood as a space that is absent from political engagement," which means that children cannot be conceived of as political actors. "As a result, children are excluded from citizenship in a substantive way, considered apolitical, and are citizens *in potentia* only. Children have no political rights, such as the right to vote or strike, limited civil rights with respect to free speech, justice, property, personal freedom, and do not participate as citizenry" (327–328). In opposition to this view, the autonomous frame "presents childhood as a space of autonomy and agency" (328): Children are presumed to "have knowledge of the world that is different, not inferior, to adult knowledge" (329). What is more, "children's ideas, values and understandings of the world can inform and improve adult understanding, and, therefore, children can partner with adults to develop new policies and practices. As a result of these conceptions, children are viewed as active political, social and economic participants in the world" (329). Lastly, the threatening framework presents "children as predatory or dangerous … in need of control and containment" (330), and the rebellious character of youth culture, for example, is interpreted primarily as contributing to youth crime and gang activity (330 fn39).

When children were for the first time recognized as a unique group in U.S. refugee law during the 1990s, they were almost exclusively viewed through the developmental/dependency lens: they were regarded as highly vulnerable, with a heightened need for protection. This manifests itself, for example, in the 1997 *Flores Agreement* as well as the 1998 *Guidelines for Children's Asylum Claims.* The latter provides asylum officers with child-sensitive interview guidelines and emphasizes the youngster's well-being during the entire asylum procedure; it was updated and improved by the 2007 *Guidelines for Immigration Court Cases Involving Unaccompanied Alien Children,* which further strengthened the use of age-appropriate measures. The *Flores Agreement* set strict limits on the duration of and the conditions under which children can be held in immigrant detention. All of these documents helped increase the understanding of and sensitivity to children's specific needs and served to promote the protection, safety, and well-being of minors in asylum procedures.

This developmental/dependency framework slowly started to change after 9/11. In the context of the U.S.'s war on terror and on drugs, as well as its heightened national security concerns, the legal conceptualization of child refugees has since then become more ambivalent: while some procedures remain "strongly protective (for example, insisting that children not be placed in facilities side by side with unrelated adults)," at other times, they have become "resolutely punitive" (Bhabha 207). This increasing tension between a protective and a punitive approach can be attributed to an increasingly ambivalent conceptualization of child migrants and refugees, resulting in a "tension between a view of children as vulnerable victims deserving of protection because of their minority, [and] a view of children as treacherous juveniles, intent on border crossing by nefarious means" (230).[12] This ambivalence is clearly mirrored in

12 Unaccompanied minors' increasingly frequent reliance on smugglers along their trip to the U.S. also "exacerbates the hostile suspicion of the immigration authorities and generates increasingly punitive practices that damage access to protection" (Bhabha 207).

post 9/11 legal discourse. On the one hand, one can note a continuation of child-sensitive protection measures for under-age refugees, such as stipulated, for example, in the document *Children Entering the United States Unaccompanied*, published by the Office of Refugee Resettlement in 2015. Moreover, in 2014, as a response to the heightened influx of unaccompanied minors from the northern triangle, former President Barack Obama launched the Central American Minors Program, which simplified the asylum application procedure by allowing Honduran, Salvadoran, and Guatemalan parents (in 2016 expanded to siblings or caregivers) with a legal residency status in the U.S. to request a refugee or parole status for their children still residing abroad. However, with respect to asylum cases not covered by this Central American Minors Program, a different development emerges.

Most Central American minors currently applying for refuge in the U.S. cannot rely on a U.S.-based parent or relative for support and hence have to go through the regular asylum procedure. A review of recent U.S. court cases, however, reveals that the vast majority of applicants is routinely denied protection even though the UN High Commissioner for Refugees had explicitly identified Central American youth fleeing gang recruitment as potentially eligible under the 1951 Refugee Convention:

> The UN High Commissioner for Refugees (UNHCR), in its March 2010 Guidance Note on Refugee Claims Relating to Victims of Organized Gangs, stated that young people, in particular those who live in communities with a pervasive and powerful gang presence but who seek to resist gangs, may constitute a particular social group for the purposes of the 1951 Refugee Convention. The guidelines reinforce that powerful gangs, like the *maras* in Central America, directly control society and *de facto* exercise power in the areas where they operate. Due to the amount of influence gangs have over agents of the State, like police, opposition to criminal acts may be analogous with opposition to State authorities, making refusal to join a gang an imputed political opinion. (qtd. in WRC 12)

However, neither the political opinion argument nor the membership in a particular social group claim currently find acceptance in U.S. courts. In July 2008, the Board of Immigration Appeals (BIA) "affirmed an immigration Judge's … denial of asylum to three young Salvadoran siblings fleeing gang violence and threats" (Harris and Weibel 5). The group consisted of two Salvadoran teenage brothers (Pablo and Rene Mira) who were beaten and threatened when they refused to join MS-13, as well as their older sister (Silvia Mira) whom the gang had threatened to rape. After a "boy in their neighborhood was killed for refusing to join," all three siblings fled to the U.S. in order to apply for asylum (8–9). Their application was denied, however, because "(1) the Miras had not suffered past persecution; (2) they had not established nexus either to membership in a particular social group or to a political opinion; and (3) … the attack and threats occurred because the gang wanted to recruit new members" (9). The BIA claimed that the Miras were not "'politically active or made any anti-gang political statements'" (9), and they "had not shown that they were in more peril than Salvadorans in general. 'Gang violence and crime in El Salvador appear to be widespread, and the risk of harm is not limited to young males who have resisted recruitment,' the board found" (Preston n. pag). Moreover, "the IJ held that the Salvadoran government's efforts to control gang disproved the Miras' contention that the government was unwilling or unable to control gangs within its jurisdiction" (Harris and Weibel 9). Harris and Weibel note that this 2008 verdict subsequently became a precedent for denying Central American gang-related asylum claims in general (5). However, as Harris and Weibel criticize, to claim, as the BIA does, that an anti-gang opinion is not a political opinion, "suggests that only those who put themselves in more danger, by openly criticizing dangerous gangs, will be eligible for asylum based on their political opinion" (9).

Yet, apart from rejecting the political opinion argument, the BIA also did not recognize gang resisters as a particular social group because the group they claimed to belong to as gang resisters was considered too large, diverse, and amorphous (Harris and Weibel 10; Hill 646). Moreover, the three Mira siblings, according to the BIA, were "'not in a substantially different situation from anyone who has crossed the gang, or who is perceived to be a threat to the gang's interest'" (Harris and Weibel 10). The BIA, however, insists that the social group argument "requires that the group has particular and well-defined boundaries, and that it possesses a recognized level of social visibility" (10). This definition was subsequently confirmed by several circuit courts. The Ninth Circuit court, for example, argued that "threats and harassments faced by individuals refusing gang recruitment" are "a 'sad part of the general criminality and civil unrest perpetrated and perpetuated by the MS-13 in Central America' and found no evidence that those recruited by gangs were socially visible" (18). The BIA thus elevated "the notion of 'social visibility' from a *factor* in the determination of a particular social group to a *requirement*" (5), yet, according to Harris and Weibel, in doing so, "the BIA misconstrued the UNHCR Social Group Guidelines" (13) because this definition of visibility would entail that "you can be a member of a particular social group only if a complete stranger could identify you as a member if he encountered you in the street, because of your appearance, gait, speech pattern, behavior or other discernible characteristics" (Hill 650–651). However, as Hill remarks, homosexuality is usually accepted as a "particular social group" criterion even if people are not overtly and visibly gay (650).

A closer look at the Eleventh Circuit court's justification of the "social visibility" factor reveals what may be the deeper reason behind this line of argumentation: the fear that "the 'particular social group' persecution basis [would] become a 'catch all' ground for all persons alleging persecution in Honduras who cannot establish refugee status under any of the other recognized grounds" (Harris and Weibel 14). In other words, recognizing the social group argument would be tantamount to opening up the proverbial floodgates, but Harris and Weibel argue that "[y]outh fleeing gang persecution are exactly the kind of group that the social group ground was intended to address – to give refugee status to those suffering persecution on account of their membership in a particular social group not otherwise covered by race, religion, nationality, or political opinion" (15).

To date, according to Harris and Weibel, only the Seventh Circuit court has questioned this insistence on the social group's visibility in a 2009 case involving a Kenyan national:

> [I]t makes no sense; nor has the Board attempted, in this or any other case, to explain the reasoning behind the criterion of social visibility. Women who have not yet undergone female genital mutilation in tribes that practise it do not look different from anyone else. A homosexual in a homophobic society will pass as a heterosexual. If you are a member of a group that has been targeted for assassination or torture or some other mode of persecution, you will take pains to avoid being socially visible. (qtd. in Harris and Weibel 22)

Yet, to date, precedents of accepted claims on the basis of this argument are sorely lacking. All in all, this means that only a small number of Central American youth was able to get protection in the form of a temporary legal residence status under the Central American Minors Program (2,714 children and adolescents from the northern triangle [Nakamura]), while the vast majority of Central American under-age asylum applicants was faced with rejection.

The situation has even worsened under the current Trump administration. While the developmental/dependency framework has been further deemphasized, the conceptualization of children as threat has become the all-dominant perspective for viewing Central American minors: they are increasingly regarded as dangerous to U.S. national security. This is highlighted by recent measures implemented by President Trump, who terminated the parole option of the Central American Minors Program in August 2017 and plans to end the entire program (as of November 2017, no new applications for the refugee option are accepted). Instead, he has proposed as an alternative the *Central American Minors Protection Act*, "which would allow minors from El Salvador, Guatemala, and Honduras with a 'qualified parent or guardian' in the United States to apply for asylum in their home countries" (Saleh n. pag.). While such a procedure has sometimes been promoted as a humanitarian alternative that could prevent children from undertaking the dangerous journey to the U.S. on their own, Trump's proposal turns out to be far more problematic as it would simultaneously eliminate the possibility for Central American minors to present themselves at a U.S. port of entry in order to apply for asylum there. Moreover, the numbers would be capped at 15,000 per year, and DHS's decision (to accept or reject an applicant) could not be appealed (Saleh n. pag.). Given that Trump's proposal does not define "qualified parent or guardian" (n. pag.), the American Immigration Council has interpreted the proposal as a "'de facto asylum ban' for the vast majority of cases" as it might limit eligibility to children of U.S. citizens or permanent residents. "Central American minors who don't have a qualified parent would no longer have a route to asylum" (n. pag.) at all under this act. Moreover, in December 2017, the Executive Office for Immigration Review also revised the 2007 *Guidelines for Immigration Court Cases*, in the process significantly reducing the emphasis on child-friendly practices and seriously weakening the "best interests of the child" standard. In this way, as Bronstein et al. have observed, the new *Guidelines* contradict both the *UN Convention on the Rights of the Child* as well as the 1998 U.S. *Guidelines for Children's Asylum Claims* "which adopt the 'best interests of the child' as a 'useful measure' for appropriate interview procedures for child asylum seekers" (Bronstein, Mendez, and Cutlip-Mason n. pag.). Various plans to revise or terminate additional existing child-friendly agreements and regulations (e.g. the *Flores Agreement*) are under way.

This shift towards an almost exclusively restrictive and punitive approach to under age refugees can be attributed to the fact that the Trump administration regards especially Central American minors as violent and dangerous, associating them directly with criminal gang activity: In a 2017 statement explaining the phasing out of DACA, for example, Trump stated:

> The temporary implementation of DACA by the Obama Administration … also helped spur a humanitarian crisis – the massive surge of unaccompanied minors from Central America including, in some cases, young people who would become members of violent gangs throughout our country, such as MS-13. ("Statement" n. pag.)

Since then, his statements have become even more radical. In 2018, he said that MS-13 gang members "exploited the loopholes in our laws to enter the country as unaccompanied alien minors. They look so innocent; they're not innocent." He continued by picturing unaccompanied alien minors as dangerous gang members:

> MS-13 is one of the most violent and formidable threats that our country faces today …. It is estimated there are 10,000 MS-13 members in the United States …. And their ranks are continually being refilled with new emissaries from El Salvador. MS-13 is infiltrating our high schools, our middle schools, even our elementary schools …. [W]e arrested, in the past year, 300 MS-13 criminal arrests here on Long Island, and more than 40 percent of those we have verified are unaccompanied alien children. So it is a problem. There is a connection. ("Remarks" n. pag.)

This "connection" between violent, criminal gangs, and unaccompanied Central American minors has also been highlighted by U.S. Deputy Attorney General Rod Rosenstein: "What we found in recent years is a resurgence of MS-13 in Maryland, in the D.C. area, and it was fueled by illegal immigration and particularly by the challenge of unaccompanied minor children" ("Remarks" n. pag.). In a cynical twist to the dependency framework, he even reinterprets these minors' vulnerability: "We're letting people in who are gang members. We're also letting people in who are vulnerable. Many of these alien children, who have no parents, no family structure – we're releasing them into communities where they're vulnerable to recruitment by MS-13" (n. pag.). This view of under-age asylum seekers is also shared by a senior U.S. juvenile immigration officer:

> unaccompanied child asylum seekers are "runaways or throwaways," petty criminals in the making. Because of their harsh backgrounds, these young migrants are considered to be threatening adults more than children "like our own." In the words of a former Republican congressman, "Denying social services to *them* is something you have to do to stop the magnet effect that all of these combined things have, the health care, free schooling. This is all a magnet that draws people into this country and I'm trying to demagnetize it." (qtd. in Bhabha 249–250)

It comes as no surprise, then, that framing Central American minors almost exclusively as a security threat results in a privileging of detention and deportation as the most suitable approaches to containing this risk. In many ways, one can thus argue that in the U.S., national security concerns have started to overrule human rights and in particular child's rights perspectives as the U.S.'s prevailing immigrant deterrence strategy also informs its asylum policy, in this way applying "a punitive migration-management system that prioritizes deterrence even [to] child migrants seeking asylum alone" (Bhabha 220). One highly problematic way in which this manifests itself is the fact that, as Bhabha notes, "the United States does not guarantee free legal representation to unaccompanied child asylum seekers" (216). The significance of this lack of legal representation becomes clear when noting that "asylum seekers without lawyers were almost five times less likely to win in immigration court than those with representation" (Lakhani 126), which might also explain the high failure rates of the political opinion and the social group arguments. This means that, due to the U.S.'s framing of Central American children as a threat to national security, the vast majority of child asylum seekers has little chance of winning their claim; instead, they face deportation back to their home countries and hence back to the gang violence they had just escaped from.

The fate of Central American deportees

Currently, 91% of all deportations from the U.S. are to Mexico, Honduras, Guatemala, and El Salvador (Menjívar and Kanstroom 17), and such deportations usually have severe consequences for the returnees. At best, it means that returnees cannot count on their own government's support in the reintegration process. As USAID observes:

> In general, neither criminal nor administrative deportees to Central America and Mexico receive any social or remedial services upon their return to their home countries. This increases the likelihood that deportees will either attempt to illegally re-enter the United States or, with particular respect to criminal deportees, continue criminal activity in their countries of origin. (18)

At worst, however, deportees coming from the U.S. are frequently regarded as criminals by default and become the targets of both the national police as well as gangs in their home countries. In this way, Central American under-age returnees are faced with exactly the same preconceptions and prejudices (i.e. being perceived as guilty unless proven otherwise) in their home countries as they are in the U.S. According to the IHRC, "[o]ne primary consequence of the Mano Dura laws and policies has been the institutionalization of police profiling enforcement efforts targeted at certain groups," including tattooed persons and deportees from the U.S. (IHRC 45–46). El Salvador, for example, had passed Anti-Gang Acts in 2002–2003 that "specifically provided for the detention of suspected gang members upon arrival in El Salvador" (58).[13] These

13 "[E]mphasis on mass detentions – carried out by police military forces with limited investigative capacity and poor human rights records – has resulted in troubling patterns of arbitrary stops and arrests by Salvadoran police" (IHRC 48).

Acts were finally declared unconstitutional by the Supreme Court in 2004, but arbitrary arrests still continue (58).[14] Moreover, returnees do not only face police abuse but also social discrimination as "politicians and the media also tend to depict deportees as dangerous gang members and criminals" (47). The former President of El Salvador, Antonio Saca, for example, almost seems to echo President Trump when referring "to deportees coming from the United States in general as 'extremely dangerous people that have to be watched'" (96). In many ways, thus, in El Salvador but also throughout the rest of the northern triangle, "deportees have become scapegoats for worsening crime and other societal problems" (95–96). Like in the U.S., they are thus routinely framed as a threat to society by their own governments.

Frequently, however, deportees do not only face discrimination, harassment, and abuse but also death threats and/or actual death upon their return. As the IHRC notes, "[i]n the same way that gang members who try to leave a gang are targeted by fellow gang members, members who return to El Salvador are considered potential traitors and are targeted if they do not rejoin the gang" (99).[15] Preston reports the case of 15-year old Benito Zaldívar who was threatened by the 18th Street Gang after he refused to join them. When his grandmother died, he fled to the U.S. (where his parents already lived). However, his asylum application was rejected on the grounds that "the threats were vague and … the petitioners' lives did not appear to be truly at risk" (Preston n. pag.). Zaldívar was subsequently sent back to El Salvador in 2010, yet two months after his deportation he was killed by gang members: "[S]everal witnesses saw a Mara-18 gunman shoot him in the face, which they understood as revenge for speaking against the gang" (n. pag.). Another example is cited by Jacqueline Bhabha. She tells the story of a Guatemalan boy named Edgar who tried to hang himself while in U.S. detention when he found out that he would get deported. He was rescued, however, and sent back to Guatemala, but "[s]eventeen days after his removal from the United States, members of Edgar's former gang murdered him" (204). And a 19-year old Salvadoran in U.S. detention explains that he, likewise, fears for his life when returning to his home country: "Once I get out of here [detention] … I'm going to go [elsewhere] to live with my aunt. If they knew where I was they'd kill me. Either my gang or the other gang" (qtd. in IHRC 81).

The IHRC has interviewed many Salvadorans whose reports confirm the dangers returnees face after deportation. As a 32-year old deportee narrates: "Here I took my daughter to a fair, and another deportee came up to me asking where I was from. I told him. He'd been deported three to four months before that, he said, and he lifted up his shirt and had bullet wounds – he had already been shot after getting back here" (IHRC

14 "In July 2006, in a particularly visible illustration of the Salvadoran police's reliance on mass arbitrary arrests, police stormed a church in a poor neighborhood outside San Salvador during a wake for three young gang members who had been killed" (IHRC 51).

15 "[T]hose gang members who leave the gang and migrate to the United States face very serious threats to their safety if they are deported back to El Salvador" (IHRC 79).

100). And a 31-year old former gang member states: "In the time that I have been here, three or four deportees have been killed. One of them [was killed] only a block away from here …. Here to kill a deportee is like a trophy" (100).

Conclusion

The transnational threat posed by gang-related violence constitutes a highly complex problem and needs to be addressed from multiple perspectives. Scholars, politicians, and NGOs in the U.S. as well as in the northern triangle countries have made a variety of proposals that focus on local, community-based measures (to address child poverty and youth unemployment, for example), as well as national changes (to strengthen judicial and criminal justice systems and tackle corruption while also establishing social reintegration programs for former gang members), and transnational forms of cooperation that move beyond the enforcement-first approach (USAID 31–32) that, so far, has only led to an escalation of the vicious circle of violence. In this concluding section, I will mainly focus on the extent to which adjustments in the current U.S. refugee practice can contribute to increasing the protection of Central American minors attempting to resist gang-recruitment while at the same time also facilitating the de-escalation of gang-related violence.

Since the 1990s, when unaccompanied minors for the first time became more visible in U.S. refugee law, we have seen several shifts in U.S. child refugee policy, which can be correlated to a range of different conceptualizations of childhood. Today, however, unaccompanied minors entering the U.S. (especially those coming from Central American countries) are framed in a highly one-dimensional and reductionist way as dangerous and violent criminals. It is crucial to note that this framework currently prevails not only in the U.S. but also throughout the northern triangle, which is why all of these countries privilege an enforcement-first (*mano dura*) approach that puts young people (especially young males) under general suspicion and treats them as gang-members by default. One of the highly problematic consequences of this is a further increase in the escalation of violence: if gang-resisters fleeing to the U.S. have little or no chance of being recognized as refugees or parolees under the current U.S. refugee regime, they will eventually be deported back to their home countries, where, in turn, they will be targeted and persecuted as criminals and gang-members solely due to the fact that they are U.S. deportees. For the majority of Central American minors, it thus seems impossible to escape this vicious circle.

The 1990s have already shown that deportations, combined with stricter enforcement policies, constituted an explosive combination that contributed nothing to a de-escalation of the gang-problem but only increased transnational gang activity and lifted it to a more sophisticated level. For this reason, in order to break this vicious circle of gang-related violence, a reconceptualization of Central American minors is sorely needed at this point, both in the northern triangle countries, but especially also in the U.S. As a first step, U.S. courts need to recognize that, while some unaccompanied Central American minors may indeed be gang-members who could potentially pose a risk, the vast majority are more likely gang-resisters in need of more extensive legal support. With respect to the latter group, U.S. courts furthermore need to "recognize the distinction between a fear of common crime and a fear of persecution at the hands of violent, transnational gangs" (Corsetti 435), and to acknowledge the latter as a form of persecution as outlined by the UN Refugee Convention. This could pave the way for reconsidering gang-resisters' claims based on membership in a specific social group as a valid argument in an attempt to apply for protection against gang-related persecution. Corsetti, who accuses the BIA and circuit courts of "willful blindness" and "willful acceptance of torturous activities" (430), proposes that such a reconsideration could be supported by providing concrete evidence that government institutions throughout the northern triangle are gang-infiltrated; that governments routinely underfund the criminal justice system; that as a result, "authorities are ill-equipped and ill-trained to battle gang members"; and that therefore authorities cannot protect individuals against torture (431–433). Corsetti suggests that specific examples of localized police corruption would also be helpful in making such a case (432). In many ways, such a line of reasoning is similar to the position that Canada has already adopted.[16] Canadian courts do not focus on the social visibility issue in asylum claims by unaccompanied Central American minors but concentrate on the individual's risk and the country of origin's ability to protect the individual instead (Harris and Weibel 27). In this context, they fully acknowledge, for example, that the state's efforts to control gangs has failed completely in El Salvador (27).

In addition to reconsidering the social group argument as a basis for refugee claims by Central American minors, the current U.S. refugee regime also needs to be opened up to include the one childhood framework discussed by Somers et al. that has – to date – never been part of U.S. refugee law at all: the notion of children as capable of agency and autonomous actions.[17] Integrating this framework would constitute a prerequisite for regarding Central American minors as political agents capable of holding an explicit anti-gang opinion. Jacqueline Bhabha confirms that some political opinion claims raised by Central American minors were denied in U.S. courts precisely because children were, on account of their age, not seen as "capable of political activism"; hence, the courts argued, they could not possibly be conceived of as "political threat" by their governments (228). Bhabha continues that "political acts by children –

16 In 1996, Canada was also the first country to issue guidelines "for the adjudication of children's asylum claims" (Bhabha and Young 85) as a response to the UN's Graça Machel Study of 1996 on the effects of armed conflict on children, which "underscored that children are no longer just innocent bystanders caught in the crossfire of armed conflict, but are subject to calculated genocide, forced military conscription, gender-based violence, torture, and exploitation" (86).

17 Bhabha cites the following example. "In the United States, adolescents without a secure immigration status who abscond from government shelter facilities to find work while their immigration cases are being decided are considered security threats rather than responsible, self-reliant young people exercising independent agency" (248).

such as stone throwing, tire burning, street protests, school strikes – are [often] discounted as not being 'really political' because prevailing judicial conceptions of political activism revolve around an adult norm" (228–229). In her view, such normative conceptionalizations of political activism are "reminiscent of decisions that dismissed women's distinctive form of political activism – providing shelter for guerillas, cooking, hiding ammunition – because they diverge from a norm of political activism that is male gendered" (229). Highlighting that "[t]he concept of a 'political act' in refugee law is still insufficiently gender- and age inclusive" (229), Bhabha emphasizes that children are often more politicized "in unstable and violent societies" (230) such as those of the northern triangle, a fact which needs to be taken into account when dealing with the asylum claims of unaccompanied Central American minors who have, after all, also been capable of making the long and dangerous journey to the U.S. on their own.

Yet, to expand the legal conceptualization of childhood in this manner does require a quite nuanced approach. In very general terms, children's rights are covered internationally by the 1989 United Nations *Convention on the Rights of the Child.*[18] Even though this Convention has not yet been ratified by the U.S., its basic principles are nonetheless consistent with a range of national U.S. laws and policies, including U.S. child welfare policy and the standards by the American Bar Association. The Convention contains four core principles: "right to life, survival and development; right to non-discrimination; the right to participation; and the best interest of the child" (Somers, Herrera, and Rodriguez 372, fn278). In relation to the latter point ("best interest"), the Convention states:

> "States Parties shall assure to the child who is capable of forming his or her own views the right to express those views freely in all matters affecting the child." … In the General Comments to the Convention, the Committee on the Rights of the Child explained that the right to be heard "constitutes one of the fundamental values of the Convention." (WRC 26).

In many ways, the best interest principle is thus of crucial importance "in foregrounding the child as an agent and bearer of rights rather than merely an object of adult concerns, particularly where – as in the asylum context – mechanisms for establishing the child's own views are underdeveloped" (Bhabha and Young 96).[19]

18 In principle, as Bhaba emphasizes, all children also have human rights, yet "apart from a single reference in the UDHR to children's special needs for protection within the article on the right to health, there is no acknowledgment of children's distinctive status. The approach of the Universal Declaration is to mandate nondiscrimination, rather than to directly promote substantive equality" (254).

19 Cf. also: "The Women's Refugee Commission has long advocated that the child's best interests be incorporated in every decision regarding custody, legal procedures and relief, and repatriation. Effective child protection policies should ensure that the child's wishes, the child's safety and the child's familial and cultural needs are in accordance with international humanitarian law and in U.S. child welfare principles" (WRC 26).

However, the current "scope of the refugee definition is narrower than a 'best interest' judgment" (Bhabha and Young 98) even though "[a]ccording to the United Nations High Commissioner for Refugees, ..., the appropriate adjudicatory standard for processing and deciding children's asylum claims is the 'liberal application of the benefit of the doubt'" (Bhabha 217), which can be seen as analogous to the best interest principle. One of the central impediments to incorporating the best interest principle in children's asylum claims, and in this way granting more autonomy and agency to under-age applicants, is the above-mentioned co-existence of competing conceptualizations of childhood, and more specifically the tension between the notion of children as being passive and in need of protection, and the notion of children as agents and bearers of rights. As Bhabha notes: "there is no satisfactory consensus on the appropriate balance between a welfare-driven notion of 'the best interests of the child' and an adolescent agency-driven notion of 'autonomy and independence'" (269). And indeed, the Convention itself seems to be ambivalent in this respect: Article 3 emphasizes the child's need for protection, while Article 12 emphasizes the child's right to voice and agency (14). Bhabha thus concludes that "[i]n child rights terms, we have to carefully calibrate the ongoing tensions between the child's need for protection and the child's evolving ability to be autonomous" (14). But child rights advocates have long criticized the current refugee regime for its age-based forms of discrimination and have argued "that children should be presumed competent unless shown to be otherwise, since it is against the best interests of the child to presume immaturity" – or a general incapacity for (political) agency (Bhabha and Young 96). In other words, children should be conceived of as political, social, and economic actors in their own right unless proven otherwise.

Adopting a more inclusive and more nuanced view of Central American minors that deems them capable of (political) action while at the same time also acknowledging them as vulnerable and in need of protection, can thus pave the way for a reconsideration of Central American minors' asylum claims in U.S. courts, which, in turn, may lead to a reduction in the number of deportations and thus a reduction in the number of young people subjected to discrimination, abuse, or even death by gangs and/or by their own governments. This seems a step worth considering at a time when both the U.S. as well as the northern triangle countries have agreed that new measures are required to break the vicious circle of escalating gang-related violence throughout this region.

Works cited

Agamben, Giorgio. *Means Without End: Notes on Politics.* Minneapolis: U of Minnesota P, 2000. Print.

Bhabha, Jacqueline. *Child Migration & Human Rights in a Global Age*. Princeton, NJ: Princeton UP, 2014. Print.

Bhabha, Jacqueline, and Wendy Young. "Not Adults in Miniature: Unaccompanied Child Asylum Seekers and the New U.S. Guidelines." *International Journal of Refugee Law* 11.1 (1999): 84–125. Print.

Bronstein, Sarah, Michelle Mendez, and Rená Cutlip-Mason. "EOIR Revises Guidance on Immigration Court Cases Involving Juveniles." Catholic Legal Immigration Network Inc. N.d. Web. https://cliniclegal.org/resources/eoir-revises-guidance-immigration-court-cases-involving-juveniles.

"Central American Minors Program." U.S. Embassy in Honduras. N.d. Web. https://hn.usembassy.gov/visas/central-american-minors-program/.

Correa-Cabrera, Guadalupe, Mariely Lopez-Santana, and Camilo Pardo. "Is MS-13 as Dangerous as Trump Suggests?" *The Washington Post*. 7 Dec. 2018. Web. https://www.washingtonpost.com/news/monkey-cage/wp/2018/12/07/trump-keeps-warning-about-ms-13-is-it-really-as-dangerous-as-he-suggests/?utm_term=.cde6563f6586.

Corsetti, Jeffrey D. "Marked for Death: The Maras of Central America and Those Who Flee Their Wrath." *Georgetown Immigration Law Journal* 20 (2006): 407–435. Print.

Flores Agreement. Center for Human Rights and Constitutional Law. 17 Jan. 1997. Web. https://www.aclu.org/sites/default/files/assets/flores_settlement_final_plus_extension_of_settlement011797.pdf.

Franco, Celinda. "The MS-13 and the 18th Street Gangs: Emerging Transnational Gang Threats?" *Congressional Research Service*. 22 Jan. 2010. Web. http://congressionalresearch.com/RL34233/document.php?study=The+MS-13+and+18th+Street+Gangs+Emerging+Transnational+Gang+Threats.

Griffith, Keith. "Barrio 18." *The Daily Mail*. 6 Aug. 2017. Web. https://www.dailymail.co.uk/news/article-4764744/Barrio-18-Meet-terrifying-gang-rivals-MS-13.html.

Guidelines for Children's Asylum Claims. 1998. KiND: Kids in Need of Defense. 17 Jun. 2015. Web. https://supportkind.org/resources/childrens-asylum-claims/.

Guidelines for Immigration Court Cases Involving Unaccompanied Alien Children. 2007. KiND: Kids in Need of Defense. 17 Jun. 2015. Web. https://supportkind.org/resources/childrens-asylum-claims/.

Harris, Lindsay M., and Morgan M. Weibel. "Matters of S-E-G-: The Final Nail in the Coffin for Gang-Related Asylum Claims?" *Berkeley la Raza Law Journal* 20 (2010): 5–30. Print.

Hill, Linda Kelly. "The Gangs of Asylum." *Georgia Law Review* 46 (2012): 639–655. Print.

Howell, James C., and John P. Moore. "History of Street Gangs in the United States." *National Gang Center Bulletin* 4 (May 2010): 1–25. Print.

International Human Rights Clinic (IHRC). *No Place to Hide: Gang, State, and Clandestine Violence in El Salvador*. Feb. 2007. Print.

Labrador, Rocio Cara, and Danielle Renwick. "Central America's Violent Northern Triangle." Council on Foreign Relations. 26 Jun. 2018. Web. https://www.cfr.org/backgrounder/central-americas-violent-northern-triangle.

Lakhani, Sarah M. "'Is This America?': Asylum-Seeking in an Era of Humanitarian Decline." *Forced Out and Fenced In: Immigration Tales from the Field.* Ed. Tanya Maria Golash-Boza. Oxford: Oxford UP, 2018. 121–130. Print.

Menjívar, Cecilia, and David Kanstroom, eds. *Constructing Immigrant "Illegality": Critiques, Experiences, and Responses.* Cambridge: Cambridge UP, 2013. Print.

Menjívar, Cecilia, and David Kanstroom. "Introduction: Immigrant 'Illegality.'" *Constructing Immigrant "Illegality": Critiques, Experiences, and Responses.* Ed. Cecilia Menjívar and David Kanstroom. 1–33. Print.

Messmer, Marietta. "Detention for Deterrence? The Strategic Role of Private Facilities and Offshore Resources in US Migration Management." *Permeable Borders: History, Theory, Policy, and Practice in the United States.* Ed. Paul Otto and Susanne Berthier-Foglar. New York: Berghahn, 2020. 136–155. Print.

Nakamura, David. "Trump Administration Ends Obama-Era Protection Program for Central American Minors. *The Washington Post.* 16 Aug. 2017. Web. https://www.washingtonpost.com/politics/trump-administration-ends-obama-era-protection-program-for-central-american-minors/2017/08/16/8101507e-82b6-11e7-ab27-1a21a8e006ab_story.html?noredirect=on&utm_term=.39a95bdc20e8.

Office of Refugee Resettlement (ORR). *Children Entering the United States Unaccompanied.* 30 Jan. 2015. Web. https://www.acf.hhs.gov/orr/resource/children-entering-the-united-states-unaccompanied.

Preston, Julia. "Losing Asylum, Then His Life." *New York Times.* 28 Jun. 2010. Web. https://www.nytimes.com/2010/06/29/us/29asylum.html.

"Remarks by President Trump at a Roundtable Discussion on Immigration." White House.gov. 23 May 2018. Web. https://www.whitehouse.gov/briefings-statements/remarks-president-trump-roundtable-discussion-immigration-bethpage-ny/.

Saleh, Maryam. "Trump's Shutdown Offer Creates a De Facto Asylum Ban for Central American Minors." TheIntercept.com. 22 Jan. 2019. Web. https://theintercept.com/ 2019/01/22/central-american-minors-trump-asylum/.

Somers, M. Aryah, Pedro Herrera, and Lucia Rodriguez. "Constructions of Childhood and Unaccompanied Children in the Immigration System in the United States." *UC Davis Journal of Juvenile Law and Policy* 14.2 (2010): 311–380. Print.

"Statement from President Donald Trump." WhiteHouse.gov. 5 Sep. 2017. Web. https://www.whitehouse.gov/briefings-statements/statement-president-donald-j-trump-7/.

United Nations. *UN Convention on the Rights of the Child.* 2 Sep. 1990. Web. https://www.ohchr.org/en/professionalinterest/pages/crc.aspx.

UNHCR. *Guidelines on Determining the Best Interests of the Child.* Geneva. May 2008. Web. http://www.refworld.org/docid/48480c342.html.

USAID. *Central America and Mexico Gang Assessment.* Apr. 2006. Print.

Women's Refugee Commission (WRC). *Forced from Home: The Lost Boys and Girls of Central America.* New York, Oct. 2012. Web. womensrefugeecommission.org.

From Color to Whiteness: Thinking the Transfiguration of the Political Body in the Americas from Evo Morales and Barack Obama to Jair Bolsonaro and Donald Trump

OLAF KALTMEIER

The end of the 1990s and the beginning of the 2000s were a heyday of multi- and pluri-culturalism in the Americas. The political impact of ethnic actors such as indigenous, Chicano, and Afro-American social movements was echoed in academia through an ongoing discussion on ethnicity, hybridity, and creolization in Cultural Studies and a socio-philosophical debate around the concepts of recognition and/or redistribution. Politically, these cultural-political dynamics found their strongest expression in the 2004 election of Barack Obama, the first afro-descendant U.S. president, and in the 2005 election of Evo Morales, the indigenous coca farmer. In the context of the research group "E pluribus unum? Ethnic identities in processes of transnational integration in the Americas," conducted by Josef Raab, Sebastian Thies, and Olaf Kaltmeier, Josef Raab wrote an article in the Journal of the Center for Interdisciplinary Studies (ZiF) comparing Obama's and Morales's diverse strategies towards identity politics. Raab points out the gravity of the situation: "The potential of these cultural transformations for conflict manifests itself in particular where the continuity of (post-)colonial structures of power is concerned: in the politicization of ethnic identities, the break-up of patriarchal social regimes, and the changes in religion-based forms of social hegemony" (7). In regards to the strategic use of ethnicity in the field of identity politics, Raab identifies two basic strategies: "While Morales emphasizes difference, foregrounding the identitarian marker of ethnicity and using it to demand changes in the distribution of resources, ownership, and capital, Obama – although astutely aware of difference – tries to unite his nation in the pursuit of common goals" (2).

In this sense, Raab diagnoses – especially in regards to the indigenous movements in Latin America – an underlying conflict between the use of ethnicity in the political field and the anti-essentialist new common sense in the academic field:

> But while demands for social and economic goods (e.g. Evo Morales) or political autonomy (e.g. the Zapatistas) tend to rely on essentialist notions of ethnicity, current academic discussions commonly de-essentialize ethnicity: concepts like 'multiculturalism,' 'new ethnicities,' 'creolization,' 'hybridity,' '*mestizaje*,' 'diasporas,' and 'post-ethnicity' articulate profound changes in our understanding of ethnic identity. (5)

Fifteen years later, the dynamics within the field of identity politics have changed dramatically. Now concepts such as whiteness, elitism, racism, sexism, and masculinity dominate the academic and political debates about this field in the Americas. This contribution analyzes these transformations in an interplay of identity politics and political representation. It draws on Josef Raab's approach to analyze the field of identity politics through the visual representation of political leaders and the seminal works of Ernst Kantorowicz and Claude Lefort on political representation. It will focus first on political representation in Bolivia in the context of the election of Evo Morales, using two film posters as points of reference; second, on the transformation of the patterns of political representation with the recent turn to the right. This essay concludes with a discussion of the political impact of the dramatically changing mechanism of political representation for those segments of the political community who have benefitted most from the democratic opening of the 1990s/2002s, namely ethnic and indigenous groups, popular/impoverished sectors of society, and women.

Political bodies – a short digression into political representation

In his seminal study of political theology, historian Ernst Kantorowicz (1957) established the theory of the "two bodies of the king" in Western Europe during the Middle Ages, from the eleventh century to the seventeenth century. The figure of the king consists of a physical, mortal body and an immortal, political body. This double figure of the royal body is exemplified in the ritualized words in the throne change: "Le roi est mort, vive le roi." This idea of a king's immortal political body in the European Middle Ages is closely connected to religious ideas, mainly by understanding the king as an earthly governor by the grace of God. This double body of the king was then provided with attributes of totality, such as omnipresence, omniscience, and immortality. Thus, the body of the king was considered an eternal and holy political representation of the community. A striking pictorial representation of this total representation of community can be found on the copperplate engraving of the original edition of Thomas Hobbes's "Leviathan."

Figure 1: Frontispiece of *Leviathan* by Abraham Bosse, with input from Hobbes. 1651.[1]

In the course of the French Revolution, there was a profound change in the models of political representation. With the end of the monarchy, the political body was literary beheaded. In democracy, it is difficult for a single person to represent a whole society. Jean-Jacques Rousseau (1988), one of the most influential political philosophers of the French Revolution, argued that the different wills of every person in society, the *volontée de tous*, must be transformed by a democratic procedure of common will, the *vontontée générale*. Nevertheless, the problem of democratic political representation has persisted. In this sense, philosopher Claude Lefort (1981) studies how knowledge, law, and power must be challenged and negotiated between different interests in civil society. In order to meet the need for political representation of the political community, Lefort refers to the ideas of Kantorowicz. But instead of the two bodies of the king and the sacralization of the king's body, political representation in contemporary democracies is realized by the secular "body of nobody." According to this thought, political power in democratic societies can no longer be defined by a historical being, since it is subject to permanent negotiation processes in civil society. There can only be a temporary fixation of political power, which is symbolically expressed in the

1 https://commons.wikimedia.org/wiki/File:Leviathan_by_Thomas_Hobbes.jpg.

body of a natural person, which can be everybody according to the democratic formula. The body of political representation has no further, transcendental meaning – it is the body of nobody. Despite this temporal fixation which usually is renewed via elections, Lefort also sees the danger in totalitarianism. This occurs when the person in power tries to make the temporal fixation permanent.

Beyond these reflections in political philosophy, it is of particular interest to analyze how the problem of political representation – relations between the political community and its representative – is resolved in regard to specific cases. As we deal with permanent negotiation within civil society, we can argue that in situations where the self-definition of civil society changes dramatically, the patterns of political representation will be transformed significantly. Saying this, it is not surprising that the multi- and pluri-cultural revolutions have deeply transformed the representation of political power.

Bolivia – debating the political body of the plurinational state

Josef Raab analyzed the conflict within the field of identity politics between strategic essentialism (Spivak) and anti-essentialism, referencing the Presidents Evo Morales and Barack Obama using the nation as a primary unit of analysis. Nevertheless, a similar conflict constellation was also present within Bolivia in 2005. The following subchapter will analyze the efforts to re-imagine the political body between (strategic) re-ethnization and anti-essentialist hybridization in the context of the "refoundation of the nation" through two influential documentary productions. In particular, I will limit the interpretation essentially to the film posters that paradigmatically express the new imagination of the political body of the nation.

Without a doubt, Bolivia underwent the deepest political transformation process of any Latin American country in its ethnic identity at the turn of the millennium. After massive protests against the neoliberal course of the government of Gonzalo Sánchez de Lozada and the privatization of gas and water, Evo Morales, the former *cocalero*-unionist and leader of the Movimiento al Socialismo, emerged as the face of the protest movement and was elected as president in 2005 (García Linera; Postero, "Andean Utopias," *Now We Are Citizens*). In 2006, he advocated anti-neoliberal politics and a "refoundation of the nation," calling for a constituent assembly with a broad participation of indigenous and popular movements. In 2009, a new constitution was approved by plebiscite. In 2014, Evo Morales was re-elected as president until 2019. This process included the indigenous majority of the population that had been structurally excluded from political participation and political-cultural recognition since the colonial conquest.

The constitution defines Bolivia as plurinational, yet a unitary state at the same time. It introduces several mechanisms of local and regional autonomy, especially for indigenous communities, and recognizes 36 indigenous languages as official languages of the state. The constitution was inspired by ideas of decolonization and places the concept of *Buen Vivir*, derived from indigenous cosmovisions, at the center of the nation's development. The central goals of Morales's government have broken with the historical state-formation and seemingly represented the refoundation of the nation. (Kaltmeier, "Politics of Indigeneity"). These goals are explicitly expressed in the preamble of the new constitution:

> We have left the colonial, republican and neo-liberal State in the past. We take on the historic challenge of collectively constructing a Unified Social State of Pluri-National Communitarian law, which includes and articulates the goal of advancing toward a democratic, productive, peace-loving and peaceful Bolivia, committed to the full development and free determination of the peoples .... We found Bolivia anew, fulfilling the mandate of our people, with the strength of our Pachamama and with gratefulness to God.[2]

The project of decolonization is epitomized in the foundation of a Vice Ministry of Decolonization. The renationalization of central industries, such as petrol and gas, has been a cornerstone in an economic strategy that has also enabled increased financing of social welfare programs. Furthermore, limited agrarian reforms have been implemented. These policies cannot be interpreted simply in terms of an indigenization of the Bolivian state, because they are also related to class-based struggles and forms of organization (we should not forget that Morales was a former union leader and no great authority on ethnic matters). This decolonization project distinguishes itself from traditional multiculturalism, as the decolonization of society and the proposed new model of *Buen Vivir* involve all segments of the Bolivian society. In part, we can claim that a revolutionary change in the elite ruling structure has taken place, insofar as there exists a clear break with the *longue durée* cycle of coloniality. The extension of full citizenship and political participation rights to the indigenous population – who were previously specifically excluded and therefore reverted to a system of clientelism – is a process that seems to have been successful and irreversible. Indigeneity is now officially defined and considered an integral part of Bolivia's political culture.

Nevertheless, in the period between 2006 and 2009, the identitarian political debate on the (ethnic/indigenous) representation was complex and multi-faceted. Two documentary films contributed to the proliferation of this debate in the field of cultural production. The first is the documentary *Cocalero* (2007) by Alejandro Landes, who accompanied Evo Morales during his presidential campaign. The second is the documentary *El estado de las cosas* (2007) by Marcos Loayza, which was produced in the context of the Bolivian United Nation Development Program (UNDP) that intervened in the debate on the reconfiguration of the Bolivian state. The first documentary was clearly produced for an international cosmopolitical audience interested in the political transformation process in Latin America, while the second was made for a Bolivian audience to empower processes of collective self-reflection.

The *Cocalero* promotional poster focuses on the figure of Evo Morales, trying to find an aesthetic solution to the problem of political representation in Bolivia. Morales

---

2 Bolivian constitution, 2009. https://www.constituteproject.org/constitution/Bolivia_-2009.pdf.

is presented as a black stencil-like image, which gives him a certain iconic look. An observer might be reminded of the iconic representation of the Che Guevara counterfeit, taken from the photo shoot by Cuban photograph Alberto Korda in 1960. With this reference, Morales is connected to other popular and left movements in Latin America. Beyond this political iconography, indigenous/mestizo elements of Morales's shape are especially noteworthy. In this sense, Morales's representation does not have a transcendent aura, but rather he is represented as a common Bolivian. In both of these aspects, Evo is represented as the popular leader of all common Bolivians. The body of the king is restored by a common citizen – the "body of nobody."

Beyond this double popularization of Evo Morales, the poster makes a significant statement on the self-definition of the nation. The black stenciled image is reproduced on a huge, multi-colored *whipala.* The rainbow-flag whipala is also known as the Inca flag and is one of the most important symbols of the indigenous movement in the Andean highlands. In particular, this chessboard whipala is related to the Katarista movement of Aymara Indians. This movement was formed at the end of the 1960s by young urban Aymaras whose parents had migrated from rural areas to the city suburb of El Alto, La Paz. The (symbolic) figure of Tupac Katari (Julián Apaza), who together with Tupac Amaru II was the leader of the indigenous revolution in Peru in the 1780s, was central to the cultural politics of the Katarista. With their "Manifiesto de Tiwanaku" of 1973, the movement gained national and international attention – in spite of the dictatorship of Hugo Banzer. It was a cornerstone in a new dynamic of decolonization and put autonomy at the center of the political organization process. Strategically, the Kataristas established themselves in the trade union movement, where they successfully introduced their political program. At the end of the 1970s, the Katarista divided into different movement fractions, but still remained influential in cultural-political terms until the end of the 1990s. This movement prepared the ground for the rise of Evo Morales to political power.

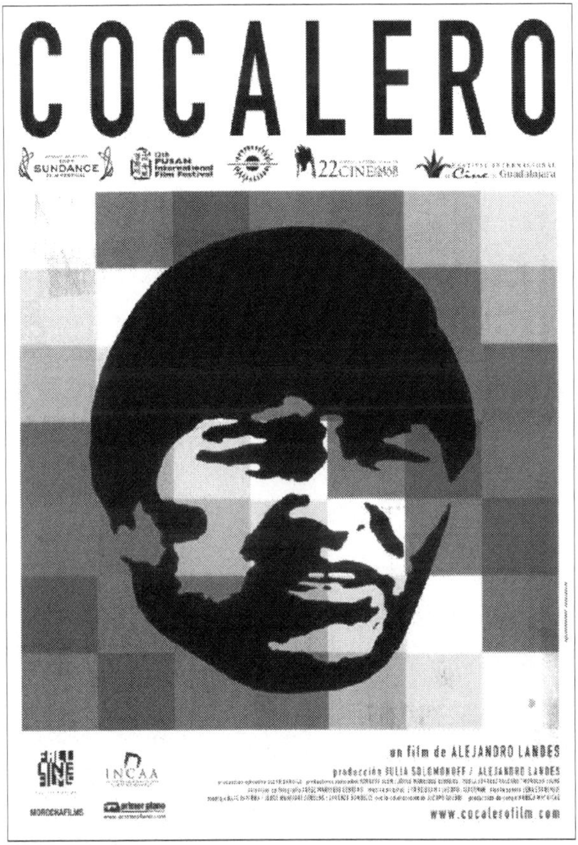

Figure 2: Film poster *Cocalero* (2007).

While the film by Alejandro Landes mainly tells the story of Evo Morales in his presidential campaign in 2005, the production of *El estado de las cosas* is intrinsically related to the United Nation Development Program for Bolivia (UNDP-Bolivia) (Kaltmeier and Thies). The UNDP intervened in the political debates around the 2007 Annual Report Constituent Assembly and inauguration of Bolivia's first indigenous president to create its own, new understanding of statehood in Bolivia to define and propagate politically (Gray Molina). The program is of particular interest since it constitutes an integral project design, a scientific study on policy advice *El Estado del Estado* [The State of the State] (UNDP 2007) and an extensive media campaign, which aimed to open up the political positions of the UNDP to a broader national audience. Components of the program are the documentary *El estado de las cosas* [The state of affairs] (2007), the television series *El laberinto* (2007), the radio broadcasts *Revista del futuro* (in Spanish and three more indigenous languages), the scientific publication series *Cuadernos del future,* and a broad campaign in the national press. The outstanding cultural-political claim of UNDP's media campaign is seen in the fact that Marcos Loayza and Juan Carlos Valdivia, two of the few internationally successful Bolivian directors, were hired for the documentary and television series.

Figure 3: Film poster *El estado de las cosas* (2007).

The poster of *El estado de las cosas* is inspired by the classic Leviathan engraving that adorned the first edition of Thomas Hobbes's groundbreaking book on early-modern state theory. The poster shows the body of a woman as a projection surface for an imaginary topography of the multiethnic Bolivia, in which complexion, color, and indigenous and mestizo garments converge, as well as ancestral and modern elements. Unlike Hobbes's version, there are no indistinguishable individuals who constitute the sovereign's political body; the figure represents an androgynous and polyvalent surface projection of a fragmented Bolivianity – a young transsexual identity that combines feminine and masculine attributes as two energies complementary to the Andean cosmovision. It is striking that the figure also refers to the issue of military uniform in the country's recent past, which still remains ambiguous. On the one hand, the uniform can be read in the Bolivian context as an allusion to popular forces' alliances with the military, as in the case with the revolution of 1952. On the other hand, the possibility of a failure of the nation-state project stands out democratic, as is the case in military dictatorships. Representing the political body in terms of a fragmented Bolivianity allows every Bolivian citizen to find an element that represents their position in Bolivian society. Simultaneously, it also makes clear that no single social group can represent the entire state. The caption "Atrevete a mirarte" is also an imperative to recognize the pluricultural character of the nation.

Both film posters reveal the promise of democratization inherent in the pluricultural politics of recognition. And they both express – in different ways – the deeply democratic promise that really anyone could represent the political community. De facto, this premonition became true in Latin America at the turn of the millennium. Common people, such as steelworker Inacio "Lula" da Silva in Brazil or coca-peasant Evo Morales in Bolivia, can become president of the republic.

"Return of the white man"

The 1990s and early 2000s were characterized by a profound process of democratic inclusion for so-called ethnic minorities, indigenous peoples, popular classes, and women into the political field. This process is now interrupted by new conservative governments with wealthy aristocrats as head of state (Kaltmeier, *Refeudalización*). There is a remarkable return of the "white man" who nostalgically insists on old privileges; as the Tea Party movement in the U.S. put it, "I want my country back!" Above all, this return of white political domination means the abolition of inclusive measures of affirmative action and mainstream actions directed against African American and indigenous groups, as well as against feminist concerns and LGBT rights.

In the U.S., Donald Trump won the 2016 presidential election with a program based on this concern. In Latin America, the Brazilian government of Michel Temer, who came to power in 2016 through a cold coup, should also be mentioned in this context. Among the members of his first cabinet, there was not a single Afro-Brazilian, Indigenous, nor, for the first time since the end of the military dictatorship, woman to be found. The InterAmerican Commission on Human Rights (ICHR) sharply criticized this composition: "The designation of a cabinet of ministers does not include any women or persons of African descent leaves more than the population excluded from the highest government offices" (Planas n. pag.). Yet, the ICHR clearly understated it. In 2015, only 43,709,136 people of a total Brazilian population of 204,855,655 were white men. Thus, the Cabinet represents only 21.3 percent of the population, as class positioning is not included here (IPEA). Temer prepared the path for the extreme right, racist, and sexist government of Jair Bolsonaro.

But the return of whiteness has also manifested in other forms. In Bolivia, the separatist Nación Camba, made up of Union Juvenil Cruceñista's right-wing, mostly white, juvenile militants, demanded the independence of the province of Santa Cruz from the Plurinational Republic of Bolivia. The ideological basis of the movement was a regionalist discourse anchored in political culture, based on racist attitudes of the white regional elite against the indigenous majority of the Andean highlands. In 2019, this movement was involved in the coup d'etat against Evo Morales, blaming him for supposed electoral fraud. The reactionary interim government, that relied heavily on white supremacy and racism, was voted out in October 2020 with a landslide win of the MAS-party and its indigenous and mestizo supporters. But even left-wing governments were not immune to the rhetoric of whiteness and the underlying feeling of racial superiority. In Ecuador, Left Social Democrat President Rafael Correa called the indigenous movement of the country, drawing on mid-nineteenth century concepts of progress, civilization, and whitening as "barbarians" and "obstacles to national progress" (Kaltmeier, *Konjunkturen der (De-)Kolonialisierung* 362). Similarly, the Chilean government refers to the Mapuche communities, which are fighting for land rights against forestry corporations, as an internal enemy and "terrorist" against the Pinochet dictatorship's anti-terror law.

These examples illustrate how much whiteness is rooted in colonialism. It is a concept that in itself often remains unclear – "unmarked" – in order to stand out all the more clearly against a colonial Other, which is marked in color. This marked difference is then given moral and cultural criteria of inferiority in relation to one's own assumed superiority. Whiteness is closely linked to class position. For example, whiteness in Ecuador, as well as in other Latin American countries with a high proportion of indigenous people, is an indicator of social status. To refer to oneself as "white" often equivalently means to refer to the middle class, differentiating it from lower classes marked as colored or indigenous. This operation also functions in Brazil. For example, the phenotypically colored son of Lebanese immigrant Michel Temer is considered "white" and treated the same way as a European-descendant white Brazilian. In this sense, Cynthia Levine-Rasky notes: "'Money whitens.' If any phrase encapsulates the association of whiteness and the modern in Latin America, this is it. It is a cliché formulated and reformulated throughout the region" (73). In this sense, the rhetorical use of whiteness has a highly strategic character, she says, but it can also be used to improve one's own position in the field of identity policy; it can also be used to invest in education, clothing, naming, place of residence, etc., in order to improve inter-generational mobility. She sees whiteness in Latin America as a secure capital investment with high returns, because of the colonial character of the Latin America. These societies had hardly been called into question by white identities until the boom of multicultural recognition policies and the associated redefinition of many Latin American states as pluricultural or even plurinational.

Only with the multicultural turnaround did white elites risk the devaluation of the identity-political capital of whiteness. Since whiteness itself had been unmarked and based mainly on the distinction of the colonial Other, there was no easy return to whiteness. Instead, a nostalgic discourse on the search for identity emerged – as shown by the example of retro colonialism – which was deeply marked by fear. Charles M. Blow also analyzed Donald Trump's political discourse in the *New York Times*: "He appeals to something deeper, something baser: Fear. His whole campaign slogan, 'Make America Great Again,' is in fact an inverted admission of loss – lost primacy, lost privilege, lost prestige" (Blow n. pag.)

Here we are dealing with a paradoxical opposite situation. The white middle class in Latin America has certainly benefited from the cycle of left-wing governments. On the other hand, they have lost their hitherto undisputed privileged position in the political field as well as in the general political culture. It is precisely this loss of power that causes a fear for a loss of privilege that can lead to violent fantasies and political aggression.

Whiteness, precisely because of its lack of definition, can serve as an "empty signifier," a hub for the articulation of fear, insecurity, and loss of identity directed against other indigenous peoples, African Americans, communists, feminists, etc. In this sense, a discursive chain of equivalences is built up, according to which the heterosexual white male embodies conservative values such as patriarchy, nation, superiority, security, and order. This chain of equivalence is diametrically opposed to other signifiers such as multiculturalism, gender, queerness, political correctness, communism, and chaos. With this operation, whiteness leaves a purely defensive position, and begins to articulate a discourse of recapture and revenge. It is amazing how fear can lead to revenge and violent fantasies. Gonzalo Portocarrero (2007) analyzed the dreams of white middle-class and upper-class children in Lima in the 1990s, during the guerrilla-state conflict. He found that children dreamed of bloody revenge and violence against alleged terrorists, who were usually imagined as Indigenous.

These concepts of power of the white middle and upper classes historically have often been implemented. The use of violence, such as rape and lynching, is deeply rooted in the colonial legacy. Furthermore, the motive of revenge can certainly be found in the orgy of violence of the military dictatorships, which oppose the participation of the popular sections of the population in the political field. In this sense, elements of discursive and non-discursive violence can also be found in today's phase of conservative backlash in Latin America, directed against three target groups that can only be hinted at here.

As the first – almost historical – target group of the revenge of the "angry white man" is the ethnically-constructed Other to call. This includes the xenophobic defense of migrants who are considered racially inferior. However, the racial-ethnic criteria are in constant flux. While the U.S. is isolating itself against migrants from Central and Latin America with racist models of justification, in Latin America – recently in Brazil – black migrants from Haiti are the target. In addition, the rights of the indigenous population, who had benefited from the recognition policies, are now again curtailed. Jair Bolsonaro in Brazil repealed the protection of indigenous territories in order to make the land accessible to the agro-industry.

A second target group of "angry white men" are women or groups targeted for gender mainstreaming and recognition of sexual rights. In Brazil, the Ministry of Women, Racial Equity, and Human Rights has also been dissolved following the illegal removal of the elected president. Just in the first five months of his term, four projects have been launched to abolish the right to abortion and to criminalize abortion (Biroli 565). In coordinated action, conservative groups, often supported by radical Protestant churches, pushed for the abolition of gender ideology in school curricula. "Gender ideology," according to Flávia Biroli, is understood as the opposite of the "natural family" and "natural sexual roles" (565).

These identity-political positions are accompanied by a fast-paced political-ethical taboo, which is expressed inter alia in public violent fantasies and hate speeches against women. For example, in 2014, conservative MP and current President of Brazil Jair Bolsonaro expressed rape fantasies and male superiority vis-à-vis MEP Maria Do Rosário. But a special target of hate speech was Dilma Rousseff. On posters that equate her with a rabid dog, it is written: "Beware of the beast! She acted in guerrilla, planned terrorist acts, used arms to implement communism in Brazil and was sentenced to 3 years in jail. She defends herself and wants to be the 'mother of Brazil.' Do you believe it?" In addition, there are vulgar sexist portrayals of Rousseff on posters, stickers, and pamphlets produced by the right movement (Biroli). The Brazilian anti-gender movement has far-reaching implications for the academic field as well. In addition to the already mentioned program cuts and changes in educational programs, individual scientists are directly defamed. A conference co-organized by Judith Butler in Sao Paulo in November 2017 (significantly entitled "The Ends of Democracy") provoked fierce protests. The demonstrators demanded, among other things, "Burn the witch!." Butler herself rationalized the incident: "The people who oppose me believe gender is a 'diabolical ideology.'" She added, "Much of the support on the right is biased. Thus, especially in the field of gender politics, the cultural-political dimension of current tendencies towards re-education, which undermine democratic and academic debates and create a climate of new 'Witch hunt'" (Johnson n. pag.).

A third target is the popular sector. In this sense, it is difficult to speak of a populism in the new legislatures, but it instead punishes the popular sectors that had supported the left-wing governments. The Universidad Católica Argentina estimates that the number of poor people in the country has risen by 1.4 million in the first quarter of 2016 following Mauricio Macri's inauguration. More and more small and medium-sized businesses are facing trouble as prices rise and the purchasing power of Argentines, even the most conservative estimates, has fallen ten percent. In addition, the poor are affected by massive price increases in basic daily necessities, while the organized workforce is affected by mass redundancies, especially in the public sector. The latter is expected in other Latin American countries as shifts from the left to the right lead to a return of neoliberal policies.

Although the Latin American revolutions in the 1820s led to independence from the European colonial powers and to the establishment of formal democratic republics in Hispano-America, there was no social revolution, with the exception of the so-called slave revolution in Haiti. There has never been a change in the composition of the elite. Through the nineteenth and twentieth centuries, a strong link between economic elites and political power has generally been maintained, only interrupted by revolutionary processes as in Cuba. But in the late twentieth and early twenty-first, people with a popular background in the political arena began to rise to presidency, embodying the hope for a real democratization. In contrast, the current massive return of the money aristocracy to the direct levers of political power represents a significant step backwards in terms of an anti-democratic re-feudalization of the political field.

"The body of money"

At the end of the 2010s, the highly democratic imaginary that Raab had analyzed in regard to identity politics has vanished. Instead, there is a return to racist, supremacist, anti-democratic tendencies which we have coined as a "return of the white man" and which, in general terms, is an expression of a broader dynamic of refeudalization (Kaltmeier, *Refeudalización*). Looking carefully at these processes, there is another aspect which must be highlighted. With the lingering cycle of Latin American left-wing governments governing in the 2010s, a massive shift to the right has taken place in the region, which represents the money aristocracy in government and partly hold the highest political office – as in Argentina with Mauricio Macri and Chile with Sebastián Piñera. In the context of a global trend to a dramatic higher social polarization – one percent of the human population is still richer than the remaining 99 % (Oxfam) – it is precisely this richest one percent that has also come to represent political communities as president. As one of the first millionaire presidents to oppose the regional left-wing trend in Latin America, Sebastián Piñera became the first conservative president in Chile in 2010 after the formal end of the military dictatorship in 1990. Upon taking office, his total assets were estimated at 2.2 billion U.S. dollars. He held large shares in the airline LAN-Chile, shares in private pension funds and real estate companies, and was owner of a TV channel. In addition, he was the Chilean representative for Visa, MasterCard, and Apple. However, during his term of office, he was unable to set any major precedents and in the course of the student protests of 2011, which were primarily directed against the privatized education system, he rapidly lost political legitimacy. Sebastián Piñera was voted out and the social democratic Michelle Bachelet again took over the presidency in 2014. After a rapid loss of legitimacy by the Bachelet government and general political party, Piñera won the presidential election again in 2017 and assumed office in March 2018.

In neighboring Argentina, the election of billionaire Mauricio Macri as President in 2015 caused a profound break with a 12-year phase of "Kirchnerismo." Under Néstor Kirchner, who served as Argentine President from 2005 to 2007, Argentina became a cornerstone of the left-turn in Latin America. Under his wife Cristina Kirchner, post-neo-liberal policies continued in her two terms of office: 2007–2011 and 2011–2015. Mauricio Macri has now taken a rapid turn to neoliberal policies, which also promote (transnational) companies and the top 10 percent. Mauricio Macri himself was born into the Argentine money aristocracy as son of millionaire Franco Macri, who has built his fortune mainly in the construction industry. The Macri Group (SOCMA) is one of the most important consortia in Argentina. In addition to the construction industry, the conglomerate includes companies from the automotive industry, post office (the Argentine post office was privatized under Carlos Menem), mining, waste management companies, and the food industry, which are also based in Brazil, Panama, and Uruguay.

Millionaires occupying the highest office of political representation is not limited to Latin America. In the U.S., the rise of Donald Trump is symptomatic of the tendency of the colonization of the political field by economic interests. Furthermore, the presidency of Silvio Berlusconi in Italy, who massively changed political communication through his media empire, should also be mentioned in this context. This tendency has deep impacts on the dynamics of political representation, as it limits the democratic principle by a colonization of the political field by economic power (Habermas). For now, it is not the body of an everyman who can fill the symbolic place of political power; rather, it is the group of money aristocracy reserved to take over political power. This process of colonizing the public and, ultimately, the political field through economic interests, as already indicated by Habermas, is a danger. Unlike what Lefort described for Western democratic societies, political negotiation is now less and less in the sphere of civil society. Instead, economic interests determine the wider social fields. For political representation, this means that the "body of nobody" is replaced by the "body of money" (Kaltmeier, *Refeudalización* 118).

Lefort (1981) foresaw a dangerous tendency inherent in democracy to totalitarianism, based on the fact that the one who temporarily occupies the political power may try to establish a supra-individual ideological fixation. In the twentieth century, Lefort keeps the examples of fascism and Stalinism in mind. Here is an attempt to fix political representation by resorting to political ideologies. This is different in the current tendency of refeudalization. The fixation of political power by the money aristocracy takes place here through references to an outside, namely economic, potency. The latter is no longer understood as a political ideology, but as a quasi-natural law-based ontology anchored in the "nature of man" as *homo economicus*. Thus, the model of the "body of money" is not only an expression of a change in the composition of the political functionaries, but it is embedded in a comprehensive tendency of the economic colonization of the political. The essentialization of the capitalist economy has become hegemonic, especially in the wake of the neoliberal economy. With elaborated governmental techniques of neoliberal governorship, economistic logics have colonized political institutions. Increasingly, state institutions are under pressure to restructure according to private-sector criteria. The private corporation serves as a blueprint for the public institution.

With reference to a quasi-natural given – the economic, purpose-rational, and benefit-maximizing anthropological constants, and the resulting economic logics – political representation experiences a fixation similar to that of the European Middle Ages. There is a danger of naturalizing, or even sacralizing, the political power of money. Latin American liberation theologians from the context of the critical think-tank DEI have referred to this connection in the theologically and politically problematic sacralization of the market. The capitalist market that stands above man mutates into a secular substitute religion. Accordingly, the political philosopher Giorgio Agamben commented on the anti-Enlightenment regress as follows: "God is not dead! God mutated into money!" (Agamben n. pag.).

Works cited

Agamben, Giorgio. Interview with Peppe Salvá, 10.09.2012. Partido Pirata. 2012. Web. http://partidopirata.com.ar/2012/09/10/dios-no-murio-se-transformo-en-dinero-entrevista-a-giorgio-agamben/.

Biroli, Flávia. "Political Violence Against Women in Brazil: Expressions and Definitions." *Direito & Práxis* 07.15 (2016): 557–589. Print.

Blow, Charles. "Trump reflects White Male Fragility." *New York Times*. 4 Aug. 2016. Web. http://www.nytimes.com/2016/08/04/opinion/trump-reflects-white-male-fragility.html.

"E pluribus unum? Ethnic Identities in Processes of Transnational Integration in the Americas." ZiF Research Group. Bielefeld University (2008–2009).

García Linera, Álvaro. "State Crisis and Popular Power." *New Left Review* 37 (2006): 73–85. Print.

Gray Molina, George. "El Estado, entre la ficción y la realidad." *Pulso*. 19.04.2007. Print.

Habermas, Jürgen. *Strukturwandel der Öffentlichkeit: Untersuchungen zu einer Kategorie der bürgerlichen Gesellschaft*. Frankfurt am Main: Suhrkamp, 1962. Print.

Hobbes, Thomas. *Leviathan: Or, the Matter, Forme and Power of a Commonwealth, Ecclesiasticall and Civil*. Cambridge: Cambridge UP, 1935. Print.

Johnson, Cade. "About 70 Protest UC Berkeley Professor Judith Butler's Conference in Brazil." 8 Nov. 2017. Web. http://www.dailycal.org/2017/11/08/protesters-gather-at-conference-organized-by-campus-professor-judith-butler-in-brazil/.

Kaltmeier, Olaf. *Refeudalización. Desigualdad, economía y cultura política en América Latina en el temprano siglo XXI*. Guadalajara, Bielefeld, San José, Quito, Buenos Aires: Bielefeld UP, 2018. Print.

——. *Konjunkturen der (De-)Kolonialisierung. Indigene Gemeinschaften, Hacienda und Staat in den ecuadorianischen Anden von der Kolonialzeit bis heute*. Bielefeld: transcript, 2016. Print.

———. "Politics of Indigeneity in the Andean Highlands. Indigenous Social Movements and the State in Ecuador, Bolivia, and Peru (1940–2014)." *Indigeneity on the Move. Varying Manifestations of a Contested Concept*. Ed. Nasir Uddin, Eva Gerharz, and Pradeep Chakkarath. Oxford, London: Berghahn, 2017. 172–198. Print.

———, and Sebastian Thies. "Boliviens Staat im Bilde. Postkoloniale Repräsentationsverhältnisse und der strategische Einsatz von Kultur in der Entwicklungszusammenarbeit." *Peripherie. Zeitschrift für Politik und Ökonomie der Dritten Welt* 113 (2009): 7–30. Print.

Kantorowicz, Ernst. *The King's Two Bodies. A Study in Mediaeval Political Theology*. Princeton: Princeton UP, 1957. Print.

Lefort, Claude. *L'invention démocratique. Les limites de la domination totalitaire*. Paris: Fayard, 1981. Print.

Levine-Rasky, Cynthia. *Working through Whiteness*. New York: Suny, 2002. Print.

Oxfam. "An Economy for the 99 %. Oxfam Briefing Paper." Jan. 2017. Web. https://www.oxfam.org/sites/www.oxfam.org/files/file_attachments/bp-economy-for-99-percent-160117-en.pdf.

Planas, Roque. "We're Starting To Get A Bad Feeling About Brazil's New Interim President." *Huffington Post*. 19 May 2016. Web. http://www.huffingtonpost.com/entry/michel-temer-brazil-president_us_573d99eee4b0aee7b8e91132.

Portocarrero, Gonzalo. *Racismo y mestizaje. Y otros ensayos*. Lima: Lima UP, 2007. Print.

Postero, Nancy. "Andean Utopias in Evo Morales's Bolivia." *Latin American and Carribean Ethnic Studies* 2.1 (2007): 1–28. Print.

———. *Now We Are Citizens. Indigenous Politics in Postmulticultural Bolivia*. Stanford: Stanford UP, 2006. Print.

Raab, Josef. "Contrary Approaches to Difference: Ethnicity and Identity Politics in the Americas." *ZiF Mitteilungen* 3 (2009): 1–13. Print.

Rousseau, Jean-Jacques. *Schriften*. Bd.1. Frankfurt a.M.: Fischer, 1988. Print.

Spivak, Gayatri. "Subaltern Studies: Deconstructing Historiography?" *The Spivak Reader*. Ed. Donna Landry and Gerald MacLean. London: Routledge, 1996. 203–237. Print.

UNDP-Bolivia. *El estado del estado en Bolivia. Informe Nacional sobre Desarrollo Humano 2007*. La Paz: PNUD, 2007. Print.

Filmography

Cocalero. Regie: Alejandro Landes. 2007.

El estado de las cosas. Regie: Marcos Loayza. 2007.

Cecilia Absatz's *Los años pares* or the Challenge of Reevaluating Autochthonous Latinamericanism

LUZ ANGÉLICA KIRSCHNER

In the Latin American continent,[1] the Jewish presence can be traced back to the Sephardic Jews that arrived to the New World with Christopher Columbus in 1492.[2] However, the Jewish Argentine community is largely the product of European migrations from East to West during the second half of the nineteenth century and the beginning of the twentieth. Jewish newcomers came to the region with the intention "to make America" rather than "to make it *in* America," implicitly expressing their view of America as a site of potentiality which was still in the making (Segal 203; original emphasis). Although in Argentina the rhetoric of immigration recognized the need for immigrants in order to face the challenges of modernization, in reality foreigners were viewed with distrust and were often the source of social tensions. For instance, Argentine social scientists, overwhelmed with polyglot immigrant crowds, acknowledged that "immigration and urbanization, the potential salvation for a barbarous country, had potential perils as well" (Rodríguez 23).

Additionally, European race discussions that followed the anti-Semitic "scientific" ideas propagated by Gobineau, Chamberlain, and Le Bon had an impact on the racial notions of the more Europeanized of the Latin American republics: Argentina and Chile. In these nations, the European intellectual influence translated into the tendency to regard "Syrian, Jewish, or Asian" immigrants with disgust" (Elkin 27) and as unqualified to culturally enlighten and racially upgrade (read: whiten) the Argentine nation. Indeed, in their bias towards Anglo-Saxon and Nordic "whiteness," Argentine state leaders and intellectuals viewed Arabs and Jews in particular as undesirables "capable of affecting the country's ethnic mix beyond recognition" (Klich 14).[3] Further-

1 A longer version of this chapter originally appeared in the volume *"Nach Amerika nämlich!" Jüdische Migrationen in die Amerikas im 19. und 20. Jahrhundert* and is reprinted by permission of the editors Ulla Kriebernegg, Gerald Lamprecht, Roberta Maierhofer, and Andrea Strutz. The article has been edited to meet the requirements of the current editors.

2 For Sephardim Jewish colonial history in Latin America, cf. Fernando Díaz Esteban's volume *América y los judíos hispanoportugueses*; Reyes Mate's and Ricardo Forster's anthology *El judaísmo en Iberoamérica*; Judith Laikin Elkin's *The Jews of Latin America* (3–22); Haim Avni's *Judíos en América: Cinco siglos de historia* (19–55). Cf. Raanan Rein's *Árabes y judíos en Iberoamérica/Similitudes, diferencias y tensiones*; and Adriana M. Brodsky's *Sephardi, Jewish, Argentine:Community and National Identity*.

3 This attitude, however, was not uniformly shared. Some pundits professed the changeability of character and thus the capacity of betterment of their "'Latin' race" (Rodrí-

more, the control of the Catholic Church on civil matters made the life of non-Catholics in Argentine territory difficult. The church, for instance, refused to provide "for the registration of births, deaths, and marriages in non-Catholic families" (Elkin 34). As Elkin reminds us, it was only in 1888 after the advancement of "secularist forces" (34),[4] which made the country seem more hospitable to non-Catholics, that mass immigration of Ashkenazim, Eastern European Jews who were escaping the pogroms in Russia and Poland, was feasible and enacted on a large scale.[5]

The first group of about 824 Ashkenazim arrived to work the land in 1889. However, the government temporally denied entrance to the impoverished immigrants who, later, often encountered harsh conditions in the agricultural settlements in the New World land that would eventually become the home for many of them.[6] Today, Argentina has the largest Jewish community of Latin America and the fifth largest Jewish community in the world. Yet, despite the fact that Argentina has become more aware of its ethnic minorities and some Argentine Jews have achieved prominence in cultural, economic, and political fields, their place in Argentine society remains marginal and indefinite as persistent "discourses of anti-Semitism" continue to be a significant force in the constitution of Argentine identity (Lesser and Rein 19).

Not surprisingly, Latin American Jewish writing in general and Jewish Argentine in particular have frequently focused "on the questions of marginality and identity" (Barr 1). Unfortunately, too often marginality and identity have been addressed from a male perspective thus positing the experience and perspective of Jewish men as both dominant and representative of Jewish life in the Latin American region. Feminist theorists have portrayed this masculine approach to experience as "male Jewish writers talking to men and about men" (2). In fact, in Argentina, where Jewish women have faced discrimination and misogyny in both traditional Jewish and Catholic communi-

---

guez 68). Prioritizing religion over race, other preferred Spaniards and Italians (cf. Elkin 27).

4 Simultaneously, often, as Elkin explains, "the forces for modernization, which favored lifting religious restrictions so as to facilitate immigration, won legal decisions that were not always put into practice because of the resistance offered by elements within Argentine society" (30).

5 Elkin explains, "Ashkenazim soon outnumbered the West Europeans and Sephardim who had preceded them, stamping Latin American Jewish communities with the East European orientation they retain to this day" (53). Nevertheless, Sephardim equally arrived to Argentina from Turkey and Morocco during the disintegration of the Ottoman Empire, and during the 1960's from Syria, Lebanon, Turkey, Iraq, and Salonika.

6 The agricultural settlements were sponsored by the Jewish Baron Maurice von Hirsch (1831–1896), who bought lands from the government and private owners. On September 10, 1891, Hirsch founded the Jewish Colonization Association (JCA), an organization that hoped to attach Diaspora Jews to the land. For the history and development of Jewish settlements as well as the ideology that supported the creation of the colonies, cf. Judith Laikin Elkin's chapter "Agricultural Colonies: The Burden of the Dream," in *The Jews of Latin America.*

ties, as Sandra McGee Deutsch states, the records on "Argentine Jewish history focus on male actions and perceptions" ("A Journey" 72). McGee Deutsch reminds us that in Argentina, there is only scarce awareness as to "what [Jewish] women did or how they perceived the events they participated in or witnessed" (72). At the same time, as members of an ethnic minority that has often been defined in stereotypes, Jewish Argentine women have had to negotiate a marginal existence as Jewish women writers in a Catholic environment frequently imbued with anti-Jewish sentiment.[7]

Cecilia Absatz is, borrowing Marjorie Agosín's words, a Jewish Argentine writer who through her writing strives to establish for herself "the complex meaning attached to being a Jewish woman of Latin America" (Agosín "Introduction," *The House* 18)[8] by reevaluating modernist identity discourses of Eurocentric as well as autochthonous Catholic, *mestizo*, *criollo* Latin American identity.[9] However, the analysis of Absatz's *Los años pares* [The Even-Numbered Years], 1985, suggests that in the context of Latin American postmodernist discourses of collective Latinamericanism, Absatz's model of Latin American identity displays the dialectical tensions, contradictions, and paradoxes that have traditionally characterized the debates about the possibility of a Latin American identity independent from imperialistic Western influences. In other words, the study of Absatz's novel reveals that though her work aims to resolve the tension between the Western "center" and the Latin American "periphery," by the end of her anti-essentialist critique her work actually builds a dialectical tension between leftist (read: political position that advocates the incorporation of marginal cultural elements) and conservative nationalistic (read: position that tends to dismiss European and U.S. American influences as utterly harmful) approaches to Latin American identity that

7 In 2010, Sandra McGee Deutsch published her groundbreaking book *Crossing Borders, Claiming a Nation: A History of Argentine Jewish Women, 1880–1955*, which reveals the strategies Ashkenazi and Sephardi Argentine women have developed, the choices they have made, the boundaries they have blurred in order to negotiate their complex identities and claim Argentineanness.

8 Cecilia Absatz, of Ashkenazic ancestry, was born in Buenos Aires, Argentina, in 1943. Absatz's father immigrated to Argentina from Poland in 1928 after losing his family in European wars. The same year, her mother came with her parents and her older brother from the Ukraine, which at that time belonged to the Soviet Union (Absatz, E-mail to the author). Absatz studied philosophy and psychology at the University of Buenos Aires. In addition to being a fiction writer, Absatz is a professional translator and a successful editor, journalist, and writer of television scripts. She has written, among others, *Féiguele y otras mujeres* [Féiguele and Other Women] (1976), *Té con canela*, [Cinnamon Tea] (1982), and *Los años pares* (1985).

9 The term "mestizo" refers to the ideology of seemingly all-encompassing Latin American *mestizaje* that celebrates the African, European, and Indigenous American racial and cultural amalgamation that took place in the American continent. Despite the apparent liberalism of *mestizaje*, which is often celebrated as the quintessential expression of "*latinoamericanismo*" (Miller 6; original emphasis; "Latinamericanism"), the ideology traditionally emphasizes the superiority of the Hispano-Catholic element to the detriment of the Native and African components of the mixture.

brings her project close to the traditional oppositional and essentialist versions of Latinamericanism that her project seeks to question.

The dominant characters in Absatz's writing are women who attempt to open up a space for an independent female identity in patriarchal Argentine society. It is a point of interest that while not all of her main characters are Jewish, they all share similar life challenges: namely, they often have to negotiate romantic relationships and claim their own identities. *Los años pares* is itself evidence against the claim that minority women writers only engage with ethnic matters, since to a certain extent the story of Clara is a universal story of the search for the self. In *Los años pares*, Absatz focuses on four years in the life of the main character, the Argentine Clara Auslender (read: clearly foreigner/outsider/alien). Absatz engages with Clara's life between the years 1976–1980, and the Dirty War (the "*guerra sucia*" also known as the *Proceso of Reorganización Nacional*: the Process of National Reorganization) serves as a backdrop for her narrative. In the work, Clara self-critically analyzes the last four years of her life and her romantic involvement with the Dutch painter Eric van der Möer. The narrative follows a traditional plot line and is divided into four chapters that create a circular structure. Clara's reevaluation of her life begins with the chapter titled "1980," followed by the chapters "1976" and "1978," and rounding up her account with a return to the year "1980."

Throughout *Los años pares*, besides attempting to assert a female identity, Absatz engages in two projects simultaneously. First, she revises and expands the official Argentine national history during the years of the Dirty War, a narrative often conveyed from the perspective of exiled artists and intellectuals to negate the commonly held belief that during this period all cultural activity had been crushed by the dictators. Secondly, as the name of the main protagonist Clara Auslender suggests, Absatz engages in the project of redefining a hybrid Latin American identity. For this project of identity reconceptualization, Absatz questions diverse ideologies that have been deployed to claim an autochthonous Latin American distinctiveness while in the process excluding non-mestizo, non-criollo elements from definitions of Latinamericanism.

Absatz's *Los años pares* attempts to present an-other face of Argentine history during the years of terror. From the first pages of her narrative, the narrative hints at the repression, intimidation, and censorship that pushed many intellectuals, artists, writers, and activists to go into exile and "huir para siempre" [run away forever] (18) in order to save their lives. However, by calling attention to the ongoing cultural life in Argentina during the dictatorship, Absatz's work more emphatically pays tribute and gives a voice to the artists and the intellectuals who remained in the country.[10] Absatz's account seems to join David William Foster in suggesting that: "[T]he exiles'

10 In fact, Absatz's autobiographical *Féiguele y otras mujeres* was censured three months after its publication by the Videla regime because one of the stories includes an explicit discussion of abortion. Despite the censorship of her work, Absatz did not leave Argentina.

visibility as spokespersons on the conditions that had forced them to seek foreign refuge led inevitably to the assumption that their voices were coterminous with all of Argentine culture, and that they were speaking for all the artists left behind whose voices had become silenced or distorted" (Foster 8).

Absatz's work emphasizes that people do suffer as a direct result of oppression. For example, Amanda's sister Mercedes has not been able to eat well for months because "le cuesta entenderse con la realidad de las cosas" [she has problems coming to terms with the reality of things] (*Los años* 36). At the same time, her account suggests that the administration of the "Teatro Municipal" [Municipal Theater] (33) has not undergone significant alterations and continues to work despite the crisis sweeping the nation.[11] Supporting Absatz's representation, literary critics illustrate that during this most bloody period of Argentine history, theater continued to thrive:

> Although any direct references to the realities of the day were prohibited, playwrights were able to use metaphors to avoid censorship. They were forced to find codes that the public could understand but would pass unnoticed by the censors (never known for their mental prowess). There was, of necessity, much symbolism and use of elliptic language. Dramatists had to be as creative as possible and the results were excellent. Cossa, Gambaro, Gorostiza, Monti, Pavlowsky, Halac, Goldenberg, Bortnik, Mauricio, Raznovich, and Kartun all were able to present some of their greatest plays, which mixed realism and vanguardism and became uniquely Argentine. They were doing so in an increasingly chaotic situation in which uncertainty reigned and disappearances were common occurrence. (Foster, Fitch, and Lockhart 139)

Absatz's narrative presents resilient Argentines who do not detach themselves from reality and who, nevertheless, try to adapt themselves to the harsh conditions of their daily lives. In addition to theater, her work calls attention to "galerías" [art galleries] (47) and numerous first-rate "exposiciones" [exhibitions] (47) that display visual art productions. In this way, Absatz likewise gives emphasis to the flourishing production in an artistic field that in Argentina has consistently been overshadowed by the tremendous "dominance of literature on the cultural landscape" (Foster, Fitch, and Lockhart 141).[12] Nonetheless, Absatz equally presents the inconsistencies and compromises experienced by resourceful people who wanted to sustain and preserve Argentine cul-

11 In relation to Argentine theater, "a true mark of Argentine pride" that has always occupied a place of utmost importance in the nation's cultural life, Foster explains, "One would have to examine the overwhelming success of the 1981 Teatro Abierto [Open Theater] movement and the parallel phenomena of Danza Abierta [Open Dance], Poesía Abierta [Open Poetry], and Cine Abierto [Open Cinema]" (139). For Open Theater, cf. Jean Graham-Jones (89–122).

12 Additionally, as Foster, Fitch, and Lockhart explain, "Argentina typically has been underrecognized for artistic achievement in spite of the fact that many Argentine plastic artists have earned international reputations for themselves. The contributions of Argentine artists to the larger body of Latin American art have been dwarfed by such giants as the Mexican muralists Diego Rivera, David Alfaro Siqueiros, and José Clemente Orozco; the pained artist cum pop icon Frida Kahlo from Mexico; the Colombian Fernando Botero; and others considered to be among the masters of Latin American art" (144).

tural production throughout the time of the Process. Her narrative acknowledges that, because of the confusion of the state of affairs in the nation, "ya nadie estaba seguro de qué erá reaccionario y qué no" [nobody was sure any longer as to what was reactionary and what was not] (110). Absatz makes reference to "un concurso de pintura" [a painting competition] (37) sponsored by a U.S. American company that is taking place at a time when it looked like "todo el mundo" [the whole world] (36) was leaving the country. Similarly, readers observe the sophisticated negotiations that the lawyer and theater legal adviser Fernando Suaya must complete in order to help the unofficial art sponsoring organization he represents stay afloat: "Suaya presionaba a los funcinarios con lenguaje ejecutivo, y al empresario anglosajón lo trataba como un secretario de la cultura" [Making use of official language, Suaya would put pressure on civil servants and would treat the Anglo manager as if he were a secretary of culture] (92).

Finally, Absatz's narrative makes the reader aware that not all artists who decide to leave the country are victims of dictatorial persecution or even in opposition to the regime. Along these lines, the novel offers the case of the affluent painter Franklin Donato. Apolitical Donato, who "pintaba flores pequeñas de colores apacibles" [painted small flowers in dull colors] (48), simply decides to leave the country of his own personal accord and whim. Hence, Absatz's work does not present the intellectual and the Argentine artistic exodus as exclusively the effect of a "draconian political program" installed by the totalitarian regime (Foster 60). Indeed, emphasizing human agency, Absatz's work calls attention to local and transnational human resourcefulness and support and requests a more contextualized study and interpretation of Argentine history during the Process.[13]

In addition to this historiographical work, Absatz's *Los años pares* also complicates the notion of stable Latin American identities. The narrative, which Absatz has described as "un homenaje a la novela policial" [a homage to the detective novel] (Flori 92), begins in 1980 on the day that Clara is having difficulties replacing her lost national identity card. At the registrar, the moment Clara says that she is single, the inspector informs her that the new official document cannot be handed out to her be-

13 As to Argentine human ingenuity under oppression, Foster expresses, "Someday someone will write the documental history of the radio programs that dared to interview the *non sancti*. The history will be written of how the best forum for sociopolitical commentary was a gutsy humor magazine, *Humor registrado* [Copyrighted humor/Humor on Record], and of how theatrical representations of foreign works became interpretative performances of national issues. It will be the story of the blooming of daily newspapers that had, at times, little mass distribution, but whose particular cultural interests transcended the purely national. The story will be about the literary and criticism workshops that functioned on the margins of the institutions to preserve and stimulate those elements that the institutions, thanks to the corruption by the military, were ignoring. It will be of all the clandestine cultural projects that, precisely for being concealed, did not attract the attention of the international community that has come to believe that the brain waves of the Argentine cultural body marked a fatal, uninterrupted horizontal line" (61–62).

cause Clara's information contradicts her old records. As Clara finds out, the document in the officer's possession dates back to 1976, when she and her Dutch boyfriend Eric had taken a bus trip through several Latin American countries. On that occasion, the couple had randomly been taken into custody under the suspicion of being dissidents. On this occasion, in response to the inquiry about her civil status, Clara spontaneously told the police that she was single, even though she had actually been divorced from her husband Leo for two years. After her marriage to Leo, Clara had never had the time to change her civil status on her identity card. During the subsequent fifteen to twenty interrogations by the police officers in Jujuy, Clara kept telling her inquisitors that she was single because she was afraid of offering contradictory information. Although Clara had nothing to hide, she was plagued by the fear that the lie could mean the difference "entre la vida y la muerte" [between life and death] (90) for her and her boyfriend Eric. Ultimately, she opened her heart to Eric and told him about her fears about not telling the police that she had been married and was now divorced.

Four years later, in the process of getting her new identity card, the officer explains to her that she is now officially identified as married. Clara finally understands why she and Eric had been released from custody soon after she had told Eric about her transgression. In fact, after all this time, Clara only confirms what she had always sensed since the random release from custody in Jujuy. Eric, the only person who had known that she had been married, had betrayed her and jeopardized her life. She now understands that Eric had made a bargain with the FBI inquisitors: he would provide them with the truth about the woman and they would let him go. Eric, who "obviamente no era su esposo" [who obviously was not her husband] (167), had told the officers that Clara was married, as the long telegram that the officer at the register was showing her, four years after it was composed, confirmed. Thus the novel traces Clara's efforts to understand how she has come to lose her ID, providing an apt metaphor for her search for identity. In this sense, Clara's pursuit for self-knowledge also allows us to view *Los años pares* as a "novel of self-discovery" (Felski 122). The work's developmental plot traces the emergence of Clara's female identity and, in the process, questions and subsequently rejects the heterosexual romance narrative.

Clara and Eric's experience in Jujuy displays how paranoid tyranny often sadistically paraded its power over Argentine citizens just for the pleasure of confirming and reconfirming the "legalidad" [lawfulness] (167) of the members of the citizenry it had decided to terrorize in its search for potential enemies. At the same time, Eric's betrayal of Clara uncovers the double standards and unsoundness of a system that defended and propagated Christian and bourgeoisie family values and is only able to acknowledge Clara's lawfulness the moment the inquisitors are satisfied with her civil status as a married woman. Most importantly, the confirmation of Eric's betrayal triggers Clara's self-critical analysis of her relationship with the European artist. In this process of self-discovery, the critique becomes an angry dialogue between Latin America and Europe in which Clara Auslender confronts issues related to her European Latin American identity as she tries to grasp why, even at a time when she did not know the dimension of Eric's betrayal, she had little by little started to hate "al tipo que el resto del mundo adora" [the guy that the rest of the world adores] (137).

Clara's auto-critique begins by recognizing that, not quite recovered from the pain that Leo's abandonment of her for another woman had caused her, from the start of the relationship with the Dutch artist she had put herself in a subordinate and vulnerable position: anticipating, waiting, cooking, cleaning, understanding, hoping to please Eric's every wish. Buying into the Western narrative of heterosexual romance and unable to believe her luck with the talented Eric, Clara had been eager not to make mistakes this time and to become the perfect partner for the painter. Looking back years later, Clara admits that the role of static art object, which she played for the painter, had been a degradation that actually had felt as if "la muerte [hubiera estado] ganando el juego" [death had been winning the game] (53). Through her recognition that Eric had never loved her, Clara extends her critique of Eric's Eurocentric disinterest in Latin American and Argentine cultures and histories. At the same time, her confrontation with Eric enables Clara to open a space that allows her to question Latin American ideologies that posit an essential and autochthonous Latin American identity.

In retrospect, Clara now understands that Eric's desire to make the bus/train trip through Argentina, Bolivia, and Peru was just his longing to have the exotic "experiencia sudamericana" [South American experience] (127). She admits that, actually, at no point on the trip had Eric tried to engage with the people and the reality he encountered during the trip across three Latin American nations, nor had this been his intention. She remembers how Eric experienced the three countries exclusively through the official narratives about an exotic Latin America region occupying an unenlightened periphery in relation to an enlightened European center.

Clara bears in mind that during the trip, because of Eric's long hair, the couple used to come across as suspicious. Again and again they would be stopped by soldiers, who wanted to see their identity cards and passports. Nevertheless, though the officers repeatedly interrogated the European, Eric always gave the impression that "esas impertinencias no le molestaban, que comprendía" [the impertinences did not bother him, that he understood] (61). Clara now sees that in his Eurocentric world view, Eric obliterated historical Western intervention in the Latin American region and remained unable to establish a cultural dialogue with the reality he encountered. For compassionate and ever understanding Eric, the Dirty War, the state of siege in Bolivia, and the perceived lack of education and backwardness of the Andean population remain the natural products of the general foolishness of the region where all its inhabitants are "locos" [crazy] (174): a perpetually unreasonable bunch of people not yet fit to govern themselves or to achieve social tranquility, progress, and civilization. Clara now believes that Eric had only been able to enjoy "su viaje" [his trip] (64) because of his historical amnesia about the disruption and exploitation that resulted from the European colonization of the region. Indifferent to the disconcerting reality they sometimes encountered, which was not his European one, Eric contemplated the exceptional Andean mountains, where "la guerrilla agonizaba" [the guerrilla agonized] (64), and immortalized them in his sketchbook. Positing two incommensurable worlds, that is, the developed First and the underdeveloped Third, Eric suppressed the fact that the emergence of Western Europe was a largely unequal "joint venture" (Shohat and Stam 14) between Europe and Latin America. In other words, the European industrial revolutions were partly financed by the exploitation of the very mountains the contemporary artist was belatedly celebrating, by the wealth generated by "Latin American mines and plantations" (14).

Hoping to locate the precise moment when her feelings for the arrogant artist started to change, Clara remembers the song called *Coroico's blues* (173), a piece that Eric had composed in a moment of lyrical exaltation in Bolivia. Exposing Eric's proclivity to homogenize and deny any form of cultural difference that might disturb his monochrome Latin American fiction, Clara stresses the irony of the fact that the artist enthusiastically celebrated "una nación a pesar de que cruzaron tres fronteras" [one nation despite their having crossed three borders] (173). Locating Latin America in a Eurocentric universalism that eradicates the context of his particular experience, Eric sings "el perfume de las retamas en Angastaco y luego inesperademente, el mismo perfume en las afueras de Oruro" [the perfume of the plants in Angastaco and then suddenly, celebrates the same perfume in the outskirts of Oruro] (173). Clara now recalls herself thinking that the decontextualized lyrical composition exposed Eric's drive for sameness; the sentimental oeuvre actually celebrated: "Idéntico paisaje, idénticas las cabelleras negras, … la gente gris, el aire limpio, la tierra alta, todo un mismo país [Identical landscape, the same black hair, … the grey people, the clean air, the highlands, everything the same country] (173). She equally remembers that Eric was constantly comparing "todo lo argentino con todo lo holandés" [everything Dutch with everything Argentine] (166). For instance, he remarked, "Los policías argentinos son diferentes de los policías de Holanda" [Argentine policemen were different from Dutch policemen] (77), but his comparisons introduced irrevocable cultural "difference" that rendered Argentina utterly "other" and unknowable in relation to Europe. By concluding that "Holanda es tan diferente" [Holland is so different] (166), Eric incidentally insinuated the singularity and superiority of Europe and erected absolute barriers between Europe and the Latin American other.

But Clara is not only critical of Eric's logic of "us" and "them." Clara articulates her discontent with her French gymnastics teacher who speaks condescendingly about her Bolivian female students to Clara, because: "En ningún momento se le había pasado por la cabeza que Clara fuera sudamericana" [at no moment did it cross her mind that Clara could be South American] (125). Equally, Clara is uneasy because she knows the French woman is by no means the only one with an *idée fixe* about the way Latin Americans are supposed to be or look. According to Clara: "A los europeos no se les ocurría que alguien de su color y con ese aspecto pudiese provenir de tierras tan bárbaras, y mucho menos lo podían concebir los mismos nativos" [It did not occur to the Europeans that somebody with her skin color and her looks could come from such barbaric lands, even less did it occur to the native inhabitants] (126). In this way, Clara starts to problematize European and Latin American cultural ideologies about an essential Latin American identity.

Among other ideas, Clara questions the Eurocentric view held by developed First World nations that the Andean region has remained resistant to the universal project of "civilizing" modernity, due to their difficulty in adapting to the emancipatory "transformations of the Western world" (Triviño Anzola 405). In Peru, Clara observes how whenever the train stopped and the Germans jumped out of it to buy the products the inhabitants of the region offered, the Germans "gritoneaban, se burlaban del producto y por fin lo conseguían a un precio que no llegaba a la mitad de lo que les habían pedido" [shouted, made fun of the product just to end up getting it for a price that was not even half of the amount initially asked for] (125) and thus celebrated their ability to take advantage of the Latin Americans. But Clara is not interested in representing the inhabitants of the region as perpetual victims of the bad European. Her evaluation does not presuppose that Latin Americans are somehow superior human beings, an intellectual move that would merely amount to turning "colonialist claims upside down" (Shohat and Stam 3). In fact, after the transaction with the Germans, Clara observes that the natives would go away satisfied in the conviction of having sold the "brutal" [stupid] (125) German something that the European "no deseaba ni necesitaba" [neither wanted nor needed] (125). However, Clara condemns the Eurocentric tendency to view indigenous practices and customs of Third World nations as symptoms of the "backwardness and barbarity" of Third World cultures in comparison to the superiority and "progressiveness of Western culture" (Narayan 17). Yet, in the same breath, Clara also starts to interrogate Latin America's essentialist reaction to the European reductionism by attempting to create a modern Latin American identity and propagate the myth of Latin American cultural authenticity in contrast with the invader by recurring to what critics have viewed as "a real cult of origins" (Ainsa 62).

This "cult of origins" manifests itself in Clara's dealings with the Peruvians, who, because of her European looks, do not recognize her as a Latin American. Moreover, even when she speaks in perfect Spanish to them, they do not listen to or answer her. In fact, with distress, she notices that the natives of the region marginalize her. Clara explains: "ellos la miraban con una desconfianza amasada durante quinientos años y en el mayor de los casos le contestaban con señas" [they looked at her with a distrust that has been accumulated for five hundred years. In the majority of cases, they answered by making gestures] (126). Clara thus questions the effort of some Latin Americans to counteract what has happened since the "encounter of two worlds in 1492" by means of an oppositional attitude that posits everything that has followed as "a long process of contamination, degradation, and destruction" of the original state (Ainsa 62). Absatz's work objects to this reactionary response to the violent impact of modernization on Latin America and does not believe that Latin America should be seen as merely a counterpart to Europe and the United States. Her work seeks to complicate intellectual discourses of Latin America that often set "young" Latin Americans fighting brutish U.S. American imperialism and the ugly European legacy of the region as a way to resist the Eurocentric essentalization of Latin American identity and come to terms with the impact of secularizing and functionalist modernity. In other words, *Los años pares* questions Latin American identity ideologies that have often been born out of the intellectual elites' uncertainty as to how to react to immigration and imperialist forces or out of their apprehension as to what values to maintain or recuperate from traditional cultures. Absatz's work challenges elitist efforts to forge a political and a Latin American identity as a mere reaction to the modernizing project that has often turned writers of the region into "prophets who speak a common language, telling stories of identity" (Rodríguez Pérsico 391).[14]

As Adriana Rodríguez Pérsico reminds us, in Argentina, there have been writers that have propagated resolute nationalism, such as the anti-Semitic Leopoldo Lugones who viewed the Indians and the immigrants as the enemies of the Argentine nation. The intellectual grieved the loss of the unity of Spanish America and longed for a return to a mythical and heroic gaucho past (392). Argentine intellectual Ricardo Rojas similarly wished to create a collective Argentine consciousness and reverse the moral degradation created by the immigrants. Doubting the capacity of Argentina to absorb difference and demanding unconditional assimilation from the foreigners, Rojas wrote: "Todo ha de ser argentino sobre la tierra argentina!" [Everything on Argentine soil must be Argentine!] (qtd. in Rodríguez Pérsico 393). Rojas's fiction of identity not only decried the "sorda hostilidad babélica" [Babelian state of mutual hostility] (qtd. in Rodríguez Pérsico 394) produced by the immigrants, it also recommended territorial expansion of the Argentine nation. In his fiction, Rojas extended the Argentine national borders all the way to Peru, thus "restoring the boundaries of Argentina to those of the ancient Inca civilization" (393). But probably the most influential expressions of oppositional Latin American identity were espoused by Uruguayan José Enrique Rodó and the Cuban José Martí. For Rodo, as Rodríguez Pérsico reminds us, it is clear: "America must be Latin … with the egalitarian spirit of Christianity" (395). For Martí, his America was solely "*mestizo*, not European, or African, or Indian," thus turning against one another the dichotomy "*meztizo* America" vs. "foreigner" (396), the other America.

Instead, Absatz's work disputes the viewpoint of an incommensurable cultural divide between "their culture" and "our culture" (43). Clara understands that this view obscures the fact that if there is some kind of national or cultural essence in the countries of the Latin American region, as Rosalba Campra suggests, "this national essence is a cultural hybrid" (qtd. in McClennen 43). Through Clara Auslender, Absatz questions narratives of essential Latin American authenticity that emphasizes mestizo 'blood' ties as a Latin American identity quintessence and instead argues for a construction of Latin American identity that is an identity-in-process and results from location of birth or long-term residence in a region.

---

14 Nelly Richard reminds us that in order to claim cultural purity: "These (versions of identity) are drawn from the opposition between self (seen as internal identity) and the 'other' (identity from outside); for instance, the regional (seen as authentic) versus the international (seen as false), the past (the vernacular roots) versus the present (seen as the destruction of the binding sense of community)" (466).

And yet, once Clara confronts Eric's betrayal and Eurocentric disrespect for her and dispels the myth of a unified Latin American identity, she concludes her evaluation (as she is finishing to clean her apartment) by saying "Eric, go home" (Absatz 174). After achieving psychological transformation in the safe retreat of her apartment, this directive signals Clara's desire to move on with her life. Disappointed in the romance plot and the persons who blindly continue to adore Eric, she now wants to be by herself and enjoy her affirmative female identity and newfound freedom. However, her experience with Eric has been an important catalyst that leads her to reevaluate and revitalize her life. Clara now "se siente fuerte y liviana" [feels strong and light] (175). In this sense, even if Clara wants Eric to leave for good, Eric remains an integral part of her existence. Clara's desire to polarize the masculine and the feminine spheres seems to propose an oppositional feminist discourse that, suggesting "a radical negation of everything that has gone before" (Felski 58), remains unaware that oppositional discourse "relies upon concepts and arguments" that originate in the very patriarchal ideology and masculine systems of representation that it seeks to undermine (59).

Moreover, by retreating to her apartment at the end of her journey of self-discovery, Clara displays vestiges of romantic individualism and seems unconscious that "the feminist critique of patriarchal values cannot occur outside ideological and social structures in some privileged space, but constantly interacts with the very frameworks it challenges" (Felski 59). By proposing gender dualism of self-sufficient masculine and feminine spheres (characteristic of the feminist "novel of self-discovery"), Clara betrays a view of gender that, instead of attempting to conceptualize adequate feminist experiences and practices, rather obscures "the complex nexus of social, ideological, and psychological relation through which gender is constructed" (132). Finally, Clara's feminist critique seems to suggest that gender is the sole variant that explains social relations. By attempting to enforce gender-based identification, irrespective of class, race, sexuality, religion, etc., Clara's apolitical and limited feminist analysis does not offer an explanation "of how existing forms of gender inequality can be changed" (59). By focusing her analysis on the variant gender to present her critique of patriarchal structures, Clara overlooks that gender inequality, as Rita Felski reminds us, "cannot be explained purely in gender terms" (59). To rely solely upon the divide female and male to explain gender discrimination fails to acknowledge that gender inequity "is related to a variety of social and cultural factors … which are not limited to women, although they will of course affect men and women in different ways" (59).

The expression "Eric, go home," not only exposes Clara's inability to engage with the complexities of the gender dialectic: her command is also symptomatic of the problems that emerge in Absatz's attempts to redefine a hybrid Latin American identity.[15] The expression "Eric, go home," in a work that questions ideologies that posit a

15 Clara's expression "Eric, go home" brings to mind the anti-imperialist expression "Green go home." Popular folklore suggests that the command "Green go home" originated in the XIX century during the time of the U.S. American invasion to Mexico when, referring to the color of the intruders' uniform, Mexicans expressed their anger at the inva-

distinctive Latin American identity (ironically, even as she utters a cliché), exposes a fundamental ambivalence and tension between conflicting forms of leftist and conservative cultural nationalism. Moreover, this directive introduces an inconsistency in Absatz's attempt to reinvent a Latin American identity that values difference. In other words, throughout *Los años pares,* Absatz displays a profound commitment and attachment to Latin America. Her work argues for a different construction of non-essential Latin American identity which affirms difference. Her anti-essentialist position posits a different construction of Latin American identity and culture and can be understood as the "leftist variation" of "cultural nationalism," which suggests an identity that does not rely "on a mythical return to origins" (McClennen 22). This leftist political position pleads for a cultural reevaluation where "forgotten aspects of the culture," like for instance the non-criollo, non-mestizo immigrants' contributions to Latin American cultures and societies, no longer have to "remain in the margins" (22).

At the same time, Absatz's expression "Eric, go home" approximates the same conservative cultural nationalist position her narrative seeks to question. Indeed, in their attempt to define themselves in opposition to the imperialism of the United States and Western influence, many Latin American writers and intellectuals have expressed the desire which Clara Auslender now expresses in relation to the European Eric. "Eric, go home," brings to mind the Latin American modernist tendency to dismiss the European and U.S. American component, influence, and experience as thoroughly negative and upsetting. This proclivity, as the analysis of Absatz's work has shown, results in attempts to find Latin American mythic origins that posit an uncontaminated past before the European disruption and the arrival of the immigrants, and has repeatedly returned to "indigenism, nationalism, thirdworldism" (Richard 466). In this sense, it is imperative that the reader rewrite the end of *Los años pares* and affirm that there is no way Eric can go home.

In the same way that the European Eric remains a constitutive part of Clara's existence, Western culture and values remain a constitutive element of Latin American identities and cultures. Europe and the European immigrants, among them the Jewish immigrants from Central and Eastern Europe, have made indelible and unquestionable contributions to the histories and cultures of Latin America and Argentina. In this way, Absatz's work exposes the unresolved dialectical tension between the Western center and the Latin American periphery that, again and again, has emerged and continues to dictate the debates on controversial and multivalent Latin American national identity; an identity that has been indisputably founded in Eastern, Central, and Western European, and incorporates Asian, Native, and African cultures and languages. As it were, it is possible to suggest, the dialectical tension between the periphery and the center

---

sion by shouting at the U.S: American soldiers to go home: "Green go home." Some arguably believe that the directive equally gave birth to the word *gringo* (green go) whose meanings vary in Latin American countries though it generally denotes a foreigner, a blond white person who speaks a foreign language. In some nations, such as Colombia or Peru, the word exclusively refers to U.S. Americans.

that emerges in *Los años pares* makes Absatz's work profoundly Latin American; profoundly Argentine.

Absatz narrates realities that confirm the accurateness of Peter Wade's observation that *mestizaje* has been based on the exclusion of "those considered unmixed" (84) and has thus promoted the marginalization of the Jewish tradition in the Latin American region where Jewish people "continue to be seen as the other, as the foreign minority" (Agosín, "Introduction," *Memory* xiv). In Argentina, where according to mainstream parlance *mestizaje* "has been judged to be negligible" (Miller 2) (very much unlike the nations of the Andean region), there has been a tendency to suppress religious, racial, and ethnic diversity in the name of Argentineness, the national ideal of a Western European white Hispano-Catholic consciousness and society (Segal; Foster, Fitch, and Lockhart 95).[16] Absatz emphasizes the need to confront Latin American societies with the presence of "other" Latin Americans who do not possess the characteristics of "rightful" members of the mythical Catholic Latin American *mestizo* race, as defined by traditional Latin American identity discourses. Her narrative questions the ideology of a hybrid *mestizo* Latin American identity that, with its tendency to favor Catholic "whiteness," presents the Western universalistic drive for uniformity that leaves no room to accommodate and acknowledge the difference introduced by non-Hispano or non-Latin Catholic, non-criollo, or non-mestizo immigrants to the region.

Works cited

Absatz, Cecila. *Los años pares*. Buenos Aires: Editorial Legasa, 1985. Print.

———. "Re: Preguntas." E-mail to the author. 5 Apr. 2006. Print.

Agosín, Marjorie. "Introduction." *Memory, Oblivion, and Jewish Culture in Latin America*. Ed. Marjorie Agosín. Austin: U of Texas P, 2005. xii–xxii. Print.

———. "Introduction." *The House of Memory: Stories by Jewish Women Writers of Latin America.* Ed. Marjorie Agosín. New York: The Feminist Press at The City U of New York, 1999. 1–25. Print.

Ainsa, Fernando. "The Challenges of Postmodernity and Globalization: Multiple or Fragmented Identities?" *Latin America Writes Back: Postmodernity in the Periphery.* Ed. Emil Volek. New York: Routledge, 2002. 59–78. Print.

16 For instance, Marilyn Grace Miller writes about the origins of the celebrated quintessential Argentine tango and its "transformation from black to white" (93). Her work problematizes "the tendency to rewrite the tango as white … and to focus selectively on its European and Euro-American features" (81). Paraphrasing Marta Savigliano, Miller states that the suppression of black roots of the tango is "at the heart of Argentine psychological repression" (94). Indeed, Miller concludes by suggesting that "[p]erhaps tango has come to stand for what it means to be Argentinean precisely because of the success with which this mestizo form has been dispossessed of its diasporic African character and spirit(s)" (95).

Avni, Haim. *Judíos en América: Cinco siglos de historia*. Madrid: Editorial Mapfre, 1992. Print.

Barr, Lois Baer. *Isaac Unbound: Patriarchal Traditions in the Latin American Jewish Novel*. Tempe: Arizona State U, 1995. Print.

Brodsky, Adriana M. *Sephardi, Jewish, Argentine: Community and National Identity*. Bloomington: Indiana UP, 2016. Print.

Díaz Esteban, Fernando, ed. *América y los judíos hispanoportugueses*. Madrid: Real Academia de la Historia, 2009. Print.

Elkin, Judith Laikin. *The Jews of Latin America*. New York: Holmes & Meier, 1998. Print.

Felski, Rita. *Beyond Feminist Aesthetics: Feminist Literature and Social Change*. Cambridge, MA: Harvard UP, 1989. Print.

Flori, Mónica. "Alicia Steimberg y Cecilia Absatz: Dos narradoras argentinas contemporáneas." *Chasqui* 17.2 (1988): 83–92. Print.

Foster, David William. *Violence in Argentine Literature: Cultural Responses to Tyranny*. Columbia: U of Missouri P, 1995. Print.

———, Melissa Fitch Lockhart, and Darrell B. Lockhart. *Culture and Customs of Argentina*. Westport, CT: Greenwood P, 1998. Print.

Graham-Jones, Jean. *Exorcising History: Argentine Theater under Dictatorship*. Lewisburg: Bucknell UP, 2000. Print.

Klich, Ignacio. "Arab-Jewish Coexistence in the First Half of 1900's in Argentina: Overcoming Self-Imposed Amnesia." *Arab and Jewish Immigrants in Latin America: Images and Realities*. Ed. Jeffrey Lesser. London: Frank Cass, 1998. 1–37. Print.

Lesser, Jeffrey, and Raanan Rein. "Introduction." *Rethinking Jewish-Latin Americans*. Ed. Lesser and Rein. Albuquerque: U of New Mexico P, 2008. 1–40. Print.

Mate, Reyes, and Ricardo Forster, eds. *El judaísmo en Iberoamérica*. Madrid: Editorial Trotta, 2007. Print.

McClennen, Sophia. *The Dialectics of Exile: Nation, Time, Language, and Space in Hispanic Literatures*. West Lafayette, IN: Purdue UP, 2004. Print.

McGee Deutsch, Sandra. "A Journey through my Life and Latin American Jewish Studies." *Memory, Oblivion, and Jewish Culture in Latin America*. Ed. Marjorie Agosín. Austin: U of Texas P, 2005. 61–74. Print.

———. *Crossing Borders, Claiming a Nation: A History of Argentine Jewish Women, 1880–1955*. Durham: Duke UP, 2010. Print.

Miller, Marilyn Grace. *Rise and Fall of the Cosmic Race: The Cult of Mestizaje in Latin America*. Austin: U of Texas P, 2004. Print.

Narayan, Uma. *Dislocating Cultures. Identities, Traditions, and Third-World Feminism*. New York: Routledge 1997. Print.

Rein, Raanan, ed. *Árabes y judíos en Iberoamérica/Similitudes, diferencias y tensiones*. Sevilla: Fundación Tres Culturas del Mediterráneo, 2008. 11–26. Print.

Richard, Nelly. "Postmodernism and Periphery." *Postmodernism: A Reader*. Ed. Thomas Docherty. New York: Columbia UP, 1993. 463–470. Print.

Rodríguez, Julia. *Civilizing Argentina: Science, Medicine, and the Modern State.* Chapel Hill: The U of North Carolina P, 2006. Print.

Rodríguez Pérsico, Adriana. "The Rhetoric of Citizenship in Modernity." *Literary Cultures of Latin America: A Comparative History.* Ed. Mario J. Valdés and Djelal Kadir. Vol. 1. Oxford: Oxford UP, 2004. 384–400. Print.

Segal, Bernard E. "Jews and the Argentine Center: A Middleman Minority." *The Jewish Presence in Latin America.* Ed. Judith Laikin Elkin and Gilbert W. Merkx. Boston: Allen and Unwin, 1987. 201–217. Print.

Shohat, Ella, and Robert Stam. *Unthinking Eurocentrism: Multiculturalism and the Media.* New York: Routledge, 1994. Print.

Triviño Anzola, Consuelo. "Andean Region." *Literary Cultures of Latin America: A Comparative History.* Ed. Mario J. Valdés and Djelal Kadir. 2 vols. Oxford: Oxford UP, 2004. 405–412. Print.

Reclaiming Voices and Bodies of the Nobodies: The Transformation of Silence into Language and Action

ISABEL CALDEIRA

Los nadies: los hijos de nadie, los dueños de nada. Los nadies:
los ningunos, los niguneados, corriendo la liebre, muriendo la vida, jodidos, rejodidos.
Que no son, aunque sean.
Que no hablan idiomas, sino dialectos.
Que no profesan religiones, sino supersticiones.
Que no hacen arte, sino artesanías.
Que no practican cultura, sino folklore.
Que no son seres humanos, sino recursos humanos.
Que no tienen cara, sino brazos.
Que no tienen nombre, sino número.
Que no figuran en la historia universal, sino en la crónica roja de la prensa local.

Los nadies, que cuestan menos que la bala que los mata.
Eduardo Galeano, "Los Nadies." El libro de los abrazos

Writing is, after all, an act of language, its practice.
But first of all it is an effort of the will to discover.
– Toni Morrison, "Unspeakable Things Unspoken"

The global devaluation of black lives: the mark of history

A different value attached to white and black bodies is one of the most enduring legacies of slavery in the Americas. And it is still visible in the global devaluation of black lives and black citizenship and the Euro-American marginalization of the people of African descent. A profound inequality persists in the white-dominant societies as available indicators have demonstrated. Across the Americas, people of African descent face unequal social and economic opportunities, as well as unequal access to political participation and other civil rights. Black women experience especially higher levels of discrimination based on gender and ethnicity, and tend to score lower on levels of economic and social rights.

In a sociological study of 2018, "Separate and Unequal: The Impact of Socioeconomic Status, Segregation, and the Great Recession on Racial Disparities in Housing Values," Melvin E. Thomas et al., regarding the particular case of residential problem, even speak of a hypersegregation in U.S society: "Hypersegregation provides a structural perspective that allows the analysis of U.S. racial stratification by highlighting the role of residential segregation and concentrated disadvantage in maintaining racial inequality" (Thomas, Moye, Henderson, and Horton 230). They conclude that segregation as a structural factor continues to disadvantage African Americans, and even the black middle class is still very fragile in this and other aspects.

Trusting the information rendered by Marialuisa Ferro (Minority Rights Group International), there are currently "at least 150 million people of African descent in Latin America and the Caribbean, with Afro-descendants especially prominent in Brazil, Colombia, and Venezuela, as well as most Caribbean islands, where Afro-descendants in fact form a numerical majority of the population" (Ferro n. pag.). However, she notes, people of African ancestry "are still rarely represented in government and usually attain lower levels of human development" (n. pag.). In the U.S., the numbers of Afro-descendants communities form a significant proportion of the population, with more than 40 million citizens identified as black or African American. According to the Pew Research Center, a "significant voluntary black migration is a relatively new development – and one that has increased rapidly over the past two decades" (Anderson and López n. pag.). Therefore, as the black population in the U.S. has grown in high numbers, black communities are now quite diverse.[1]

In spite of all the transformations in social status since the 1960s in the U.S., and even though several countries in Latin America have adopted legal and institutional measures to combat ethnic discrimination towards Afro-descendants, the available indicators still showcase levels of profound inequality, even if social welfare has improved. Throughout the Americas, poverty is pervading; in the U.S. today, more than a quarter of the black American population live below the poverty level, compared to less than a tenth of the white population, access to justice remains poor, police brutality is common, and the barriers to political participation and other civil rights still persist; in Latin America, as can be found in many reports, the black population represents the majority of poor people in the region, and according to a World Bank report of 2018, they are 2.5 times more likely to live in chronic poverty than whites or mestizos. They also have fewer years of education and are more often victims of crime and violence.[2] As Margarita Sanchez and Maurice Bryan assert in their study for Minority Rights Group International,

---

1 African American society has begun to reflect this change even making the designation African American ever more fluid. In New York, the Roman Catholic diocese has added masses in Ashanti and Fante, while black men and women from various Caribbean islands march in the West Indian American Carnival and the Dominican Day Parade. In Chicago, Cameroonians celebrate their nation's independence day, while the DuSable Museum of African American History hosts a Nigerian Festival. Black immigrants have joined groups such as the Egbe Omo Yoruba (National Association of Yoruba Descendants in North America), the Association des Sénégalais d'Amérique and the Fédération des Associations Régionales Haïtiennes à l'Étranger rather than the NAACP or the Urban League. https://www.smithsonianmag.com/history/the-changing-definition-of-african-american-4905887/#9hsKHqeXyX2kBpt7.99.

2 Cf. Denise Ferreira da Silva who, in a study focusing the state military police's and the Brazilian Army's occupations of the city of Rio de Janeiro's black and brown economically dispossessed neighborhoods (*favelas*), observes that "the racial violence that cap-

> communities of African descent (Afro-descendant communities) in Latin America are often marginalized as part of a legacy of colonialism and 'racial democracy.' The latter has promoted the notion that racism does not exist in Latin America because, in these multi-ethnic societies, an inherent state of harmonious relations supposedly prevails. Afro-descendants have been 'invisible' in relation to development. (3)

Nobody can deny that the history and ancestry of Afro-descendants are prevailing factors for their continued discrimination. The vast majority of Afro-descendants in the Americas derive from the slave traffic that fed the wealth of the several European empires. The racialized labor and the racialized communities established by colonial capitalism denied humanity to Africans and their descendants and concurred to their invisibility and inaudibility throughout history, leaving their sequel until the current days.

Along with inequality in access to civil rights and discrimination, Afro-descendants are also marked by invisibility and silencing in the historical records. The most tragic instances of not only invisibility, but a literal disappearance of dehumanized black bodies in the context of slave traffic are the many lives lost at sea, either thrown overboard by the decision of slavers because of death or disease caused by the horrid conditions of sanitation in the holds of the ships, ill-treatments and rapes by the crew, and as result of rebellions, or by the Africans' own decision to commit suicide because of depression and desperation.[3] There were also the infamous cases of owners of ships involved in the transatlantic slave trade who threw the slave cargoes overboard and then sued the ship's underwriters. There was the famous legal case in London, in 1783, involving the Liverpool owners of the ship, the Zong, who sued the ship's underwriters for the value of 132 Africans lost on a voyage from Africa to Jamaica. The Africans had been thrown overboard when the ship had run short of water because of an unexpected extension of the journey due to a navigation error. To save the healthy, the sick (or those who were said to be sick) were killed. The decision of the crew was to sacrifice part of the 442 enslaved Africans. Before this case, no other case is known to have made an insurance claim for slaves deliberately killed. The jury decided that the underwriters were obliged, under law, to pay, but they asked for a second trial, which was recorded at Granville Sharp's request,[4] thus preserving the

---

tures how raciality immediately justifies the state's decision to kill certain persons – mostly (but not only) young men and women of color – in the name of self-preservation. Such killings do not unleash an ethical crisis because these persons' bodies and the territories they inhabit always-already signify violence" (213).

3 There would also be occasions when black enslaved people would be discarded because they didn't have market value on account of their age, as the case cited in Mustakeem: "The Woman's Hands being tied behind her, and her Feet across," several designated men put her "into the Cannoe, and carried [her] off about half a Mile from the Shore." They steered into deeper waters, casting the enslaved woman overboard, after which they witnessed some "voracious Fishes" begin to "tear her to pieces in an instant" (1).

4 It was Olaudah Equiano who called on the anti-slavery campaigner Granville Sharp with news of this horrid event. The subsequent outcry would have a profound effect on the course of abolition, as testified by the founding of the Abolition Society in 1787.

memory of this sad episode. The argument presented in court by the solicitor general John Lee well illustrates the outrageous level of dehumanization of those lives:

> What is this claim that human people have been thrown overboard? This is a case of chattels or goods. Blacks are goods and property; it is madness to accuse these well-serving honourable men of murder. They acted out of necessity and in the most appropriate manner for the cause. The late Captain Collingwood acted in the interest of his ship to protect the safety of his crew. To question the judgement of an experienced well-travelled captain held in the highest regard is one of folly, especially when talking of slaves. *The case is the same as if wood had been thrown overboard.* (The Zong Case Study n. pag., emphasis mine).

Much of the experience related to the lives of slaves was never registered or was erased, like the information contained in the Zong mate's log, which mysteriously disappeared.[5] Were it not for the initiative of the two abolitionists, Olaudah Equiano and Granville Sharp (cf. note 4 above), the Zong massacre might not have reached our ears. As we read in the Zong case study, "The people who remembered it best were, of course, the 200 African survivors sold at Black River, Jamaica, who had heard the screams of their drowning shipmates" (The Zong Case Study n. pag.).[6] But their voices were silenced.

Memory and the role of the artist

Therefore, of utmost importance is memory, the rewriting of history, and the claiming for voice. In a symposium hosted by Small Axe and the Caribbean Literary Studies Program at the University of Miami (June 2007), scholars met to reflect on "Archaeologies of Black Memory." Patricia J. Saunders summarizes the focus of that forum: "the work of memory in producing knowledge, in this case knowledge about black people who have been [sic] disappeared, nowhere to be identified or localized, except (of course) in the archives of history" (n. pag.). In *Memory, History, Forgetting*, Paul Ricoeur exalts poetry for preserving memory while the instances of power often silence and obliterate it for political interests:

However, after the abolition of the slave trade by Britain in 1807, new massacres of Africans occurred whenever suspected illegal slave ships were chased by the Royal Navy vessels and the slavers needed to get rid of the illegal cargo before being caught.

5 Literature also represents this loss of information, specially the intentional erasure of documents related to the experience of slaves, as a factor for the invisibility of people of African descent in the Americas. We find an example in the voice of the old woman passing on the testimony of a generation of women to her great-granddaughter: "They burned all the documents, Ursa, … we got to keep what we need to bear witness. That scar that's left to bear witness" (Jones 62).

6 Today, a memorial in Black River stays as a reminder of one of the bleakest episodes in the history of the transatlantic slave trade.

> only poetry preserves the force of unforgetting ... Poetry knows that the political rests on forgetting the unforgettable ... the voice of the unforgetting memory, excluded from the arena of power by the forgetful memory bound to the prosaic refounding of the political. ... The fortifying use of dissensus, the echo of the unforgetting memory of discord. (501)

Édouard Glissant also believes that the writer alone provides forms of memory capable of transcending "nonhistory" (*Poetics of Relation* xvi). Literature is a privileged source to reveal the writers' ability to read the future of their communities and their nations in a reassessment of the past and tradition (Caldeira, "Toni Morrison"; "Memory"). We thus owe to literature and also to other forms of art the socially-engaged objects that give voice to silence – "a silence broken, a void filled, an unspeakable thing spoken at last" (Morrison, "Unspeakable Things Unspoken" 149).

In a time of dramatic contradictions and hypocrisy, when hundreds of people drown in the Mediterranean or languish in detention centers under subhuman conditions, when borders are closed and new walls are being built to negate hospitality to millions of refugees and immigrants who try to escape war or famine; in a world of systemic global injustice, on which mainstream media have chosen not to focus, preferring sensational images disconnected from history, "the struggle to find words is among the most profound struggles in which one can engage, it is ultimately an ethical struggle" (Schmidt 131). I argue that literature may enact this ethical struggle and furnish us with "the transformation of silence into language and action" (Lorde 40) which Audre Lorde speaks about ([1997] 2007).[7] For, as she claims,

> we share a commitment to language and to the power of language, and to the reclaiming of that language which has been made to work against us. In the transformation of silence into language and action, it is vitally necessary for each one of us to establish or examine her function in that transformation and to recognize her role as vital within that transformation. (43)

For people of African descent in the Americas, the search for memory may be assumed as a form of paying respect to the suffering and the resistance of their ancestors, and a form of ethical responsibility to claim the bodies that were lost in the Atlantic as well as the voices that were silenced. I take as my example in this text the way literature and art have responded to the Middle Passage, and in particular to the Zong massacre. In the different representations artists and writers chose, I search for the transformation of silence into language and action.

As Sowande' M. Mustakeem makes clear in her groundbreaking book *Slavery at Sea: Terror, Sex, and Sickness in the Middle Passage* (2016), slavery as a "human manufacturing process" (4), which made and unmade slaves didn't start when Africans landed on the coasts of the Americas; it already started during the Middle Passage. That explains her introduction of the concept of "slavery at sea": "Slavery at Sea cen-

7 From a paper originally delivered at the Modern Language Association, Chicago (1977; then it was published in *Sinister Wisdom* 6 (1978), and later in *The Cancer Journals* (1980), and *Sister Outsider* (1997)).

ters the terrain of political struggle not only on ocean going ships but also on the diverse and vulnerable bodies of captives continuously unmade by their transporters and the human manufacturing process" (7). In the slave traffic, the Atlantic, a "zone of death,"

> also became a central conduit for how bondage unfolded and consequentially devastated lives. Yet, the sea represented an important open arena of struggle for power and agency as captives jumped to their deaths and sailors flung slaves overboard knowing about, and in many respects relying upon, the presence of sharks and other dangerous sea creatures lurking beneath. (5)

Mustakeem's attention to the inter-relations of power is what strikes me as a very important focus. She analyses the interior of the merchant ships as "vital sites of power sailors used to dehumanize captives, enforce dependency, inflict pain, establish authority, and prohibit any sense of control over one's personal life in the near and far future" (Mustakeem 7). But when captives orchestrated rebellions or committed suicide against all odds, those acts are read as acts of resistance. "Slaves conceived ideas of defiance in secrecy, yet the body became the terrain and public space where and how violence was performed" (99). Slavery, "a commercial industry anchored on terror" (4), really generates an inter-action of violence. In spite of the clear unbalance of the power relations within the ship – and here I consider it useful to regard the ship as a Bakthian chronotope, i.e., a space that condenses the historical time of slave trade –, I think it is vital the way Mustakeem looks at the shipboard interactions as a shared language of violence: "Violence operated as a shared language through which bondpeople were routinely victimized, but one they repeatedly used against their transporters by disrupting the slaving process through the pursuit of freedom" (81). By doing it, the author gives agency to the bondpeople turned into passive objects (81).

Representations of the Middle Passage

In the nineteenth century, the English painter J.M.W. Turner left us the painting entitled "Slave Ship" (1840), whose longer title is "Slavers Overthrowing the Dead and Dying – Typhoon Coming On." The intense shades of red and yellow bleed through the painting, fading the limit between sea and sky; pieces of bodies seem to struggle with the sharks in the rough waves, taking the foreground of the picture, while the ship is already moving away. The title given to the painting is already an interpretation through the choice of allegory in the figure of the monster, Typhoon. The art work was first exhibited along with a poem by Turner himself: "Before it sweeps your decks, throw overboard/The dead and dying – ne'er heed their chains/Hope, Hope, fallacious Hope!/Where is thy market now?" (n. pag.). The question in the last lines reinforces for me the irony of the poet's political interpretation, addressing the lost value of those discarded lives thrown overboard, still in chains, soon to be devoured by the sharks.

The poetic language of the Martiniquan poet and philosopher Édouard Glissant gives us the most eloquent representation of those lives deprived of their identity as human beings, reduced to the "corroded balls and chains" lying in "the depths of the sea" (*Caribbean Discourse* 6) as the only testimony to their existence. Ironically contrasting with the usual pleasures offered by the ocean to vacationers and tourists, the poet may also be interpellating their/our proverbial indifference:[8]

> Navigating the green splendor of the sea – whether in melancholic transatlantic crossings or glorious regattas or traditional races of yoles and gommiers – still brings to mind, coming to light like seaweed, these lowest depths, these deeps, with their punctuation of scarcely corroded balls and chains. In actual fact the abyss is a tautology: the entire ocean, the entire sea gently collapsing in the end into the pleasures of sand, make one vast beginning, but a beginning whose time is marked by these balls and chains gone green. (*Caribbean Discourse* 6)

Glissant addresses the Atlantic passage as an abyss of water, and the slave ship as a "womb abyss" (*Caribbean Discourse* 6). Glissant no longer thinks of the origin, once he chooses to focus on the idea of the abyss. He uses expressions of negation, loss, and stasis for his definition of abyss: "nonworld" (6), "the unconscious memory of the abyss" (7) and of the petrification caused by the horror of the unknown: "For the Africans who lived through the experience of deportation to the Americas, confronting the unknown with neither preparation nor challenge was no doubt petrifying" (5).[9]

The African American poet Robert Hayden also addresses the "voyage through death" in the poem "Middle Passage" (1962):

> Jesús, Estrella, Esperanza, Mercy:
> Sails flashing to the wind like weapons
> sharks following the moans the fever and the dying,
> horror the corposant and compass rose.
>
> Middle Passage:
> voyage through death
> to life upon these shores.
>
> 10 April 1800 –
> Blacks rebellious. Crew uneasy. Our linguist says
> their moaning is a prayer for death,

8 This deep contrast between the common tourist's indifference and the colonial memories of continued exploitation in the places they visit explored by the writer for the sake of political awareness reminds me of Jamaica Kincaid in *A Small Place*, 1988.

9 This confrontation with the unknown for Africans kidnapped or sold into slavery reminds me of Toni Morrison and her justification for the abrupt way she chooses to begin her novels. Specially related to the way she starts *Beloved*, she comments: "It is abrupt, and should appear so. No native informant here. The reader is snatched, yanked, thrown into an environment completely foreign, and I want it as the first stroke of the shared experience that might be possible between the reader and the novel's population. Snatched just as the slaves were from one place to another, from any place to another, without preparation and without defense. No lobby, no door, no entrance – a gangplank, perhaps (but a very short one). And the house into which this snatching – this kidnapping-propels one, changes from spiteful to loud to quiet, like the sounds in the body of the ship itself may have changed" ("Unspeakable Things Unspoken" 160).

> ours and their own. Some try to starve themselves.
> Lost three this morning leaped with crazy laughter
> to the waiting sharks, sang as they went under. (48)

In the last strophe, the imagined lines of a mate's log, the poet registers one among the many untold stories. The poem recreates the multiple sounds and voices within a slave ship, and then at a court hearing, after a slave rebellion that led to the loss of human cargo. The juxtaposition of records without an apparent logic makes me think of a summoning of different perspectives on reality. Notwithstanding, we miss the perspective of the captives, reduced to a mere object of the others' perception. They are perceived either as threatening " the jungle hatred/crawling up on deck" (Hayden 49), or the image of complete degradation and abjection ("A charnel stench, effluvium of living death/spreads outward from the hold,/where the living and the dead, the horribly dying,/lie interlocked, lie foul with blood and excrement" [51]).

Melville's *Benito Cereno* (1855) comes to my mind. It also focuses on a slave rebellion along the Middle Passage. The author recreates the environment in the slave ship through the different sound of various languages. The cacophony engendered offers a symbolic frame for the theme of uncommunication in Melville's short novel. Just as human behavior, made of codes often illegible, different cultures in their disencounters do not try or do not manage to find a translation. It is then that silence is the most significant language, as Melville seems to convey by ending *Benito Cereno* focusing on the African, killed for his act of resistance and displayed at a plaza in Lima as an example to discourage such acts of rebellion. However, the text, instead of depicting just a barbaric black body as perceived by the colonial eyes, does justice to Babo's intelligence, skillfulness, and leadership:

> As for the black – whose brain, not body, had schemed and led the revolt, with the plot – his slight frame, inadequate to that which it held, had at once yielded to the superior muscular strength of his captor, in the boat. Seeing all was over, he uttered no sound, and could not be forced to. His aspect seemed to say, since I cannot do deeds, I will not speak words. (Melville n. pag.)

And further offers him the dignity of which he was deprived: "Some months after, dragged to the gibbet at the tail of a mule, the black met his voiceless end. The body was burned to ashes; but for many days, the head, that hive of subtlety, fixed on a pole in the Plaza, met, unabashed, the gaze of the whites" (n. pag.).

The text of *Benito Cereno* incorporates by the end the records of the investigation that followed the slave rebellion in the San Dominick, which caused the death of most of the crew, including the hearings of Captain Benito Cereno and elements of his crew. The contrast with the silenced voices of the Africans is clear. Along with it we have the Melvillian characteristic emphasis on the difficulty or even impossibility of settling the truth of the facts. The sentence that links the two kinds of registration is significant: "If the Depositions have served as the key to fit into the lock of the complications which precede it, then, as a vault whose door has been flung back, the San Dominick's hull lies open to-day" (Melville n. pag.). Melville's ambiguity attached to 'if' clause makes us interrogate the discourse of the law and order. Will it be able to disentangle the complex meanings of what happened? Will the key "fit into the lock"?

Nevertheless, the ship's hull lies open for future generations to try to understand. Glissant offers us a similar metaphor in the image of the "Open Boat," the title of the first section of the first chapter, "Approaches" of *Poetics of Relation*. He dedicates this section to imagining the violence of the first encounter of the captives with the unknown, as they are faced by the unfathomable abyss of the sea and are taken into the belly of the slave ship, the "womb abyss," a womb for dying, rather than birthing. It is worth noting that the emphasis in the double idea contained in the original French expression used by Glissant, "gouffre de l'abîme marin," is erased in the English translation, "abyss": "the belly of this boat dissolves you, precipitates you into a nonworld from which you cry out. This boat is a womb, a womb abyss. It generates the clamor of your protests" (Glissant, *Poetics of Relation* 5). However, the chronotope of the slave ship silences the cries and the clamor: "Within the ship's space the cry of those deported was stifled, as it would be in the realm of the Plantations" (5). It is left to the poet the imaginative possibility of filling the deathly hush of millions of lives perceived as precarious just because they were perceived as different and inferior, and thus completely vulnerable to the powers that be.[10]

A poet from Trinidad-Tobago, based in Canada, NourbeSe Philip, also addresses the Zong massacre in her book *Zong!* (2011). In the acknowledgments, Philip refers to the production of her work as an act of responsibility to her ancestors, since she feels "Haunted by 'generations of skulls and spirits'" (201) settled at the bottom of the Atlantic Ocean. Philip, a practicing lawyer before devoting herself entirely to writing, takes advantage of her competence in Law and convenes both discourses, since she observes, "Law and poetry both share an inexorable concern with language" (191). As the court records of the Zong case are the only source available to shed light on the case, serving as the gravestone for the untold story of the sacrificed Africans, the poet appropriates the legal discourse, or the imperialist imposition by the colonial language, as she calls it. She uses it as a "word store" (191), but makes its grammar explode on the page: words randomly taken out from the source and randomly scattered (just as the African bodies were randomly kidnapped by the traders, gathered without any logic (just as the African bodies were gathered in the forts or factories along the western coast of Africa), breaks the text into pieces (just as the African lives were ripped to shreds by the sharks, or as the meaning of their existence was torn to pieces by the colonial aggression) (192–193).

Philip's poems fill page after page in an anxious attempt to find the right words, but there's only an accumulation of frustration ("words gone astray" [198]), until the moment she realizes that "[her] urge to make sense must be resisted" (193). There is, after all, no meaning and no possibility of communication, only the urgency (the sense of debt and obligation) to speak the unspeakable because it was unspoken: "the not

10 On the notion of precarious lives, cf. Butler ("Precarious Life"; *Precarious Life*).

telling of the story that must be told" (197), an expression repeated throughout the whole epilogue. As the author declares in the final section – Notanda –, the only one that is conventionally readable, "Zong! is chant! Shout! And ululation! Zong! is moan! Mutter! Howl! And shriek! Zong! is 'pure utterance.' Zong! is Song! And Song is what has kept the soul of the African intact when they 'want(ed) water … sustenance … preservation.' Zong! is the Song of the untold story; it cannot be told yet must be told, but only through its un-telling" (207).

Philip's book is made of 180 pages of floating words on the sea of the pages. It masks an artistic intervention, the artist offering a visual challenge more than a formal readability: "I question the transparency of language. … I use the text of the legal report almost like a painter uses paint or a sculptor stone" (Philip 198). Besides the explosion of the grammar "the mechanism of force" (193), scattering tattered pieces of language, different languages, and different characters sculpt dis-encounters: Latin, Greek, or Arabic meet the languages of the colonizers and languages of the African continent. Proper names in Yoruba are cited in successive footnotes: "what the Africans on board the Zong become – dicta, footnotes, related to, but not, the ratio"; "They will be ghostly footnotes below the text" (200). Later, the names appear again, but this time on the page, after the Apocalypse, as if suggesting that the pieces of the bodies finally assembled together resurrect to receive justice in the Final Judgement, as showcased by the epigraph taken from Ezequiel: "and the bones came together, bone to his bone … the sinews and flesh came upon them … and the skin covered them above … and the breath came into them … and they lived, and stood upon their feet" (Ezequiel 37:7, 8, 9, 10; Philip 126).

When, at the end, Philip, as if authenticating her text, declares herself to be a descendant of slaves and her work a metaphor for slavery, she shares with us a deeply emotional feeling of responsibility towards the memory of her ancestors, a sense of moral obligation[11] to acknowledge[12] them and restore the dignity they were deprived of. The only way she has left to humbly pay her debt is to register a series of African names in a footnote, symbolically engraving on the page the names of the dead that could not be engraved on tombstones, the liquidity of language memorizing claiming to be more permanent than tombstones. All the bodies sunk into the ocean throughout the three centuries of the slave traffic were not entitled to the dignity of a tomb. There is not even a word to say it, as the word "bury" means to cover with earth. Philip feels that she has not the proper words. To what may correspond the word exhume ("ex

11 Obligation (n.) c.1300, from Old French obligacion "obligation, duty, responsibility" (early 13c.) and directly from Latin obligationem (nominative obligatio) "an engaging or pledging," literally "a binding" (but rarely used in this sense), noun of action from past participle stem of obligare. The notion is of binding with promises or by law or duty (Online Etimology Dictionary).

12 Acknowledge (v.) 1550s, a blend of Middle English aknow (from Old English oncnawan "understand," from on + cnawan "recognize") and Middle English knowlechen "admit, acknowledge" (c.1200) (Online Etimology Dictionary).

hume"), when we need to describe the act of collecting corpses from the sea? To exhume means to unearth but it also has the metaphoric meaning of to save from oblivion. But in this case we cannot speak about a burial, just a "liquid grave" (Philip 201). Like Antigone, pleading for the moral obligation to bury the dead, the poet too intends to restore the dignity to the dead, but language, her métier, is not prepared to express that reality – ex-humu, not ex-aqua. In the six sections (or movements) of her book, the poet carefully tries to recreate the symbolic locus of that watery tomb: bones (*Os*), spread under the salty water (*Sal*), its surface roughened by the wind (*Ventus*). The logic of the "European project" (*Ratio*) deprived those creatures of the possibility to be, reduced them to cargo dumped into the sea so that their value in money could be claimed. The last two books are *Ferrum* and *Ebora*, the former evoking the chains and the shackles, the latter representing the "underwater spirits," according to the meaning of the Yoruba word translated in the glossary. In *Ebora*, words appear faded on the page, as if underwater or very far from us, some of them are juxtaposed, preventing us from the possibility to read, spaces between them shrink and all this becomes more dramatic on the last page: is the poet calling up the spirits of the Ancestors and they are gathering to meet her? Is poetry finally succeeding in exorcising the dead and giving them back the life they lost? The poet declares: "I think of these poems as the flesh – the earlier 26 poems are the bones" (201).

The graphic image of the poem throughout the pages is in itself a representation. The words, loose and scattered, are spaced out on the page, creating room (which the imprisoned bodies lacked being cramped in the hold of the ship) and giving them air to breathe (which they did not have in the filthy and smothering atmosphere of the hold of the ship):

> Some – all the poems – need a great deal of space around them – as if there is too much cramping around them, as if they need to breath .... The poet's struggle with the language of empire to subvert it is tough: "I mutilate the text as the fabric of African life and the lives of these men, women and children were mutilated. I murder the text, literally cut it into pieces." (Philip 193–194)

But she is determined to reach its heart and take "a new life" (Philip 193). She comes out of this painful venture with blood in her hands ("hands bloodied" [193]). Although she is only capable of producing a "language of grunt and groan, of moan and stutter" (205), she feels at last that she has conquered the language and made it her own – "I feel that I do have a language" (205), in spite of only being able to produce fragments, like the fragment she herself is: "And, in its fragmentation and brokenness the fragment becomes mine. Becomes me. Is me" (205).

The effort has been too hard. Specially, because the writer as inheritor and interpreter struggles with ambivalence. To possess the language she has, on one hand, to compromise with the language of power and replicate the authority she is trying to combat; on the other hand, she has to invent the memory she intends to respect and legitimize the voice she gives to the voiceless. We feel a deep awareness of the ethical question involved in the poet's task of telling a story that can only be told by not telling (Philip 191). Distrusting the transparency of language (197), the poet needs "to seek permission to bring the stories of these murdered Africans to light" (202), and fears she may be imposing meaning (199). In the "disorder and mayhem" she tries "to release the story that cannot be told, but which, through not-telling, will tell itself" (199).

Identical ethical concern we find in Toni Morrison ("This is not a story to pass on" is the concluding sentence in *Beloved*) and also an identical effort with language to find the best word, the right word, an effort that feels painful. Morrison's most recent publication's title *Mouth Full of Blood* (2019) gives utterance to this painful act of tying together, as she says, aesthetics and ethics while staying truthful to the most vulnerable and wronged.

We may not find in these various and rich representations of the Middle Passage an optimistic prospect for the future for the racialized nobodies in our global world. But we certainly find the sense of respect and acknowledgment they deserve and the political awareness we need to disturb our indifference. Therefore, they also accomplish the tying together of aesthetics and ethics to be able to effectively reclaim the lost bodies and the silenced voices.

Works cited

Anderson, Monica, and Gustavo López. "Key Facts about Black Immigrants in the U.S." Pew Research Center. 24 Jan. 2018. Web. https://www.pewresearch.org/fact-tank/ 2018/01/24/key-facts-about-black-immigrants-in-the-u-s/.

Butler, Judith. "Precarious Life, Vulnerability, and the Ethics of Cohabitation." *The Journal of Speculative Philosophy* (2012): 134–151. Web. https:// muse.jhu.edu/article/486301.

———. *Precarious Life: The Powers of Mourning and Violence*. London, New York: Verso, 2004. Print.

Caldeira, Isabel. "Toni Morrison and Edwidge Danticat: Writers-as-Citizens of the African Diaspora, or the Margin as a Space of Radical Openness." *The Routledge Companion to Inter-American Studies*. Ed. Wilfried Raussert. London, New York: Routledge, 2017. 207–218. Print.

———. "Memory is of the Future: Tradition and Modernity in Contemporary Novels of Africa and the African Diaspora." *e-cadernos CES* 26 (2016): 68–91. Web. https://journals.openedition.org/eces/2126.

Ferro, Marialuisa. *Minority Stories. Minority Rights Group International*. 2015. Web. http://stories.minorityrights.org/afro-descendants/chapter/301/.

Glissant, Édouard. *Caribbean Discourse: Selected Essays*. Trans. and with an Introduction by Michael Dash. Charlottesville: The UP of Virginia, 1996. Print.

———. *Poetics of Relation*. Trans. Betsy Wing. Ann Arbor: The U of Michigan P, 2010. Print.

Hayden, Robert. "Middle Passage." *Collected Poems*. Ed. Frederick Glaysher. New York, London: Liveright Publishing Corporation, 1985. 48–52. Print.

Jones, Gayl. *Corregidora*. Boston: Beacon Press, 1986. Print.

Lorde, Audre. *Sister Outsider*. New York: Crossing Press, 2007. Print.

Melville, Herman. *Benito Cereno*. (1855, 1856). The Walt Whitman Archive. 2019. Web. https://whitmanarchive.org/resources/teaching/dickinson/analogue7.html.

Morrison, Toni. *Mouth Full of Blood: Essays, Speeches, Meditations*. London: Chatto & Windus, 2019. Print.

———. "Unspeakable Things Unspoken. The Afro-American Presence in American Literature." Tanner Lectures On Human Values. The University of Michigan, 1988. Web. https://tannerlectures.utah.edu/_documents/a-to-z/m/morrison90.pdf.

Mustakeem, Sowande' M. *Slavery at Sea: Terror, Sex, and Sickness in the Middle Passage*. Urbana/Chicago: U of Illinois P, 2016. Print.

Philip, M. NourbeSe. *Zong!*. Middleton: Wesleyan UP, 2008. Print.

Ricoeur, Paul. *Memory, History, Forgetting*. Trans. Kathleen Blamey and David Pellauer. London/Chicago: The U of Chicago P, 2004. Print.

Sanchez, Margarita, and Maurice Bryan (with MRG partners ADEPHCA, Asociación Proyecto Caribe, ASOMUGAGUA, Movimiento de Mujeres Negras, ODECO and ORBOAFRO). "Afro-descendants, Discrimination, and Economic Exclusion in Latin America." Minority Rights Group International. May 2003. Web. https://minorityrights.org/wp-content/uploads/old-site-downloads/download-78-Afro-descendants-Discrimination-and-Economic-Exclusion-in-Latin-America.pdf.

Saunders, Patricia J. "Fugitive Dreams of Diaspora: Conversations with Saidiya Hartman." *Anthurium: A Caribbean Studies Journal* 6.1, Article 7. 2008. Web. http://scholarlyrepository.miami.edu/anthurium/vol6/iss1/7.

Schmidt, Dennis J. *Lyrical and Ethical Subjects: Essays on the Periphery of the World, Freedom and History*. Albany: State U of New York P, 2005. Print.

Silva, Denise Ferreira da. "No-bodies: Law, Raciality, and Violence." *Griffith Law Review* 18.2 (2009): 212–236. Print.

The World Bank. "With More 'Afro' Visibility, Latin America Redefines the Color Black." 29 Aug. 2018. Web. https://www.worldbank.org/en/news/feature/2018/08/29/afrodescendants-in-latin-america.

The Zong Case Study. USI Project. 2011. Web. http://www.understandingslavery.com/index.php-option=com_content&view=article&id=373&Itemid=236.html.

Thomas, Melvin E., Richard Moye, Loren Henderson, and Hayward Derrick Horton. "Separate and Unequal: The Impact of Socioeconomic Status, Segregation, and the Great Recession on Racial Disparities in Housing Values." *Sociology of Race and Ethnicity* 4.2 (2018): 229–244. Print.

Turner, J.M.W. "The Slave Ship." 3 May 2016. https://www.bartleby.com/essay/The-Slave-Ship-J-M-W-Turner-PKR7RS5H3UEZ.

Saint or Scoundrel? Remembering and Representing Padre Martínez in Early (Auto)Biography and Fiction

ASTRID HAAS

The eminent New Mexican religious leader and politician Padre Antonio José Martínez (1793–1867) became known to wide audiences for this religious-political opposition to the first bishop of New Mexico, Jean Baptiste Lamy, that plays a key role in Willa Cather's novel *Death Comes for the Archbishop* (1927). Born and raised in colonial New Mexico, Martínez attended the theological seminary in Durango. After his ordination in 1823, he returned to New Mexico, where he became the parish priest of Taos three years later. In 1837 he sided with federal forces against the Chimayó Rebellion of New Mexican farmers and ranchers against the Mexican governor. Witnessing the animosity Anglo settlers and soldiers displayed toward Mexicans and Amerindians in the region, he engaged in the Taos Rebellion of 1847 against the United States occupation of New Mexico. Soon after the U.S.-Mexican War, however, he swore loyalty to the United States, possibly hoping to achieve benefits for the region's Mexican population. The clash ensuing between Martínez and Lamy since the 1850s over social, theological, and legal issues finally led to the padre's excommunication in 1858.[1]

In contrast to the thoroughly negative portrayal in Cather's novel, Martínez is held in high esteem among Latina/o New Mexicans to this day as a community activist and educator in the region (Cohen 147, 152; Mares 107, 127–128). Scholarly biographies of the priest – almost unanimously published since the emergence of the Chicano movement in the 1960s – have retrieved him from oblivion or denigration in (Anglo-)U.S. American public memory (Francis; Chavez; Mares). But what about earlier and "non-scholarly" portrayals of the padre's life and work? How do they represent their subject and for which purposes? In the following, I will analyze selected (auto)biographical and fictional representations of Padre Martínez from the mid-nineteenth through the mid-twentieth century. Discussing them against the backdrop of the changing historical contexts, I argue that they paint a complex and contradictory picture of this historical figure that articulates shifting political agendas for distinct target audiences.

(Self-)Representations of Padre Martínez during his lifetime

Almost a century before Cather published her famous fictional account of the padre, the priest of Taos published his own account of his life. Printed in 1838 by his own

1 Cf. Chavez; Francis; Mares. On the Chimayó and Taos Rebellions, cf. Reséndez (172–196, 239–240, 253–264).

press in New Mexico, his *Relación de Méritos del Presbítero Antonio José Martínez: Autobiografía y Apología* [Apologia of Presbyter Antonio J. Martinez], re-narrates Martínez's life story from his childhood through his early years as priest, educator, publisher, and politician. As the title of the text indicates, it follows in the traditions of both the Spanish *relación* and the (Christian) apology. The former designates a "report that is generally made in writing and presented to [a secular or religious] authority" (Real Academia, my trans.). Since the colonial era, the *relación* became one of the best-known genres of Spanish writing from and about the Americas. The (auto)biographical subgenre of the apologia, or apology, on the other hand, encompasses the argumentative explanation of a person's deeds or theological position, especially in defense against criticism or accusations (Harp).

Martínez's narrative combines both text types. As the author explains in his introduction (328), he was motivated to penning his story by the desire not only to provide an edifying example to his students and followers but also to testify to his merits in order "to defend himself against charges of sedition by reviewing all his procedures in every field since the start of his public career" (Chavez 53, 61, 131). To verify his account, Martínez enclosed factual documents as well as the testimony of a legal expert with his text (Martínez 329–230, 335–341, 346). In the introduction and conclusion of his third-person *Relación*, he further engages in a discourse of modesty that emphasizes his humble origins (327–328, 343, 345; Chavez 61–62). This strikingly contrasts with the self-confidence, even pride, in his intellectual capacities and professional accomplishments which characterizes the main body of his narrative (Martínez 327–343). According to Genaro Padilla, by "citing the library of doctrinal texts which constituted his intellectual personality, the *Relación de méritos* describes Martínez's socio-intellectual formation and … theological knowledge" (162; cf. Martínez 329–335). The padre justifies the detailed description of his attainments as providing his readers with an example of the personal achievements and societal benefits hard work and dedication can bring forth. In so doing, he legitimizes his continuing ecclesiastical ambitions (Martínez 343).

In addition to his knowledge in Scholastic Theology and Canon Law (334–335), Martínez particularly stresses his competence and fulfillment of his pastoral duties as a parish priest. He explains his not having been nominated *cura propio* [irremovable pastor] of a congregation solely with administrative reasons – his lack of required *formal* qualifications postponements of nominations due to political instability – rather than admitting personal character flaws that may have played a role here (Martínez 337–340; Chavez 22, 31–33, 41). The desire to receive a nomination as *cura propio* or even as vicar of Santa Fe (Chavez 42, 44) was possibly another reason for Martínez to compose the account of his achievements. In his text, he repeatedly emphasizes that it was solely for his socio-political commitment as a priest and educator that he had fallen into disgrace with Mexican secular and Catholic Church authorities (Martínez 340; Chavez 41). The padre explicitly counters the accusation – only hinted at in his text – that he played an active role in the Chimayó Rebellion. He points out that he served as political advisor to the governor of New Mexico and as a field pastor to troops fighting against the insurgents (Martínez 340–341, 344; Chavez 53, 57; Mares 116). In line with the apologetic autobiography of a priest, Martínez concludes his argument with an affirmation of his faith, which he presents as the source of his strength and thus as justification for continuing his way (Martínez 344–346). By choosing this genre and blending it with the *relación*, the padre sets himself in the traditions of Christian apologetics and the Spanish colonial endeavor. He thus claims the secular and spiritual authority of these established types of writing to justify his at times controversial life and work as valuable and unjustly burdened.

The sense of struggle expressed in Martínez's *Relación* found an even stronger echo in another account of his life and work, possibly authored by the padre himself (Weber 21; for a different view, cf. Chavez 17, 156). As Genaro Padilla observes, "the rupture of everyday life" that the Mexican population of the territories added to the United States after the U.S.-Mexican War experienced "opened a terrain of discursive necessity in which fear and resentment found language," among others, in (auto)biography: "Memory – shocked into reconstructing the past of another socio-national life set squarely against experience in 'an alien political system in an alien culture' – gave rise to an autobiographical formation in which the desire for historical presence was marked" (Padilla 153; 172–174).

In 1861, the short pamphlet *Historia concisa del cura de Taos Antonio José Martínez* [Concise History of the Curate of Taos, Antonio José Martínez] was published in Taos under the pseudonym "El Historiador." The piece emphasizes the priest's accomplishments in serving the needs of New Mexico's Mexican population with some consideration for Anglo concerns but at the expense of the indigenous population (El Historiador). In contrast to the earlier *Relación*, this pamphlet also reveals a problematic side of Martínez: in line with the Mexican policy of his time (Hernández), he endorsed the violent subjugation of nomadic native nations in the name of "civilization" and to curtail their raids on Mexican settlements. Even though the padre blamed increasing indigenous raids on the pernicious presence of Anglo traders in the region, the text does not target Anglos as culprits to be fought against (El Historiador 2; Chavez 66–67; Weber 19). In so doing, it downplays the religiously and ethnoculturally motivated Anglophobic attitude the historical Padre Martínez repeatedly voiced (Reséndez 83).

According to El Historiador, the priest's main antagonist was Bishop Lamy. The *Historia concisa* directs particular attention to the padre's repeated critique of the Church's tithing practice in New Mexico, especially the bishop's threatening to deny the sacraments to families too poor to pay the tithe. The text argues that it was solely the padre's theological opposition to Lamy's strict regime in the diocese that led to Martínez's excommunication, and the text also supports its position through citing written evidence – this time Canon law and the Scriptures (El Historiador 2; Francis 274–277, 284–286; Mares 127). El Historiador thus continues the padre's earlier self-defense in his *Relación*, addressing the two major lines of conflict, Martínez's attitude toward Anglos and Natives in New Mexico, on the one hand, and the growing conflict with his bishop, on the other, with the clear intention of preserving, or even re-establishing, his reputation among Mexican readers.

Padre Martínez in early Mexican American biography

Soon after his death in 1867, Padre Martínez became the subject of a first biography. In 1877, Santiago de Jesus Valdez, the priest's foster child – and possibly illegitimate biological son (Damico par. 1–2) – penned his "Biografía del Presbítero Antonio José Martínez, Cura de Taos" [Biography of the Presbyter Antonio José Martínez, Curate of Taos]. The never-published manuscript renders an "undoubtedly romanticized" (Reséndez 195) homage to its subject and explicitly intended to publicize the padre's "arts, expressions, and writings" (Damico par. 8). It may also have informed the first published biography of the priest (par. 8).[2]

Written by a student and relative of Martínez's and claiming to be based on his personal remembrance of his mentor (Sánchez 24–25; Chavez 137), Pedro Sánchez's *Memorias sobre la vida del presbítero don Antonio José Martínez* [Recollections of the Life of the Priest Don Antonio José Martínez] is an apotheosis of its subject. The biography opens with a gesture of auctorial modesty that seeks to claim the authority of the personal testimony, assure audiences of Sánchez's altruistic motivation for writing, as well as justify the publication of the book by stating its intention of edifying and inspiring especially young readers (Sánchez 24–27). The text emphasizes that Martínez advocated political and religious liberty, which the padre hoped the Mexican Republic – "now independent of intolerant Spain" (36–37) – would pursue and believed the United States to do so. His endorsement of a secular state and critique of the power of the clergy in the *Memorias* probably results from the anti-Catholic sentiments prevailing in the United States in Sánchez's days as much as from Martínez's own views (Chavez 31–32): "You can say that in comparison [to Mexico] the American government is like a burro, but on this burro ride the lawyers and not the clergy" (68–69; 86), the priest is cited to have told his students. As a politician, the Martínez of the *Memorias* embodies the very democratic values he admired in the United States: "He treated everybody equally," Sánchez writes. "'Equal rights to all, special privileges to none'" (78–79).

Time and again, the biography dwells on how the padre's love of his region and its Mexican population moved him to engage in education, journalism, philanthropy – even calling him "the greatest philanthropist New Mexico has ever produced" (Sánchez 82–83) –, and politics, opposing both Catholic Church and Mexican government practices at times, but never impairing the padre's fulfillment of his clerical duties (30–31, 38–45, 58–67, 78–83). The text argues that it was this strong dedication to his faith and his ministry, on the one hand, and to his fellow citizens, on the other, that turned Martínez into a fierce critic of tithing and other Church fees: "The priest, observing that such obligations instead of edifying the faithful and promoting the well-being of society solely served to corrupt the Christian citizen, raised his voice" (42–43; 40–41). At the same time, the *Memorias* crucially omits the padre's conflict with Bishop Lamy

2 Damico par. 8. Valdez's "Biografia" can be accessed in the Henry H. Huntington Library, San Marino, CA, Ritch Collection, Microfilm, Reel 1, NMSRCA.

and ensuing excommunication but, instead, claims that Martínez's clerical activities were always in line with Catholic doctrine (80–83).

Particularly striking is Sánchez's depiction of the Chimayó and Taos Rebellions. In both instances, the biography sides with the New Mexican government opposing the uprisings, the position Martínez had also taken (Sánchez 46–57, 72–77; Chavez 52, 57, 84). The text articulates this especially by characterizing the insurgent Chimayoses as cowardly and violent (Sánchez 48–49, 54–57) and their leader – historically incorrect – as illiterate and elected to his position only for his hunting abilities (50–51). Their opponents, on the contrary, appear as heroic and humane, with the padre serving as clerical counsel, peace negotiator, and benefactor (50–51, 56–57). In a similar vein, the description of the Taos Rebellion emphasizes Martínez's humanitarian but also military activism: In his house, the *Memorias* states, "there were reunited all the peaceful citizens of Taos ... and all without distinction of race, color or religion found in the priest's home a heart full of goodness and a spirit of consolation and peace. He provided food for all and arms to those who could use them. ... He placed himself at the head of his guests, in their defense" (72–73).

This gesture of hospitality is complemented by another one, in which Sánchez describes – historically only partially accurate – how Martínez also housed the leader of the government forces as well as served to hold the court-martials of the captured rebels (Sánchez 74–77). Here and elsewhere in the biography, Sánchez highlights Padre Martínez's strong dedication to and manifold labor for the Mexican population of his region in order to preserve and/or revive his reputation and function as a role model in face of increased anti-Mexican and anti-Catholic sentiments in the United States Southwest.

Padre Martínez in Anglo U.S. American fiction

Sánchez's endeavors would soon be undermined by the fundamental change the wider public image of Padre Martínez underwent in Anglo American fictional representations, which began with the appearance of Willa Cather's novel *Death Comes for the Archbishop* (1927). The volume is a fictionalized autobiography of Bishop Lamy – here called Jean Marie Latour – with a particular focus on his endeavor to strengthen Rome's authority in New Mexico.[3] In line with prevailing anti-Catholic and anti-Mexican stereotypes (Rinke 212, 214) in the United States as well as with the Eurocentrism of Catholic historiography (Francis 266), Bishop Latour tends to regard the Mexican population of his diocese as either pious, puerile "poor natures" (Cather 208; cf. 141–142, 206, 211) in need of guidance or as frivolous, lazy, selfish, and/or cruel opponents of orthodox Catholicism that had to be subdued (83–84, 139, 147; Cohen 150; Stout 240). The key antagonist to Latour, Padre Martínez emerges in *Death Comes for the Archbishop* as the epitome of the latter category. Constantly

3 For a detailed analysis of the novel, cf. Haas.

breaking his priestly vows, tyrannizing his congregation, and fighting both Washington's secular and Rome's religious rule (32, 139–153, 159–164; Cohen 151–152), the fictionalized priest represents a threat to the religious-political changes the bishop and the novel as a whole endorse; "Both the priest and people [of Taos] were hostile to Americans and jealous of interference" (Cather 139), Latour notes – historically incorrectly (Francis 271, 278–279; Chavez 93–94, 104) – in the novel.

Cather's narrative acknowledges Padre Martínez's pastoral presence, high intellect, and profound theological and historical knowledge (Cather 150–153; Cohen 152). Yet, the text predominantly depicts the priest as a sinister figure, whose physical features aptly express his character: "he gave the impression of being an enormous man. His broad shoulders were like a bull buffalo's, his big head was set defiantly on a thick neck," and "his mouth was the very assertion of violent uncurbed passions and tyrannical self-will" (Cather 140–141). In line with that description as well as following the anti-Mexican views the historical Bishop Lamy shared with many Anglo New Mexicans (Chavez 94–96), Cather's Martínez is a morally repugnant abuser of political and religious ideas for worldly personal gains. Accordingly, it is solely his personal conduct – rather than, historically accurate, matters of theology, politics, and Canon Law (Francis 268, 272–288; Chavez 104–111, 116–117, 120–124, 129–150) – that triggers his conflict with the bishop (Cather 139–147, 158–159, 162–163; Cohen 151–155). Tellingly, the novel also "repeats the rumor that Martínez instigated the 1847 revolt of the Taos Indians" (Cohen 151; cf. Cather 139–140). In so depicting this figure, *Death Comes for the Archbishop* discredits not only the historical priest but also the Native and Mexican acts of resistance against the U.S. occupation of their territory during and after the U.S.-Mexican War (Padilla 162; Stout 32, 239–240, 245). This represents a conscious choice on Cather's part, which subordinates historical accuracy and complexity to the positive depiction of the French bishop's pioneer work on the United States frontier and the Americanization process of a multicultural contact zone in a much-contested border region.[4]

The dangerous otherness Martínez embodies in the novel particularly manifests itself in differences in religious practice and theological thought, which are connected to notions of ethnocultural otherness. Where the historical Martínez in his religious tracts and essays was primarily concerned with defining religion in a Republican state and with criticizing the Church's harsh policy of tithing a rather poor populace (Chavez 32, 135–136, 151–156), the fictionalized padre challenges the Vatican's general authority in defining doctrines for Church members all over the world (Cather 145–47; Cohen 151–152):

> We have a living Church here, not a dead arm of the European Church. Our religion grew out of the soil and has its own roots. … We do not require aid from the [Roman] Propaganda, and we resent its interference. The Church the Franciscan Fathers planted here was cut off; this is the second growth, and it is indigenous. (Cather 146)

4 According to Cohen (156–57), Cather had access to historical sources providing alternative depictions of both Bishop Lamy and Mexican culture in New Mexico.

Cather's Martínez particularly argues for accommodating Catholic religious practice to local cultures in order to fully reach out to people. He warns Latour:

> You know nothing about Indians or Mexicans. If you try to introduce European civilization here and change our old ways, … I foretell an early death for you. I advise you to study our native traditions before you begin your reforms. … The dark things forbidden by your Church are part of Indian religion.[5]

Interestingly, Martínez's argument as presented in *Death Comes for the Archbishop* – though not the historical padre's theological writings – anticipates key tenets of Indigenous Theology, a branch of theological thought developed since the late 1960s in Latin America, which seeks to revalue Amerindian traditions and integrate them into Catholic religious practice to make the Church serve its indigenous communities rather than vice versa (Cleary).

Unlike Cather's novel, Maxwell Anderson's almost-forgotten (Avery, "Maxwell" 30) tragedy in verse, *Night Over Taos* (1932), paints a more benign picture of Padre Martínez. Set during the 1847 Taos Rebellion, although not concerned with historical detail or accuracy, the play depicts the struggle of New Mexico's Spanish elite against the U.S. occupation of the region through a generation conflict between a wealthy rancher and leader of the insurgents and his sons (Anderson; Dukore 82–83; Gilbert 65-75). The drama presents Anglo Americans as "unscrupulous and mercenary" (Avery, "Maxwell" 30), but at the same time portrays the United States as a land of liberty and opportunities for everyone, regardless of race, class, or gender (45–46, 76, 128). It hereby suggests that, justified criticism notwithstanding (83–84), the shift from the "old order" of New Mexico's semi-feudal, patriarchal Spanish society which the rancher Pablo Montoya represents (23, 55–60, 74–78, 86, 114–117, 94, 119–120, 124, 130–133; Gilbert 65–75) to the "new order" of U.S. American rule and broader political participation Montoya's sons stand for in the play was inevitable (18, 127–128; Dukore 82–83).

Padre Martínez appears in *Night Over Taos* as advisor and confidant of Taos's Spanish elite, whose own life, in contrast to *Death Comes for the Archbishop*, is not addressed at all in the play. This falls in line with Anderson's practice in his historical dramas of "using historical incident and character to exhibit a human being in the process of 'spiritual awakening or regeneration'" (Lee 11; 5, 12, 24). Considering the looming U.S. annexation of New Mexico as a threat to the region's Mexican civilization (Anderson 11, 21–26, 56–58), Anderson's fictionalized priest supports the insurgents and even encourages their resistance. He asks: "What would happen to Taos … and New Mexico?/We are the farthest arm of an old civilization here" (11; ellipsis in the original). The preservation of New Mexican cultural identity manifests itself for Martínez primarily in defending his city. "What we have is Taos. Losing our city,/We have nothing left" (Anderson 35; 114–115; Gilbert 67), he argues in *Night Over Taos*. Despite his concern for maintaining Spanish culture, on the one hand, and his conde-

5 Cather (147). On New Mexican Catholicism, cf. Reséndez (77–83, 177).

scending attitude toward New Mexico's lower classes (Anderson 11), on the other, the padre recognizes the need to face the political transformation of New Mexico. Tellingly, he identifies the originating of these changes in Mexican society as well as in the United States: "The times are changing," he acknowledges in the drama. "Mexico's a republic./The English from the north broke from their kings. We're here/Like a little island of empire, and on all sides/The [common] people have a share in what happens" (75–76; Dukore 83). As a consequence, he argues, the patriarchal family structures and autocratic regime of the Spanish elite in New Mexico will have to give way to more democratic forms of social and political life (Anderson 116–118).

However, this attitude stems from Martínez's intention "to save/What we have" (76; Gilbert 66) and from the conviction that "an enlightened people/Could be ruled more simply" (Anderson 77) rather than from a true critique of the social and political injustice of the "old order." This somewhat pragmatic attitude turns the padre into a key mediator between Montoya, who rejects the change, and his sons, who seek it (11–19, 27–35, 75–78, 114–118; Gilbert 65–68). Given this function, it is a logical solution to *Night Over Taos* – and a conciliatory one, considering the rather negative Anglo attitudes to Mexicans, both in the mid-1840s and when Anderson wrote his play (Gonzales 67–68, 82–84, 146–147) – that in the final speech the dying Montoya entrusts the priest with guarding New Mexico's Spanish culture through the inevitable transformation: "Martinez – /I leave you my world. Save it, keep it alive,/There are those who care to live" (Anderson 133; Avery, "Conclusion" 319). Thus, while Anderson's *Night Over Taos* follows Cather's *Death Comes for the Archbishop* in endorsing the Anglo-Americanization of New Mexico as the harbinger of civilization and progress, the play crucially positions Padre Martínez not as an antagonist to this process but as an important mediator accompanying the Mexican population on their path. The play thereby provides a connection to the subsequent body of scholarly biographies of the padre, which seek to correct Cather's distorting image of his charter and to restore his standing as an important theologian, educator, and advocate of Mexican culture in his native region.

Conclusion

While Willa Cather's novel *Death Comes for the Archbishop* paints a uniquely positive picture of the proponents of Eurocentric Catholic orthodoxy, Manifest Destiny, and U.S. Americanization, it vilifies those who oppose these paradigms, most notably the Taos priest Antonio José Martínez. In so doing, Janis Stout points out, the narrative "define[s] in exaggerated terms the conflict between [Anglo and Spanish] cultures" in a way that supports the novel's "legend of enlightened American expansion" (245–246; Cohen 147, 152, 155–156). Written only five years later, Maxwell Anderson's tragic drama *Night Over Taos* uses the historical context of the Taos Rebellion of 1847, in which Martínez functioned as a mediator, as little more than a background for the unfolding tragedy of the fictional(ized) Montoya family. Nonetheless, the play depicts Padre Martínez more accurately than Cather's novel as a confidant of New Mexico's Spanish elite and as an arbiter in their struggle with the impending Anglo dominance in the region.

In contrast to these Anglo-authored, fictionalized biographical sketches of the priest, the padre's Relación as well as El Historiador's and Pedro Sánchez's (auto)biographies of Martínez unanimously praise the priest's deep concern with the well-being of New Mexico's Spanish population and his achievements as parish priest, theologian, educator, and politician. The padre's apologetic memoir moreover draws upon two established text types to support its secular and spiritual discursive authority: Emphasizing his theological knowledge as well as his dedication to his ministry, the text justifies Martínez's political activities and theological thoughts against charges of insurgency against both political and religious authorities and doctrines. However, where Cather's novel presents him as an advocate of Amerindian cultures and an early proponent of Indigenous Theology, the historical Martínez, as revealed by the early Spanish-language (auto)biographies, not only held ambivalent views of Anglo culture but also actively supported the Mexican and U.S. governments in suppressing the Native autochthony they considered a threat to their hegemonic civilizations.

Taken together, the analyzed texts articulate a complex picture of Padre Martínez as a thoughtful theologian and committed activist but also as a political strategist. As much as, or even more than, the priest's own views and actions, the different texts express the religious-political positions of their respective times, cultures, and individual authors. Hence, while publicly remembering Padre Martínez, they simultaneously use him as a lens through which to (re)present ideas about the political, ethnic, and religious conflicts that marked New Mexican – and in a larger sense also Mexican and U.S. American – history in a period of profound change, when the region shifted from being a Spanish-dominated province of newly independent Mexico to a multiethnic state within the Anglo-hegemonic United States.

Works cited

Anderson, Maxwell. *Night Over Taos: A Play in Three Acts*. 1932. *Eleven Verse Plays, 1929–1939*. 11th print. New York: Harcourt, Brace, & World, 1968. 1–133. Print.

Avery, Laurence G. "The Conclusion of *Night Over Taos*." *American Literature* 37.3 (Nov. 1965): 318–321. Print.

———. "Maxwell Anderson." *Dictionary of Literary Biography*. Vol. 7.1: *Twentieth-Century American Dramatists: A-J*. Ed. John MacNicholas and John Houseman. Detroit: Gale, 1981. 23–35. Print.

Cather, Willa. *Death Comes for the Archbishop*. 1927. New York: Vintage, 1990. Print.

Chavez, Fray Angelico, O.F.M. *But Time and Chance: The Story of Padre Martínez of Taos, 1793–1867*. 1981. Santa Fe: Sunstone Press, 2001. Print.

Cleary, Edward, ed. *Resurgent Voices in Latin America: Indigenous Peoples, Political Mobilization, and Religious Change*. New Brunswick, NJ: Rutgers UP, 2004. Print.

Cohen, Judith Beth. "Father Martinez: Folk Hero or Dangerous Infidel? Rereading Willa Cather's *Death Comes for the Archbishop*." *Rethinking American Literature*. Ed. Lil Brannon and Brenda M. Greene. Urbana, IL: National Council of Teachers of English, 1997. 146–159. Print.

Damico, Denise Holladay. "Santiago Valdez." *New Mexico History.org*. Santa Fe, NM: New Mexico Office of the State Historian. 23 Jan. 2014. Web. http://newmexicohistory.org/2014/01/23/santiago-valdez/.

Dukore, Bernard F. *American Dramatists, 1918–1945*. London: Macmillan, 1984. Print.

Francis, E.K. "Padre Martínez: A New Mexican Myth." *New Mexico Historical Review* 31.4 (Oct. 1956): 265–289. Print.

Gilbert, Robert L. *The Thirties Verse Tragedies of Maxwell Anderson*. Ann Arbor, MI: University Microfilms International, 1977. Microfilm.

Gonzales, Manuel G. *Mexicanos: A History of Mexicans in the United States*. Bloomington: Indiana UP, 1999. Print.

Haas, Astrid. "Borderlands Identities and Borderlands Ideologies in Willa Cather's *Death Comes for the Archbishop*." *American Studies Journal* 57. May 2012. Web. http://www.asjournal.org/57-2012/willa-cathers-death-comes-for-the-archbishop/.

Harp, Jerry. "Apologias." *Encyclopedia of Life Writing* vol. I. Ed. Margaretta Jolly. London: Fitzroy Dearborn, 2001. 44–45. Print.

Hernández, José Angel. "From Conquest to Colonization: *Indios* and Colonization Policies After Mexican Independence." *Mexican Studies/Estudios Mexicanos* 26.2 (Summer 2010): 291–322. Print.

El Historiador. "Historia consisa del cura de Taos Antonio José Martínez." 1861. *Northern Mexico on the Eve of the United States Invasion: Rare Imprints Concerning California, Arizona, New Mexico, and Texas, 1821–1846*. Ed. David J. Weber. New York: Arno Press, 1976. N. pag. Print.

Lee, Henry Glenn. *The Use of History in the Historical Plays of Maxwell Anderson*. Ann Arbor, MI: University Microfilms International, 1977. Microfilm.

Mares, E.A. "Padre Martinez and Mexican New Mexico." *New Mexican Lives: Profiles and Historical Stories*. Ed. Richard W. Etulain: U of New Mexico P, 2002. 106–130. Print.

Martínez, Antonio José. *Relación de Méritos del Presbítero Antonio José Martínez: Autobiografía y Apología*. 1838. Trans. by Cecil V. Romero as "Apologia of Presbyter Antonio J. Martinez." *New Mexico Historical Review* 3.4 (Oct. 1928): 325–346. Print.

Padilla, Genaro M. "Recovering Mexican-American Autobiography." *Recovering the U.S. Hispanic Literary Heritage*. Ed. Ramón Gutiérrez and Genaro Padilla. Houston: Arte Público, 1993. 153–178. Print.

Real Academia Española. "Relación." *Diccionario de la lengua española*. 23nd ed. 2014, rev. 2019. Web. https://dle.rae.es/relación.

Reséndez, Andrés. *Changing National Identities at the Frontier: Texas and New Mexico, 1800–1850*. Cambridge: Cambridge UP, 2004. Print.

Rinke, Stefan. "Grenzwahrnehmungen – Grenzüberschreitungen: Selbst- und Fremdbilder in der Geschichte der Beziehungen zwischen den Amerikas." *Grenzen der Macht – Macht der Grenzen: Lateinamerika im globalen Kontext*. Ed. Marianne Braig, Ottmar Ette, Dieter Ingenschay, and Günther Maihold. Frankfurt/M.: Vervuert, 2005. 207–238. Print.

Sánchez, Pedro. *Recollections of the Life of the Priest Don Antonio José Martínez/ Memorias sobre la vida del presbítero don Antonio José Martínez*. English/ Spanish. Trans. and introd. Ray John de Aragon. Santa Fe: Sunstone Press, 2006. Print.

Stout, Janis P. *Willa Cather: The Writer and Her World*. Charlottesville: UP of Virginia, 2000. Print.

Weber, David J. "Introduction." *Northern Mexico on the Eve of the United States Invasion: Rare Imprints Concerning California, Arizona, New Mexico, and Texas, 1821–1846*. Ed. David J. Weber. New York: Arno Press, 1976. 3–31. Print.

Of Love Songs, Open Wounds, and (Almost) Everything In Between: Borderlands and InterAmerican Literature

SASKIA HERTLEIN

"We are all 'grenzgangers'" (xii). As Roland Hagenbüchle and Josef Raab rather provocatively begin their *Negotiations of America's* [there limited to] *National Identity*, all of us cross borders in some ways, since we "(whether we like it or not) are part of specific national, regional, and local cultures, but more than ever before we also happen to *live in between and across cultures* – in a global environment, first of all, but also in intranational and intraregional contexts of sociocultural diversity" (xiii, emphasis in original). These crossings as well as the liminal subjects are explored and reflected in many ways in literary and cultural productions, embedded in diverse contexts.[1] Borderlands – in the broadest possible sense of the term[2] – and related concepts have therefore been studied from various perspectives, and in these studies, a wide range of potential foci have been explored. And while one might be tempted to believe in allegedly shrunken distances or instant access because of recent developments, Koshy cautions us not to assume that ideas nowadays consequently travel well – or even better – across borders (302).

1 For example Kerstin Eksell connects borders and wanderers in Arabic literature, but her findings may be transferred to interAmerican literature as well: "The borders between geographical regions, ethnical groups or historical periods are easily outlined, and to define the consequences for those moving across them adds to our understanding of the world. Yet, the outer experiences of clashes, ruptures and confusion, appear in a mirror world as a mental borderland, in which the wanderer is able to try his identity and prove his potential. For the individual, such a borderland is both a loss and an opening; for the other, it holds an ambiguity which may produce a new and rich literature" (7).

2 Besides the above-mentioned use by Eksell (Fn 1), for example Raab highlights that the multi-leveled complexity of the borderlands can only be understood if various dimensions of the term ("ideological, value-based, psychological, class/gender/ethnicity-based") are considered (*The Borderlands* 4). (For more dimensions, cf. "Hemispheric" (219, Fn 11). He therefore conceptualizes "'[b]orderlands of identity' [as] all those realms in which the individual or group has to negotiate her/his/its position vis-à-vis what surrounds it (spatially, ideologically, historically, etc.). Some forms which this negotiation can take are varying degrees of acceptance and rejection, assimilation and resistance, the return to older models or the conceptualization of future ones" (*The Borderlands* 4). Johann Schimanski propose[s] using the term "'symbolic border' … about differences concerning the lived life of humans and other agents, either in its social aspects (*gender*, *religion*, *class*, *ethnicity*, *hegemony*, etc.), in its individual aspects (*being*, *body*, *psyche*, etc.), or in the in-between of interpersonal relationships. Literature to a large extent deals with precisely the crossing or the transgression of such symbolic borders" (55, emphasis in original).

In scholarly work, border crossings in the sense of (re-)conceptualizations of established and emerging fields and reference frameworks – such as interAmerican perspectives – provide us with opportunities to reflect on established, normalized conceptions and thinking modes. As will be explored below, the challenges inherent in the endeavor to pursue the to-some-extent still emerging field of InterAmerican Studies and literature[3] may provide us with incentives to continue to expand our schemata,[4] and to recognize the inherent diversity of materials and approaches, beyond potentially oversimplifying thinking modes. A habitual but diversified practice of collaboration may thereby contribute to (re-)considering potential blind spots in our engagement with both interAmerican literature and literature in our respective fields, emphasizing the reciprocal contribution such a mode of thinking may provide to both InterAmerican Studies and other fields from which individual scholars originate or in which they are engaged.

Aside from the general ambiguities behind the concepts of "America,"[5] "Inter-American," and "literature," the combination "interAmerican literature" may already be difficult to conceptualize.[6] Nonetheless, the general idea behind such an approach may be characterized by Chang-rae Lee's words from his novel *Native Speaker*, "Let us think differently!," that Raab transfers to the approach Mexican American culture has recently taken with regard to borders ("Symbiose" 171). As Raab highlights in several contributions about interAmerican approaches, "Let us think differently!" is at their core because instead of thinking only within the frameworks of a particular nation or region of the Americas in line with disciplinary and language boundaries, interAmerican approaches include a hemispheric perspective ("InterAmerican Studies") and transdisciplinary practices ("Thinking" 21), thereby crossing numerous borders.

As becomes clear, however, when considering the implications of studying the Americas, an interAmerican approach provides scholars with a number of challenges, ranging from linguistic proficiency to academic training in either comparative or specific national or regional fields. Nonetheless, one might recall for example the then

3 Claudia Sadowski-Smith traces the development back to the early 1900s with Martí and Bolton ("The Place" 106), and Sophia McClennen explores the historical development more extensively. Moreover, Earl E. Fitz reminds us that interAmerican literature also already has a comparably long history of closer scholarly attention, since "the International Comparative Literature Association (ICLA) officially declared interAmerican literary studies to be a major new field of inquiry" in 1982 ("Then" 15).

4 In a social psychologist's sense of the term. For more explorations of schema expansion via close reading, cf. for example Moya (esp. 142–6, 35–37, 63, 79–80, and 163–165).

5 As Olaf Kaltmeier rightly points out, "it seems impossible to find a common ground to define the Americas. And indeed, it might not be necessary to find the essence of the Americas. Instead, it is necessary to focus on the 'variable geography,' and thus, in a self-reflexive way, on the strategic construction of areas like the Americas" (6).

6 For some proposals, cf. for example Fitz (*Rediscovering*; *Inter-American*, esp. "Introduction" 2).

president of the American Studies Association (ASA)[7] Shelley Fisher Fishkin's emphasis on the attractiveness of a rather multifaceted field: "indeed, one of the reasons many of us were attracted to American studies [sic] in the first place was its capaciousness, its eschewal of methodological or ideological dogma, and its openness to fresh syntheses and connections" (19). Some of these "fresh syntheses and connections" are highlighted by Gabriele Pisarz-Ramírez when she observes that "[i]n recent decades, the various notions of nationalism on the American continent have increasingly been questioned by theoretical approaches that have emphasized the historical and cultural links between the different regions of the Americas" (285). She then mentions "'New American Studies,' 'Postnational Studies,' and 'Hemispheric Studies' [as examples] that have pointed to the multiple historical and cultural connections between the various regions of the continent" (285). These connections are included in both Fisher-Fishkin's idea of a transnational version of American Studies and in current definitions of InterAmerican Studies. Fisher Fishkin explains:

> As the transnational becomes more central to American studies [sic], we'll pay increasing attention to the historical roots of multidirectional flows of people, ideas, and goods and the social, political, linguistic, cultural, and economic crossroads generated in the process. These crossroads might just as easily be outside the geographical and political boundaries of the United States as inside them. We will increasingly interrogate the "naturalness" of some of the borders, boundaries, and binaries that we may not have questioned very much in the past, and will probe the ways in which they may have been contingent and constructed. (22)

This shift in – or added – perspective within American Studies has been debated over the years,[8] and as Raab argues,

> [n]ot every research topic in North American, Latin American, or Caribbean Studies requires a hemispheric consciousness. Also, transatlantic, transpacific, and global interconnections may in some cases outweigh the relevance of other parts of the Americas for exploring a particular topic. But the recent movement toward transnational American Studies and InterAmerican Studies reflects a growing awareness that the analysis of many phenomena grounded in a particular space and time will benefit from a recognition of their hemispheric contexts. ("Hemispheric" 219)

Different from a transnational or hemispheric approach within a field such as American Studies, InterAmerican Studies emphasizes the in-betweenness already in its name and may not be as obviously traced back to a U.S. American endeavor only, as American Studies have been, if one considers, for example, the history of the field or the self-understanding of the ASA and other similar associations. Instead, an inter-

---

7 The "American" in American Studies Association refers exclusively to the United States of America; even if Fisher Fishkin argues for a transnational version of American Studies, a reference to the United States remains at its core (ASA). Cf. Fitz ("Then" 15–16) or Messmer.

8 Cf., for example, Leo Marx for an urge to "submit America as a nation to the closest possible scrutiny" (372), or Messmer (esp. 11) summarizing major trends in the debate in the ASA and beyond.

American perspective on transnational Americas emphasizes a focus on "the multiple dimensions of interAmerican integrations. Therefore, an interAmerican approach involves understanding cultural and political elements not bounded by a closed national space but instead situated in a space of entanglements" (Kaltmeier 3).[9]

Nonetheless, interAmerican approaches may still invite the dangers of similarly maintaining hierarchies, of oversimplifications, or homogenizations. Alexia Schemien therefore argues that

> InterAmerican Studies … highlights the interconnectedness between the two Americas: North and South. While acknowledging that there are two distinct parts of the American continent that are connected but still can also be treated as separate entities, Inter-American Studies opens up the field of 'American' studies [sic] and at the same time acknowledges the diversity that North, Central, and South America have to offer. The differences and similarities between the countries of the American continent are used productively and always in conversation with each other. (23)

Moreover, Raab cautions that "[a]n inter-American approach … does not imply any kind of homogenization. Differences and similarities between and within North America, the Caribbean, Central America, and South America have to be kept in mind" ("Introduction" 7). As becomes clear from the emphases presented above, a critical interAmerican perspective may instead "transcend the limitations inherent in studying one nation in isolation and can successfully address the multifaceted economic, political, and cultural interrelations of the Americas in an age of global interconnectedness" (Messmer 12). Criticism concerning a potential hierarchical thinking is challenged by Schemien, who points out that:

> [c]ritics of the term [interAmerican] have argued that it implies a hierarchical structure of U.S.-America in the center of the research and public interest which then is challenged and confronted with other American nations, as the ones of Latin America in the South and Canada in the North. This is, however, not the way that InterAmerican Studies is designed and acted out today. Many scholars working in the field are for example Latin Americanists and do not even come from the field of U.S. American studies [sic]. interAmerican approaches, therefore, concentrate on the nations on the American continent and their mutual political involvement and their intercultural exchanges. (25)

Generally, as we might conclude from the above, America may be conceptualized "as a multifaceted continent marked by inequalities and interconnections [with a variety of] spaces, communities, and discourses in [it which] are treated … as socially constructed" (Hertlein and Raab 5). Especially the inequalities and their legacies, however, may nonetheless cause potential unease or even "open wounds" about the general concept of InterAmerican Studies or literature. In practice, therefore, such concerns need to be considered and, where necessary, negotiated and addressed. Fitz attempts to reconcile the opposing views by arguing that

> while we understand how and why the phrase, "interAmerican literature," can be offensive and objectionable to some, its practitioners mean it only as a useful methodological

9 Cf. Fitz ("Finding").

> framework within which different cultures can be studied together and within which defining characteristics are to be recognized, valued, and maintained. ("Native" 143)

Consequently, an interAmerican approach such as that used in this contribution should be understood as being aware of such inequalities, interconnections, and potential challenges, and in its approach attempts to find more suitable ways to study inter-American interconnections. The question remains, however, how to proceed in this endeavor,[10] especially considering Fitz's warning to not just voice good intentions, but rather to practice them ("Then," for example, 16–17).

Due to the limitations inherent in any InterAmerican Studies academic training – the inability of any scholar to gain sufficient access to all potentially necessary specific and comparative perspectives[11] –, this contribution proposes that the particular strength of this field may lie precisely in its awareness of the inherent need for collaboration across multiple borders. By means of such collaboration, scholars may not only bring together their own diverse backgrounds and trainings, but also need to continuously (re-)negotiate all those points that might otherwise be overlooked. This proposal, however, does not mean to imply that it is impossible to provide specific training with an interAmerican focus, but rather emphasizes an openness to potential dangers and limitations without broader and varying collaborations since in such a context, even more obviously than in many others, neither an all-encompassing training nor a full awareness of potential pitfalls appears otherwise possible.

These multifaceted collaborations[12] may then continue to "challenge the ways of thinking about the Americas" much as Wilfried Raussert ("Introduction" 3) or Fitz –

---

10 Fitz proposes to classify prominent contemporary approaches as "the American Studies/ International American Studies …, the Latin American literature …, and the comparative literature approach" ("Then" 15).

11 To some extent, such limitations (linguistic, methodological, etc.) apply to many fields, but InterAmerican Studies – with this specific focus on its awareness of its own limitations because of the multiplicity of languages, cultures, and interrelations in the Americas which simultaneously need highly specialized and comparative perspectives – may be even more obviously affected than some other fields. As Raab argues, "[w]hile an interAmerican approach runs the risk of glossing over differences and while few scholars can claim expertise on the whole Western Hemisphere, InterAmerican Studies maintains that the relevance and impact of many of the phenomena we study in our academic practice do not stop at national borderlines. Nor do they stop at social, political, gendered, ethnic, religious, educational, economic, historical, ideological, or any other borderlines. Intent on exploring what Herbert Eugene Bolton called the 'wider horizons,' InterAmerican Studies proposes a departure from insular thinking and an espousal of hemispheric contexts" ("Hemispheric" 219). For further aspects, cf. Fitz (*Inter-American*, esp. "Introduction" 6–8; "Then").

12 Generally, many of the regional, national, or broader comparative or disciplinary associations have included interAmerican foci in their conferences. In addition, one fairly recently added potential forum that has not been founded in the context of a particular regional, national or disciplinary association is the International Association of Inter-American Studies|Asociación Internacional de Estudios Interamericanos (IAS).

the latter mentioning the "concepts of *Americanity, americanité, americanidad, americanidade,* and, most recently, *américité*" ("Then" 15) as examples –, propose Inter-American (Literary) Studies has already done. Practicing "Let us think differently!" (Lee qtd. in Raab, "Symbiose" 171) may expand the schemata of the scholars involved and thereby support ever new perspectives on otherwise potentially overlooked interAmerican or interdisciplinary "open wounds," "love songs," and "(almost) everything in-between."

While, however, the border has been identified as one of the key tropes in Inter-American Studies,[13] neither "love songs" nor "open wounds" may, at first sight, seem related to the study of "borderlands" or "interAmerican literature." Considering the implications of the above-mentioned potential challenges within the approach though, they may provide a worthwhile framework encompassing not only topics within inter-American literature, but also those framing the study of it.

Both terms, the "love song" and the "open wound," have been inspired by the Mexico-U.S. border, a region that is being extensively researched in comparison to other national or regional borders on the American continent.[14] The "open wound"[15]

---

13 A list of such tropes provided by Raussert, Brian Rozema, Yolanda Campos García, and Marius Littschwager in their publication with the same title includes Colonial/Neocolonial, Independence, Religion, Border, Mobility, Race/Indigeneity, Gender, and Decolonial Reflections ("Selected" 5–10). Conscious of the above-mentioned attempt of InterAmerican Studies to be critically diversity literate (for example sensu Steyn 19–20), Raussert provides this essay in English and Spanish ("Selección") simultaneously. This is by no means intended to imply that English and Spanish were the only languages spoken in the Americas, but as Raussert explains, it reflects the linguistic development of the IAS journal *fiar* from English/Spanish to including French and Portuguese ("Selected" 5). While there are more languages on the American continent than the languages of the European colonizers, the current coverage mirrors an awareness that reaches beyond English as an [academic] lingua franca and exposes the complex challenges of providing for example a journal that is both as widely accessible and all-encompassing as possible, thereby reflecting the continuous challenges the field of InterAmerican Studies, including literature, faces. This chapter is written in English because of my academic background and training, but acknowledges the consequently inherent limitations, and invites further perspectives.

14 This observation applies to all other national borders in the Americas (explored for example by Fitz in "Then"). For the Canadian-U.S. border, for example, cf. Sadowski-Smith ("The Centrality," esp. 161, or "The Place" 106) or see Pisarz-Ramírez, who argues that "[t]he huge majority of interAmerican critical discourses focus on the border between the USA and Mexico as a prototypical site of interculturality and transnationality and as a source of theoretical approaches that question national narratives of monoculturality and exclusivity. Gustavo Pérez-Firmat's provocative question in his 1990 collection *Do the Americas Have a Common Literature?* was almost completely directed at the links between the United States and Latin America" (285, emphasis in original). A somewhat more inclusive approach can for example be found about 10 years later in *Do the Americas Have a Common Literary History?* (Buchenau and Paatz), while for example Sadowski-Smith ("The Place") – despite calling for more di-

refers to Gloria Anzaldúa's[16] characterization of this region as being a "1,950 mile-long open wound" (24), "*una herida abierta* where the Third World grates against the first and bleeds" (25, italics in original). In this quotation the specificity of this particular national border is highlighted, not only by providing its length, but by defining it further, for example as a hurt. Beyond the wound, this particular space can also be understood as a space for multiple explorations of hybrid or otherwise non-essential identities,[17] for example in Richard Rodriguez's pondering over a "North American" who embodies some aspects of a potentially "interAmerican identity" due to his multiple entanglements and mobility (n. pag). In both explorations, the U.S.-Mexican border may be regarded as an "open wound," but equally provides a chance for further conceptualizations, for example as a "contact zone" (Pratt, *Imperial*; "Arts"), and even as potentially inspiring a "love song" (Urrea, interview at KeplersBooks, n. pag.).

While Luis Alberto Urrea's work most obviously also includes references to some aspects of the "open wound" when referring to the U.S.-Mexico border, as for example in his non-fictional *The Devil's Highway*, in which he tracks a 2001 desert border crossing which proved fatal for half of those men attempting it, in his fictional novel *Into the Beautiful North* (almost simultaneously also published in Spanish, *Rumbo al Hermoso Norte*), Urrea deliberately chooses to write "a love song to both Mexico and the United States" (KeplersBooks n. pag.), exposing harsh and beautiful realities on both sides of the border. Thereby, he challenges a variety of essentialist schemata – a strategy he also uses in other texts such as *The House of Broken Angels*, in which a family gathering exposes the multifaceted borders within a transnational, interAmerican family.

Obviously, numerous more examples from the vast corpus of interAmerican literature may provide such references, and in an interAmerican interdisciplinary conversation a question resulting from such examples would ask how other American literatures conceptualize and otherwise explore borders and related interAmerican issues – a conversation that cannot be part of this short and limited article, but deserves to be continued in the future. The examples given here – both restricted to English and

---

versity – equally highlights the importance of this particular borderland for Inter-American Studies.

15 For more explorations of wounds in an interAmerican literary and cultural studies context, please refer to contributions such as Berndt Ostendorf's "Introduction: Wounds as Collective Memory," in which he highlights the function of wounds as for example explored by Nietzsche (275) or, with a special focus also on borderlands, Maritza Cárdenas.

16 Raab evaluates Anzaldúa's "hybrid autobiography *Borderlands/La Frontera* (1987)" as "groundbreaking," "represent[ing] a new postcolonial beginning in charting the borderlands of Mexican American identity" (*The Borderlands* 26, emphasis in original), and emphasizes its importance for the study of multiple borderlands.

17 As Raab and Butler argue, "the polyphony and simultaneity of cultural practices – no matter whether they contest one another or are joined together into a new cultural discourse, whether they illustrate or constitute contacts, contrasts, or confluences – account for the general departure from essentialist notions of cultural identity" (4).

Spanish and to a limited geographical and thus specific reference framework – were used because the notions of the border referred to in the title of this contribution were taken from them. More generally though, the borderlands in their many different conceptualizations as well as literature with its multiple perspectives and its invitation to expand one's schemata may both mirror the challenges an interAmerican approach inherently has as well as providing some potential strategies for facing them.

In the attempt to "Let us think differently!" (Lee qtd. in Raab, "Symbiose" 171), interAmerican literary scholars study a diverse field that encompasses "love songs," "open wounds," and "(almost) everything in-between." For practical purposes and from a future-oriented perspective, Fitz proposes that

> the issues confronting [interAmerican literature in the 21st century] will be seen as more methodological than conceptual, that is, they will speak less to its validity as a field (which now enjoys wide acceptance) than to issues of making these new and productive approaches to interAmerican study work together for our common hemispheric good. ("Then" 27)

This outlook includes the continuing need for the development of more diversified bibliographies and inclusive collaboration in order to expand all interAmericanists' schemata, resulting in fewer "blind spots" such as those Fitz ("Then") points out – which persist despite already existing good intentions. Moreover, as interAmerican "grenzgangers" (Hagenbüchle and Raab xii), we might strive for Aurora Levins Morales's conclusion in "Child of the Americas"[18]: after referencing the both painful and positive legacies of her diverse heritage, she concludes: "I was born at the crossroads and I am whole" (3028). Currently, however, as Raab concludes, "the field remains wide open" ("Inter-American Perspectives" 95), and after all, despite the fact that "the challenges of an interAmerican academic practice are numerous, the rewards are even more so" ("Hemispheric" 219).

Works cited

Anzaldúa, Gloria. *Borderlands/La Frontera: The New Mestiza*. 3rd ed. San Francisco, CA: Aunt Lute Books, 2007. Print.

ASA American Studies Association. *About*. N.d. Web. https://www.theasa.net/about.

Buchenau, Barbara, and Annette Paatz, eds. *Do the Americas Have a Common Literary History?* Frankfurt a.M.: Peter Lang, 2002. Print.

Cárdenas, Maritza. "A Central American Wound: Remapping the U.S. Borderlands in Oscar Martinez's *The Beast*." *Symbolism: An International Annual of Critical Aesthetics* 17 (2017): 13–30. Print.

18 Raab further explores this poem and other border-crossing, interAmerican literary examples, in "Colonial" and "Inter-American Perspectives."

Eksell, Kerstin. "Introduction." *Borders and Beyond: Crossings and Transitions in Modern Arabic Literature*. Ed. Kerstin Eksell and Stephan Guth. Wiesbaden: Harrassowitz, 2011. 7–14. Print.

Fisher Fishkin, Shelley. "Crossroads of Cultures: The Transnational Turn in American Studies – Presidential Address to the American Studies Association. 12 Nov. 2004." *American Quarterly* 57.1 (Mar. 2005): 17–57. Web. http://muse.jhu.edu/article/180093.

Fitz, Earl E. *Rediscovering the New World: Inter-American Literature in a Comparative Context.* Iowa City: U of Iowa P, 1991. Print.

———. *Inter-American Literary History: Six Critical Periods*. Frankfurt a.M.: Peter Lang, 2017. Print.

———. "Finding the Americas in American Studies. Inter-American Studies as an Emerging Field: The Future of a Discipline." *RIAS* 3 (2008): 1–2. Web. https://journals.us.edu.pl/index.php/RIAS/article/view/985.

———. "Native American Literature and Its Place in the Inter-American Project." *Comparative American Studies: An International Journal* 11.2 (2013): 124–147. Print.

———. "Then and Now: The Current State of Inter-American Literary Studies." *The Routledge Companion to Inter-American Studies*. Ed. Wilfried Raussert. London/New York: Routledge, 2017. 15–30. Print.

Hagenbüchle, Roland, and Josef Raab. "Preface." *Negotiations of America's National Identity*. Ed. Roland Hagenbüchle, Josef Raab, and Marietta Messmer. Tübingen: Stauffenburg, 2000. xii–xvi. Print.

Hertlein, Saskia, and Josef Raab. "Spaces, Communities, and Discourses in Inter-American Studies." *Spaces – Communities – Discourses: Charting Identity and Belonging in the Americas*. Ed. Josef Raab and Saskia Hertlein. Trier: WVT/Tempe, AZ: Bilingual Press, 2016. 1–20. Print.

International Association of Inter-American Studies/Asociación Internacional de Estudios Interamericanos. *About*: *History*. N.d. Web. http://www.interamericanstudies.net/?page_id=16.

Kaltmeier, Olaf. "Transnational Americas: Envisioning Inter-American Area Studies in Globalization Processes." *Transnational Americas: Envisioning Inter-American Area Studies in Globalization Processes*. Ed. Olaf Kaltmeier. Trier: WVT/Tempe, AZ: Bilingual Press, 2013. 1–14. Print.

KeplersBooks. Luis Alberto Urrea at Kepler's Books, 2009. Web. https://www.youtube.com/watch?v=LsqKWgwhI-M.

Koshy, Susan. "Postcolonial Studies after 9/11: A Response to Ali Behdad." *American Literary History* 20.1/2 (2008): 300–303. Print.

Marx, Leo. "Reflections on American Studies: From the 1950s to the Present." *American Vistas and Beyond: A Festschrift for Roland Hagenbüchle*. Ed. Marietta Messmer, Josef Raab, and Roland Hagenbüchle. Trier: WVT, 2002. 361–373. Print.

McClennen, Sophia A. "Inter-American Studies or Imperial American Studies?" *Comparative American Studies* 3.4 (2005): 393–413. Print.

Messmer, Marietta. "Introduction: Transcending Borders: The International Turn in American Studies." *The International Turn in American Studies*. Ed. Marietta Messmer and Armin P. Frank. Frankfurt a.M.: Peter Lang, 2015. 7–44. Print.

Morales, Aurora L. "Child of the Americas." *The Heath Anthology of American Literature. Contemporary Period. 1945 to the Present*. Ed. Paul Lauter and Richard Yarborough. 5th ed. Boston et al.: Houghton Mifflin, 2005. 3027–3028. Print.

Moya, Paula M. L. *The Social Imperative: Race, Close Reading, and Contemporary Literary Criticism*. Stanford: Stanford UP, 2016. Print.

Ostendorf, Berndt. "Introduction: Wounds as Collective Memory." *Negotiations of America's National Identity*. Ed. Roland Hagenbüchle, Josef Raab, and Marietta Messmer. Tübingen: Stauffenburg, 2000. 275–282. Print.

Pérez-Firmat, Gustavo, ed. *Do the Americas Have a Common Literature?* Durham, North Carolina: Duke UP, 1990. Print.

Pisarz-Ramirez, Gabriele. "African-Canadian Literature and the Americas." *Americanisms: Discourses of Exception, Exclusion, Exchange*. Ed. Michael Steppat. Heidelberg: Universitätsverlag Winter, 2009. 285–300. Print.

Pratt, Mary L. "Arts of the Contact Zone." *Profession* 91 (1991): 33–40. Web. http://www.jstor.org/stable/25595469.

———. *Imperial Eyes: Travel Writing and Transculturation*. 2nd ed., reprint. London/New York: Routledge, 2009. Print.

Raab, Josef, and Martin Butler. "Introduction: Cultural Hybridity in the Americas." *Hybrid Americas: Contacts, Contrasts, and Confluences in New World Literatures and Cultures*. Ed. Martin Butler and Josef Raab. Münster: Lit/Tempe, AZ: Bilingual Press. 2008. 1–18. Print.

Raab, Josef. "Colonial and Decolonial Thinking: Race Discourses in Literatures of the Americas." *De/Colonization in the Americas: Continuity and Change*. PUCP: Lima, Perú. 6 Aug. 2014. Conference Paper.

———. "Hemispheric Intersections in Toni Morrison's *A Mercy*." *The Routledge Companion to Inter-American Studies*. Ed. Wilfried Raussert. London/New York: Routledge, 2017. 219–227. Print.

———. "Inter-American Perspectives." *Handbook of the American Novel of the Twentieth and Twenty-First Centuries*. Ed. Timo Müller. Berlin: De Gruyter Mouton, 2017. 84–97. Print.

———. "Inter-American Studies: Why and Whither?" *FIAR: Forum for Inter-American Research* 7.3 (2014). Web. http://interamerica.de/volume-7-3/raab/.

———. "Introduction: Contested Americas." *New World Colors: Ethnicity, Belonging, and Difference in the Americas*. Ed. Josef Raab. Trier: WVT Wissenschaftlicher Verlag Trier/Tempe, AZ: Bilingual Press, 2014. 1–32. Print.

———. "Symbiose, Hybridisierung und Entgrenzung in der zeitgenössischen mexikanisch-amerikanischen Kultur." *Abgrenzen oder Entgrenzen: Zur Produktivität von Grenzen*. Ed. Markus Bieswanger, Manuela Boatcă, Joachim Grzega, Claudia Neudecker, Stefan Rinke, and Christine Strobl. Frankfurt am Main: IKO-Verlag für Interkulturelle Kommunikation, 2003. 171–195. Print.

———. *The Borderlands of Identity in Mexican American Literature*. Habilitationsschrift. Katholische Universität Eichstätt, 1999. Print.

———. "Thinking Beyond the Nation: The Project of Inter-American Studies." *Cruzando Fronteras en las Américas. Las Dinámicas del Cambio en la Política, la Cultura y los Medios. Fronteras Simbólicas: Cine, Media, Música. Crossing Boundaries in the Americas: Dynamics of Change in Politics, Culture, and Media*. Ed. Yolanda M. Campos García, Margarita Ramos Godínez, and Wilfried Raussert. Guadalajara: Universidad de Guadalajara, 2015. 21–51. Print.

Raussert, Wilfried. "Introduction." *The Routledge Companion to Inter-American Studies*. Ed. Wilfried Raussert. London and New York: Routledge, 2017. 1–12. Print. Routledge Companions to Literature.

———. "Selección de tropos claves en los Estudios Interamericanos: Formas de mirar a las Américas entrelazadas." *Key Tropes in Inter-American Studies: Perspectives from the* forum of inter-american research (fiar). Ed. Wilfried Raussert, Brian Rozema, Yolanda Campos García, and Marius Littschwager. Trier: WVT/Tempe, AZ: Bilingual Press, 2015. 12–24. Print.

———. "Selected Key Tropes in Inter-American Studies: Ways of Looking at Entangled Americas." *Key Tropes in Inter-American Studies: Perspectives from the forum of interamerican research* (fiar). Ed. Wilfried Raussert, Brian Rozema, Yolanda Campos García, and Marius Littschwager. Trier: WVT/Tempe, AZ: Bilingual Press, 2015. 1–11. Print.

Rodriguez, Richard. "Go North, Young Man." *Mother Jones* 1 Jan. 1995. Web. www.motherjones.com/politics/1995/07/go-north-young-man.

Sadowski-Smith, Claudia. "The Centrality of the Canada-U.S. Border for Hemispheric Studies of the Americas." *Key Tropes in Inter-American Studies: Perspectives from the* forum of interamerican research (fiar). Ed. Wilfried Raussert, Brian Rozema, Yolanda Campos García, and Marius Littschwager. Trier: WVT/Tempe, AZ: Bilingual Press, 2015. 161–178. Print.

———. "The Place of the Canada-U.S. Boundary in Border and Inter-American Studies." *The Routledge Companion to Inter-American Studies*. Ed. Wilfried Raussert. London/New York: Routledge. 2017. 106–116. Print.

Schemien, Alexia. *Of Virgins, Curanderas, and Wrestler Saints: Un/Doing Religion in Contemporary Mexican American Literature*. Trier: WVT/Tempe, AZ: Bilingual Press, 2018. Print.

Schimanski, Johan. "Crossing and Reading. Notes Towards a Theory and Method." *Nordlit* 19 (2006): 41–63. Web. 8 Sep. 2010. https://septentrio.uit.no/index.php/nordlit/article/view/1835.

Steyn, Melissa. "Critical Diversity Literacy. Diversity Awareness in 12 South African Organisations." *Being Different Together: Case Studies on Diversity Interven-*

tions in some South African Organisations. Ed. Melissa Steyn. ebw.co: EBW, 2010. 15–42. Web.

Urrea, Luis A. *Into the Beautiful North: A Novel*. New York: Little, Brown and Company, 2009. Print.

———. *The Devil's Highway: A True Story*. New York: Back Bay Books, 2014. Print.

———. *The House of Broken Angels: A Novel*. First Back Bay paperback edition. New York: Back Bay Books/Little Brown and Company, 2018. Print.

Political Organization at the Grass-Roots Level in Oscar Zeta Acosta's *The Revolt of the Cockroach People*

FRANCISCO A. LOMELÍ

When Chicano literature re-emerged during its Renaissance period from 1965 through 1980, it was commonplace to identify works that did not mince words in terms of their message and contentious political content as a result of the social turbulence of the era – i.e. cultural rifts, a strong anti-war sentiment, ethnic demands of vindication, an acute sense of discrimination, and of course a keen awareness of civil rights. The American academy generally viewed such ethnic literature with considerable suspicion and some disdain, oftentimes displaying a cold shoulder of scorn or simply indifference. Chicano writings' working-class origins, cultural nationalist leanings, and barrio-centric texts rubbed the academic establishment the wrong way and, consequently, universities initially were not prepared to deal with such an emerging phenomenon that challenged the canon. Anglo America felt generally immune to ethnic writings, particularly as it related to the low expectations from Chicanos, due in part to racial biases, institutional stuffiness, and socially unaffected conventions. The nation was experiencing an intense ethnic divide of tensions, polarizations, and conflicts couched within what could be called an epidemic of cultural-historical indigestion embedded within a revolutionary and messianic zeal that truly marked a watershed period of unrest and quest for fundamental social change. A mushrooming Civil Rights Movement, consisting mainly of Black, Chicano, and Native American progressive crusades, was unfolding as part of a historical backdrop of rampant discrimination and long-standing social injustices that were wittingly being tested. Works such as Oscar Zeta Acosta's openly political novel, *The Revolt of the Cockroach People* (1973), faithfully reflect the deep-seated turmoil of the late 1960s and early 1970s through metaphor and stark agitprop prose in a graffiti-style narration that mirrors much of the swirling madness and sharp conflicting interests of that era.

Acosta first left an indelible mark with his existentialist fictional autobiography titled *The Autobiography of a Brown Buffalo* (1972) which chronicles the protagonist's identity search as a self-destructive chameleon, who consistently exhibits a sense of self-loathing toward his Mexicanness until reaching a sudden surge of social consciousness at the very end. The transformation, however, is too abrupt to be believable unless we assume the change is only symbolic of things to come. This Chicano classic is created through the lens of gonzo literature (a style of journalism popularized by Hunter S. Thompson in the 1970s[1]), written with the claims of objectivity, including a

1 Upon reading Hunter S. Thompson's article "The Kentucky Derby is Decadent and Depraved" for the *Scanlan's Monthly* in June 1970, Bill Cardoso of *The Boston Globe*

counter-cultural first-person narrator, Brown Buffalo, who tells the story. Much of the intent is to construct a social critique via self-satire (more collective than personal), thanks in great part to sarcasm, exaggeration, and frequent profanity as strategic forms of distraction, which he then continues in his second novel. Confused and often lost in his own excesses of drugs, liquor, and sex, the protagonist endures various self-appointed labels, starting from a beatnik to a Samoan and from there to a buffalo, or anything non-Mexican, but eventually he has an epiphany about his Mexican ancestry which before he had avoided like the plague. The transition from his first novel to the second is relatively seamless with only slight variations on the protagonist situated in a totally different social environment that tests his true commitment to his community. A definite conversion occurs from a state of paranoia in his first novel to discontentment about societal institutions in his countercultural sequel, *The Revolt of the Cockroach People* (1973), an impactful testimonial novel that Joe D. Rodríguez categorizes as a thinly "veiled autobiographical" ("United States" 270) narration that documents where fictional and historical characters easily and deliberately coexist. The narrator, whose nerves are often raw, travels to Los Angeles in search of a story given his aspirations as a writer, thus recounting gripping highlights and lowlights of his involvement in the gestation of a local movement that has various fronts, allowing fiction and reality to teeter or, better yet, oscillate between one and the other.

Although beleaguered as an unreliable narrator in both works (in part because of his embellishments, hyperboles, and carefully orchestrated smokescreens regarding legally sensitive activities), the enigmatic and sometimes misogynistic protagonist in *The Revolt of the Cockroach People*, known now as Zeta Brown, an obvious allusion to the empirical author, makes painstaking efforts to convince the reader of his genuineness, fervor, and social allegiance to a greater cause other than himself despite his intensely egocentric tendencies. His participation in the Chicano Movement in the heart of an urban backdrop (East Los Angeles, California, comprised of nearly 98% Chicanos) at the peak of inter-city political activity between 1969 and 1972 coincides with the various timely issues the Movement was addressing in that era, namely his community's impoverishment, disenfranchisement, and dissatisfaction. As a result, he develops a new mantra with a religious zeal by professing a revolutionary spirit in the name of his people, although in one surprising moment he makes a stunning admission: "Politically, I believe in absolutely nothing" (Acosta, *Cockroach People* 28), which seems to undermine his overt pronouncements and actions. He openly displays a public persona of a steely confidence, yet, when alone with his own thoughts, he continues to be dragged down by an ingrained suppression of doubts and insecurity, as

---

Sunday Magazine vol. 1 (1970) coined the style as "gonzo" in reference to this unique genre of a non-objective journalism with renditions of lived experiences on the basis of the personal and the emotional. The style became epitomized in Thompson's novel *Fear and Loathing in Las Vegas and Other American Stories* (1996). The article was later reprinted in Tom Wolfe's anthology *The New Journalism* in 1973 and Thompson's work *The Great Shark Hunt* in 1979.

evinced so profoundly in Acosta's first novel. As a narrator and rebel of many faces, he repeatedly shares his secret thoughts, irreverence, insolence, hyper-masculinity, and intimate experiences (cf. Lomelí and Urioste 39). In part, he is hounded by a sense of guilt for becoming a "super" activist attorney (almost a rock star among Chicanos in East L.A.), a profession that offers him some material privileges, notoriety, and status which he ultimately despises yet desperately needs to overcome and compensate for an empty private life that ultimately depends too much on pure ego, adrenaline, and testosterone. But his wild impulsive persona of unrelenting drugs and a lascivious desire for sexual encounters while constantly distracted by objectifying women, along with his contradicting convictions, make it clear once again that he needs to address his personal misgivings while living in the present much like a typically anguished existentialist character. When encouraged to take the mantel of a Chicano leader in the struggle for barrio self-determination, he readily hesitates in a revealing self-reflection: "I who have been lost in my own excesses, drowned in my own personal confusion. A faded beatnik, a flower vato [barrio dude], an aspiring writer, a thirty-three-year old kid full of buffalo chips is supposed to defend these bastards? … My knees feel like pillars of smoke blowing out from under me" (Acosta, *Cockroach People* 53).

This self-deprecating confession seems almost out of character compared to the macho self-portrayal throughout the novel. So we find an internal as well as an external dilemma of opposing forces that are on balance within Zeta himself. The reader is driven to ask: who is the real Zeta Brown? The bullish maverick lawyer who masterfully manipulates the court scenes with his histrionics or the insecure and vulnerable activist who huffs and puffs in public in order to compensate for his inner weaknesses and uncertainties? Either way, the protagonist's actions mirror what Oscar Zeta Acosta did in real life by cleverly insulating himself from scrutiny and the potential legal repercussions of his radicalism by insisting that the narration is fiction. Zeta here is often portrayed as larger than life, an action hero for social justice who oozes with confidence one minute followed by retreat and reluctance the next minute. In many ways, he is a slippery character of any culpability because he possesses a slick and cunning demeanor that overpowers those who might want to penetrate the smokescreens he creates around him.

This hard-hitting satire holds back few punches by first and provocatively referring to Chicanos, and any marginalized people – including Vietnamese and other ethnic groups – as "cockroaches" or "cockroach people," "the little beasts that everyone steps on" (Acosta, *Cockroach People* 135), for their uncanny resilience as survivors among those who prefer them to either be invisible or annihilated. Curiously, such a characterization by Acosta both defies the establishment while also rattling Chicanos into a new level of consciousness. Cockroaches are universally understood to represent peskiness, filth, and long life, thus portraying them as the lowest creatures of the animal world, despised, trampled on, and blemished, unmistakably suggesting a high level of undesirability. The analogous epithet or double entendre is striking, even disturbing, but equally effective for its blunt nature, thereby leaving no doubt in its critical stance toward mainstream society's apathetic and condescending as well as dehumanizing view of Chicanos. The use of the term "cockroaches" in the novel becomes a double-edged sword that cuts across a sanitized outlook by a society that ultimately ignored Chicanos in the late 1960s and early 1970s, but it also refers to the common soldier from the Mexican Revolution (1910–1920) who sacrificed everything to pursue real social change. The Revolution's popular anthem song, properly titled "La cucaracha," precisely makes this analogy of the common soldier on the brink of exhaustion, requiring as a last measure marijuana to pass the time when facing imminent death. Again, the depictions are often testy and controversial in nature, accompanied by cockroach drawings in the margins of one out of every ten pages – in the process providing a visual for the reader that goes beyond the abstract.

The action unfolds in the eye of a political storm in East L.A. in which Zeta operates as the rudder who drives the strategies and direction of an emerging social movement, partly echoing the ideology of questioning the mainstream as represented in the Mexican Revolution novel par excellence titled *Los de abajo* (1916) by Mariano Azuela. We soon see his role as the mastermind of a volatile uprising, turning the work into a documentary and testimonial of an urban grass-roots struggle at the same time that we can penetrate a mentality and psyche of a conflicted militant. Rebelliousness and protests become rampant in the streets, calling for fundamental change to an overdue oppression that has stifled the community vis-à-vis the three main guilty sources (what might be considered the diabolical trinity of a prolonged subjugation): the schools, the church, and police in conjunction with the overall environment of politics and representation. In the midst of all this radical activity, oftentimes such action becomes secondary or obscured by Zeta's inflated sense of self. The lawyer narrator then serves as the main filter through which we witness his machinations to guide Chicanos toward organizing a resistance movement against the three aforementioned Anglo American institutions that generally excluded Chicanos from decision-making or from forging their own destiny. The "cockroach people," it is suggested, are apparently unable to overcome institutional obstacles (racism, discrimination, hegemony, etc.) that are so entrenched to block them from any social mobility.

By effectively creating a protest novel through the depiction of ground zero of Chicano discontent, Acosta allows Zeta to move through the various domains in schools, churches, and court rooms, and political circles while providing alternative forms of contestation in order to denounce the way these institutions have shaped and contributed directly to Chicanos' plight. This required leaders who could intelligently channel discontent and even rage into constructive forms of social transformation and historical agency. In that regard, Mr. Buffalo Brown becomes Buffalo Zeta Brown, thus adopting "Zeta" much like a modern Zorro would slash a Z on those who mistreat the poor and vulnerable. Technically speaking, the protagonist is inspired by General Zeta – a source of mimicry – who was the hero of an old movie classic from the Mexican Revolution, appropriately called *La Cucaracha*. He also views himself as a kind of Humphrey Bogart, every man's man who can conquer all with his charm, emphasizing

Joseph Campbell's concept of the "hero with a thousand faces."[2] Curiously, the narrative avoids using real names whenever they might be controversial or possibly guilty, thus shielding them from prosecution and civil liability. Clearly, some of the strident militant companions of Zeta are neither boy nor girl scouts, at times plotting violent actions or throwing bombs, usually orchestrated by our clever but also manipulative protagonist. In the midst of this docu-drama, the protagonist assumes a role of part Robin Hood, part quasi-super hero, and part messiah, but his fear of failure rises as the expectations of him become magnified and heightened. He also likes to model himself after another historical but definitely chameleon figure of filmic fiction, Anthony Quinn, a film star who specialized in portraying virtually any ethnic group from Zorba the Greek to Emiliano Zapata or from Lawrence of Arabia's sidekick to Italian strongmen. In other words, we discover that as convinced as Zeta is of his resolute and unrelenting commitment and consciousness, much of his actions can be reduced to a temporary impulsive act.

At the same time, he tries to team up with the famous rural labor leader of the time, César Chávez, along with the best known urban organizer, Rodolfo "Corky" Gonzales, but the coordination between them is somewhat stifled by the police forces, school administrators, and political obstacles. What could have functioned like a fine-tuned triumvirate for the Chicano Movement for the sake of instilling radical change in Los Angeles shows instead some of the fissures between them because our protagonist is too self-absorbed by his lawyerly rhetorical defenses and exacerbated by his slippage into self-indulgence via immediate gratifications through drugs, sex, and hedonistic sessions. In other words, Zeta is constantly distracted and ultimately unable to overpower his vices and demons – manifestations of his long-standing paranoia and other psychological complexes – as the hubris of his actions. Although social renovation is supposed to be the ultimate objective, he cannot focus sufficiently on such goals for the sake of the collective good.

The narrative is essentially divided into two dimensions or directions between the external and the internal: a series of well-known protests at the height of the Chicano Movement in which Zeta finds himself in the middle as a media savvy defense lawyer but as someone still plagued by his inner turmoil. In his role as central instigator, mobilizer, and part-time trickster, he becomes the axis of the story from whose vantage point we witness the political mobilization and engagement of his community, consequently constructing an in-depth insider's view of radical militancy from the 1960s and 1970s – that was intentionally hidden from the public and especially police and other authorities. He exhibits a gallant exterior with a special knack as an organizer, thanks to his unmatched leadership skills and charisma mixed with aggression and capability of bringing together opposing forces with contrasting interests in order to focus on the main goals at hand. Much of the narration focuses on his exceptional achievements as an attorney and organizer. For example, he first successfully defends the St. Basil

---

2 Consult his famous book, *The Hero with a Thousand Faces* (1949).

Twenty-One, consisting of three priests, two nuns, and 16 young Chicano militants who had disrupted religious services on Christmas Eve in 1967 – a historical event that is dramatized here somewhat like a Greek tragedy – and who are acquitted. Other overt acts of violence on the part of the suspects are glossed over, thanks to Zeta's clever defense by deflecting fault and identifying contradictions in the cross-examinations of witnesses. In another occasion, he defends the Tooner Flats[3] Seven indicted on "charges of arson, firebombing, inciting to riot and conspiracy" (Acosta, *Cockroach People* 209) – another historical happening modified considerably by fictionalizing the barrio where it happened to protect the not-so-innocent by suggesting their response was inspired by self-defense. This parallels the Walkouts of 1968 led by educator Sal Castro when thousands of high school students "spontaneously" walked out of their classes, protesting their inferior educational curriculum in substandard schools in the heavily Chicano section of Los Angeles. The third case involves the East L.A. Thirteen who were arrested for conspiracy, having also protested against the education system by disrupting traditional procedures and were subsequently arrested for contaminating young minds, disturbing the peace, and threatening schools. The last instance is when he solves the mysterious death of Roberto Fernández, a Chicano prisoner who purportedly committed suicide in his cell. He proves that the coroner had essentially covered up important evidence to prove that he had been strangled.

These four cases catapult him into a celebrity status among Chicanos because he seems to be invincible in court due in great part to his verbal ingenuity, rhetorical flair, and oratorical skillfulness. His community sees him as a pied piper, savior, and spokesperson for denouncing police brutality and widespread discrimination while deep inside he considers himself a pretender. He also enquires into the puzzling death of Roland Zanzíbar who was killed by a stray teargas canister in a bar when the Chicano Moratorium against the Vietnam War was unfolding in 1970 – another historical event with an explicit allusion to Rubén Salazar, a highly regarded journalist and martyr who championed Chicano civil rights through mainstream media in the *Los Angeles Times*. However, Zeta was unable to solve the mystery, although his efforts were nonetheless praised, allowing his fame and reputation to grow even more to the point that he gained enough confidence to run for sheriff of Los Angeles county, a post he didn't win.

Near the end of this camouflaged novel, or what Joe D. Rodríguez insists in calling a "legal account" of events between 1969 and 1972 (cf. Rodríguez, "United States"), the events add a touch of an ominous and foreboding overtone. First of all, his past of deep insecurities and personal doubts haunt him at the same time he relishes his new-found fame and notoriety. Zeta's faith in what used to be called the "system" of respected institutions, such as those in legal, educational, political, religious, and economic areas, is tacitly shattered and undercut when he unveils widespread moral corruption that seems to target Chicanos through persistent stereotyping and stigmatization, consequently undermining any possibility of ever having justice serve his peo-

3 Tooner Flats is a fictional barrio that is supposed to represent Garfield High School where the student walkouts actually occurred in 1968.

ple. Through "[s]catological details, ribald remarks, and gallows humor" (Rodríguez, "Oscar Zeta Acosta" 9), the protagonist raises a series of questions about methods, strategies, and approaches to changing society from within through group action or calculated rebellious deeds. Those responsible for acting out in violent ways via fire-bombs, carrying guns, destruction of property, guerrilla tactics, promoting riots, etc. (i.e. Pelón, Frog, Sailor Boy, Lady Feathers, Black Eagle, and Gilbert) are generally protected with pseudonyms or nicknames to protect the potentially guilty, given that the author knew that the Los Angeles Police Department and their detectives sought any shred of evidence of self-incrimination, be it in real documents or literary narratives on what appears described in the novel as the Chicano Liberation Front. Again, fiction and reality paint a fine line of interaction. Therefore, we find the aforementioned institutions on high alert as Chicanos rally to achieve a new kind of liberation and self-realization they had been unable to pursue before, which clearly reflects the Chicano Movement's prescribed ideological aims and aspirations. In that regard, the Movement becomes a central character who hovers throughout the narration while Zeta becomes profoundly disenchanted and disillusioned with capitalism (bringing back memories of his old dropout days chronicled in his first novel, *The Autobiography of a Brown Buffalo*) due to its structured hierarchies and exclusive politics that drive its desire for profit at the expense of human advancement. His idealism for social reform takes a definite hit to the point of not ever quite recovering in the narration, making him realize that perhaps his moral fortitude is not quite up to snuff as required by the extraordinary circumstances that demand an unwavering commitment toward social change. In other words, his hero status is crushed.

As an astute, yet, dissident lawyer, Zeta truly exercises the function of a catalyst and intermediary, although some accuse him of being the mastermind of the three occasions of Chicano rebellion in East L.A. He denies any connection with such actions of spearheading acts of overt violence while biting his tongue. Either way, he stands out as a bridge between those who are filled with rage for their oppressive social condition and those responsible for running the institutions of order, authority, and subjugation. He relishes the role of a go-between, but the lack of fundamental change gnaws at his every action while increasing his frustrations. The choices seem to be irreconcilable: to overthrow or destroy a system or to give in and be coopted by it. He does not appreciate the odds nor the alternatives because his nature is not one so much of a single-minded rebel, but rather more as an instigator as a provocateur, stating: "I was just one of a bunch of Cockroaches that helped start a revolution to burn down the stinking world. And no matter what kind of end this is, I'll still play with matches" (Acosta, *Cockroach People* 257–258). While fiction and history become intertwined in the novel, his dilemmas deeply distress him and make him wonder if it is all worth it, foreshadowing the eventual disappearance of the empirical author in 1974 off the coast of Mazatlán one year after the novel was published.

The novel's anarchistic underpinnings sometimes distract from the seriousness of the protagonist's struggles to balance his militant commitment and his inner trepidations. His spirit of advocacy for those oppressed and colonized is noble but his windmills of idealism easily get derailed by immediate desires, flashbacks of inadequacy, and self-doubts. As an instrument of defense of Chicanos by galvanizing those in greater need, he is indeed masterful but he also recognizes he is a product of his era: he wonders how one individual lawyer can truly instill social change to lessen the insurmountable obstacles a second-class citizenry has to face and resolve. The work raises many questions while suggesting options and alternatives, including best practices, except that a realization quickly emerges: there is no simple manual on how to fundamentally change long-standing structural habits of inequality and limited opportunities within entrenched social mores and unfair economic conditions. Zeta implies that Chicanos have to take their rebelliousness into their hands because they can't count on mainstream society to do it for them. Should violence be exercised? That is a central question that gnaws at Zeta's consciousness while remaining mindful of and torn with César Chávez's non-violent teachings. Although the protagonist does not openly promote violence nor is he totally immune to using it, he seems to accept it as a last resort as long as it is done surreptitiously and strategically given the magnitude of the oppression. In other words, for him the end can justify the means.

But, ultimately, the protagonist does not let the reader trust this strident lawyer completely because he has only learned how to react at the moment because his positions are not defined by a well-articulated ideology nor any premeditated thought process. His impulses are genuine and socially redeeming on the surface, but he does not view himself as part of a liberated future, so it is difficult for him to envision the same for others. He realizes he is too much of an individual – and less so part of a group – and therefore he fundamentally has a hard time grappling with the collective psyche of a grass-roots movement. Zeta certainly enjoys the adrenaline rush spurred by such epic happenings where he feels history is unfolding before his very eyes. In his mind, collective action also has its merits, but he is a realist while conceding that he cannot be everyone's Don Quixote, and perhaps less so in this East L.A. tale of protest and rebelliousness. He cannot live up to those kinds of expectations because he does not profoundly seek liberation due in great part to his weighty sense of self. His authenticity does not let him become anyone else's savior because he is still bewildered by having to exorcise his extensive personal baggage as part and parcel of an unfinished personal project. He acknowledges his talents and verbal dexterities, but it is clear he lives more through fantasies – be they sexual or social – and less so by concrete projections into well-calculated future plans. In other words, he functions best as a catalyst or a conduit but not as an ideologue because he does not really generate new creative ideas. He reacts to immediate circumstances impulsively and decisively, but he does not know how to construct a far-reaching visionary proposal for the future of his people. In sum, he appears proactive on the surface but he does not seek permanency for fundamental social reforms because he obsessively concentrates on the means instead of focusing on a well-defined end.

Acosta's *The Revolt of the Cockroach People* changes thematically from beginning to end, wading through a series of events that give the impression of seeking different forms of justice for the underdog – in this case, the "cockroach people." But, there is considerable substance of intrigue beneath the narrative surface when the narrator-protagonist unveils two parallel stories: an insider's view on the Movement in trying to achieve immediate liberation by promoting a spontaneous revolution for Chicanos within an East L.A. barrio while providing insight into his own individual struggles with who he truly is within an America that has traditionally rejected him and his ethnic cohort. The novel, therefore, develops into a full-blown paradoxical satire – even self-referential – about the difficulties of achieving political gains at the grass-roots due in part to the mixed messages and contradictions. The work outlines the political exigencies involving grass-roots movements of the late 1960s and early 1970s that required renewed strategies for survival and for transforming an intransigent American society and economic system. The protagonist indulges in considerable exhibitionism as a way of achieving social advocacy while also chronicling an inner chaos as part of his own fantasies as well as the zaniness of the period. But, the central question reverts to this: is he indeed the model and champion of a Chicano Movement in need of leaders within the context of the novel? Does he possess the necessary convictions to promote such social reforms or is he a temporary fix? If he is not willing to sacrifice himself (die?) for such a cause and its ideals, might he then be more of a charlatan? In addition, historical allusions and characters impregnate the narration with the objective of chronicling an ambience of extreme tensions and unpredictability.

The central goal evolves into overcoming institutional oppression from the social, religious, economic, political, and especially educational establishments that, according to Zeta, have coordinated and conspired to keep Chicanos in a prescribed social position of inferiority and lack of opportunities. This politically charged countercultural fictional chronicle offers an incisive symbolic representation of finding a viable voice at a time most needed in order to overcome deep-seated oppressive conditions via empowerment and networking that only grass-roots techniques can allow. However, disillusion permeates the narration at the end because Zeta is unable to readily achieve the desired results in the social struggle. First of all, he concludes that the capitalist system is a daunting competitor, forcing minorities to end up with minimal advances, and, second, in a slowly developing irony at the end of the narrative, the protagonist, who is prone to conversions, might not embody the most sustainable and exemplary figure to unleash this movement within a complicated Chicano urban environment. Therefore, his delusions (of grandeur) and complex as a messiah in *The Revolt of the Cockroach People* come tumbling down when he is exposed as a flawed character. In this respect, the novel unveils a dark side of such a movement for the many challenges it faces through its agents of revolutionary actions, realizing that fundamental social change requires a complete multiple-pronged overhaul from the bottom up and from the inside out. If not, it could simply be another failed attempt at partial or temporary gains.

Works cited

Acosta, Oscar Zeta. *The Autobiography of a Brown Buffalo*. San Francisco: Straight Arrow Books, 1972. Print.

——. *The Revolt of the Cockroach People*. San Francisco: Straight Arrow Books, 1973. Print.

Azuela, Mariano. *Los de abajo*. Mexico City: P. Robredo, 1938. Print.

Campbell, Joseph. *The Hero with a Thousand Faces*. New York: Pantheon Books, 1949. Print.

Cardoso, Bill. Editorial. *The Boston Globe* Sunday Magazine. Vol. 1 (1970): n. pag. Print.

Lomelí, Francisco A., and Donaldo W. Urioste. *Chicano Perspectives in Literature: A Critical and Annotated Bibliography*. Albuquerque: Pajarito Publications, 1976. Print.

Rodríguez, Joe D. "Oscar Zeta Acosta (8 April 1935-?)." *Dictionary of Literary Biography: Chicano Writers*. Vol. 82. Detroit: Gale Research, 1989. 3–10. Print.

——. "United States Hispanic Autobiography and Biography: Legend for the Future." *Handbook of Hispanic Cultures in the United States: Literature and Art*. Ed. Francisco A. Lomelí. Houston: Arte Público Press, 1993. 268–290. Print.

Thompson, Hunter S. *Fear and Loathing in Las Vegas and Other American Stories*. New York: Modern Library, 1996. Print.

——. *The Great Shark Hunt*. New York: Summit Books, 1979. Print.

——. "The Kentucky Derby Is Decadent and Depraved." *Scanlan's Monthly* 1/4 (Jun. 1970): 2–12. Print.

Wolfe, Tom. *The New Journalism*. Manhattan: Harper & Row, 1973. Print.

The Politics of Remembering in Carmen Aguirre's *The Refugee Hotel*[1]

GABRIELE PISARZ-RAMIREZ

"It takes courage to remember, it takes courage to forget.
It takes a hero to do both." (Aguirre, *The Refugee Hotel* 18)

The sentences that open Canadian-Latina playwright Carmen Aguirre's play *The Refugee Hotel* emphasize the difficulties of remembering and forgetting both on a personal level and in the public sphere. Nearly 30 years after General Augusto Pinochet seized power in Chile, Aguirre in her comedic drama revisits the history of Chilean exiles who fled in the wake of the September 1973 military coup that overturned the government of Salvador Allende. Written in 2000, *The Refugee Hotel* was produced by Marilo Nuñez and the Alameda Theater Company in Toronto where it premiered at Theatre Passe Muraille in October 2009. It received a nomination for the prestigious Dora Mavor Moore Award, an important Canadian theater prize, for Outstanding New Play in 2010. Set in Vancouver, the play dramatizes the agony, concerns, and survival strategies of a group of Chileans who come to Canada after their escape from the military regime and who are sheltered in a residential hotel. Aguirre explores the individual forms and public politics of remembrance and interrogates the trauma of exile, while her play and its production history also address questions of (in)visibility with respect to the Latina/o community in Canada and within the field of Latino/a and InterAmerican Studies.

Demographically, the Canadian Latino/a population is a relatively small but growing minority of 400,000 to 500,000 people. In the 1970s, when Aguirre came to Canada, the majority of Latin American immigrants to the country came as political refugees and exiles from dictatorships in their home countries. Carmen Aguirre was five years old when she and her parents fled from Chile shortly after the overthrow of president Allende. Her plays[2] foreground experiences of inbetweenness, dislocation, and marginalization in similar ways as texts by border writers from the U.S. Mexican border have done. However, her texts are also shaped by the exilic experience of loss, trauma, and survival, experiences that can only partially be addressed by the paradigms of border studies.

1 I would like to thank Carmen Aguirre for kindly sending me a post-production script of the play and Marilo Nuñez for taking the time to meet me in Toronto in October 2010 and provide me with a video recording of a performance of *The Refugee Hotel.*

2 Aguirre has written and co-written 25 plays, among them *Qué Pasa Con La Raza, Eh* (produced by the Latino Theater Company in Vancouver in 1999), *In a Land Called I Don't Remember* (1995), *Chile con Carne* (1995), *The Trigger* (2008), and *Blue Box* (2012).

In an interview that Carmen Aguirre gave to a Canadian radio station on launching her autobiography *Something Fierce: Memoirs of a Revolutionary Daughter* (2011), she talked about the psychological burden of living as a refugee abroad and working in the *resistencia* and about the toll it took on her family. When Aguirre was 11, her mother took her and her sister from Canada back to South America. While living in Bolivia and Peru, the mother and her partner worked for the underground resistance movement. The family, including the children, had to adhere to rules of secrecy, meaning that most contacts were anonymous and the danger of arrest was always imminent. Aguirre remembers her parents telling her: "If 24 hours pass and we don't come back, call this number and say you're with the Tall One and Raquel. Then hang up. Within an hour someone will knock on the door. Answer it, and then you and (your sister) go with that person" (Aguirre, *Something Fierce* 16). While her sister remained apolitical, Aguirre joined the resistance movement when she was 18, hoping to help reinstall a socialist system in Chile. After the plebiscite in 1988, when Pinochet was denied a further eight-year term in office, and the 1990 elections when Chile officially returned to democracy but Pinochet retained many of his offices, she, like many of her fellow underground activists felt that they had lost their cause. "It is only now, i.e. many years later that people have started to talk about the effects of that on their psyche and on their bodies. A lot of people died quite young … because of the stress of what it was like to be in the resistance and then to have lost and then to have been lost to their own devices" (16).

What Aguirre describes as the 'lost cause' of the Chilean resistance movement may account for the long silence about the psychic and mental burdens carried by those who had left the country in 1973. Aguirre has stated that *The Refugee Hotel* came out of her reaction to two events: the 1998 arrest of Pinochet in London and the 1995 death of her uncle, a Chilean exile, who drank himself to death on Vancouver's skid row (Aguirre, "The Refugee Hotel" n. pag.). Both events are significant in the context of the play: Pinochet's arrest for many exiled Chileans opened a wound that had never been allowed to heal, since Pinochet ruled Chile for 17 years, and even after his arrest was never made fully accountable for his crimes. The victims of his dictatorship who escaped death in Chilean concentration camps suffered the traumatic effects of torture and institutionalized violence without ever being able to completely work through their traumas, given the amnesia and displacement of Pinochet's crimes in Chile.

The play retrospectively tells the story of eight Chilean refugees gathered in a small hotel in Vancouver, from the point of view of one member of the group, Manuelita who was an 8-year-old child upon her arrival in Canada. Manuelita who in the play appears as an *alter ego* of Carmen Aguirre, opens and closes the play that looks back on what happened in the refugee hotel thirty years ago and remembers the first week in the life of the Chileans in Vancouver. Before the actors come onto the stage, she introduces the play's key theme of remembrance speaking the words: "It takes courage to remember, it takes courage to forget, it takes a hero to do both"

(Aguirre, *The Refugee Hotel* 18). These sentences also conclude the play when Manuelita transforms from her child's persona into her adult self in the play's epilogue. *The Refugee Hotel* dramatizes the psychic and mental pain the residents have suffered as a result of displacement, torture, violence, and the loss of their homes, as well as their ways of coping in an environment largely ignorant of their plight.

The members of the group of residents in the hotel are all affected by traumatic memories. Among them are La Flaca, Manuelita's mother, a university teacher who joined the resistance in Chile, got caught and tortured and narrowly escaped death, and her husband, Fat Jorge, a former bank accountant who was largely apolitical until he got arrested by the secret police and broke under torture, giving away information about a colleague. There is Manuel, a 17-year-old student who has been severely tortured in the infamous concentration camp Pinochet established on Dawson Island, and who will later try to commit suicide. There is Isabel, who remains mute throughout most of the play, the loss of her voice signaling her state of shock and her inability to speak about her memories. Other residents include Cristina, a Mapuche Indian whose parents were arrested by the Chilean secret police and "disappeared," never to return, and Juan, a miner and unionist who escaped prison after several months of incarceration. Finally, there are La Flaca's and Fat Jorge's two children, eight-year-old Manuelita and her ten-year-old brother Joselito who were torn from their relatives in Chile and who struggle to understand what has caused their parents to leave their homeland.

The play explores the traumas the characters are suffering as the memories of the coup and its aftermath reemerge in nightmares, flashbacks, and hallucinations. The pathology of trauma, as Cathy Caruth has observed, consists in the structure of its reception: the traumatizing event is assimilated only belatedly, in its repeated *possession* of the one who experiences it. According to Caruth, to be traumatized is to be possessed by an image or an event (Caruth 4–5). This "possession" is particularly evident in Fat Jorge's recurring nightmares in which he relives the days he spent in prison and under torture. In these dreams, he hears the screams, wailing and moaning of the other prisoners, and he remembers conversations with fellow-inmates. Absorbed in their individual recollections, Jorge and his wife La Flaca have difficulties in reestablishing their relationship or even to communicate their experiences to each other. Both need to cope with unspeakable memories, while they also have lost trust in each other. Other characters display different effects of trauma, such as Isabel, who has lost her voice and whose only way of expression is to rock her body rhythmically back and forth. Memories are also embodied in the torture marks some residents carry: La Flaca has scars where her nipples used to be and Manuel's body is covered with burn marks from cigarette stubs. The violence archived in their bodies reminds the characters constantly of their past and their own horrible experiences. When Manuel is examined by a physician upon his arrival, he recalls the various forms of torture he was subjected to:

> Cigarette burns. Blow torches. Electricity. Many blows to the head. Heart failure. Brought back to life. Fingernails pulled out. Raped by men. Raped by dogs. Electricity.

> To the gums. To the eyes. To the tongue. To the anus. To the testicles. Starvation. Dehydration. Hypothermia. Solitary confinement. Many blows to the head. And I'm alive. (Aguirre, *Refugee Hotel* 56)

Only few days after coming to Canada, Manuel decides to end his life by jumping out of a window of the hotel. Before taking this step, he explains: "Is it possible to have lived too long at the age of seventeen? … Enough is enough. Ya basta ya! Basta. My mother used to say, nothing belongs to us, Manuel. Absolutely nothing. Not even our bodies. We come from the dirt and when we die we go back to the dirt" (76).

Aguirre's play does not only address the effects of torture on the refugees but also the disorientation and uncertainty the residents feel as exiles in Canada. Feelings of guilt over leaving Chile and their responsibility towards those who stayed back dominate many dialogues in the play. For some of the characters, the question if leaving the country was a form of treason looms large. In a crucial scene, two of the exiles struggle openly with their feelings of anger, guilt, and fear, accusing each other of cowardliness. Cristina, the Mapuche woman who recalls how her parents were taken away by the secret police, points to the specific marginal situation of her community in Chile. In her eyes, the Mapuche have always needed courage to survive in Chile, whereas other Chileans were cowards because they did not interfere when their immediate neighbors were arrested:

> CRISTINA: I've come to the conclusion that our country is a country of cowards – … They just sat and watched my parents being taken away, nobody helped, they just sat and watched like they were watching TV.
> JOSELITO: (CONFUSED) TV?
> CRISTINA: My parents. They took them away and the neighbours, all of them, the very ones that saw me being born just sat and watched. I was at the craft market, trying to sell some pottery, that's all –. (Aguirre, *Refugee Hotel* 72)

While for Cristina the arrest of her parents was another incident in the long history of oppression and displacement the Mapuche community in Chile has suffered, Fat Jorge in her eyes has led a life of privilege. Indeed, Jorge was never involved in any political activity until he was arrested while working at the bank by police who were looking for his colleague. Forced into exile by accident, he has just recently become radicalized and calls for action in an appeal to the other refugees:

> FAT JORGE: I refuse to believe that Chile's done for. I refuse, I don't care if I have to go sneak back in tomorrow, I don't care about the fucking blacklist –
> CALLADITA KEEPS ROCKING.
> FLACA: (GETTING UP) Fat Jorge, you're drunk.
> FAT JORGE: I see it clearly now! Thank you, comrade Cristina, for the clarity! I see it so well! Here we are, in a hotel, a HOTEL – that's just too fucking ironic – in a goddamn hotel, in the heart of the monster, as refugees, REFUGEES, do you hear me? Since when do refugees stay in hotels and watch TV and learn English? I see it now! This is all a set up! That's what it is! Exiles, my ass. If we had balls, we'd be there, we'd be living in the underground, helping out. I'm leaving. Come on! Get up! All of you! You too, comrade Bill! We're leaving this place right now! (73)

Fat Jorge lacks the resilience and conviction of his wife La Flaca; when under torture, he gave away information about his colleague, leading to the man's arrest. He tries to compensate his feelings of guilt by blaming Cristina of a lack of moral courage and by pleading with the others to return to Chile and take action:

> FAT JORGE: I can't stay here, Flaquita. I can't. Everything smells the same here. They spray everything.
> (TO CRISTINA): And you! You call our people cowards? What about you? If you're so goddamn brave, then why did you leave? Why?
> CRISTINA: They killed my parents.
> FAT JORGE: So you leave? Just like that?
> CRISTINA: No! Not just like that!
> FLACA: Fat Jorge, don't.
> FAT JORGE: Why didn't you stay and join the underground?

Cristina's reply highlights the gulf that separates their experiences as well as their racial and social positions:

> CRISTINA: You white ass fuck! You live your cushy life in downtown Santiago and now all of a sudden 'cause you found out there's a fence that divides the rich from the poor, now all of a sudden 'cause you decided to jump to the side of the fence that the rest of us have always been on, now all of a sudden you can look me in the eye with no shame whatsoever and ask me why I love life so much that I decided to live it?! Fuck you.
> FAT JORGE: Answer the question.
> FLACA: Leave her alone, Fat Jorge. Can't you see she's a kid?
> CRISTINA: (TO FAT JORGE) 'Cause I'm scared. Okay? You satisfied now? 'Cause I'm so scared that I haven't slept or eaten for months and I was afraid of myself. Afraid of what I might do. I was afraid of turning into a traitor. From sheer fear. So when I saw the opportunity to run, I ran, okay? Satisfied? Now, you may know a little bit about fear, comrade. But I know a lot about it. I am a Mapuche. We've lived in fear for four hundred and fifty years. And I've seen what fear can do. It can turn you into a traitor or into a hero.
>
> …
> FAT JORGE: She's not a traitor. But I am, Flaquita. I am. I'm here when I could be there. Oh, my God. (RUNNING HELPLESSLY AROUND THE ROOM) I'm stuck here. I'm stuck here. I'm stuck here …. (75)

The scene foregrounds the characters' confusion about their role in Canada and their uneasiness about staying in a refugee hotel while their friends and relatives back home are being tortured and killed. It also posits different positions against each other – Cristina's, whose people have developed resistance strategies over centuries because the Mapuche were persecuted from the colonial era onwards, and Fat Jorge's, who only recently discovered his political consciousness.

In another scene, the play stages the children's disorientation: Manuelita and Joselito consider leaving the hotel and traveling back to Chile in search for their grandmother and away from their parents whom they suspect to be criminals. They are shown to have partially internalized the ideological doctrine of the regime: Joselito, convinced that his parents are "crazy" and "communists" (Aguirre, *Refugee Hotel* 95) because otherwise they would not have ended up in jail, argues that "[g]ood people don't leave their kids behind just like that. With no word" (95).

Aguirre's play is driven as much by the project of uncovering the personal stories of trauma that have been left untold by Chilean exiles in Canada as by the larger endeavor to break the long silence concerning the 17 years of Pinochet's rule. The play presents a representational site to approximate an unrepresentable reality in a context – democratic Canada – that is largely oblivious to the historical reality of September 11, 1973 and to the experiences of Chilean exiles, with grave human consequences. The silenced histories that Aguirre privileges in her play can be read as communal trauma narratives about a forgotten and thus ghostly period in the history of the Americas.

In her study *Where Memory Dwells*, Macarena Gómez-Barris has extensively written on the cultural productions emerging from the national trauma created by the coup in Chile. As she takes the reader on a journey through what she calls "the complex memoryscape of terror" (Gómez-Barris 72), she points to the evacuation of stories and details about the dictatorship from the public sphere in Chile, an absence that has accounted for the haunting character and the ghostliness of these stories and details. The works of artists and writers, as Gómez-Barris argues, have been a major site of "socially breaking through and witnessing the hegemony of public silence, concealment, or the flattening of the complex subjectivities of loss and survival" (106). If we contextualize *The Refugee Hotel* in the body of texts that do this work of remembering, we are made aware that the amnesia and the silencing of violence in the coup's aftermath was not only true for Chile but also for most other countries, including Canada.[3] The play's survivor characters bring the history of the coup to the Canadian public in all its tragedy and disastrous mental impacts.

Aguirre recalls that when she came to Canada in the 1970s, she was largely unable to share her experiences with her new classmates because nobody could even remotely imagine the reality that she had escaped from: "We learned never to talk about what was happening in Chile. From the moment when I told some classmates very matter-of-factly in grade two that my stepfather and some of my family members had just come out of a concentration camp that was the national soccer stadium, I was Crazy Carmen" (Gallant n. pag.). The ignorance in Canada about what happened in Chile in 1973 echoes the historical amnesia in Chile itself where governments after the end of the dictatorship were ready to "move on" quickly without attempting to deal with the

3 There was a significant difference in the way this period in Chilean history was represented in the former "Eastern bloc" countries many of which solidarized with the Allende government and its socialist goals. To give an example, in the former German Democratic Republic the atrocities of the Pinochet junta were highly publicized and widely discussed in the media. While the media coverage of the events in Chile was clearly driven by an ideological agenda that supported leftist governments worldwide, "Eastern bloc" countries, like many Western democracies, also offered asylum to numerous political refugees.

atrocities of the past and the violence perpetrated by the Pinochet regime. Significantly, it took Aguirre nine years to be able to put the play on stage in Canada, as she found it extremely difficult to get theater companies interested in a topic that for Canadians seemed far too remote. The forced preemptive closure on the past of the Chilean Pinochet dictatorship gave added significance to the play that, when it was staged in 2009, provoked highly emotional reactions among Latino/a audiences, especially from Chilean exiles. As producer Marilo Nuñez recalls, audience members gave their own testimonies, describing their own encounters with state violence and torture, as well as their ways of survival: "The response to the show was unbelievable. People would come up to me, hug me tightly, crying, sobbing, couldn't speak … the way that this play made people feel … was kind of cathartic … ("Making The Refugee Hotel Part 10" n. pag.).

The play and its production implicitly also interrogated Canada's self-image as a benevolent player in global affairs. Montreal activist Yves Engler in *The Black Book of Canadian Foreign Policy* has observed that the then Canadian president Pierre Trudeau was quick to politically recognize General Pinochet's coup regime when it seized power on September 11, 1973, after a period of diplomatically isolating and financially boycotting the democratically elected Allende government:

> In 1964, Eduardo Frei defeated openly Marxist candidate Salvador Allende in Chile's presidential elections. Worried about growing support for socialism, Ottawa gave 8.6 million to Frei's Chile, its first aid to a South American country. When Allende won the next election Canadian assistance disappeared …. In 1972 Ottawa joined Washington in voting to cut off all money from the IMF to the Chilean government. When Allende was first elected all Western banks, including Canada's withdrew from Chile … Allende invited Pierre Trudeau to visit Santiago. Ottawa refused "for fear of alienating rightist elements in Chile and elsewhere" …. Within three weeks of the coup, Canada recognized Pinochet's military junta. (Engler 99)

While Canada did offer asylum to thousands of Chileans who fled the Pinochet dictatorship, at the same time it provided massive economic assistance to the regime. Just after the coup, Canada "voted for a US$ 22 million interAmerican Development Bank loan" and "endorsed sending 95 million from the IMF to Chile and supported renegotiating the country's debt held by the Paris Club" (Engler 100). While the play stages the support given to the refugees by Canadians, it also makes clear that this help came largely from Canadian human rights organizations and individuals who sympathized either with the refugees' situation as exiles from their country or with their political views.

The Refugee Hotel does not only foreground the agony and suffering the exiled Chileans live through in their first week in Canada, it also shows how they develop strategies of survival. The characters in the play mainly do so by employing humor, by stressing their community bonds and by reasserting cultural traditions. *The Refugee Hotel* is a comedic drama, although the humor is a somber one. The play contains several episodes that stage absurd situations, as when Fat Jorge attempts to talk to the coke machine in the hotel's foyer to get a soft drink, or when Pat Keleman, the social worker who takes the refugees to the hotel, tries to explain to Jorge and Flaca in a hilarious mixture of French and rudimentary Spanish where they are and that they do not have to pay for lodging. A few scenes later, when Manuel tries to commit suicide by jumping out of a third story window he is unaware that beneath the window a huge garbage container full of pink cotton fibers will abate the impact. The others who have watched him fly by their windows and witness his miraculous survival start calling him Condor Passes, an allusion to the famous Andean song "El Condor Pasa." At the same time that Manuel jumps out of the window, fellow refugee Cristina pushes her head into an oven in her room, hoping to die from asphyxiation:

> FAT JORGE WALKS RIGHT INTO THE ROOM. EVERYONE FOLLOWS. THEY SEE CRISTINA WITH HER HEAD IN THE OVEN, SURROUNDED BY SMOKE.
>
> FAT JORGE: Holy shit.
> THEY RUN TO HER AND PULL HER OUT. HER HAIR IS BURNT. HER FACE IS BLACK.
> FAT JORGE: Woman! If you're gonna commit suicide like that, as least make sure it's a gas oven!
> JOSELITO: Yeah! This is electric!
> MANUELITA: Your hair's burnt.
> JOSELITO: And your face is all black!
> FLACA: Would everybody just shut up and take pity on the poor girl?
> CRISTINA: Shit. This is an electric oven?
> FLACA: Yeah.
> CRISTINA: How the hell was I supposed to know that?
> ...
> FAT JORGE: Hey! We'll have to call you Condor Passes! Flying by our window like that like the King of the Andes. And you! Wanting to bake your head like that! We'll just have to call you Cakehead! (Aguirre, *Refugee Hotel* 79–80)

Humor serves as a form of relief from the memory of terror, an escape from trauma and a way to build community with others. As Freud has shown in *Wit and Its Relation to the Unconscious*, there is a connection between 'wit' and unconscious passions and fears. Freud's interpretation of humor as an expression of suppressed thoughts and feelings elucidates how humor can be seen as a way to express what cannot be said otherwise. Since wit uses many of the same strategies as dreams do in order to interpret reality and turn it on its head, it can be subversive in a similar way and allows for the representation of the unspeakable.

Cultural traditions and their preservation also prove enormously significant in the process of remembering and healing. One of the tropes that reemerge in the play is dance and especially the figure of the sole *cueca* dancer that is visible only to some of the characters. The *cueca*, a traditional folkloric dance, is usually interpreted as a courting ritual. The dance is generally associated with rural culture, and particularly with the culture of the *huaso*, the Chilean version of the Argentinian gaucho or the U.S. American cowboy. Pinochet tried to turn the *cueca* into a national dance in the late 1970s, making it part of military parades, while persecuting and prohibiting other forms of popular music such as Andean flute music that had served as a major source of inspiration for the leftist *Nueva Canción* movement. While previously *cueca* had celebrated love, laughter, and country life, under Pinochet and military rule it came to be an emblem of his dictatorship. The *Cueca Sola* emerged among the wives of political prisoners and families of the disappeared as a symbolic gesture of resistance against Pinochet. It was danced alone by women in city centers and town commons, evoking the spirit of those who were missing, who had been detained and never returned. The *Cueca Sola* thus served as a haunting form of remembrance and an assertion of the disappeared's presence not only in the memory of their loved ones, but in public memory. The sole cueca dancer, a *huaso* in traditional dress, emerges at the play's beginning and does his *zapateos*. As the audience cannot see his face in the dim lighting and a hat conceals his face, the figure conveys a sense of ghostliness. He reappears in several scenes where La Flaca and Fat Jorge try to reestablish their relationship, and in a scene in which Cristina and Manuel are shown to discover the attraction they have for each other. The *cueca* dancer is also a symbol of cultural survival, a piece of popular culture that the refugees have brought from Chile and preserve in Canada, something that they have reappropriated from the dictator's grasp. In one scene of the play the *cueca* dancer hands Fat Jorge a record of Inti-Illimani, a popular music group that had emerged from the song movement *Nueva Canción Chilena* and that was strongly associated with the resistance to Pinochet. Inti-Illimani, who were on tour abroad at the time of the coup, continued to develop their careers in exile and supported the resistance movement with their songs. The play's *cueca* dancer handing Jorge the record thus links the *cueca* to the celebration of a resistant musical tradition.

Community is of key importance for the refugees. At the play's beginning, even the members of the family – Flaca, Fat Jorge, and their two children – find it hard to communicate with each other. The others also seem utterly lost in an environment that they barely understand and that has very little knowledge of their situation. As the play progresses, though, both the similarity of their experiences and their common cultural memories of Chile enable at least some of the group's members to slowly establish or re-establish emotional connections of love and trust with each other. It is this trust that causes Isabel (whom the others have affectionally started calling "Calladita" [little silent one]) to regain the capacity of speech towards the end of the play. By sharing stories and by listening to Chilean music and dancing, the refugees start a gradual process of healing. Moreover, the play also suggests that the story of the Chilean refugees is part of a larger story of exile, migrancy, and marginality that unites many Canadians. The gay receptionist of the hotel who in the beginning is completely indifferent to their situation, in the course of the play develops genuine empathy and interest in their lives. As they prepare to leave the hotel for more permanent lodgings he reaches out to them, giving Fat Jorge his record player and offering Cristina a job in the hotel. Pat Keleman, the social worker who brings the refugees to the hotel is the daughter of Hungarian refugees and her memory of her own story of exile enables her to relate to them emotionally and to provide not only practical help but human warmth.

The play's end once again points to the fragile balance the refugees have struggled to regain in Canada as Manuelita (now again looking back as an adult) tells the audience in the epilogue what has become of each of them over the course of the past thirty years. Some of the former residents of the hotel have succeeded in making a life for themselves in Canada while continuing the work of remembering, like Isabel (Calladita) who now runs a successful bakery where she sells gingerbread houses "depicting real-life experiences, such as people attempting suicide by sticking their heads in electric ovens" (Aguirre, *Refugee Hotel* 125). Others did not escape the long-term consequences of the abuse and torture they suffered, like Manuel who died from a brain aneurism when "all those blows to the head finally caught up with him" (125), or Fat Jorge who died a homeless alcoholic. The refugee hotel becomes a place of remembrance itself as the receptionist "filled a wall with photographs" of the many refugees who followed the Chileans there, "[f]rom Guatemala, El Salvador, Vietnam, Iran, Ethiopia, Somalia, Yugoslavia, Colombia, Iraq ..." (126). The play thus offers a point of reference to many social groups in Canada who look back on experiences of exile and dislocation and who have fled from a multitude of terror-ridden places.

When director Marilo Nuñez set out to put the play on stage in Toronto, she soon realized there was no company in the city that was able to promote Canadian Latino/a theatre. At a reading of the play where Nuñez participated, it turned out that the cast was predominantly non-Latino because the organizers could not find a sufficient number of professional Latino/a actors who were qualified to do the job. This eventually brought Nuñez to found the Alameda Theater Company in 2006, the first Latino-Canadian theater company in Toronto. Alameda Theater Company called itself "an avenue for Latin voices" (Alameda Theater Company), and strove to establish itself as a network of professional Latin Canadian theatre artists in Canada. The company over eight years created visibility for Canadian Latino/as and developed the new work of Canadian Latin American playwrights, similar to the Latino Theater Group in Vancouver, that was founded by Carmen Aguirre in 1994 and that consisted of nonprofessional actors. Both companies have provided Canadian Latin American artists with the chance to produce plays such as Aguirre's *Chile con Carne* and *The Refugee Hotel* which bring the histories of the various Americas together in the stories of their exilic people. *The Refugee Hotel* as staged by Alameda Theater Company was a truly inter-American event – actors from various Latin American countries enacted a story of trauma and survival, unearthing memories that not only Chileans but many other Latin Americans can relate to.

While the issues of political violence and trauma link the play with much of Latin American writing, *The Refugee Hotel* also resonates with questions that are relevant in Latino/a artistic productions in the U.S., especially as it foregrounds immigrant experiences of disorientation and marginalization. Although *The Refugee Hotel* obviously does not fit many of the paradigms of border theory, it invites a dialogue between Latin Americans in Chile and elsewhere, Latinos/as in the United States, and Latinos/as in Canada. So far, Canada has been largely ignored in Latino/a Studies as well as in interAmerican discourses in the United States. The majority of critical Latino/a Studies have focused on the border region between the U.S. and Mexico, rarely considering the other border that links the U.S. with its northern neighbor. However, plays such as *The Refugee Hotel* point to the necessity of incorporating Latino/a Canada as a space of inquiry into Latino/a and hemispheric studies to enable broader discussions about Latino/a culture on the continent. It is a conversation that is sorely needed to gain a more comprehensive view on border and hemispheric issues in the various parts of the Americas.

Works cited

Aguirre, Carmen. *Chile con Carne and Other Early Works*. Toronto: Talon Books, 2019. Print.

———. *Something Fierce: Memoirs of a Revolutionary Daughter.* Vancouver: Douglass and McIntyre, 2011. Print.

———. "The Refugee Hotel." N.d. Web. http://talonbooks.com/books/the-refugee-hotel.

———. *The Refugee Hotel*. Toronto: Talon Books, 2010. Print.

Alameda Theater Company. An Avenue for Latin Voices. Web. N.d. https://web.archive.org/web/20141008030924/http://www.alamedatheatre.com/.

Caruth, Cathy, "Introduction." *Trauma: Explorations in Memory*. Ed. Cathy Caruth. Baltimore: Johns Hopkins UP, 1995. 3–12. Print.

Engler, Yves. *The Black Book of Canadian Foreign Policy.* Black Point (Nova Scotia): Fernwood Publishing Co., 2009. Print.

Gallant, Paul. "Ghosts of Revolutions Past. Carmen Aguirre's New Play, The Refugee Hotel, Peers into Personal and Shared Refugee Experiences." N.d. Web. http://www.eyeweekly.com/theatre/article/71191.

Gómez-Barris, Macarena. *Where Memory Dwells. Culture and State Violence in Chile.* Berkeley: U of California P, 2009. Print.

"Making The Refugee Hotel Part 10." Oct. 2009. Web. http://www.youtube.com/watch?v=VwS90j8hKNM.26.

Silence and Voice in Villanueva's *Scene from the Movie GIANT*

JULIANA FILLIES TESTA MUÑOZ

The poetic imagination is as persistent as a cactus flower.
– Cordelia Candelaria (xi)

Introduction

Tino Villanueva can be considered one of the most important – if not the most significant – Chicano poets of our time. His work is internationally acclaimed by critics in the field and is now part of various anthologies. In addition, Villanueva received the American Book Award in 1994 for the poetic collection *Scene from the Movie GIANT* [Escena de la película GIGANTE]. To date, he has published a total of five poetry books, written in English and Spanish: *Hay otra voz: Poems* (1972); *Shaking off the Dark* (1984); *Crónica de mis años peores* [Chronicle of My Worst Years] (1987); *Escena de la película GIGANTE* [Scene from the Movie GIANT] (1993); *So Spoke Penelope* (2013) (Heide 91; Miguélez 237).

Villanueva's poetry is characterized by being intimate and personal. However, it does not only express the poet's sincere feelings but also reflects the anguish experienced by the Chicano community, which represents a minority in the United States and is often cornered into anonymity. It is, therefore, a radical poetry that wants to give visibility to the marginalization endured by Mexican Americans. The hypothesis that the present work raises is that, in *Scene from the Movie GIANT*, Villanueva is gradually breaking the silences imposed by Anglo-Saxon society on the Chicano subject. In this process, he insistently draws on his memories of the movie *Giant*. Since voice, silence, and memory are central components in Villanueva's poetry, we will employ in our analysis the conclusions reached by the scholars Juan Bruce-Novoa, Maher A. Mahdi, and Julián Olivares on these concepts. In addition, we will draw on the idea of memory proposed by Walter Benjamin. These theories contribute to a better understanding of the growth process of the voice in *Scene from the Movie GIANT*, which this study has the purpose of analyzing.

Tino Villanueva

Born in 1941 in the college town of San Marcos, Texas, Villanueva endured great difficulties during his childhood and adolescence. The son of Mexican immigrants who worked in the fields, Villanueva faced poverty and heavy work on the cotton farms in this hot and humid region of the state. In addition, he suffered racism and hostility from Anglo-Americans towards Mexicans and Mexican Americans. This experience marked him deeply and is evident throughout his work. However, despite all the difficulties, Villanueva finished high school. After working four years in a furniture factory, he decided to enroll in the military, serving from 1964 and 1966 as a supply clerk on the Panama Canal. This is a significant experience in the poet's life since, through contact with fellow Panamanians, he was exposed for the first time to poetry written in Spanish. At the age of 24, Villanueva had returned to his hometown in Texas and was admitted to South West Texas State University, where he found his true vocation: poetry. During the following years, the young poet took classes in Hispanic and North American poetry and discovered in the works of Dylan Thomas a source of inspiration for his writing. His first poetic work entitled *Hay otra voz: Poems* was published in 1968 (Pérez, "Tino" 527–528). The title, a mixture of Spanish and English, emphasizes the characteristic bilingualism of Chicano works. However, the true importance of the title lies in the affirmation that there is another voice, which has been silenced but needs to be heard. Giving voice to this discriminated, excluded, and forgotten group is Villanueva's main objective in all his poetic work, and this overarching theme continues in *Scene from the Movie GIANT.*

Silence, voice, and memory

The presence of the silence-voice dichotomy in Villanueva's poetry has been noticed by various critics.[1] Juan Bruce-Novoa makes the following observation:

> he himself, his people, and humankind in general struggle to break their silence and express their particular reality. Silence essentially characterizes life's victims, while sound pertains to the oppressors. Human silence searches for expression, yet must not become empty sound, noise. Time, death, and silence in constant conflict form the dynamic of this poetry, the voice of which is faithful to the silent essence of life's victims with whom the poet identifies. Finding a voice of silence he makes it his own. (Bruce-Novoa 131)

The desire, as well as the difficulty, of breaking the silence and of manifesting one's reality is presented here as a particularity of the human condition. However, a central difference separates those who have power from those who do not. While the oppressors have the privilege of expressing their opinions, the victims are destined to live in silence. Through his poetry, Villanueva resists this dynamic by making the voice of the oppressed his own voice. Even when he talks about his most intimate experiences, as in the case of the poetry book that we will analyze below, the poetic "I" expresses a collective anguish. The young Villanueva who articulates his grief and cries out for justice in *Scene from the Movie GIANT* could be any other Chicano teenager in any movie theater in the country. For Bruce-Novoa, Villanueva's poetry is, therefore, "unspoken silence," a language that becomes ritual for his people and in which they can

---

1 Cf. Bruce-Novoa; Mahdi; Olivares; Pérez-Torres; Stock.

recognize themselves and feel represented (149). Although collective, that voice is not polyphonic, but articulates the common yearnings of an entire community; aspirations of justice, equality, and respect.

The idea of a break in silence in Villanueva's poetry has also been elaborated by Maher A. Mahdi. According to the scholar, the poet acknowledges that the Chicano people have been marginalized and silenced for several years and, therefore, makes his poetry a mechanism to articulate the voice of his community (114). Mahdi states that the poet expresses the Chicano silence "simply through the depiction of the presence of this silence" (114). This aspect is evident in the poems that compose *Scene from the Movie GIANT*, since Villanueva insists here on portraying the silence that invades and takes over the adolescent in the cinema, immobilizing and oppressing him. A silence that results as a reaction to the voice articulated by the oppressor, in this case, a fictional character from the movie *Giant*. However, Mahdi highlights that, more than simply identifying with the oppression suffered by the Chicano people, Villanueva instrumentalizes his poetry in search of social transformation. The author highlights that the poet composes his poems in order to destabilize the status quo and break the hegemonic division. The awareness of the social inequality existing in the society in which he lives, makes Villanueva transform the silence expressed in his poems into a "subversive political act" (114). Mahdi, therefore, emphasizes the importance of Villanueva's work in claiming a space that has been denied to the Chicano community.

Finally, Julián Olivares also emphasizes that the silence imposed on the Chicano people "is tantamount to death-in-life," since it relegates the Mexican American to anonymity, preventing him from affirming his existence (98). If we start, therefore, from the premise that silence is the equivalent of death, we can assume that voice would be analogous to life. Following that equation, we could propose that Villanueva gives life to the Chicano subject by breaking the silence imposed by their oppressors. His poetry would, therefore, be a vindication of the recognition of the existence and voice of the Mexican Americans. In sum, we can conclude with Olivares that Villanueva's poetic work is a moral gesture, "it is a committed poetry; it is a 'literature engageé' in which we often note the voice of wrath" (103). Thus, it is a poetry of protest, which demands justice. That voice of resentment and anger is also present in *Scene from the Movie GIANT*.

Furthermore, it is of primary importance that we briefly present the concept of memory proposed by Walter Benjamin, since it is through the recovery of memory that Villanueva builds his poems and gives space for his voice to grow and find expression. Benjamin defines "memory" as follows: "Memory is not an instrument for exploring the past, but rather a medium. It is the medium of that which is experienced, just as the earth is the medium in which ancient cities lie buried" (576). Benjamin uses the image of the earth to create an analogy. In the same way that the archaeologist works the earth intending of finding old objects, those who look for their own buried past must act like a man who excavates. Digging without fear, the investigator comes across loose images that appear to him as in a "gallery" (576). For Benjamin, more important than the content of the memory itself is the awareness of the moment in which this memory was born:

> In this sense, for authentic memories, it is far less important that the investigator report on them than that he mark, quite precisely, the site where he gained possession of them. Epic and rhapsodic in the strictest sense, genuine memory must therefore yield an image of the person who remembers, in the same way a good archaeological report not only informs us about the strata from which its findings originate, but also gives an account of the strata which first had to be broken through. (576)

Benjamin claims that memory says something about that individual who remembers. The memory, embodied in *Scene from the Movie GIANT*, exposes not only something about Villanueva's past, but it also states something about his present. Poet and memory are, in a sense, one. Villanueva is a product of what he has experienced in the past, which also includes the traumatic experiences of racial exclusion. This idea is key to the present work since we start from the premise that all of Villanueva's poetry was born from the work of "excavation" of memory carried out by the poet. Like an archaeologist who carefully works the land, Villanueva repeatedly returns to his memories to articulate, in his poetry, what is most intimate of his being.

The collection

Scene from the Movie GIANT is a collection of 19 poems, published in 1993. Narrating from different perspectives, the lyrical "I" gradually reconstructs a specific scene from the movie *Giant* (1956) by filmmaker George Stevens. In this scene, Bick Benedict (Rock Hudson), a Texan rancher, fights with Sarge (Mickey Simpson), the racist owner of a small restaurant, after witnessing how Sarge discriminates against a Mexican family by refusing to serve them. The poems in that collection speak about how the 14-year old Villanueva feels when he sees this scene in the cinema. They portray the painful, scarring, and transforming experience in which he assimilates himself and his history in the Mexican family that, without a voice, is expelled from the establishment. The narrative voice is that of the adult who learned to express in words the feelings that he did not know how to exteriorize, or was not able to pronounce when he first saw the movie. It is a resentful, but empowered voice that grows gradually throughout the poems. When interviewed by Robert Lee, Villanueva reflects on the reason that leads him to write years later about this scene. The poet makes the following statement:

> I wanted to give that inarticulate boy of fourteen a voice. The boy who went to see the movie that day was overwhelmed by the next-to-the-last scene that showed people who looked like him being shoved around for the simple fact of being Mexican American and for the simple act of wanting to dine at a roadside café in 1950 in rural Texas. It had unsettled him … reminded him of his social and racial standing in his home state. (Lee 178)

The memory is recovered and placed at the service of poetry that seeks to do justice to this child who was lost, helpless, and discriminated against. Recognizing oneself in the Mexican family projected on the screen can be considered a significant moment in the poet's personal and intellectual career. These are the moments that will serve as inspiration in the future when Villanueva begins poetizing the difficulties and prejudices suffered by the Mexican American people.

However, the collection does not focus only on the description of the scene and the teenager's feeling of helplessness. The poems also portray the adolescent's growth and development into a poet, whose role is to name this sentiment, while expressing his indignation and criticism towards racism by people like Sarge. As Rafael Pérez-Torres aptly observes, "the poem offers a vision of the poet rising majestically above adversity as a giant finally able to speak" (163).

Scene from the Movie GIANT is divided into five parts that are preceded by an introductory poem bearing the same title as the collection. Like all other poems, this one is also written in free verse. According to Rafael Cabaña Alamán, the "free verses … justify the strength of the poetic and restless voice that composes them, to reaffirm the writer's own identity" [versos libres … justifican la fuerza de la voz poética e inquieta que los compone, para reafirmar la propia identidad del escritor] (13). Villanueva pauses where the reader would not normally do so, forcing him to stop and think about each image that the poet draws on the paper.

The introductory poem, "Scene from the Movie GIANT," is very expressive in images and has the function of contextualizing the poems that will follow. It introduces the base theme that gives life to the collection of poems (the scene from the film) and reveals the poet's motivation in dealing with that theme. In this first poem the lyrical "I" starts by making the following statement:

> What I have from 1956 is one instant at the Holiday
> Theater, where a small dimension of a film, as in
> A dream, became the feature of the whole. It
> Comes towards the end … the café scene. (Villanueva, *Scene* 18)

The act of viewing this scene, which becomes the most emblematic of this film for Villanueva, is presented as "the instant" that has been etched in his memory out of so many moments lived that year. The poet emphasizes the impact that this experience has on him. From the first verse, it becomes clear to the reader that the poems to come will thematize something rescued from memory, something that Villanueva carries with him from a distant past. Although the memory of this scene is presented as something very real, it also emerges to him like a dream. The poet feels trapped and is determined to fight against these images, seeking to give expression to this feeling that has haunted him since his youth. The writing process is an arduous healing process in which the poet conquers his space and his voice with each word placed on the paper.

Already in this first poem, "Scene from the Movie GIANT," silence emerges as a powerful entity capable of taking over the entire space and scene:

> Juana, from barely inside the door, and Sarge,
> Stout and unpleased from behind his counter, clash
> Eye-to-eye, as time stands like heat. Silence is
> Everywhere, acquiring the name of hatred …. (Villanueva, *Scene* 18)

The silence that hangs in the air between the innocent eyes of Juana and the voracious eyes of Sarge, is portrayed as a destructive force. Identified as "hatred," the silence consumes the environment and leaves its devastating trace on the characters. It is a silence that, *de facto*, has a voice that expresses racism and attacks Juana. In this scene, therefore, the absence of words is perceived by the poet as an act of violence that immobilizes the character who "cannot bear the dread" and, in turn, terrifies the young Villanueva who sees himself attacked in the cinema hall by that same agonizing silence (*Scene* 18). The distressing experience "locks" him in the armchair of the theater and makes him recognize his insignificance and helplessness in the face of Sarge's discrimination. This is the driving force that leads him to break the silence and to give life to the poetic "I" that questions whether "[he] can ever live enough to tell/The after-tale" (20).

The first part of the collection consists of five poems. In these, the characters are introduced in a dualistic form. While Sarge and the waitress represent evil, Juana and the Mexican family are presented as positive characters, victims of racism. We could accuse Villanueva of offering a simplistic image of the characters on the scene, but the poet introduces the individuals in a binary way because he has a specific purpose in mind. He wants to advocate for the class that suffered racial discrimination and to protect the characters with his shield of words by presenting them in a strictly positive way. To present racists as fully negative characters is to take away the possibility of excusing or justifying their behavior in some way. Lee Bebout highlights that Villanueva does not identify with Bick Benedict, Sarge's opponent, but with the Mexican family in the scene. Bebout claims that the film offers a paternalistic solution to racism. The negative image that whites have of Mexicans and Mexican Americans is not deconstructed. Racism, in the movie *Giant*, can only be fought through the use of what Bebout calls the "white benevolence" (26–30), that is, Anglo-Saxon benevolence. What Villanueva does in his poetry, thus concludes Bebout, is to challenge "the system of whiteness and white benevolence that undergird the 1956 film. His telling fundamentally alters any re-viewing of the film, responding in a way to construct new, more complex layers of meaning" (30). In this first part of the poetry book, therefore, we observe how Villanueva creates a representational space for Mexicans that had been denied to them in the scene of the film.

"The 8:00 O'clock Movie," the first poem of part I of the collection, begins with a spatial and temporal localization. The poetic "I" is in Boston and the year is 1973 (Villanueva, *Scene* 24). Seventeen years have passed since the young Villanueva experienced the anguish of seeing himself projected on the screen (18). Villanueva is no longer a child; however, that scene insists on chasing him. The images that "came into [his] room" remind him of the plot (24). In the verses that follow, Villanueva rebuilds the image of the characters according to his memory and interpretation. He starts with the stage: livestock, oil, dust, and heat. In this environment the characters intersect and class differences become evident. Moreover, he mentions the characters Ángel, Juana, her "color of dark amber" son, and finally, the Mexicans who are denied service. This last memory is perceived by Villanueva as "a roaring of light" that enters without permission and breaks the silence, making him remember "words spoken and unspoken" (26). And although the poet resists the memory that storms him, he knows, deep down, that this memory will not disappear. What remains is to put it at the service of his poetry. The recovery of memory is an essential feature of the poet's work, who in an interview states:

> I am of the belief, however, that for some creative writers, to simply recollect something is an incomplete process. The next step is to write it down. If it's significant enough – judged from afar in time, and from the writer's perspective – commit it to paper, I say. Make memory serve as inspiration – memory as muse, and ultimately, memory as identity. So you see, memory, for me, becomes a useful device to go back in time to recover a history which would otherwise be lost – a personal or communal history, no matter how lackluster or unsettling that history might have been. (Lee 176)

The four poems that follow in part I present the Benedict family, the restaurant waitress, and Sarge. In all the poems, the image of Sarge as representative of the vileness and of Juana as the victim of Sarge's gaze that "fire[s] upon the heart" is emphasized (Villanueva, *Scene* 28). The main theme of these poems is the racial discrimination experienced by Juana and the family of Mexicans in the restaurant. By painstakingly reconstructing this scene and emphasizing the racist expressions that come out of Sarge's mouth, Villanueva desires the reader to reflect on Sarge's attitude. The poet writes a whole book so that this scene, which has a duration of no more than a few minutes in the film, stands out with importance and value. It is crucial to remember, reflect, and write, even if this is a painful process, to finally be able to achieve a change in society. All of Sarge's racism is captured in the poem "The Serving of Water" when Bick Benedict orders ice cream for his Mexican American grandson:

> Afternoon when Sarge, moved by deep familiar
> Wrath, talks down: "Ice-cream – thought that kid'd
> Want a *tamale*." An angry mass of time travels
> Back and forth the distance between Sarge and
>
> Rock Hudson, as I sit, shy of speech, in a stammer
> Of light, and breath not fully breathed. (*Scene* 32)

The irony in Sarge's speech and his contempt for the Chicano boy are obvious. The image of the "tamale" as a representative of the Mexican community is violent because it offers a simplistic and prejudiced idea of this group. A stereotype is created and affirmed that has the function of depersonifying the Mexican individual and presenting him as an inferior being. While viewing this scene of outrage, the 14-year-old Villanueva is motionless, unsure of his existence, violated by the words that steal his voice and air.

In the poem that follows, "Claiming the Air," Villanueva seeks to do justice to Mexicans on the scene and describes them as follows:

> Courteous hat. The women, in uneventful-street clothes,
> How their faces do not glow back from themselves, yet
> Beckon with the color of sepia subdued – his also. Slow
> In their gait toward the nearest booth by the door, they
> Show a tired look as if from a journey begun long ago, one
>
> Only their heritage could know. A woman I could be nephew. (*Scene* 34)

Villanueva expresses in these verses his admiration for these resilient people who are persecuted for not having the socially accepted skin color. He refers to the difficult trajectory of part of the Mexican people, which have undertaken a long journey in search of a better life. It is a reality that only those who have lived it, like Villanueva's ancestors, can understand in its full sense. Here, the poet refers to the historical experience of conquest, migration, and diaspora of the Mexican American people. The identification with these characters could not be more explicit: a migrant woman who could be his aunt is represented in the scene.

Gradually, Villanueva moves away from narrating the scenes in the film. He begins to focus on describing his feelings as a Chicano spectator of the scene projected in the movie, and which he reconstructs in the first part of the poetry book. In fact, the second part of the collection, which is also composed of five poems, offers a look at what is most sensitive to the poet. The entire traumatizing experience is embodied as a swallowed shout, a plea for help not pronounced at the time, but that never stopped clamoring to be heard.

A characteristic of this collection of poems is the constant oscillation between the fictional and the real plane. In some cases, both are presented even in the same sentence, as we observe in the prose verses of the poem "The Existence of Sarge":

> Then the
>
> Very way the tight-wound voice of Sarge
> Echoes through the café walls, out onto the
> Street, and back inside the Holiday Theater
> Where I sit alone in the drop-shadows of the
> back – : "Your money is no good here. Come on,
> Let's go. You too," he says to the women,
> Their torment half inside me.[2] (Villanueva, *Scene* 42–44)

This symbiosis of the physical and the chimerical emphasizes the degree of immersion of the young Villanueva in the projected scene and the impact that it has on him. Sarge's "tight-wound" voice has a resonance that extends far beyond his café and reaches the Holiday Cinema. When Sarge tells the Mexicans that their money has no value in his establishment, Villanueva feels as if he is saying it directly to him. The first reaction of the poetic "I" to this outrage is to cry out in his heart to "*Put the*

2 All citations follow Villanueva's original script-setting.

film/in reverse .... Tear out these frames/From time-motion and color; run the words/ Backward in Sarge" (*Scene* 44). Within the poem, the young Villanueva desires to make racism non-existent; he refuses to accept the brutal discrimination against the ethnic community to which he belongs. Recognizing one's own marginalization is a painful and traumatic process that the poet goes through, but it is also a crucial moment in the formation of his Chicano identity.

The poems of part II demonstrate Villanueva's intense desire to resist the images that are imposed with violence on his heart. The second poem in this part, "On the Subject of Staying Whole," tells how the adolescent arrives at the cinema hall with an "orange soda and scoops of popcorn" (*Scene* 46). The child's innocence will be lost forever. As the film progresses, Villanueva's desire to scream grows, but he suppresses it, aiming to endure the pain. However, something very significant begins to emerge within him: "a small/Fire began to burn" (46). In 1956, the teenager was not able to express his feelings using words yet, but a seed of poetic inspiration had been planted.

In this second part of the collection, Sarge is the one who owns the word. And the word has power, as we can see in the poem "Stop-Action: Impression":

> And Sarge, absolute, stressing the plane
>
> Of outward fact, as when the screen
> Gives up the deep-in-air-rooted sound
> Of his voice, the strong ejectives
>
> And glottals; as when he unifies his
> Muscle with the blunt instrument of
> His words with which he tries to purge
>
> His roadside dominion. (Villanueva, *Scene* 48)

In these verses, Villanueva uses specific terms from the linguistic field (ejectives, glottals), accentuating the process of the construction of the words that are harshly poured against the Mexican family. Words, in Sarge's mouth, are an instrument to impose his dominance and violence. The power of those words terrifies the child Villanueva who fears that someone like Sarge could do the same with him, expelling him "from the rest of [his]/Life not yet entered" (48). The teenager feels immobilized and helpless before the sound that Sarge emits through his words.

An image that is present in the entire collection of poems is *light*. Light is often something that invades the poet with its strength and intensity. It emerges as something that insults the eye and forces the poet to see, recognize, and deal with the scenes and his memories (Villanueva, *Scene* 48). In the poem "Fallingrief of Unpleasure," the poetic "I" plays with the light-shadow duality to express the internal conflict that he is experiencing when seeing that scene in the film: "The eye surrenders to the light," and by surrendering, by yielding, the child Villanueva loses some of his ingenuity, of his childhood. The fragments are burned and "each frame rises into consciousness with the meaning/Of failed belief" (50). There is no way to escape the light that insists on persecuting, although he desires to "dissolve [himself], fade to black" (50).

The cry trapped in the throat and the anxiety to pronounce his indignation is particularly evident in the last poem of part II of the collection. In "Without a Prayer at the Holiday Theater," Villanueva recognizes:

> Without words, the child
> Began to feel mortal, his mind breaking into awfulness:
> A pulse-beat of dread worked itself down from his
>
> Temples – there was, in his throat, a tightening dry
> Knot and his mouth could not make spit. (*Scene* 52)

The process of disillusion, of recognizing oneself as mortal and vulnerable, is directly manifested in the poet's body. The images of the knot in the throat and the lack of saliva emphasize the sensation of anguish that the young Villanueva felt, making it more palpable and real. At the same time, these images highlight the child's silence, his inability to express his feelings. Therefore, the traumatic experience of recognizing oneself as a small and fragile being (or as "a thin, flickering/Helpless light") before the fearsome Sarge, lord of a cruel repertoire of words and sounds, is lived as a moment of psychological as well as physical distress (20).

As mentioned above, in the second part of the poetry book Villanueva insists on expressing the set of feelings that arose in his heart when he saw the film; feelings that would mark him profoundly. In the five poems that compose this section, Villanueva allows the reader to access the deepest part of his soul so that, in this way, the reader can understand, or at least assimilate, what discrimination causes in its victims. The poetic introspection reaches its apex in the second half of the last poem, "Without a Prayer at the Holiday Theater," in which Villanueva prays to God. These verses are unspoken desires, crying out for mercy, protection, and justice:

> *O Saviour, release*
> *me from this fear; give me cool waters to temper*
> *the heat of his wound which the back-row darkness*
> *hides. Send forth your swift light of compassion*
> *into the places of my woe. Climb down and be seated*
> *next to me, All-Merciful, bearer of the world's pain.*
> *Increase the faith in me that your deep justice will*
> *triumph on the screen. I need to see it done.* (*Scene* 52)

In the three poems that compose part III of the collection, Villanueva dedicates himself to narrating in detail the scene of the fight between Sarge and Bick Benedict. In these poems, too, reality, memory, and fiction amalgamate as if one were constitutive and dependent on the other. Once again the light bursts forth impetuously coercing the poet to remember the unforgettable (62). The poetic "I" is in the year 1973 and struggles against the images that memory imposes on it. In the poem "Fight Scene: Final Frames," the young Villanueva wants to help Bick Benedict in his battle, but he feels helpless and questions:

> When may I learn strongly to act, who am caught
> In this light like a still photograph? Can two fighters
>
> Bring out a third? To live, must I learn how to die? (*Scene* 66)

Some verses later, Villanueva declares that: "a victory is not over until you turn it into words" (Villanueva, *Scene* 66). Sarge is victorious in the film not because he defeats his physically inferior opponent, but because he manages to legitimize his aggression with words by displaying the sign:

> WE RESERVE
> THE RIGHT
> TO REFUSE SERVICE
> TO ANYONE. (66)

This victory, the one of Sarge's cruel words, is the one that was inscribed in Villanueva's heart and memory. However, the cathartic conclusion reached by the poet is that only the transformation into language attests victory. Sarge may have emerged triumphant in this scene, but in poetry, the one who has the power of words is the poet and it is through this recognition that Villanueva gradually conquers his voice. He will put it at the service of the defense of Mexicans and Mexican Americans.

Part IV of the collection consists of a single poem entitled "The Trailing Consequence: A Triptych." This poem is subdivided into three parts in which the poet describes how he felt as he left the cinema hall. In the first part, "Journey Home," the poet narrates how "vexed at the unwinding/course of truth" he wanders around the city, lost and helpless in a "world [that] seemed enormous around [him]" (Villanueva, *Scene* 70). It was the same world, but the young man had changed. He could no longer escape the violent and insistent light. A memory was formed. The adolescent walks aimlessly, in circles; he had lost all sense of direction in his life. He crosses the railroad tracks; passes by the lumber yard and the cement bridge over Purgatorio Creek (73). These familiar places no longer help him locate himself and are now part of this strange and gloomy world. During this errant walk, the feeling of revolt grows in the poet, which then manifests in his body: he clenches his fists tightly and a scream begins to grow in his mouth:

> I think I must have made a fist
> in desperation, as though as the years
> to my name
> and there grew in my mouth
> a great shout which never came. (*Scene* 72)

That shout, however, is not articulated, since "a child at that age/ falls short of endowing dumb misery with speech" (72).

In "Observer and observed," the second part of this poem, the poet highlights the loneliness and emptiness experienced by the child when leaving the theater. No one walks with the teenager who silently roams the city. He cannot yet fully understand the transformation he went through, and the trees, the houses, and the neighbors do not notice his despondency. The adolescent lets himself be carried away by the "soft-hollowed steps," without being able to resist this feeling that consumes and hurts him (Villanueva, *Scene* 74). In these verses, the poetic "I" is passive, an unprotected child whose fantasy of equality had been destroyed. What remains is the emptiness of disillusion, which, in time, will be replaced by poetry in the adult Villanueva.

The feeling of absence, this longing for something that no longer exists, is also present in the first verses of the third section of this poem: "Dusk with Dreaming." Feeling that he "was nothing/other than [his] name," he accepts that something inside him had been lost (Villanueva, *Scene* 76). Giving in to reality creates a space for the poetic imagination to germinate. It is by recognizing himself as marginalized and discriminated against that Villanueva wants to surrender himself to dreams. Dusk, the home of the romantic poets, also represents a change of state, the passage from day to night. It is not by chance that Villanueva dreams in the twilight which symbolizes the internal change that the poet is going through. With the following verses Villanueva encloses the poem:

> I remember the clock ticking
>
> and my breathing
> when finally
>
> my mouth took ethnically again
> sustenance in solace.
> The rest of me began to dream and my mind
> flew off and I became, for that instant:
>
> Another boy from another land, in another time,
> another time, which is also home. (*Scene* 78)

The image that Villanueva draws to the reader is quite graphic, the clock ticking transmits, as in a scene in a movie, the idea of a static, or very slow advancing time. The real and the imaginary plane merge between the physical sensation of taste in the mouth and dream in the mind. The poetic "I," still in the year 1956, is in a moment of transition. The sphere of dreams is still a space of refuge. With the arrival of poetic maturity, the words will gradually occupy this place.

In the four poems that compose part V of the poetry collection, Villanueva moves away from the scene of the film to make room for the birth of poetry. In "That Autumn," the first poem in this part, the poet explains why he decided to transform that experience in the theater into poetry. This is how the poetic "I" expresses himself:

> Now I think: *the*
>
> *poem's the thing wherein I'll etch the semblance*
> *of the film.* So the mind becomes involved again with
> after-sight, with frames as large as screens … and
>
> without wearing it as too much knowledge, something
> out of reach gets underway and the two-sided act of
> myself (in the available light) behaves into words …. (*Scene* 82)

In these verses, the interior monologue is graphically indicated by the use of italics. These verses say something about Villanueva's creation process. Poetic production is, on the one hand, a decision that involves work (writing, recording); on the other, it is also something involuntary, something out of reach that starts by itself (Villanueva, *Scene* 82). Tino Villanueva is very meticulous when constructing his poems and the words used are the result of rigorous elaboration work. In an interview with Pérez, Villanueva reflects on his writing method, which he describes as follows:

> I am too much of a perfectionist, it seems to me, and so my poems require a long incubation time. I am what Unamuno would call an oviparous, non-viviparous writer, that is, the writer who does not birth a live poem, but rather comes up with an idea for a work, and then gradually adds other ideas to the original idea and, changes, deletes, and amends, until the poem is ready … and it is born.[3]
>
> [Soy demasiado perfeccionista, me parece, y por eso mis poemas requieren mucho tiempo de incubación. Soy lo que llamaría Unamuno un escritor ovíparo, no vivíparo es decir, el escritor a quien no le nace el poema ya vivo, sino que le nace una idea para una obra, y luego va paulatinamente añadiendo otras ideas a la idea original y, cambiando, suprimiendo y enmendando, hasta que el poema está listo… y nace.]. (Pérez, "Entrevista" 602)

In the second poem, for which Villanueva chooses a title related to the cinematographic field, "Fade-Out-Fade-In," the poet narrates how language arises. The play of light and shadows, already noticeable in the title, is present throughout the poem. The poetic "I" relives in memory the moment when the film ended, as "the bright blankness of the screen" descended on him and the boy came out into the corridor "in the yielding chiaroscuro" (Villanueva, *Scene* 84). The teenager, stunned and wounded, finds himself lost in the blurred light of his new reality. Language arises through the years, with maturity and with memory, and it is writing that rescues the poet. "Now I am because I write," declares Villanueva, as a consolidated poet (84). He has found a place of significance. Poetry is where he manages to name the feelings that he intensely desired to forget. Writing is therefore something intrinsic and inseparable from his being. In that quoted verse, poet and poetry are one.

The penultimate poem in the collection, "The Slow Weight of Time," expresses the poet's liberation through poetry. In this poem, Villanueva is no longer a prisoner of his memories and speaks to himself:

> You draw air, press these
> thoughts to paper and release your daily
> self from the lost fragments of the past.
>
> Now: in the conquered vigil of your
> days, all distance weeps for you as you
> drift out from the journey through the
>
> Slow weight of time, and you claim
> that you are safe forever in the
> very words you have chosen to become. (*Scene* 86)

The poet rests in poetry where he finds salvation. Poetry is the refuge in "the slow weight of time." Writing is a decision; it is something that the poet chooses to do. Words are his shield and sword, it is through them that the poet acquires a voice capable of expressing repressed feelings and freeing himself from the rancor of discrimination felt on the skin.

---

3 English translation by the author.

Villanueva names "The Telling" the last poem in the collection *Scene from the Movie GIANT*. That is a self-reflective and introspective poem at its highest expression. In it, the poet expresses what it means for him to poeticize his emotions and memories. The "anxious truth," as an "unction," runs through his body (89). Poetic inspiration is something that emanates with strength and urgency and takes over the poet. The idea of poetry as an unction, as a blessing, had already been worked on by Villanueva in previous poems, as we observe in the poem "Anointing words," from *Chronicle of my Worst Years* (Villanueva, *Chronicle* 73). In Villanueva's intimate verses, poet and poetry unite into a single entity: "when the teller is the tale being told" (*Scene* 88). *Scene from the Movie GIANT* is based on a personal experience that rests on the past, like much of Villanueva's poetry. For this reason, memory occupies a central position in his work. It is in memory that poetic inspiration is born, which, in turn, becomes language:

> (when the teller is the tale being told),
> the ash of memory rises that I might speak,
>
> that I might tell what I tell with words,
> which are the past falling from my mind. (88)

The existence of memory is the reason why the poet writes. Memory is what makes the birth of the poem possible. It is the memory and the consequent act of narrating that enables the healing of the poet. By processing his experience of discrimination, the poet appropriates his memories, masters them, and puts them to work at the service of his poetry.

> Let the script reveal: that in the telling
>
> I am cast in the time forward, wherethrough runs
> the present – one track of light triumphant,
>
> the sum of everything that ignites this room
> with life, *vida que no olvida*, calling out
> my name. (*Scene* 88)

It is in the act of telling that the memory bursts into the present and materializes itself as poetry. It is through writing, through words, that the poet triumphs. The *vida que no olvida*, that is, memory requires the poet to express in words what has been lived and what is impossible to forget. Here, we see once again how Villanueva uses the metaphor of light: "one track of light triumphant" (88). However, contrary to what we observed in the initial poems, the light in this poem is not something that assaults the poet. On the contrary, it is responsible for filling the room with life. The disturbing and violent light that haunts the poet in the first poems of the collection, transforms into a benevolent luminosity that helps Villanueva remember and narrate the pains and the memories.

Villanueva concludes the poem "The Telling" with the following verses:

> O life, this body that speaks, this
>
> repetitious self drawn out from *la vida revivida,*
> *vida sacada de cada clamor*. Home at last, I am
>
> trusting the light that attends me and the
> natural physic of breathing, with words to
> show the measure. *Oh vida vivida y por venir….* (*Scene* 88)

The repetition of the vocative "O life" underlines the idea of clamor. The "body that speaks," a body suffered, lived, waits, and trusts in the future, in the life to come. At last home, safe, the poet hopes that time will heal him. In that process, the right words are essential. Light, once again, plays a central role in these verses. The poet trusts it to heal his wounds.

One last observation is important to mention. In this poem, Villanueva uses the two languages that form his identity: three sentences in Spanish emerge between the verses in English: *vida que no olvida; la vida revivida, /vida sacada de cada clamor* and *Oh vida vivida y por venir*. Bilingualism is a common feature of Chicano literature and is also present in Villanueva's writing. According to Mahdi,

> language, in Villanueva's poems, plays a twofold role. First, language, especially bilingualism, reflects the polyglossic nature of Chicano subjectivity, hence, its ability to be incarnated in hybrid and heterogeneous cultural spaces. As a reflection of hybridity and heterogeneity, on the other hand, Villanueva's language assumes the shape of a bonding substance that prevents Chicano subjectivity from falling under the postmodernist sway of the sense of unbelonging. (166)

As Mahdi observes, the use of both languages expresses a rejection of a simplistic definition of the Mexican American as belonging to one culture or another. Also in the specific poem discussed above, "The Telling," the use of Spanish is not accidental. It expresses a singular condition of the Mexican American: the life suffered, not forgotten, but which resists and creates, through poetry, the life to come.

Conclusion

The poetry collection *Scene from the Movie GIANT* by Tino Villanueva narrates the poet's trajectory from the moment he sees the scene of racism projected on the screen of the cinema in 1956, passing through the moment of remembrance in Boston in 1973, until reaching the present (1993), when the poet, in his maturity, finally manages to express in words the experience that marked his life and impacted his being. What the present essay has demonstrated, relying on theories about voice, silence, and memory, is how the process of conquering the voice occurs gradually throughout the poetry book. Like a good excavator, to use Benjamin's metaphor, Villanueva works with his memories throughout the entire creative process. The result is Villanueva's transformation as he is finally able to poetically express what he lived, pouring it into the verses of the 19 poems that compose the collection.

The initial poems denounce racism and express Villanueva's aversion to Sarge's behavior. As the reader delves into the poetry collection, he is increasingly invited to learn the poet's interior who, through inner monologues, expresses the anguish experienced when seeing the scene. At first, unable to translate his feelings into words, the poet suffers with the light (memory) that haunts him. It is only when maturing that Villanueva will be able to free himself from pain, that is when he manages to transform the traumatic experience in the Holiday theater into poetic expression. This is evident in the last poems of *Scene from the Movie GIANT* when the light becomes a poetic inspiration and the poet feels safe in the "words [that he has] chosen to become" (86). This collection, therefore, is presented as a journey in which the poet breaks the silence and seizes his voice. A healing voice that is determined to be heard.[4]

Works cited

Alamán, Rafael Cabaña. "Introducción." *Escena de la película GIGANTE*. Ed. Alamán. Madrid: Catriel. 2005. Madrid: Catriel, 2005. 11–14. Print.

Bebout, Lee. "Troubling White Benevolence. Four Takes on a *Scene from Giant.*" *Melus* 36.3 (2011): 13–36. Print.

Benjamin, Walter. "Excavation and Memory." *Selected Writings*. Ed. Marcus Paul Bullock, Michael William Jennings, Howard Eiland, and Gary Smith. Vol. 2, part 2. Cambridge, MA: Belknap P of Harvard UP, 2005. 576. Print.

Bruce-Novoa, Juan. *Chicano Poetry: A Response to Chaos*. Austin: U of Texas P, 1982. Print.

Candelaria, Cordelia. *Chicano Poetry. A Critical Introduction*. Westport, CT, London: Greenwood P, 1986. Print.

Heide, Markus. "The Poetry of Tino Villanueva: Texas, the Chicano Movement, Memory, and Ekphrasis." *Comparative American Studies An International Journal* 15.1–2 (2017): 91–98. Print.

Lee, Robert. "'The Breath is Alive/With the Equal Girth of Words': Tino Villanueva in Interview." *Melus* 35.1 (2010): 167–183. Print.

Mahdi, Maher A. *The Rediscovery of Chicano Culture and Self in Selected Poetry of Alurista and Tino Villanueva*. Philadelphia: U of Pennsylvania, Ph.D. Dissertation, 2001. Print.

Miguélez, Armando. "Tino Villaneva, la voz lírica de Norteamérica." *Poesía hispana en los Estados Unidos*. Ed. Ana Valverde Osan. Madrid: ALDEEU, 2011. 236–248. Print.

Olivares, Julián. "Self and Society in Tino Villanueva's 'Shaking' off the Dark." *Confluencia* 1.2 Literatura Chicana (1986): 98–110. Print.

---

4 I would like to thank Tiffany Blasdel and Eduardo Muñoz for their detailed and careful proofreading.

Pérez, Alberto Julián. "Tino Villanueva (1941-)." *Latino and Latina Writers*. Ed. Alan West-Durán, Maria Herrera-Sobek, and César Augusto Salgado. Vol. 1. New York: Scribner's. 2004. 527–536. Print.

———. "Entrevista con Tino Villanueva." *Alba de América* ILCH 23.43–44 (2004): 597–605. Print.

Pérez-Torres, Rafael. "Chicano Ethnicity, Cultural Hybridity, and the Mestizo Voice." *American Literature* 70.1 (1998): 153–176. Print.

Stock, Ann Marie. "Talking Back, Looking Ahead: The Revisionist Cine-Poetry of Tino Villanueva." *The Bilingual Review/La Revista Bilingüe* 23.3 (Sept. 1998): 237–247. Print.

Villanueva, Tino. *Chronicle of My Worst Years*. Translated by James Hoggard. Evanston: TriQuartely Books/Northwestern UP. 1994. Print.

———. *Scene from the Movie GIANT*. Translated and edited by Rafael Cabaña Alamán. 1a ed. (Bilingual edition). Madrid: Catriel, 2005. Print.

Filmography

Giant. Directed by George Stevens, performances by Elizabeth Taylor, Rock Hudson, and James Dean, Warner Bros., 1956.

Piedra Rodante: The Memory of the Musical Consumption of a Generation of Mexican Youth in the Seventies

YOLANDA MINERVA CAMPOS GARCÍA

Introduction

Piedra Rodante emerged as a Spanish-speaking franchise of the mythical and long-lived North American publication *Rolling Stone*. The publication's identification slogan reads, without qualms: *Piedra Rodante* (with special material from 'Rolling Stone'). On the second page of the magazine, which introduced the editorial team, in one column it named the local editorial team and in a second column introduced the 'Rolling Stone' team in San Francisco, thus underlining the relationship with the 'original.' The design of the editorial format was in line with that of the original and introduced itself with the subtitle: "The newspaper of emotional life."

The magazine was the perfect showcase for the countercultural manifestations of the moment; rather than limiting itself to the translation of articles published in the North American original, it promoted journalism focused on both the music and the counterculture that served as a backdrop for the musical sector. *Piedra Rodante* acted as a one-way bridge for the U.S. pop culture of the time and connected perfectly with its Mexican audience and, with each additional issue, opened up the possibility of creating locally produced music, which was not always imitative of the North American culture.

In the aftermath of the Festival de Avándaro, the publication was halted for several months when the local editorial team came up against the wall of intolerance that characterized the Mexican State at the start of the seventies. In total, only eight issues were published between May 1971 and January 1972.[1] According to the editor of *Piedra Rodante*, Manuel Aceves, issue Number 9 remained in negative form only (Aguilar Sosa 235–240).

Piedra Rodante was a welcome addition to the range of magazines dedicated to musical journalism, which included *México Canta* and *Pop*, whilst offering a different approach to the style of Mexico's first musical publication: *Notitas Musicales*, which was launched in 1955. However, what set *Piedra Rodante* apart from its contemporar-

1 In the collection housed in the *Hemeroteca Nacional* (National Newspaper Library), there are eight issues of *Piedra Rodante*. However, in an article signed by Beto Cronopio, it was announced that there was also an issue numbered '0;' published in December 1970, it even shows the cover of the issue with a photo of the group Credence Clearwater Revival. http://www.eslocotidiano.com/articulo/tachas-276/meros-peldanos-son-peligr-osos-ahora-primer-libro-cuentos-fue-editado-2012-san-roque-ir-portada-tachas-276/20180922231815048182.html.

ies was the marked influence of the counterculture that came directly from *Rolling Stone* with regard to theme selection, the type of publicity, and the irreverent tone with which it exercised journalism. At this point, it is important to mention that we are reading between the lines, interpreting the writing, and contextualizing what the magazine reproduced. Some parts are more descriptive, others more analytical.

The counterculture in *Piedra Rodante*

One of the peculiarities of the countercultural concept is the difficulty to define it given that it is a social manifestation, it is thus impossible to subscribe it to one particular era since alternative culture has always existed throughout the different stages of history, governed by its own parameters and acts in opposition to the *establishment* of the day; at one point it is considered as avant-garde until later being adopted by the hegemonic culture of the times, which is why we subscribe to the definition put forward by Timothy Leary:

> Counterculture flourishes wherever and whenever certain members of a society choose a specific lifestyle, artistic expression and forms of thought, the common factor being that it wholeheartedly embraces the old axiom that the only true constant is change. The mark of counterculture cannot be defined as a social form with any particular structure, but is rather the evanescence of forms and structures combined with the dazzling speed and flexibility with which it appears, mutates, transforms and disappears. (IX)

In the context in which *Piedra Rodante* was published, the youth cultures of the time manifested their views from different trenches against an authoritarian state which, in its discourse appealed for reconciliations and a "democratic opening," whilst in practice it utilized its repressive apparatus to limit, and in some cases actually reduced the different forms of coexistence and expressive forms that it considered contrary to "family values." In this sense, *Piedra Rodante* made its mark by projecting different voices from alternative cultures on several fronts, not only in the musical context, but also regarding themes such as sexual freedom, the consumption of drugs, avant-garde literature, and even denouncing cases of censorship, along with political events such as the repression that took place in Mexico on June 10, 1971.[2] Topics and discussions that appeared in *Piedra Rodante* aimed to provide a stage for a declaration of principles in common with countercultural phenomena in other latitudes, thereby being in tune with the explosion of youth culture from around the globe.

New journalism sneaks into Mexico

The analysis of periodical publications makes it necessary to construct a methodology that takes into account the mediating role played by the medium itself: "they are neces-

2 *Piedra Rodante* reported on the student repression that occurred on June 10, 1971. Cf. "*Jueves de Corpus. Bronca de tres años*" by Observer (*Piedra Rodante* 4, July 1971).

sary and omnipresent mediators between social events and individuals" (Gutiérrez 170), and according to Eliseo Verón: "Social events are not objects that are created in some part of reality and whose properties and vicissitudes are not immediately published by the media, with greater or lesser fidelity. They only exist to the extent that these media elaborate them" (qtd. in Gutiérrez 172).

In this sense, periodic publications are social constructions in which a specialized editorial team chooses a fragment of reality and decides what an event can or cannot be:

> The informational input chosen by the journalist allows him/her to construct a story that takes into account certain instances of an event and discards others. By way of this discursive practice "the enunciating subject transforms the objective facticity of a subjective structure of meaning." (Sosa qtd. in Gutiérrez 172)

The editors of *Piedra Rodante* were very clear from the outset regarding the public to whom their publication was directed, and based on that, they constructed a subjective structure that gave meaning to the demands of the youth of the day. In a natural way, the contents of the publication were devoted to offering information on the current affairs that connected with specific youth cultures of certain sectors of society. As a declaration of principles, the first issue defined its editorial line, thus acquiring a commitment to this sector:

> They represent a highly complex public that can at no time be taken for a ride. They must be provided with authentic, objective information. Most advertisers underestimate the new consumer. We cannot.
>
> Rock today is undoubtedly the catalyzing element of the only truly important movement of our time, that of young people, and it is more than their music: it is expression, whilst at the same time acting as a vehicle for the values, style, philosophy and religion of the latest generation of youth.
>
> Therein lies the strength and success of 'Rolling Stone,' its editor and contributors belong to this movement, it is their starting point and their point of return. "Nothing can substitute being "connected," says Wenner: "If the kids trust us, it is because we know what we are talking about, that we are going after the good groups."[3] (qtd. in Aceves 5)

In addition to referring to the emergence of the parent (*Rolling Stone*), three aspects stood out: the conviction that rock music was more than just a musical genre, but rather a way of life; the need to make an ethical commitment to young people and the recognition of a potential consumer sector. As can be seen, beyond the commercial aspect, which was also mentioned, there was an increasing sensitivity towards the feelings of young people, perhaps also because it was a publication produced by young people.

---

3 Regarding the latter, from the pages of *Rolling Stone* came reports on Anglo-Saxon musicians who were at their peak, either because of their record releases or because they had been "news," such as the unfortunate deaths of Janis Joplin and Jimi Hendrix that occurred in the year prior to the publication of *Piedra Rodante*, plus that of Jim Morrison in July 1971. Posthumous reports were reproduced on these musicians.

We feel it is of great importance to point out that the context in which *Piedra Rodante* came into being is particularly special for rock in Mexico, given the fact that it was during the months previous to the celebration of the "Festival de Rock y Ruedas, Avándaro" [Festival of Rock 'n Roll, Avándaro] which, according to the chroniclers and scholars of this musical phenomena, was the first mass rock concert in Mexico (Urteaga 70) and was a watershed moment for the musical consumption of this genre. After Avándaro, rock in Mexico became marginal and thereafter followed a long phase of confinement in underground clubs called Hoyos Funkys (De la Peza 40).

Before entering into the analysis of the themes and sections of the magazine, it is worth mentioning its affiliation with respect to the other publications of the time. First of all, it should be noted that *Piedra Rodante* was a magazine whose field of interest was music and culture in its extended form; the type of journalism produced was more analytical than informative. Initially being published on a monthly basis and later bi-weekly, immediacy was far from its reach. However, it must be said that events such as the Avándaro Festival were covered with speed close to the time of the event, in this specific case with a complete issue dedicated to the concert.

From the parent company, that is, from the North American magazine *Rolling Stone*, came the tradition of the so called 'New Journalism,' the journalistic style that emerged in the U.S.A. during the mid-sixties, which reduced the boundary between literature and journalism and thus enabled a more flexible way to present stories in novel ways. The new style placed the journalist's particular voice in a new position, therefore achieving greater interaction with the readership. The magazine's collaborators, more than journalists, were in some cases writers who continued their career in the literary narrative (José Agustín, Parménides García Saldaña, Juan Tovar), so it was not by chance that the casual language of the *Literatura de la Onda* slipped through in the tone of the magazine, especially in the headlines, running heads, and even in the articles themselves.

Piedra Rodante, "a rolling stone gathers no moss"[4]

Piedra Rodante was launched in May 1971, out of Mexico City. For its first seven issues, it adopted a tabloid format, like the original *Rolling Stone* and in its final issue (#8), in January 1972, it changed to a smaller, magazine-like supplement. Each issue had around 50 pages, except for the last one, which reached 90; a good portion of the

4 It is important to draw attention to the name of the magazine: *Piedra Rodante*, the verbatim translation of 'Rolling Stone,' which is a very significant concept related to the history of music by those who have used it; the term was coined by the mythical Muddy Waters song 'Mannish boy,' by Bob Dylan in his song 'Like a Rolling Stone,' and also as the name of the English group 'The Rolling Stones.' Jann Wenner recalled, in 2007, in the anniversary issue of *Rolling Stone*: "When I named the magazine after songs by Bob Dylan and Muddy Waters, not to mention the band, I did not foresee this development. If I had, I might have named it something else, because I'm really tired of this moss shit …." (*Rolling Stone*, 14 May 2007 (7)).

pages were dedicated to advertising and there were fixed sections from its inception; other sections were added on the fly, in the same way as its contributors.

In the following pages we refer to two themes that we consider central to exemplify the articulation of the musical memory of the context: La Onda Chicana [The Chicano Wave] and the Avándaro Festival.

La Onda Chicana

Rock was the musical genre that featured as the central theme in *Piedra Rodante*, and although most of the articles were dedicated to groups and singers from the Anglo-Saxon world, the Mexican groups that were beginning to achieve recognition in the musical environment were also included in the magazine, thus acting as a projection medium to connect with its fans. Extensive interviews with the groups were included, and in the 'Records' section, the editors reviewed their recordings in different formats.

This coexistence between Anglo-Saxon and national musicians in the pages of *Piedra Rodante* shows the generational connection of the readers, because at the same time that they were informed about the news of what was happening in other latitudes, they were also updated regarding the groups that had been baptized as the *Onda Chicana*, in other words, the national groups that entered the scene in the "professional" musical environment. Through these interviews, latent influences and tastes appeared that were later reflected in their musical styles, which, as a general rule, were from Anglo-Saxon musicians and singers.

Many of the criticisms, when approaching the existence of countercultural manifestations in the Mexican society of the sixties and seventies, were focused on the fact that the records came to Mexico with an 'imported' seal and so from the (political) left were seen as a form of cultural colonialism (Monsiváis, *Amor* 227).

Eric Zolow, in his essay on the phenomenon of the Onda Chicana, questioned its true significance in the context of the seventies:

> In effect, the imagined community created by La Onda Chicana filled a discursive (and participatory) moment during which Mexico's political regime had lost its credibility among the nation's middle-class youth. Intellectuals, however, naturally viewed English-language Mexican rock with deep suspicion and cynicism, and, in turn, attacked the movement as inauthentic and imperialist. (Zolov 33)

This distrust towards the cultural manifestation that was rock, significant with regard to the emergence of youth cultures, was ultimately detrimental since it interrupted the process of the development of Mexican rock, whose maximum expression was the *Rock and Ruedas Festival*, more commonly referred to as just Avándaro, a point to which we will return in the following pages. For the moment, we wish to highlight the words of Zolov regarding the dimension of the blindness of intellectuals: "This disconnect between the native rock enthusiast and Mexican intellectuals contributed to the failure of La Onda Chicana remaining as a vibrant avant-garde cultural force into the 1970's and thus played an important role in the suppression of cultural memory in subsequent generations" (30).

However, we consider that the existence of La Onda Chicana was highly significant for young people in Mexico in the 1970s because it was a form of generational identification with national groups; despite the fact they sang in English, it was a way of being connected on a global level. More precisely, the tendency of *Piedra Rodante* was to act as a forum to encourage that feeling of ownership, when the local and national fell into sync with the global:

> Still, for the first time, however briefly, native rock now resonated with a broad and growing segment of the population, not only in Mexico City but also throughout the provinces. Hundreds of thousands of youths discovered a sense of empowerment through La Onda Chicana music, along with the discourses of a reinvented sense of community. (Zolov 30)

Continuing with Zolov, the groups named as La Onda Chicana represented an important moment in the history of Mexican rock because "*La Onda* had come to stand for 'Cultural Revolution,' rebellion against patriarchal authority, self-discovery, and solidarity" (30).

For all the above reasons, we consider it of great importance to review the treatment and information published by *Piedra Rodante* regarding the groups that were included in La Onda Chicana; reading between the lines about the reception of this sector of the press towards the said groups, and through this content highlighting the new experience, which was also of importance for young journalists reviewing records produced by local groups.

The first issue of *Piedra Rodante* contained an article about an event called "El Festival del Naranjazo," organized by *Acción Social*, a government body from the official party. This report, written by Gustavo Castañeda, provided a good pulse for the understanding of the relationship of local rock with the authorities and the public, because it provided the author with a guideline for making a tally of the number of concerts held by foreign musicians in Mexico up to that moment. In fact, he raises the question of whether there really was a receptive culture for mass concerts.[5]

La Revolución de Emiliano Zapata

This group from Guadalajara was mentioned in the first issue of *Piedra Rodante*. The magazine's collaborators Alfonso Perabeles, Josefo Ruiz Esparza, Gustavo Castañeda, and Federico Camphel, along with the photographer Marisa López, interviewed the group La Revolución de Emiliano Zapata when they were in Mexico City to receive an award. The freshness of the musicians who recounted the story of the emergence of the

---

5 The author cites the concert of 'The Byrds' held at the *Ciudad Universitario Stadium* (in Mexico City) on March 9, 1969. Cf., in this regard, Monsiváis ("For all things" n. pag.).

band is striking, which was, as it so often used to be, a group of neighborhood friends who got together and learned to make music, motivated by the groups they were listening to. In the case of La Revo, they recognized The Rolling Stones as their main influence.

A recurring theme in the interviews with national groups was the disadvantageous conditions that the record companies had to overcome due to their inexperience in the business area. They learned through trial and error since they were not privy to any advice on how to negotiate contracts with record labels and thus often ended up signing burdensome contracts.

La Revo was also mentioned on one occasion in the column "The album of the month" (González Reimann, "El disco del mes" 5), whereby the album and group that had been given that distinction was framed in a box. The album "La Revolución de Emiliano Zapata" was reviewed by Luis González Reimann; this review, in addition to musical criticism, put on the discussion table a central problem shared by other groups: the difficulty of being accepted by the radio networks and the necessary movement of musicians seeking places to play outside of their localities of origin.

La Revo was projected as a group that started out strong, because according to Reimann it was the first native group to be heard on national radio. In issue #3 of *Piedra Rodante*, a 'Hit Parade' was released, prepared by the magazine itself, which positioned two of the group's songs: 'Nasty Sex' and 'Shit City,' at position two and four, respectively (*Piedra Rodante* 3 (10)).

El Brujo, Javier Bátiz

In the second issue of *Piedra Rodante*, the interview that Alfonso Perabales and Luis González Reimann held with Javier Bátiz from Tijuana was published. In a long interview, the musician recounted his early beginnings in music and his career: he arrived in Mexico City in 1962 in search of places to play. By 1971, Bátiz was probably the musician with the longest time on stage in Mexico, with a passionate predilection for the blues. In the interview, he denotes being knowledgeable about the genre and the use of chords. And through his arguments he shows that he was a musician who always insisted on being professional and looking for originality.

However, in his narrative, there is a notable lack of empathy, he comes across as very individualistic, if not egocentric. When talking about other national and international groups, everything seemed to him as if it lacked quality. He was outraged to be compared to Hendrix, he hated The Rolling Stones; among the national groups, he gave slight recognition to La Revo and Los Dugs Dugs.[6]

---

6 The attitude of the musician outraged a reader who sent a letter to the section "Letters of love and fury," in which he expressed his opinion about the interview: "Bravo, Batiz, bravo! You're the best, you're the only one, the others are worth nothing. You're so good that only Martians would understand your blabbing, your three pianos, your applause.... But what else can you expect from *Nacolandia* [Ignoramousland]? There are

Tinta Blanca

In #3 of *Piedra Rodante*, the album with the same name as the group, *Tinta Blanca*, was reviewed in the 'Records' section, in the 45 rpm (revolutions per minute) column that covered records in that format. Gustavo Castañeda made a favorable review of the "first single on the market" (24). As an unavoidable device, the canon critics used was to find influences and similarities with Anglo-Saxon groups. In this case, Castañeda cites sounds from 'Rare Earth' and 'Chicago,' when he refers to the song "Everything is gonna change." "... moderate jazz-rock, with enough momentum to justify the title of the song. The somewhat elementary texts say much less than the outstanding guitar solo, which is well worth the full production of this side. The only unfortunate detail in this composition (good for the achievements presented to date) is the breathing ... (24).

However, the critic ended up expressing good omens for Mexican rock and determined that Tinta Blanca needed a producer to help them fulfill the idea they were looking for and that, probably, that was also the case with the other groups:

> At this level (and thanks to these two or three minutes) we can deduce that Mexican rock is lacking, not a higher level, but rather details to correct. The themes can be condemned (*verbatim*) for being pretentious, the productions for a lack of presence and, in general, there is the lack of someone to say to the boys: "Well, what do you want to do? ... Let's discuss it and we can choose the factors that will achieve your idea perfectly." (24)

It seems very important to highlight several things from this review: The authors of the review found themselves with a dilemma when analyzing Mexican groups, since the rock music references that they themselves had were from the English and North American groups. On the one hand, they expressed that the Anglo-Saxons and national musicians could not be measured by the same standard, however, since there was no precedent for *La Onda Chicana* groups, they had no choice but to make use of that canon; this occurred with the reservation that they could not be so severe with the local groups just starting out. On the other hand, the Mexican groups that were beginning to perform on the stages of the Mexican capital could hardly be measured on the same scale with regard to the professionalism that musicians from countries showed since music constituted an entire industry in the English-speaking world.

---

other places where they can understand what your about, for example in *Gabacholandia* (the USA). Ah! But in Los Angeles there are only two or three people who catch your wave; however, don't get lazy, kid, you're still among the best guitarists in the world, you and who else? Oh yeah B.B. King, Clapton? No, he's a cheater. Hendrix? Don't mention him. Anyway, who can surpass you, comrade? Relax, don't get hung up on bad vibes. By the way, I congratulate you on your newspaper. It is very hip." Alfonso López Rodríguez, Guadalajara, Jalisco, Mexico (*Piedra Rodante*, "Cartas de amor y furor" 5 (5)).

Los Spiders

Under the title: Guadalajara: *Capital of Rock*?, an interview conducted by Arno Reim with Los Spiders was published in the 4th issue of *Piedra Rodante*. The group showed more experience than other groups, perhaps because they had a longer, though not constant, trajectory. They mainly comment on their relationship with record labels, but also provide an assessment of the musical environments in Mexico City and Guadalajara. In their opinions, the burning moment that rock was undergoing in Mexico at the beginning of the seventies was evident. However, they themselves were aware of the 'intermediate' level that Mexico had in the development of musical activity, regarding concerts and recordings.

Dugs Dugs

In the 7th issue of *Piedra Rodante*, Luis González Reimann reviewed the album of the original group from Durango. The critic comments again that one must be indulgent to criticize a Mexican group "… is to put the album on the turntable bearing in mind that very recently there was no one in these parts who was interested in recording a rock group with their own vibe. Only a few albums have come out so far and looking back there is nothing, everything is just beginning" (González Reimann, "Discos" 30).

Reimann also makes a distinction between groups that sound great at a live concert and comments that it is another experience listening to their music on a studio-recorded album. In the case of the Dugs Dugs, the critic highlights the vitality of Armando Nava on stage, but above all the good production of the album, which denotes serious work. Overall, the criticism is favorable, and he ends up recommending the album.

Piedra Rodante had a certain ally in *La Onda Chicana*, though not unconditional, since the texts show that they did not like everything, and those who exercised criticism did so from within their own possibilities and scope. However, it is noteworthy that, for the publishers, it was important to promote local rock, and given the fact that their recordings were included in the 'Disc' sections alongside the consolidated musicians, the obvious conclusion is that they were aware that the national rock bands were at a disadvantage, especially in terms of time on the scene, meaning many things were still to be done.

In this same vein of promoting national rock, the column "De tocho un pocho" [A Little of Everything] was created, written by Pepe Cornejo and Jesús Luis Benitez, which was a miscellany section in which concerts and festivals that took place in Mexico City were reviewed. It is evident that, although the information was centralized, an attempt was made to inform the readership about the organization of musical events in schools and different forums, using a youthful language that connected with young people. Unfortunately, this column appeared only once, since it was not introduced until the 8th issue of *Piedra Rodante*, the final issue.

Regarding the record labels, in issue 4 of *Piedra Rodante*, information was released from a press conference entitled "Polydor launches the Power Records series," whereby it was announced that the brand was going to dedicate a collection to international rock records. The first titles were produced and it was ensured that they would be released with their original covers, which prompted the editor to comment:

> The decision to launch the 'Rock Power' series without revisions or mutilations, as well as the original graphic presentations already reflects a more honest attitude to rock than in the past, as it will be remembered there were those who destroyed the LPs to make collections of hits, and hits according to their criteria, thus distorting the purposes of both authors and producers. (*Piedra Rodante* 4 (8))

Later, the note acknowledges Polydor's interest in launching national groups. This meant that the arrival of records from foreign groups was also conditioned by a censoring practice that intervened regarding the original album covers.[7]

A further aspect that we consider important to highlight is the invitation to young people to collaborate with *Piedra Rodante* in different ways: as correspondents in the provincial cities, in the sale of *Piedra Rodante*, as well as by sending a review of their favorite albums.

Regarding this point, the final issue included an article on the advantages of being a music critic, entitled "How to shine in the world of rock criticism," by Greg Shaw, in which the author referred to a series of advantages enjoyed by those who dedicate themselves to this profession:

> You too can be a Rock critic. Perfect! If you are between 12 and 30 years old, great opportunities await you in the dynamic field of Rock criticism. You can build a very well-paid career where you listen to records all day, dine with the stars in big restaurants, and publish your articles. You can be envied by all your friends, become the idol of all the groupies and girls in your school!. (Shaw 76)

The (above) text was the introduction to a training course as a music critic that was offered by correspondence; later, the author gave basic advice, such as subscribing to the best music magazines, and once the budding critic got an article published and became known, the next step was to create links with the record companies that would send them news of the fashionable musicians. Although it was an article translated from *Rolling Stone*, and depicted an idyllic life working as a rock critic, he continued giving good tips to get into music journalism professionally.

One section that also served to expand its readership was "El bazar. Medium-use and new things," which included the column "Free classifieds (Musicians without a job)." In this section, both musicians looking for work and groups looking for musicians were advertised; it also served the purpose of advertising the sale of sound equipment and musical instruments.

7 The note alludes to what the Peerless brand did to the album 'Their Satanic Majesties Request' by the Rolling Stones a "supreme example of mediocrity and bad taste" (*Piedra Rodante* 8 (1972): 77).

Another interactive section was the column "Letters of love and fury," in which letters from readers were published giving their opinion about the magazine. Most of the letters expressed a positive reception, encouraging the editorial team to continue in that line and not fall into harmless commercialism. The letters were sent from different parts of the Republic and the odd one or two were received from abroad. The feeling of the readers can be summarized by stating that they considered *Piedra Rodante* as a publication with which they fully identified; they enjoyed both the content and the editorial line.

Avándaro, The Festival de Rock y Ruedas[8]

The Monterey Pop (1967) and Woodstock (1969) music festivals held in the United States had a great impact on the youth culture of the 1970s in Mexico. Without a doubt, they influenced the organization of the legendary Avándaro *Rock y Ruedas* Festival [Rock and Wheels], better known simply as Avándaro. On the weekend of September 11 and 12, 1971, around 250,000 people gathered in the town of Valle de Bravo, in the State of Mexico (approximately two hours from Mexico City), to listen to national groups that were beginning to express a style of their own, capable of competing with the invasion of the so-called "English Wave" that predominated on radio stations and on some national television channels (Campos García).

For years prior to 1971, when the said Festival took place, the Avándaro Circuit car race had been held in the same town, in the State of Mexico. For the year 1971, the plan was to accompany the automobile event with a rock concert. That is why at first it was known as the "Rock and Wheels Festival." However, in the weeks prior to its performance, the musical part began to grow and the car race ended up being canceled the day prior to the event (Del Llano 110–120).

The Festival was held in September 1971, when four numbers of *Piedra Rodante* had already been published. As expected, the magazine covered the event extensively, prior to and after the event. In issue 4, corresponding to the month of August 1971, the Festival was publicized for the first time and three free tickets were offered with the purchase of a subscription. Then, on August 5th (1971), the special issue on Avándaro (#6) was announced, which would finally be published on October 30, 1971.

The *Piedra Rodante* team traveled to the State of Mexico to cover the event on different fronts. The impressions of the concert were outlined to initiate the legend of the mythical weekend, in which young people took over a public space and enjoyed their newly learned freedom under their own rules.

The information that was published in *Piedra Rodante* was highly varied in terms of the types of notes: reports, chronicles, interviews and opinion articles, and included a large quantity of photographs. The editorial line, in general, tended to be favorable to

8 The detailed chronicle on the *Festival Rock y Ruedas de Avándaro* is not the central theme of this article, for more information, cf. Agustín; Rubli; del Llano Macedo.

the organization and final result of the event. Unlike other publications, it did not subscribe to the trend of discrediting and condemning the event as was the case in the national press.[9]

On the first page, the article "*Avándaro y la esperanza*" [Avándaro and Hope], signed by *El Observador*, was published. The cover photo is highly significant, a woman carrying a baby outside a makeshift tent in Avándaro, what better way to take a stand than to present a woman who enjoyed the festival with her son, thus demonstrating that she was living in a responsible manner!

El Observador interviewed a policeman who was in charge of monitoring the Festival, and whose only complaint was about "the plague of journalists," thus providing the author with the opening for the article:

> The pirates of journalism, the gazetteers, the tabloid publications and those who just pretended to be journalists, constituted, in effect, the worst plague. Some of these so called journalists attended the concert with the sole purpose of taking note of the negative aspects so as to discredit the Festival, with the knock-on effect of putting the youth back in the place they belong as their old enemies, and from which they refuse to release them, a place that corresponds to a social stratum unworthy of exercising their rights and that only deserves to suffer all kinds of defamations. (*Piedra Rodante* 6 (8))

Not only these sectors of the press proved to be the ones who caused Avándaro's success or failure, *El Observador* also pointed out other groups that were interested in ruining the festival: "Gang members at the service of the extreme right, who definitively wanted to discredit the current government, also traveled to Avándaro. Their aims were similar, to make the rock festival degenerate into bloody chaos. But neither the soldiers nor the police, fortunately, fell into the trap…" (6).

El Observador highlights the sentiment that prevailed among the young attendees: "forging the spirit of Avándaro," as subjective as it may sound, it seemed to be summarized as follows:

> The youths had set out to forge the spirit of Avándaro; they succeeded, staying united by their enthusiastic fondness for music, by friendship, by the ideals of peace and by the longing for love. The spirit of Avándaro reduced the emissaries of prefabricated anarchy to passivity, they were unable to put into motion the plans of those who were responsible for the massacres of 1968 and of the not yet forgotten June 10th. However, they refused to acknowledge their failure; didn't the Avándaro festival give enough pretexts to fight it? Aah, so you had to invent them …. (6)

Later, the journalist refers to an article published in the *Heraldo de México* and signed by Enrique Ahmed: "But there is no fix, Independence Celebrations: 21 dead, 665 Injured, 275 Arrested" (Ahmed 10) which points out the double standard that prevailed among the corresponding authorities, contrast the excesses caused by the Independence celebration, in which the unfortunate balance is normalized compared to Avándaro's results:

9 For some mentions regarding the press, cf. Campos García.

> In an official government bulletin issued on Thursday by the Attorney General's Office of the District and Federal Territories, it was reported that during the 48 hours of the festivities for the 161st Anniversary of our Independence, 21 people were killed, 665 injured and 275 arrested for violating the law. (10)

The journalist and rock critic, Oscar Sarquiz, in his article "Humiliation, Fraud with the Musicians," referred to the mistreatment suffered by the participating groups, who did not receive what had been agreed with the organizers regarding the provision of accommodation and meals during the Festival, because they were overwhelmed by the crowd.

However, Sarquiz's analysis of Avándaro was positive and especially important because he outlined a more empathetic vision in which generational strength stood out: the discovery of a public eager to listen to native groups and the potential shown by the groups, without discounting the failures:

> The Festival, despite its great flaws, was a success in which 150,000 fans (the official figure within the music area) proved capable of getting on, despite having met in the most precarious conditions.
>
> In Avándaro it was demonstrated, without any doubt, that there is a significant nucleus of young Mexicans who like Rock, freedom and peace, and who are willing to fight for their ideals, whilst enduring all kinds of hardships.
>
> For this reason, national musicians have an audience that deserves respect and for which it is worth working energetically. The future of Rock in Mexico is, in the eyes of performers, brighter than ever. (Sarquiz 10)

Sarquiz also warned about the smear campaign that was unleashed at the conclusion of the Avándaro Festival, whilst echoing the force that was manifested in different aspects regarding the coexistence of the young people:

> All have agreed in stating that the tabloid campaign that most of the upper-class media have unleashed is unfair and tendentious: they enjoy disseminating the negative aspects of Avándaro but ignore the positive: the music, the coexistence. The issues highlighted by journalists do not say much about Avándaro, but rather about their own personalities. No matter, the smear campaign of the newspapers can no longer stop the process that for so many young people began in Avándaro; as Alejandro Lora from Three Souls said: "We already realized that there are many of us, nobody can stop us, because we are right." (10)

In the article "Ceremonia cósmica y poca música," Luis González Reimann first highlighted the spirit of brotherhood that was experienced and how technical failures were dispensed with in order to achieve communication between the audience and the participants on stage, from where, at dawn on Friday, the attendees witnessed the rock opera 'Tommy,' produced by the English group The Who:

> Perhaps here began to form what was to become known as the "Avándaro wave," a true spirit of brotherhood and of the "we already did it" feeling that floated in the air until the last moment. It was very clear that the kids (all aged twenty or under) had heard so much about the Woodstock Festival (and others) and seen the photographs that they needed to experience it themselves. Reading the newspapers was no longer enough. We had to invent our own tribal gathering. And we did it. (González Reimann, "Ceremonia" 18)

This chronicle also highlighted the performance of the police and soldiers who, incidentally, chose to have a cooperative attitude:

> At first, there was a certain insecurity caused by the police who circulated around the place, but it didn't last long. It became clear that they were not there to annoy, but to help. The police from the State of Mexico, with their rifles slung over their shoulders, seemed to be having as much fun as all the kids, and at no time were there any problems. When everyone wants, things work out well. There were also soldiers, but nobody saw them because they were at a good distance from the music venue; they didn't move, thus avoiding any paranoia their presence might have generated. (18)

Paraphrasing González Reimann, what had been achieved was to show that the young people who congregated in Avándaro appropriated a public space to live in a joyous and peaceful way, this mass concert revealed their generational strength. Despite the close surveillance of the army and the infiltrated police, the spirit of brotherhood referred to by Reimann remained in the memory of the attendees, it was conceived as a victory for the young, despite the fact that the official version articulated a black legend that gravely harmed the process of rock development in Mexico.

Later, González Reimann referred to the musical part of the Festival as follows:

> All the music from the Mexican groups was pretty mediocre in general. Most of the local groups presented quite a similar sound and have not yet managed to identify themselves as groups with their own style. Two of the best-known groups that had been announced didn't not show up: Brujo Batiz and Love Army. Too bad, but there were some good moments, and in reality, the music itself was actually secondary, the important thing for everyone was the fact of actually being there together, spending time together; there would be time for music. In other words, the energy and emotion that a group could provide was more important than the quality of their music, and there were many high points …." ("Ceremonia" 18)

González Reimann highlighted the performance of Three Souls in My Mind, and referred to the fact that Alejandro Lora mentioned the unfortunate recent events of June 10; in this way, the journalist focused on the spirit of social empathy and announced that it could also have a place in rock:

> Before playing 'Street Fighting Man' by the Stones, they presented it as follows: "in this festival there has been a lot of talk about love and peace and those things are very cool, but that's not Rock, and to show that we care about things like June 10th, we're going to play a Stones song called 'Street Fighting Man.'" ("Ceremonia" 22)

The editor concluded his note by making a comparison with Woodstock, citing a note alluding to the North American festival published at the time in the *New York Times*:

> That was the Avándaro wave. For a long time there had been a vibe in the air, a meeting was needed, and everyone went with the idea of coexistence, as in the case of the Woodstock model, with the idea of being with the brothers, no violence, quite the opposite: understanding and good vibrations. And perhaps something that the *New York Times* said in an editorial about the legendary Woodstock, in the state of New York, is pertinent here: "The meeting was essentially a phenomenon of innocence … they came, it seems, to enjoy their own society, to live a lifestyle that constitutes its own declaration of independence." (22)

Luis González Reimann's chronicle seems very revealing to us, firstly, because it is a testimony of someone who lived through the Avándaro experience; secondly, because he was a connoisseur of the musical development of rock in Mexico, and thirdly, because when citing Woodstock, and the perception of the North American press, he was highlighting the cultural and social influence from North American pop culture, whose transmission route was undoubtedly rock music, and *Piedra Rodante* was certainly adding its influence in that field too.

From a rather different perspective, you can read the article by Enrique Marroquín, a Catholic priest who attended Avándaro and wrote a chronicle of his experience, entitled "God wants it to rain to unite us!" The liberation theorist focused more on trying to give meaning to the collective experience that the festival had been. Without diminishing the excesses, but also recovering the positives of coexistence, he referred to the mixture of social classes:

> When we arrived, the majority were young boys from proletarian colonies, vocational and high school students who alternated getting to know each other with listening to the music: "What colony are you from?" "No, the good vibes are in *Santa Maria*." "The boys from *Naucalpan*." "The vibes of *Roma*" .... Curious thing; during the festival, I met very few Mexican hippies of the relaxed, mystical vibe. The few that did exist were far back, in shelters loosely built from branches. Those of the more affluent classes wouldn't arrive until Saturday night, in their Mustangs. Hippies from the USA provided the folk note and sported the most colorful outfits. The Mexican kids, for their part, had improvised "gala" costumes as best they could for the occasion. Only a few birds. Few but cool .... (Marroquín, "Dios" 10)

Among the articles that dealt with the Avándaro Festival in *Piedra Rodante*, it is surprising to find two notes originally published in the newspaper *Excélsio*r, the first by Carlos Monsiváis and the second by Carlos Solórzano and entitled "Monsi and Solórzano: Carlos, Not Relatives" (*Piedra Rodante* 7 (30)).

> We would like to focus on Carlos Monsiváis, who was in England when the festival of the Avándaro took place and from that place had sent a letter celebrating the appearance of *Piedra Rodante* months before, which was reproduced in the section "Letters of love and anger." In that letter, Monsiváis expressed among other things: "Enough with the decrepit publications where people give their opinion alternately about the decadence of the customs and the customs of decadence ... you will elaborate a utopia to create a semi-underground press in Mexico, a praise of the Counterculture in a country that does not usually consent even to culture .... Will you have enough Mexican material? That is the enigma and the challenge – to not repeat colonial schemes." (*Piedra Rodante* 4 (2))

However, his views on Avándaro are considered controversial to this day. It is surprising that an intellectual and defender of social movements such as Monsiváis should have stirred up opposition to the festival, because he found forms of "cultural colonialism" in Avándaro reprehensible:

> What is the Nation of Avándaro? Groups that sing in a language that is not their own, innocuous songs; rejection of the Vietnam War, but not of the exploitation of the Mexican peasant; long hair and astrology, but no critical readings and confrontation. I believe that the Nation of the Avándaro is the greatest triumph of the American Mass Media: it

> is the Mr. Hyde of articles, reports and chronicles about Woodstock. It is one of the great moments of mental colonialism in the Third World. (*Piedra Rodante* 7 (30))

He addressed the issue in other essays but never changed his first opinion. As for the controversy that arose in *Piedra Rodante*, Monsiváis had retractors in the face of the lack of empathy with the Jipitecas (Marroquín, *La Contracultura* 28), Alfonso Perabeles (*Piedra Rodante* 7 (2)), and a Tapatian reader, Alejandro Santamaría (*Piedra Rodante* 8 (3)).

Published under the title "*Avándaro, Amor y Pasón*," [Avándaro, Love and Passion] was the chronicle of Parménides García Saldaña, one of *Piedra Rodante*'s most assiduous collaborators. The writer had just arrived from California, having been invited by Fito de la Parra from the group Canned Heat, who expressed a certain skepticism regarding the upcoming Festival:

> Festival of Rock and Wheels, Peace and Love, Avándaro 71. A festival, here? And the government allowed it, can you believe that? Go for it mate: just twenty-five Pesos! Cash, any teacher can drop him. Who will be playing? Only groups from here? What a bad scene, Rock without Americans isn't rock! I mean really, Rock is not Mexican. I say bring Canned Heat and others. Santana or anybody, whoever. Are the rest of the staff coming. But they are going to pay the groups here a pittance, three thousand pesos. What about television rights?. (García Saldaña 34–36)

The comparison with Woodstock was apparently inevitable, for those informed of the 'Woodstock' and 'Monterrey Pop' festivals, the possibility of experiencing their own festival in Aztec territory was somewhat difficult to believe, given the experience of other concerts held in Mexico which had ended in excesses and people being arrested:

> A festival is something very dangerous. Staff can get violent. The '*Halcones*' (the paramilitary group) can go disguised as hippies. Remember the riot at the *Ciudad de los Deportes* (Sports City Stadium) when The Byrds played… In reality, Mexican Rock is not sufficient to create the necessary vibe for a festival. Rock has been repressed a lot in Mexico. Who relaxed? Well, the point is that the government allowed it …. (34–36)

However, Parménides García Saldaña wrote a chronicle in his peculiar journalistic style that reveals his passion and knowledge of rock, combined with sociological notes on "the staff":

> On Friday morning I'll be going to Avándaro by bus, to the Rock and Wheels Festival, Love and Peace, Mexico 1971. Will Avándaro be our national Woodstock? No way, it has nothing to do with Woodstock. Great. Woodstock is the wave. But at Woodstock there were cool groups, stars. In the truck the rockers who participate go there happy, stoned. Give us a drag mate, cheers. A quick one, or two or three. Mexican rockers chatter about our squalid Rock and Roll showbiz …. (34–36)

Several aspects can be highlighted in García Saldaña's article. The writer does not find the Avándaro concert comparable with Woodstock, simply because more consolidated musicians played in the North American concert than at Avándaro. This is a discussion that continued for a long time, which led to another conversation: the political and cultural references in both contexts were different, Woodstock was constituted as a pacifist and countercultural demonstration, the concept of "Love and Peace" was, above all, antiwar. While the hippies who came to Avándaro wanted to listen to rock and have a good time. However, this did not prevent it from also becoming a countercultural manifestation of "self-discovery," of rebellion against an authoritarian state that failed to understand the rights of young people. The founding of the Avándaro Nation (Monsiváis, *Amor perdido* 247) signified a form of recognition for the attendees, of youth identification that was not destroyed, despite the smear campaign in the national press.

"La Santa Pasadena or the Nudist of Avándaro"

One of the most memorable anecdotes from the festival was the striptease performed by a girl on stage whilst the group División del Norte (Rubli 18) was playing, who was baptized as the "Nudist of Avándaro." Spontaneously, to the rhythm of the music, she stripped off her shirt and then took off her pants, before the astonished gaze of the audience. However, there were actually several young people who undressed in Avándaro, though only she became famous, and for a long time her identity was unknown. In the last issue of *Piedra Rodante*, issue 8, corresponding to the month of January 1972, a long interview with the alleged girl was published.

The interviewee spoke in an uninhibited way about her nudism in Avándaro, the consumption of narcotics and her stance on sexual freedom. She had only made a stop at the *Piedra Rodante* newsroom because she was heading to Huautla to experience a mushroom trip. She also spoke of having left the family home due to her dalliance in Avándaro, adding that she was interested in studying nursing.

The interview was deemed to be true for a long time and, without a doubt, in its time it was a very powerful commercial strategy for the magazine. Imagine, finally, the identity of the famous "Avándaro Stripper" was revealed. However, years later, the veracity of the interview was questioned by one of the magazine's collaborators, Oscar Sarquiz, who kicked off a controversy with the director, Manuel Aceves, accusing him of having encouraged the publication of a fictitious interview signed by the writer José Luis Benítez, otherwise known as *El Buker* (*La Jornada,* 2001).[10]

However, in the files that are kept in the General Archive of the Nation, the police report of the interrogation of the girl can be consulted, since she had been arrested, and the identification data does not correspond to the name and place that was printed in the magazine *Piedra Rodante*. Regardless of whether the interview was fictitious or not, the fact is that the article paved the way for the possibility of projecting female imaginary on the rock music experience of this sector in public spaces.[11]

---

10 Regarding this controversy, on the occasion of the 25th Anniversary of Avándaro, two notes were published alluding to the controversy between Manuel Aceves and Oscar Sarquiz, and the intervention of Carlos Martínez Rentería (cf. *La Jornada*, September 14 and September 18, 2001).

11 In this same vein is the article published in issue 7: "But, do Chicano groupies exist?," signed by *El Observador* (*Piedra Rodante*, November 15, 1971).

In the same issue, the article "*Las chavas y el catre*" [Women and the Cot] (*Piedra Rodante* 6-22) was published, which was an extensive report on the sexual practices of Mexican women, based on a study carried out at the Nutrition Hospital in Mexico City, whereby contraceptive pills were provided to a group of volunteers. It is an article that vindicates the pleasure of women to sexual enjoyment, questions the fact that the sexual act is only tolerated for procreation and adds that the right of women to sexual pleasure is not recognized.

Later on, interviews with women of different ages and social strata are reproduced. The fortunate paradox is that the women interviewed claim their right to sexual freedom for themselves, not only as a theory, they also speak of already putting it into practice. There is even mention of abortion. Of course, it is only a representative sample and it is difficult to imagine that the "practitioners" were in the majority.

It is a pity that this column appears in the final issue of *Piedra Rodante*, however, it is still important to recognize that the magazine was concerned about bringing young people's sexual practices to the table for discussion, among other important issues that we cannot address in this article due to the limit on space.

By way of a closing

Without a doubt, *Piedra Rodante* was a magazine that was ahead of its time (Ramírez 155), the historical, political, and social context which saw the publication of its eight issues was governed by the emergence of a new social actor that manifested itself with great power: young people. The editors of *Piedra Rodante* created an editorial line that, over time, managed to distance itself, to a certain extent, from its franchise seal of the North American magazine *Rolling Stone*, because the editors, headed by Manuel Aceves, provided local content very consistent with the youth culture of the moment. They knew how to read their time, and thus placed topics on the discussion table that had rarely been approached with minimum impartiality and empathy. In this way, rock music, drug use, sexual freedom, and the Avándaro Festival were offered a forum for information and analysis in the magazine *Piedra Rodante* that sought to provide a correlation with the perception of its readers.

Despite its short life, from a distance *Piedra Rodante* can be seen as a publication with a marked countercultural accent, a recipient of the political and cultural events of the moment. The magazine itself grew and managed to achieve a balance in the style of its reporting, since it always tried to show an intermediate point of view on the issues considered to be controversial, without falling into paternal or moralistic speeches. Unfortunately, it disappeared when it was becoming more confrontational and provocative or perhaps because of it.

The cultural journalism that *Piedra Rodante* put into practice remains as a testimony to the social practices of Mexican society at the beginning of the 1970s, in which the thrust of the youth cultures of the time was revealed, which, despite the authoritarian state, found several forms of expression that the magazine knew how to channel in excess. *Piedra Rodante* is a publication that, almost fifty years after it started, looks fresh, irreverent, bold, and committed to young people.

Works cited

Aceves, Manuel. "Rolling Stone." *Piedra Rodante* 1.1 (15 May 1971): 5. Print.

Aguilar Sosa, Yanet. "La Onda fue una en la vida y no más. Entrevista con Manuel Aceves, director de *Piedra Rodante*." *La cresta de la ola. Reinvenciones y disgresiones de la Contracultura en México*. Ed. Carlos Martínez Rentería. Jalisco, CULagos: Casa del Poeta, 2009. 235–240. Print.

Agustín, José. *The Counterculture in Mexico*. Mexico: Debolsillo, 2007. Print.

Ahmed, Enrique. "Pero no hay fijón. Fiestas: 21 muertos, 665, heridos, 275 arrestados." *Heraldo de México*, qtd. in *Piedra Rodante* 1.6 (30 Oct. 1971): 10. Print.

Campos García, Yolanda Minerva. "The Institutional Memory on the Avándaro Festival. The Documents on the Festival in the General Archive of the Nation and the Avándaro Report of the Government of the State of Mexico." 2019. Web. *FIAR: Forum for Inter-American Research*. http://interamerica.de/current-issue/campos-2.

Castañeda, Gustavo. "El Festiva del Naranjazo." *Piedra Rodante* 1.1 (15 May 1971): 1; 6. Print.

García Saldaña, Parménides. "Avándaro, Amor y Pasón." *Piedra Rodante* 1.6 (30 Oct. 1971): 34–36. Print.

González Reimann, Luis. "Discos (rpm)." *Piedra Rodante* 1.1 (15 May 1971): 46. Print.

———. "El disco del mes (La Revolución de Emiliano Zapata)." *Piedra Rodante* 1.2 (11 Jun. 1971): 5. Print.

———. "Ceremonia cósmica y poca música." *Piedra Rodante* 1.2 (11 Jun. 1971): 17; 18; 22. Print.

Gutierrez Vidrio, Silvia. "Discurso periodístico: una propuesta de análisis." *Comunicación y Sociedad* 2010: 169–198. Web. http://www.comunicacionysociedad.cucsh.udg.mx/index.php/comsoc/article/view/1285/1162.

"Las chavas y el catre." *Piedra Rodante* 1.8 (Jan. 1972): 6–22. Web. http://digital.library.stonybrook.edu/cdm/compoundobject/collection/rodante/id/252.

Leary, Timothy. "Foreword." *Counterculture Through the Ages: From Abraham to Acid House*. Ken Goffman and Dan Joy. New York: The Random House Publishing Group, 2005. IX–XI. Print.

Llano Macedo, Luis del. *Expedientes Pop*. México: Planeta, 2016. Print.

Marroquín, Enrique. *La Contracultura como protesta*. México: Joaquín Mortiz, 1975. Print.

———. "Dios quiere que llueva para unirnos." *Piedra Rodante* 1.6 (30 Oct. 1971): 10–11. Print.

Monsiváis, Carlos. *Amor perdido*. México: Bolsillo Era, 2005. Print.

———. "For All Things There is Seasoning, a Rock Chronicle by Monsi." 21 Oct. 2010. Web. https://www.milenio.com/cultura/laberinto/carlos-monsivais-cronica-fallido-concierto-byrds, Recovered from the issue printed on 21/10/2010.

Perabeles, Alfonso, Josefo Ruiz Esparza, Gustavo Castañeda, Federico Camphel, and Marisa López. "La Revolución de Emiliano Zapata." *Piedra Rodante* 1.1 (15 May 1971): 22–25.

Peza Casares, Carmen De La. *El rock mexicano. Un espacio en disputa*. México: UAM-X, 2013. Print.

"Polydor lanza Serie Rock Power." *Piedra Rodante* 1.4 (Aug. 1971): 8. Print.

Ramírez, José Agustín. *La contracultura en México. La historia y el significado de los rebeldes sin causa, los jipitecas, los punks y las bandas*. México: Debolsillo, 2017. Print.

Rubli, Federico, *Yo estuve en Avándaro*, Mexico, Trilce Editores, UNAM, *Fondo Editorial del Estado de México*, ENGRANDE, 2016. Print

Sarquiz, Oscar. "Humillación, fraude con los músicos." *Piedra Rodante* (30 Oct. 1971): 10. Print.

Shaw, Greg. "Cómo sacar buena luz en la crítica de rock." *Piedra Rodante* (Jan. 1972): 76. Print.

Urteaga, Maritza. "Imágenes juveniles del México moderno." *Historia de los jóvenes en México. Su presencia en el siglo XX.* Ed. José Antonio Pérez Islas and Maritza Urteaga. México: Instituto Mexicano de la Juventud/Centro de Investigación y Estudios sobre Juventud/Archivo General de la Nación, 2004. 33–89. Print.

Wenner, Jann S. "Four Decades on Our Own with no Direction Home." *Rolling Stone*. New York: Bondi Digital Publishing, 2007. 7–12. Print.

Zolov, Eric. "La Onda Chicana. México's Forgotten Rock Contraculture." *Rocking Las Americas. The Global Politics of Rock in Latin/o America.* Ed. Deborah Pacini Hernández, Héctor Fernández L'Hoeste, and Eric Zolov. Pittsburgh: U of Pittsburgh P, 2004. 22–42. Print.

Sonic America(s): Politics of Recognition and Recent Trends in Music Documentary

WILFRIED RAUSSERT

Sound- and imagescapes from the Americas have shaped and performed the social in the Americas. These scapes at times supersede language as mediators and commentators of the social. In the late twentieth century, MTV music/video culture established musical sound and image as interconnected and almost inseparable expressions of youth cultures (Edgar, Fairclough-Isaacs, and Halligan). The music documentary and its growing presence in TV programs, film festivals, cinema programs, and museums of popular culture point toward the genre's increasingly important role in endorsing celebrity culture and rewriting music history. The music documentary provides a matrix to rethink music historiography in narrative forms where image, sound, and word interact intensely. It also lends itself to relocating music in history and at the intersection of entertainment, commerce, and heritage politics. Likewise, as I argue in this chapter, the music documentary reflects the interrelation of music and the social on a grander scale.

A proliferation of documentaries as well as other non-fiction or reality formats characterizes recent developments in media industry. And they reveal new tendencies in redefining the documentary mode. In global network society with its inclination toward hyperreality, simulacrum, and media saturation (Baudrillard 9ff.), the flourishing of the documentary mode responds to a newly awakened desire to come to terms with the real, the social, and with history at large. Popular documentary series for television like Martin Scorsese's *The Blues* (2003), a compilation of seven blues documentaries directed by renowned film directors from around the globe, reveal the attractiveness of the genre for fiction and nonfiction filmmakers. The documentaries highlight a new level of interaction of music and documentary film as a mix-media historiography between education and entertainment. It is safe to say that documentary filmmaking has hit the big screen and successfully rid itself of its former confinement to noncommercial distribution. Filmmakers like Michael Moore and Marilyn Agrelo have produced multi-million revenues. Documentary films like *Fahrenheit 9/11* (2004) and *An Inconvenient Truth* (2006) raised public consciousness of political and ecological issues. Music documentaries like *Searching for Sugar Man* (2012) and *20 Feet from Stardom* (2015) rose to Oscar-winning fame, achieving critical and popular acclaim. Mitchell Block emphasizes that with the beginning of the twenty-first century, "theatrical exhibition of documentaries became a business" (n. pag.) for the larger film and entertainment industry. Documentary film not only flourishes in the contemporary digital age but adds to the creative representation of actuality through new hybrid and participatory formats. We encounter documentary modes crossed with staged performances and animation. An intensified presence of hyperreality (Baudrillard) and performativity (Bruzzi 53–56) shapes the narrative modes of music documentary film and shows that the line between fiction and non-fiction film is nothing but thin and porous. Against the backdrop of these dynamics, selective approaches to truth and forms of eclectic and fragmentary narration of content and context are highlighted. Increasingly, actuality is pressed into narrative modes and patterns geared toward popular narrative and public success. "The long-cherished idea that truth in documentary film is established in a process exclusively controlled by the documentarian seems increasingly untenable," as Thies maintains (168). Music documentaries are deeply embedded in the mechanisms of the cultural industry at large (Yúdice 9–39). Sheila Curran Bernard emphasizes that "in today's documentary marketplace, story is what commissioning editors are looking for, and training in storytelling is deemed necessary for filmmakers" (6).

Tony Palmer's 1970s TV series *All You Need is Love* may be seen as a starting point to create large span music documentaries geared toward education embedded in entertainment (Long and Wall 25–26). In the twenty-first century, music documentaries like Wim Wenders's *Buena Vista Social Club* (1999) and Martin Scorsese's *Shine a Light* (2008) have popularized the genre, interweaving moments of political actuality, nostalgia, and musical history into documentary success stories. Standing out as box office successes, they illustrate the music documentary's newly gained popularity for and within the cultural industry (Yúdice 9–35).

Part of the documentary revival in recent years is the growing production of documentaries on music in the Americas. One striking tendency among filmmakers is the selection of hotbeds of social crisis and change like Havana in Cuba, Detroit in the U.S., and the U.S.-Mexican borderlands as background to the music historiography they want to present. Havana, for instance, has become a most popular site for music documentary makers. As Geoffrey Baker has documented, some dozen documentaries on the hip hop scene in Havana alone have moved the focus from traditional Cuban music to hip hop in Cuba and its relations to global subcultures.

The documentary approach varies from film to film. Some documentaries pursue a high degree of objectivity and historicity in a conventional sense (*Cuban Hip Hop Desde el Principio* [2006]), others openly embrace politics and polemics (*Guerrilla Radio* [2007], *A Short Radiography of Hip Hop in Cuba* [2004]), and a third group follows artistic and symbolical patterns to create new narratives based on hip hop's cultural significance (*Havanyork* [2009]). Their differences and meanings cannot be understood without comprehending their cultural, economic, or political agendas. Many of the documentaries, such as Mexican director Luciano Larobina's *Havanyork*, are made by cultural outsiders and demonstrate the filmmaker's awareness of music's key role in performing and reflecting social change. These films not only give voice to the hip hop scene in Cuba but also shape it by narrating it anew in the mode of tourist, nostalgic, or romanticizing gazes. The link between image and music and their significance for rethinking the social in music documentaries particularly thrives in those films that create cultural narratives that transcend the notion of the musical expression or genre. *Havanyork* represents a filmic journey between New York and Havana and conveys Larobina's objective to bridge the gap between the U.S. and Cuba cinematically and musically. Oscillating between images from both cities, inserting the individual stories from hip hoppers in New York and Havana, and narrating connected subcultures beyond Cold War political divisions, the documentary creates a tapestry of interconnected Southern and Northern hemispheres. As Baker puts it, "the idea behind this film is as much to create a bridge between New York and Havana as to describe one" (n. pag.). While the desire for objectivity may fall prey to narrative vision, music in *Havanyork*'s visual and sonic representations serves as cultural memory and template for a new socio-cultural vision.

Music documentaries are increasingly present in film festivals, such as in Los Angeles and Montreal. The Guadalajara International Film Festival, one of the most influential film festivals in the Americas, started to dedicate a whole section to documentaries on music in 2009. In a rubric labeled "Son de Música," the festival organizers presented a wide array of documentaries on music genres, individual artists, bands, and the migration of music in the Americas and extended global contexts. Among the films shown were Barbara Kopple's *Woodstock: Now & Then* (USA, 2009), Jacki Reem Salloum's *Slingshot Hip Hop* (Palestine/USA, 2008), Guto Barra's *Beyond Ipanema* (Brasil/USA, 2009), Luciano Larobina's *Havanyork* (Mexico, 2009), and Bestor Cram's *Johnny Cash at Folsom Prison* (USA, 2008). While these films differ strikingly in their use of camera and narrative, they all mediate the representation of "otherness" in music be it ethnic, racial, class-based or counter-cultural.

My focus in this chapter lies on a recent wave of music documentary films that have gained commercial as well as critical success. In the U.S. context, for instance, documentaries like *Standing in the Shadows of Motown* (2002), *The Wrecking Crew!* (2008), *Muscle Shoals* (2013), *A Band Called Death* (2012), *Searching for Sugar Man* (2012), *Charles Bradley* (2012), and *20 Feet from Stardom* (2013) represent a fairly recent direction in music documentary of making unheard voices heard. These films are frequently linked with urban, regional, and community sites in crisis and change. They attempt to fill gaps in music history and correct standardized narratives about music genres. Unlike canonical music documentaries that take for their subject matter celebrities like Harry Belafonte, Bruce Springsteen, Neil Young, Eric Clapton, Ruben Blades, and most recently Whitney Houston, these films focus on the stories of minor figures. In spite of their historical and political interest, they unfold music historiography as entertainment; they do not hide their ambition to create narratives to reach larger audiences and popular acclaim. They seem to share what Jean-François Lyotard labels the postmodern "incredulity toward metanarratives" (1). Looking into minor and puzzling stories of music history, they tend to produce postmodern knowledge that "refines our sensitivity to differences and reinforces our ability to tolerate the incommensurable" (1).

Knowledge production and music have long been recognized as close allies in the formation of the social. According to George Lipsitz, popular music functions as a "vital repository for collective memory" (vii). Although they may not consciously or intentionally see themselves as historians, songwriters frequently provide "alternative archives of history" (xi) emerging from the artist's experience, memory, and vision. Popular music, in particular, functions as a "vital repository for collective memory" (vii). Music functions as an excellent medium for representing communal values, since music can be enjoyed across the otherwise strict divisions of different languages and customs. For this very reason, music is adaptable to different cultural and social contexts, which also means that music can be appropriated for the purposes of exposing, narrating, and reflecting the social beyond local, regional, and national boundaries. The music documentary, then, is an additional medium to emphasize the historicizing power of music.

The recent wave of music documentaries unravels music historiography within a complex network of education, history-making, entertainment, and politics of recognition. More intensely than ever, the topics and sites chosen are embedded in a larger politics of recognition. Certainly, recognition is a highly debated concept, but it still holds a strong position in theories of subject formation. As Winfried Fluck puts it with a nod to Althusser and Butler, "by means of interpellation … recognition remains crucial …. Recognition is not gained in reciprocal acknowledgement of others but in an act of hailing (interpellation) that turns individuals into subjects" (170–171). Current films like *Searching for Sugar Man*, *20 Feet from Stardom*, and *A Band Called Death* engage with interpellation as "a performative practice whose effectiveness is based on iteration" (171). In these films, musicians, singers, and composers gain an identity (perhaps fluid) by a form of recognition. Despite their at times incomplete and eclectic narrations, these films share a desire to correct flawed representations of others and expose social, political, and cultural conditions in music history. In recent years, as Wendy Martineau, Nasar Meer, and Simon Thompson point out, "the idea of the politics of recognition has become an increasingly popular way of thinking about a wide range of political phenomena from the logic of social struggles to the nature of social justice" (1). Music history has been shaped by recognition and absence, the latter often reinforced by the misrecognition of others. Such misrecognition Richard Rorty reads as a lack of solidarity (190). The positioning of musicians in music history has also to do with certain group affiliations. That musicians from various ethnic, racial, and gender backgrounds have played a subordinate role or suffered absence in music histories has also to do with what Charles Taylor defines as the consequences of group entrapment and asymmetrical relations: "If a certain group is demeaned or held in contempt, its members will face forms of neglect, exclusion, and subordination" (25–26, 24).

By selecting several representative documentaries, this chapter looks at how politics of recognition shape new minor narratives in contemporary music documentary at the intersection of historiography and mass entertainment. To narrow the focus of the relation between music, music documentary, and the social, I select documentaries related to music emerging from sites of crisis like Havana, Detroit, and the U.S.-Mexican borderlands.

***Buena Vista Social Club* (1999)**

Let me begin with Wim Wenders's well-known 1999 documentary *Buena Vista Social Club*, which arguably is not only a late-twentieth-century beginning of a wave of music documentaries feeding on nostalgia and a politics of recognition in the twenty-first century but also a striking manifestation of the politically charged mobility of music. The music documentary thematizes the long broken ties between Cuba and the Western World through the lens of music. Many of the filmic elements serve as a reservoir to rethink music through the social and the social through music. Wenders's film is a transcultural product bringing together the musical experience of Buena Vista Social Club musicians and singers such as Compay Segundo, Eliades Ochoa, Ruben Gonzalez, Ibrahim Ferrer, and Omara Portuondo; the music ethnography and creative spirit of American musician Ry Cooder; the production talents of Nick Gold, and Wenders's cinematographic mastery of narrative progression. By providing intimate looks into the lives and minds of musicians aged 80 and more, who are seemingly far beyond the possibility of new musical success, the film narrative takes an affectionate approach to music historiography that evokes empathetic responses from the spectator.

Old age, Cuban music history, and long forgotten musicians find recompense in Wenders's narrative of Cuban *son*'s late global success. The film's title is a borrowing from the album that Ry Cooder had produced with Buena Vista Social Club in 1997. Both album and film emerged toward the end of the Cuban crisis in the 1990s, the so-called Special Period, and helped bring Cuban music and culture back into Western circuits. While Wenders's film did not rediscover the Buena Vista Social Club, it distinctly expanded the international recognition that the above musicians had already gained from the album and show. As I argue, Wenders's film establishes central strategies for music documentaries in the twenty-first century to rethink music and the social as interrelated. His narration of Cuban music is one that tells and partly idealizes Cuba's musical emergence after a cultural freeze during the cold war period. In a nostalgic twist, Wenders reloads Cuba's music culture that had its heydays in the 1940s and 1950s before the Cuban Revolution. This nostalgia for the golden days of Cuban music that flourished in the context of a totalitarian and repressive regime, though, is paired with stories of a new cultural recognition exemplified by the Amsterdam and Carnegie Hall concert in New York and a mythic recreation of the West as arbiter of world music. Cuba is culturally reintegrated in the larger world order of Western '*gusto*.' When the Cuban musicians walk the streets of Manhattan in awe, it is not only a celebration of newly gained mobility but also of New York as the cultural hub of the modern world. Emblematically, the show window scene of the encounter of Buena Vista Social Club musicians encountering replicas of American greats like Louis Armstrong, Ray Charles, and Miles Davis illustrates both the rupture that had characterized U.S.-Cuban relations and the lingering admiration from the South for the globally successful culture of the North.

The Buena Vista band of aging Cuban musicians, once affiliated with a prominent 1940s' social club in Havana of the same name and cast into oblivion in Castro's

Cuba, provides fortunate material for a culturally and politically motivated American success story, this time, however, transnationally produced. With the release of Wenders's film, the band's global success skyrocketed. The scenes from and around the concert in New York illustrate a politically engaging story that envisions a new connectedness between Cuba and the U.S. and demonstrate that Wenders's narrative is loosely embedded in a larger context of historical conflict and change. Whereas comments of admiration for the Manhattan skyline by musicians like Ibrahim Ferrer insert a desire to embrace U.S. culture, the filmic representation of Havana evokes a sense of nostalgia for a decaying political and economic system on the brink of collapse beneath the weight of the West. The camera light surrounds the decaying colonial architecture of Havana in a shimmering vintage style. Musicians from the Buena Vista Social Club walk the streets as a public memory lane while the streets of Manhattan promise the future. Wender's narrative stages Ry Cooder's arrival on motorbike in Havana as a friendly but firm cultural conquest. Rewriting musical history gets paired with a desire for participatory appropriation. In most concert and recording scenes, Cooder takes center stage as mediator and producer. This gesture is sanctioned by also telling the story of a latent desire of Cuban musicians and artists to finally immerse their products into markets of the Western cultural industry. Wenders's fascination with Cuban and American culture is honest. His rendering of politics of recognition cannot avoid revisiting hegemonic cultural relations. Declared forgotten, Cuban music is heard again, but now channeled through Western music venues and film production.

Both, album and film, illustrate the political work of cultural production. In retrospect, the Buena Vista Social Ckub musicians' role as messengers of traditional Cuban music and culture played a significant cultural part in the improvement of political relations between Cuba and the U.S. The fact that the musicians finished their Carnegie Hall concert with a proud presentation of the Cuban flag in the midst of one of the cultural cathedrals in the U.S. underscores the film's desire to create a relational narrative for a future U.S.-Cuban connectedness. The documentary film as box office success revealed that the culture industry, too, had recognized the image-sound connection as a gateway for Cuban traditional music to enter global music circuits. It is significant that these political and economic opportunities were made possible by a musical and cultural exchange between Cuba, the U.S., and Europe, leading to a Cuban musical success story on a global scale. Wenders's example shows that the documentation of music in the late twentieth and early twenty-first century is inextricably related to nostalgia and a politics of recognition, as well as to the production of knowledge for consumption in Western markets. *Buena Vista Social Club* also demonstrates that the visual documentation of music can go beyond furnishing a subject matter and soundtrack; it can serve as a way to reinvent the social, as we see with this film's reappropriation of music for new historiographies of Cuban-U.S. American cultural entanglements.

Standing in the Shadows of Motown (2002)

Detroit, the first U.S. American city that ever had to declare bankruptcy, is home to an increasing number of music documentaries. With its historical cycles of social and political crisis on the one hand, and of tremendous music output on the other, Detroit represents an ideal matrix for dynamic and tension-driven documentaries that rethink music historiography in a larger context of social relations and development. Music documentaries like *Standing in the Shadows of Motown*, *20 Feet from Stardom*, *A Band Called Death*, and *Searching for Sugar Man* create soundscapes as cityscapes providing a strong identification between city, music, and musicians. Twenty-first century U.S. music documentaries tend to follow templates that translate politics of recognition into a creative process of rewriting music historiography, while at the same time presenting carefully crafted storylines to keep the audience entertained. These templates bring musicians, background singers, and performers largely ignored by the music industry into the spotlight.

Allan Slutsky's book *Standing in the Shadows of Motown: The Life and Music of Legendary Bassist James Jamerson* (1989) forms the basis for the Grammy award winning music documentary *Standing in the Shadows of Motown* (2002) directed by Paul Justman. The film's mode is predominantly poetic, the script written by Walter Dallas and Ntozake Shange. The film is set in Detroit, the home of Motown and witness to many Civil Rights marches and street dances inspired by Martha and the Vandellas. The film adds alternative historiography to the cultural music histories told by critics like Suzanne Smith in *Dancing in the Street: Motown History and the Cultural Politics of Detroit* (2009). Smith portrays Motown's evolution from a small local record company in Detroit's black community to a global player in the music industry and establishes Motown music as cultural agent in politically turbulent times. The story of Motown as a music industry and successful sound enterprise is also a story of black Detroit and a microcosm of black America. Complementary to Smith's narrative, the music documentary places minor stories within this larger picture by highlighting the talents and fates of lesser known musicians involved.

Justman's music documentary tackles the Motown music history from the economically privileged position of a budget film production. The film's agenda is to create a counter-narrative to the standardized success stories of 1960s music history and expose a band of largely ignored black studio musicians as local cultural heroes. High production values are enlisted to present a highly entertaining cinematographic historiography. The documentary represents and elevates the skills of studio musicians and their significant role in shaping the sound of Motown. The film's protagonists comprise the Motown studio musicians Earl Van Dyke, Joe Hunter, Johnny Griffith, Eddie Willis, Joe Messina, Robert White, William Benjamin, Uriel Jones, Richard Allen, James Jamerson, Bob Babbitt, Jack Ashford, und Eddie Brown, a group also known as The Funk Brothers. Adopting strategies used by Wenders in *Buena Vista Social Club*, Justman's documentary unites many of the former Funk Brothers with the purpose of unraveling their musical grandeur and releasing them from long-time oblivion. The documentary stages the musicians' iteration of masterful performance skills. Exaltation follows iteration in the film's progression so that the storyline moves back and forth between documentation and celebration.

Most of the musicians portrayed had been gathered by Berry Gordy from many jazz and blues clubs in Detroit from the late 1950s to the early 1970s to record the musical tracks for his Motown label. According to the film's narrative, The Funk Brothers' studio performances were the key to the success of Motown music. They accompanied Motown luminaries, only to be all but abandoned when the label moved to L.A. in the early 1970s. At the time of filmmaking, many band members, including Benjamin, Jamerson, Brown, Van Dyke, and others had experienced bankruptcy and oblivion; some had already died. City and music historiography complement each other seamlessly. Race riots, class struggle, and exploitative practices in the Detroit music industry form the backdrop to the marginalization of Motown studio musicians. *Standing in the Shadows of Motown* allows the surviving Funk Brothers to tell their own story against the social reality of city decay and Motown's dubious business dealings.

The music documentary installs voiceover commentary as a bridge to line up historical reenactments, several interviews of the Funk Brothers' members, and the reunion concert as an assemblage and final climax of recognition. The film is a blend of archive footage, oral history, vivid reenactments, and concert film. The voiceover by Andre Braugher addresses the audience directly with the "recount history" (Nichols 105) of Motown Records and a brief introduction of the Funk Brothers. In the opening scenes, the documentary unfolds the history of the Funk Brothers in its relation to larger social and economic developments in the industries of Detroit. The story line emblematically situates the origin of the Funk Brothers within the migration of tens of thousands of workers to Detroit after World War II. Images of migrant workers and the blossoming car industry form the backdrop to an intersectional narrative addressing race and class. Interviews with musician Joe Hunter about his original jobs in the car factory and his motivation to play music emerging from the working experience provide a master narrative that establishes a close link between the socio-economic context, musical expression, and the evolving music business in Detroit.

Beyond the "argumentative frame" of documentary making (Nichols 105), *Standing in the Shadows of Motown* adopts poetic as well as performative patterns to tell a story of resurrection and recognition (Renov; Bruzzi). In Nichols's reading of documentary practice, the poetic mode permits the exploration of "associations and patterns that involve temporal rhythms and spatial juxtapositions" (102). Justman fuses recent musical material by the Funk Brothers with archive footage of dead band members to create the impression of a cultural continuum. The reunion concert in the present gets intersected by band members' memories and archive footage. Thus, the music documentary fuses the storytelling function of Braugher's voiceover with the performativity of the concert, creating a mix of telling and performing the social history behind the Motown sound.

The storyline emerging around the deceased bass player James Jamerson is arguably the most illustrative for the generational narrative of *Standing in the Shadows of Motown*. The voiceover about James Jamerson's boyhood emerges against the background of a short video clip of the bass player's former school site. A reenactment scene of a little boy playing a self-made instrument follows the archive footage before the interview of James Jamerson Jr. telling his father's story takes center stage. In the reenactment scene, Jamerson is shown as a little boy creating a makeshift bass out of a stick strung with a rubber band. Jameson Jr. is shown reenacting the one-finger plucking that marked the late bass player's unique and captivating style. Among its other stories, the film here provides an uplifting story of a little known bass player legend through family narrative, replacing the musician's actual decline into alcoholism and oblivion with a story of a musical continuum from father to son. This is a major storyline among many other minor ones that give voice to the sounds, rhythms, and people behind the globally successful Motown sound.

Similar to Wenders' *Buena Vista Social Club*, Justman's music documentary is driven by a strong nostalgia for the past and a desire to perform music history anew. The documentary film celebrates the Funk Brothers as principal creators of the Motown sound behind seemingly endless number one hits in the U.S. charts. With the Funk Brothers as the mastermind of one of the greatest soundtracks in music history, the film uplifts working class and race in an alternative historiography and rethinks the social from the perspective of the dispossessed (Butler and Athanasiou 4–5).

20 Feet from Stardom (2013)

A decade later, aspects of Motown and Detroit music history, within a larger context of rock music history, were revisited from a transcultural and gender perspective in the Academy-award-winning music documentary and box office hit *20 Feet from Stardom* by Morgan Neville, one of the most prolific documentary producer/directors of American pop culture, credited with documentaries on Muddy Waters, James Brown, and James Taylor among others. The music documentary mixes archival material, TV footage, concert clips, recent interviews, recording scenes, and private and public scenes from the lives of the portrayed female vocalists. Beginning with the story of Darlene Love, who, with her trio The Blossoms, helped tear down the color barrier for black backup singers in the early 1960s, the film revisits black female artists in the context of rock music but looks at musical history through a sharpened lens of gender and race. Arguably, background singers in rock music historically contributed to "politics of racial alterity" (Fast 171ff.). A great number of black female background singers performed aside or behind white male rock icons like Bruce Springsteen, Mick Jagger, Sting, Joe Cocker, and African American icons like Ray Charles, Ike Turner, and Stevie Wonder. As Susan Fast reminds us, the stage scenario reinforced persisting patterns of "heteronormativity and whiteness" (174) even at a time when the feminist movement took full speed in the 1960s. With reference to the title '*20 Feet from Star-*

dom,' David Scott Diffrient maintains that "those … twenty feet also hint at the larger history of race relations and sexual politics in twentieth-century America" (26). Concert venues and recording sessions frequently reproduced "divisionist discourses and segregationist policies" (26) from larger society in the realm of music. *20 Feet from Stardom* clearly addresses the power structures visible in the performance culture of popular music along the lines of gender and race and presents itself as a revisionist documentary to bring this issue to the foreground. Similar to music documentaries such as *Muscle Shoals* and *The Wrecking Crew*, all of which narrate the histories of largely unknown instrumental backing groups, *20 Feet from Stardom* seeks to tell the silenced history of female background vocalists and their respective roles in concert performances and recordings of R&B and rock since the early 1960s.

20 Feet from Stardom's proclaimed protagonists are primarily African American female background singers such as Merry Clayton, Darlene Love, and Lisa Fischer. While their stories stand in the foreground, they equally serve as gateway to introduce other female vocalists, including Afro Caribbean Tata Vega, who tours with Elton John; Cindy Mizelle, who backs up Bruce Springsteen; and Janice Pendarvis, who collaborates with Stevie Wonder. Against the backdrop of skyrocketing music careers like those of Ray Charles, Ike and Tina Turner, and others, the film thus brings out previously marginalized members of rock music groups and provides a generational panorama of female back-up vocalists whose overlapping careers span a roughly sixty-year period (1950s–2010s). Many of these performers share similar histories of starting out as singers in gospel choirs, mastering the call-and-response techniques essential to background performance, and eventually pursuing their own musical careers in the realm of R&B and rock music. The film permits them to recount their own stories and add histories to counter the standard historiography of R&B and rock music. Concert and recording clips, and interviews that offer insights into the female vocalists' everyday lives fuse the public and private persona to create a series of minor portrayals.

Admittedly, the film chronicles a shift from white to black female back-up vocalists in the 1960s and also addresses the consequences of complex racial politics in the musical industry. One of the female protagonists in the film is Tata Vega, whose ethnicity and multiracial background (her family hails from Puerto Rico and the Dominican Republic) complicated her access to contracts and performances. Zaineb Mohammed cites Vega in her film review: "I did have a hard time finding gigs because of the way I looked," she said. "Either I was too white, not white enough, too black, not black enough" (n. pag.). As this example shows, the film does not shy back from highlighting the complexity of changing racial and gender politics in the 1960s. Still, its take on the social dimension of musical performance remains framed by heteronormative patterns of recognition. Orthodox music historiography keeps creeping into the film's overall narrative when voices of rock icons complement the female histories, applauding the singers through a male gaze and voice. The talking-head interviews with rock stars such as Bruce Springsteen, Mick Jagger, and Sting effectively provide recognition of the women's histories by male authority figures. Their voices overlay archival footage and frame recently recorded studio performances in which the female backup vocalists now take center stage.

With a nod to Andrew Flory, I argue that while questions about gender differences, inequalities, and power asymmetries are raised by the music documentary, thus pointing toward the imbrication of musical performance, many remain largely unanswered:

> Why did rock musicians, who were mostly white and male, start to value the "insertion" of female vocal blackness (or a 'gospel vocal sound') into their music? How did this "syncretic sound" represent the changing cultural identity of rock during the 1960s and 1970s? Finally, what are we to make of the issues of race, gender, and power implied by this characteristic representation? (Flory n. pag.)

Instead, the music documentary drifts off in domestic stories, explores gender issues in relation to career making, addresses racial issues in a predominantly personal context, and plays with personal erotic attractions between black female vocalists and white male front singers.

It is fair to say that the documentary uncovers neglected and largely unknown voices whose musical power and expressivity get full aesthetic recognition. The film also shows that linking gender, race, and music reveals new historiographies, thus making us see the interrelatedness of social developments and music history in a more complex light. Still, historiography in *20 Feet from Stardom* gets framed, limited, and controlled by the film's high-budget necessity to appeal to an imagined, predominantly heteronormative mainstream. The film demonstrates that despite their best intentions, alternative music historiographies struggle to come to terms with the asymmetrical power hierarchies deeply inscribed in the market policies of the music industry, which encourages narratives of music history that maximize profit.

Searching for Sugar Man (2012)

Oscar award-winning music documentary *Searching for Sugar Man*, directed and written by the late Malik Bendjelloul, tells a story of transnational music flows with the songs of Sixto Díaz Rodríguez and their countercultural impact on white South African middle-class youth culture in the 1970s and 1980s. In 2012, the film premiered at the Sundance Film Festival. The documentary, produced by Simon Chinn and John Battsek as a Swedish-British transnational project, gained further fame by winning the World Cinema Special Jury Prize and the Audience Award for World Cinema Documentary. A year after its release, the documentary won the Award for Best Documentary Feature at the 85th Academy Awards.

Searching for Sugar Man is a multifaceted documentary that is more about music and social relations than music itself. The music documentary catapults imaginaries of Detroit working class hardships in the late 1960s and early 1970s and glimpses into white youth protest culture in apartheid-era South Africa in the late 1970s and 1980s. Key figure is Sixto Díaz Rodríguez, a musician born in Detroit of Mexican and Native

American descent. He recorded two albums with Sussex, *Cold Fact* in 1970 and *Coming from Reality* in 1971. Combining the story of Rodríguez's minor music career with Detroit's working class history and a changing South African social and historical landscape, the documentary links three thin narratives in an aesthetically-crafted plotline that stylizes and mystifies Rodríguez as an icon for white youth protest in South Africa and socially active artist-citizen of the Detroit working class. The documentary reads like a "fairytale of a Mexican American working class hero finding recognition amongst his unknown fans in far-away South Africa" (Hyslop 491) and "derives its appeal, in large part, from the way it allegorizes and dramatizes South Africa's emergence from an isolated, censorious pariah state to a participant in an increasingly globalized world" (Lewsen 456). In the figure of Rodríguez, recognition becomes threefold: first, there is a personal recognition for him as musician with the climax of his first concert in Cape Town in March 1998, second, there is a recognition of Rodríguez as embodiment of the enduring spirit of the Detroit working class, and, third, there is a recognition of South Africa as member of a global society exemplified by its participation in cultural exchange.

In a highly eclectic manner, the film not only connects these three narratives but builds a postmodern minor success story in which a lot of idealizing and mystifying takes place around a few 'cold facts' about Rodríguez's life. The spectator learns about his different jobs as hard-working laborer in Detroit, his role as a caring father, his political engagement in his Detroit community, and his performances in run-down local clubs. As the story puts it, it was the combination of voice and lyrics that opened the doors to the recording industry. However, his two albums sold few copies in the U.S., and consequently Sussex dropped Rodríguez before he could release a third album. Sussex itself closed shortly after in 1975.

While Rodríguez never gained recognition by the American public and larger music industry in the U.S. during the 1970s, the film and earlier re-release of the albums *Cold Fact* and *Coming from Reality* by Light in the Attic Records brought Rodríguez to the attention of critics and fans in the U.S. and Europe in the twenty-first century. The film's unusual American success story created prominent news coverage and ushered in a new fan culture around a musician whose modest and humble personality made him an uplifting representative for the working class of the economically battered Detroit. Arguably, his songs of working class experience and urban melancholia finally found better hearing in the twenty-first century U.S., a time when the U.S. myth of a classless society continues to be heavily challenged by social reality.

Like *Buena Vista Social Club* and *20 Feet from Stardom*, *Searching for Sugar Man* proves that while the American Dream may have lost some of its appeal, new transculturally produced success stories in the 'American style' continue to sell well. The story reads like a modern myth inserting elements of suspense, enigma, and animation to create a poetic and performative mode of documentary. Roe detects in the combination of animation and documentary "an odd couple" (1). Their opposite positions in portraying the real, however, offer a unique perspective in how we view the world, she argues. This odd coupling in particular underscores the cinematic power to construct and perform the social within a documentary mode that seeks to expose, convince, and entertain. The film reflects and performs the social by connecting working class endurance in the U.S with countercultural politics in anti-apartheid South Africa through global music circuits. It is the traveling of sound and word as means for identity and resistance that crosses barriers between classes and nations and that exposes the social as flexible and fluid (Bauman 2–3).

Bendjelloul's film explicitly treats the medium of documentary as "not being reality but a construct" (Rabiger 68). The search for the true story behind Rodríguez, as it unfolds in the film, permits "the possibility of alternative forms of knowledge to the straightforward transfer of information, the prosecution of a particular argument or point of view" (Nichols 103). As for the film director, mythmaking appears to be an appropriate means for coming closer to the truth to be conveyed. Drawing upon a well-structured mix of talking-head interviews, archival footage, and several melancholic animation scenes, Bendjelloul creates a narrative based upon unity of tone and effect (E.A. Poe). The opening narrative announces the potentially greatest suicide story in the history of rock about a musician who presumably had put himself on fire while on stage. The camera shifts from distant views of Cape Town, South Africa, to night shots of Detroit in thunder and lightning. Dramatic music, narration, and image create a spooky atmosphere to open the film's narrative of rediscovery and recognition. Every piece of information from various interviews adds new mystery to the puzzle and holds the viewer in suspense about who was or is Rodríguez. While his persona is initially kept a mystery, the songwriter's mournful urban laments accompany the mythmaking storytelling of the compiled interviews as background music. The tone of mystery is confirmed by interviews with the producers of Rodríguez's record and a bartender who vaguely remembers the protagonist as a peculiar musician wandering the streets of Detroit and performing with his back to audience.

Since the documentary holds back and then reveals information only step by step, it also narrates bits and pieces of the archival work behind documentation on a meta-level, spicing it with elements of suspense and mystery. The rumors of Rodríguez's suicide, for instance, are encouraged rather than questioned by the wave of early interviews. Driven by the melancholic mood of Rodríguez's songs, the film unfolds a quest story whose narrative elements are the selected interviews with music producers, music fans, Rodríguez's daughters, and Rodríguez himself. Going through a timespan of over thirty years, *Searching for Sugar Man* portrays a romanticized search for the true history behind Rodríguez. The music documentary moves back and forth between South Africa and Detroit, revolving around the archival work of the two Cape Town music fans, Stephen "Sugar" Segerman and Craig Bartholomew Strydom, who embark on a voluntary mission to find out whether the rumored death of Rodríguez is true. Segerman and Strydom are ultimately led to the daughter of Rodríguez and a phone call with the musician himself. The film follows a carefully crafted storyline of Rodríguez's emergence from putative death to an animated and, eventually, real flesh and blood musician. From rumors to a scene of reenactment, from animated images of Rodríguez walking in the snow to his voice on the phone, from his voice in the songs to the final physical presence of Rodríguez, the film slowly unveils the secrets about the composer and musician behind the songs "Sugar Man" and "I Wonder." We learn later in the film that Rodríguez spent most of his life as a construction worker in Detroit who was active in local politics; interviews with selected locals build the narrative of an 'inner-city poet,' a 'wandering spirit,' and even a 'prophet' in the local community of Detroit.

The documentary, on different levels, moves from invisibility to visibility. In many ways it unfolds a narrative of the dispossessed and alienated (Butler and Athanasiou 5), linking examples from industrial Detroit with anti-apartheid Cape Town with a clear appeal to all those who share similar social and economic experiences. Rodríguez's lyrics and melancholic tone reflect harsh living and working conditions for the lower classes in Detroit. His music appeals to a younger white generation of South Africans disenchanted with mainstream control and conservatism and appalled by apartheid politics that are dividing society and oppressing the black population. As Peter Bradshaw puts it, the film functions partly as an "interesting footnote to a species of secret or denied cultural history: the history of South Africa's white liberal classes, the fabric of whose lives may be overlooked by social historians .... Many were trapped by history and fate and the apartheid laws they detested" (n. pag.).

According to the film's narrative, a bootleg copy of *Cold Fact* found its way to apartheid-era South Africa where it became a hit among the white liberal classes and a soundtrack for the white anti-apartheid movement. South African record labels picked up distribution rights from Rodríguez's U.S. label, Sussex Records, and while some songs were banned on South African radio the record sales, according to witnesses interviewed, equaled the success of Simon and Garfunkel's *Bridge over Troubled Water* and the Beatles' *Abbey Road* album in South Africa.

Rodríguez himself is portrayed as a victim of the corrupt music industry, Sussex never sharing royalties for high record sales in South Africa and other African countries. The documentary reflects on different levels of inequality and social injustice, linking class, race, youth issues, and music industry politics loosely and transnationally. While all this provides material for empathy it is the story of redemption and recognition that touches the spectator. While it is not a classical story from 'rags to riches,' it is still conceived as an uplifting story that moves the protagonist from oblivion to recognition. Recreating the social transnationally, the music documentary shows Rodríguez's communal presence and impact in two geopolitically and geographically distant locations characterized by uneven temporalities. The reflection and the transformation of the social, as *Searching for Sugar Man* wants us to convince, is possible through the power of music to cross national, cultural, and class boundaries both by music industry channels and idiosyncratic underground music circuits.

Flor de Muertos (2011)

Flor de Muertos [Flower of the Dead] performs and narrates the interrelation of music and the social in and against the background of the U.S.-Mexican American borderlands. Danny Vinik – film director, film producer, film distributor, writer, web developer, and founder of BRINKmedia – thoroughly remolded an original set for a concert film into a performative documentary that contains a wide range of interviews: for example, journalist Charles Bowden observes social issues on the U.S.-Mexican border, community worker Gustavo Lozano attributes the heightened risk of death to the border fence, writer Margaret Regan explores immigration issues, and visual artist Salvador Duran paints to mourn the loss of life.

Most interviewees express their opinions of the United States immigration policies, the violence and destruction from a seemingly ceaseless drug war, and the search for spiritual comfort in the *Santa Muerte* religion, the growth of which can be observed on both sides of the border. Voices of interviewees take turns with Calexico's music and thus create an aesthetically and musically multifaceted documentary film that exposes social injustice while at the same time celebrating contemporary spectacle culture as a venue for performing cross-border flows of culture, music, and religion. The film revolves around a concert performance by Calexico in the historic Rialto Theater in Tucson, Arizona. Calexico is a Tucson-based band named after a small border town in rural California. As a loosely knit, constantly changing collective of musicians, they adopt and assemble a great variety of musical styles like indie rock, Portuguese *fado*, Cajun jazz, and Southern folk ballads. Additionally, they incorporate elements of *mariachi* sounds, *cumbia* waltzes, and a broad range of other Latin American musical forms (Roddy; Schacht; Engelschalt) into what can be called a truly trans-American musical vision. Their hybrid approach to cultures is also reflected in their use of English and Spanish in their lyrics. Their songs are politically conscious and address issues of social, economic, and environmental crisis. Many of their songs express an activist standpoint that is critical of U.S. foreign and social policies as well as of the treatment of migrants and political activists in Latin American countries. For example, songs cover the disastrous impact of hurricane Katrina on the U.S and Mexican Gulf Coast, human rights issues of indigenous tribes in the borderlands between Mexico and the U.S., issues of drug und human trafficking in the Americas, and the violence and oppression used against activists like the assassination of protest singer Victor Jara by CIA agents in Chile (Schacht; Engelschalt).

Calexico's concert performance in the Rialto Theater represents the point of departure from which Vinik expands the original set for a concert film to include documentary footage about the Mexican Day of the Dead (Thomas). The film reflects the liminal experience of the social and the cultural in the borderlands sonically and rhythmically through the fusion music of Calexico, visually through vivid images from the All Souls Procession in Tucson, Arizona in honor of the dead and Day of the Dead cultural practices in Mexico, and discursively through various borderland expert interviews. By inserting and editing seven performances from the Calexico concert, including the songs *Roka, Faker Fur, Inspiración, Victor Jara's Hands, Guero Canel, None of This is Mine*, and *Frontera/Trigger*, Vinik keeps the emphasis on a primarily performative mode to relate a hybrid musical world from the borderlands – whose contribution to popular music frequently goes unacknowledged – to a conflicted social world at the U.S.-Mexican border. The documentary makes use of music as spectacle and part of spectacle culture to reflect on violence, disappearance, and death in the borderlands.

Vinik's documentary highlights that "[p]erformative documentary underscores the complexity of our knowledge of the world by emphasizing its subjective and affective dimensions" (Nichols 131). The film effectively draws viewers into "subjective qualities" (131) and underscores that "[p]erformative documentaries primarily address us, emotionally and expressively, rather than pointing us to the factual world we hold in common" (132). The musical pieces from the concert function as a bridge to connect images, scenes, and cultural expressions from both sides of the border. The border itself holds an omnipresence in the film, as the camera repeatedly inserts images of it in the narrative. *Flor de Muertos* commences with the Mexican celebration of the Dia de los Muertos and ends with the All Souls Procession, an annual spectacle in which thousands of locals turn out in skull face to parade through the streets of downtown Tucson, Arizona, to honor and dance with the dead. Flor de Muertos – the Aztec marigold, 'cempasuchil' – spreads on both sides of the border and becomes the visual bond between the cultures from the natural world. Repeatedly, the film inserts images of this flower whose strong transcultural impact on religion in the borderlands appears in the resurgent *Santa Muerte* religious tradition. In this religious context, the scent of marigolds forms a path that the souls of the dead can follow back to the living on the annual Day of the Dead. Symbolically, marigolds personify the compression of time in which past and present merge. As a unifying image throughout documentary, marigolds in the fields sharply contrast with the dividing border.

With estimates of the border death toll climbing, *Flor de Muertos* ultimately manages to associate the Day of the Dead ceremony with U.S. immigration policies. As Nichols puts it, "[r]ecent performative documentaries try to give representation to a social subjectivity that joins the general to the particular, the individual to the collective, and the political to the personal" (133). Individual, often anonymous fates in the South and the North gain a collective voice in the film's visual and sonic narration of the All Souls Procession and the cultural practices related to the Day of the Dead. *Flor de Muertos* is a good point to close the essays' reflections on the interrelations of music and the social. In *Flor de Muertos*, music speaks to and about the living and the dead in the borderlands. In the film, music propels the social to stay dynamic, versatile, and hybrid beyond representation. With Calexico's sonic spectacle on the Rialto Theater stage – a performance that echoes the tones of sound sculpture artist Glenn Weyant, who turns the border fence into a gigantic percussion instrument – *Flor de Muertos* expresses music as a performance of entangled American histories that are conflictive, yet relational and in process. The social discursively evolves in and around sound and image and is bound to keep moving even in the face of violence and death. So at least the sonic and visual performances in *Flor de Muertos* make us want to believe.

Works cited

Baker, Geoffrey. "Represent Cuba: Havana Hip Hop under the Lens." *Alter/Nativas – Latin American Cultural Studies Journal* 2 (Spring 2014). Web. https://www.alternativas.osu.edu/en/issues/spring-2014/essays1/baker.html.

Baudrillard, Jean. *Simulacra and Simulation*. Michigan: U of Michigan P, 1994. Print.

Bauman, Zygmunt. *Liquid Modernity*. Cambridge: Polity Press, 2000. Print.

Block, Mitchell. "Docunomics: The Money, Markets, and Business of Non-Fiction." *IDA International Documentary Association*. 2007. Web. https://www.documentary.org/feature/docunomics-money-markets-and-business-nonfiction.

Bradshaw, Peter. "Searching for Sugar Man: Review." *The Guardian*. 26 July 2012. Web. https://www.theguardian.com/film/2012/jul/26/searching-for-sugar-man-review.

Bruzzi, Stella. *New Documentary*. London/New York: Routledge, 2006. Print.

Butler, Judith, and Athena Athanasiou. *Dispossession: The Performative in the Political*. Cambridge: Polity Press, 2013. Print.

Curran Bernard, Sheila. *Documentary Storytelling. Creative Nonfiction on Screen*. Amsterdam: Focal Press, 2010. Print.

Diffrient, David Scott. "Backup Singers, Celebrity Culture, and Civil Rights: Racializing Space and Spatializing Race in 20 Feet from Stardom." *Black Camera: An International Film Journal* 8.2 (Spring 2017): 25–49. Print.

Edgar, Robert, Kirsty Fairclough-Isaacs, and Benjamin Halligan, eds. *The Music Documentary: Acid Rock to Electropop*. London/New York: Routledge, 2013. Print.

Engelschalt, Julia. "Straddling the Crystal Frontier: Reworkings of the U.S.-Mexican Border in the Lyrics of Calexico." *FIAR: Forum for Inter-American Research* 11.1 (2018): 34–46. Web. http://interamerica.de/current-issue/engelschalt/.

Fast, Susan. "Genre, Subjectivity, and Back-Up Singing in Rock Music." *The Ashgate Research Companion to Popular Musicology*. Ed. Derek B. Scott. Surrey: Ashgate, 2009. 171–188. Print.

Flory, Andrew. "20 Feet from Stardom: Entertainment or History." 21 Feb. 2014. Web. http://musicologynow.ams-net.org/2014/02/20-feet-from-stardom-entertainment-or.html.

Fluck, Winfried. "The Concept of Recognition and American Cultural Studies." *American Studies Today. New Research Agendas*. Ed. Winfried Fluck, Donald E. Pease, and John Carlos Rowe. Heidelberg: Winter, 2014. 167–208. Print.

Hyslop, Jonathan. "'Days of Miracle and Wonder'?: Conformity and Revolt in *Searching for Sugar Man*." *Safundi* 14.4 (2013): 490–501. Web. https://www.tandfonline.com/doi/full/10.1080/17533171.2013.841066?src=recsys.

Lewsen, Simon. "On Music, Censorship, and Globalization." *Safundi* 14.4 (2013): 455–466. Web. https://www.tandfonline.com/doi/abs/10.1080/1753317.

Lipsitz, George. *Footsteps in the Dark. The Hidden Histories of Popular Music*. Minneapolis: U of Minnesota P, 2007. Print.

Long, Paul, and Tim Wall. "Tony Palmer's All You Need is Love: Television's First Pop History." *The Music Documentary: Acid Rock to Electropop*. Ed. Robert Edgar, Kirsty Fairclough-Isaacs, and Benjamin Halligan. London/New York: Routledge, 2013. 25–41. Print.

Lyotard, Jean-François. *The Postmodern Condition: A Report on Knowledge*. Minneapolis: U of Minnesota P, 1997. Print.

Martineau, Wendy, Nasar Meer, and Simon Thompson. "Theory and Practice in the Politics of Recognition and Misrecognition." *Res Publica* 18 (2012): 1–9. Print.

Mohammed, Zaineb. "New Film Puts back Singers in the Spotlight." *Mother Jones*. 17 Jun. 2013. Web. https://www.motherjones.com/media/2013/06/20-feet-stardom-documentary-backup-singers/.

Nichols, Bill. *Introduction to Documentary*. Bloomington: Indiana UP, 2001. Print.

Rabiger, Michael. *Directing the Documentary*. London: Focal Press, 2004. Print.

Renov, Michael, ed. *Theorizing Documentary*. London: Routledge, 1993. Print.

Roddy, Nikki. "Calexico's Joey Burns – Interview." *Country Music Pride RSS*. 1 Nov. 2008. Print.

Roe, Annabelle H. *Animated Documentary*. Basingstroke: Palgrave MacMillan, 2013. Print.

Rorty, Richard. *Contingency, Irony, Solidarity*. Cambridge: Cambridge UP, 1989.

Schacht, John. "The Musical Mixing Pot of Calexico." *Pastemagazine.com*. 10 Feb. 2003. Web. https://www.pastemagazine.com/articles/2003/02/the-musical-mixing-pot-of-calexico.html.

Slutsky, Allan. *Standing in the Shadows of Motown: The Life and Music of Legendary Bassist James Jamerson*. Wisconsin: Hal Leonard, 1989. Print.

Smith, Suzanne. *Dancing in the Street: Motown History and the Cultural Politics of Detroit*. Cambridge: Harvard UP, 2009. Print.

Taylor, Charles. "The Politics of Recognition." *Multiculturalism and the Politics of Recognition*. Ed. Amy Gutman. Princeton: Princeton UP, 1994. 25–73. Print.

Thies, Sebastian. "United Colors of Belonging? Participatory Culture and Diversity 2.0 in the Crowd-Sourced Documentary *Life in a Day*." *Mobile and Entangled America(s)*. Ed. Wilfried Raussert and Maryemma Graham. London/New York: Routledge, 2017. 167–187. Print.

Thomas, Bryan. "'Flor de Muertos': A Love Letter to the Sonoran Desert where Life, Death and Cultures Collide with Calexico." 26 Aug. 2016. Web. http://nightflight.com/flor-de-muertos-a-love-letter-to-the-sonoran-desert-whose-life-death-and-cultures-collide-with-calexico/.

Yúdice, George. *The Expediency of Culture. Uses of Culture in the Global Era*. Durham: Duke UP, 2004. Print.

Filmography

A Band Called Death. Directed by Mark Christopher Covino and Jeff Howlett. Drafthouse Films, 2012.

A Short Radiography of Hip Hop in Cuba. Directed by Ricardo Bacallao. Cubafilms, 2004.

All You Need is Love. Directed by Tony Palmer. Television, 1977.

An Inconvenient Truth. Directed by Davis Guggenheim. Paramount Classics, 2006.

Beyond Ipanema. Directed by Guto Barra. 2009. IMDb.

Buena Vista Social Club. Directed by Wim Wenders. ARTHAUS, 1999.

Charles Bradley: Soul of America. Directed by Poull Brien. 2012. IMDb.

Cuban Hip Hop Desde el Principio. Directed by Larissa and Vanessa Diaz. 2006. IMDbPro.

Fahrenheit 9/11. Directed by Michael Moore. 2004. IMDb.

Flor de Muertos [Flower of the Dead]. Directed by Danny Vinik. Brink Films, 2011.

Guerrilla Radio: The Hip-Hop Struggle Under Castro. Directed by Thomas Nybo. 2007. IMDb.

Havanyork. Directed by Luciano Larobina. Acitron, 2009.

Johnny Cash at Folsom Prison. Directed by Bestor Cram. 2008. IMDb.

Muscle Shoals. Directed by Greg Camalier. Magnolia Pictures, 2013.

Searching for Sugar Man. Directed by Malik Bendjelloul. NonStop Entertainment, 2012.

Shine a Light. Directed by Martin Scorsese. Paramount Classics, 2008.

Slingshot Hip Hop. Directed by Jarki Reem Salloum. 2008. IMDb.

Standing in the Shadows of Motown. Directed by Paul Justman. Artisan Entertainment, 2002.

The Blues. A Musical Journey. Directed by Martin Scorsese. Television, 2003.

The Wrecking Crew. Directed by Denny Tedesco. 2008. IMDb

20 Feet from Stardom. Directed by Morgan Nelville. Studiocanal, 2013.

Woodstock: Now & Then. Directed by Barbara Kopple. 2009. IMDb.

Noir Aesthetics, Institutional Racism, and Social Critique: Anthony Mann's *Devil's Doorway* and the Denial of Legal Rights to First Americans

CHRIS LIPPARD

In 1949, shortly after completing their brutal immigration border noir, *Border Incident*,[1] Anthony Mann directed and Jon Alton shot *Devil's Doorway*, one of the few acknowledged noir westerns and one of the earliest films – along with *Broken Arrow* also released in 1950 – to sympathetically address the plight of the indigenous population of the American West. The film still casts a white man – the politically conservative Robert Taylor – as the American Indian, civil war hero Lance Poole aka Broken Lance; nevertheless, the application of traditionally noir aesthetics to iconic western locations, both indoors (the saloon, the cabin) and outdoors (the land, the porch), effectively works to express the denial of human/land rights to the Shoshone during the era of post-civil-war colonizing settlement through homesteading land laws in 1870 Wyoming when the first Land office opened there. In addition, I would argue, its critique of settler-colonial practices comments on 1950s termination policies and contemporary land use debates in the American West.

Lance's opponent, the villain of the piece, is eastern lawyer Verne Coolan (Louis Calhern). We first see him, backlit, in extreme close-up and on the extreme left of the frame, as Lance enters the bar. He is huge in the frame but still – and for a few seconds we may not register his presence. Looming unseen and unspeaking, he dominates the scene and establishes his power long before his first words which express his racism explicitly "Did you notice how sour the air got when the Indian came in." His language here and throughout serves to infantilize the indigenous subject and to present him as savage, a classic instance of long-standing racist description. Classified a ward of the state and denied the right to run cattle on his ancestral lands, Lance seeks another lawyer in town who turns out to be a woman, Orrie Masters (Paula Raymond). Overcoming his prejudice, he hires her, thus providing Hollywood with a potential love-interest in addition to another figure for Coolan to dismiss as he manipulates the townsfolk to oppose both racial and gender equality. Thus, like almost all Hollywood

1 In between these two collaborations with Alton, Mann directed *Side Street*, a New York City-set noir, starring Farley Granger and Cathy O'Donnell, reunited after the success of the previous year's *They Live By Night*. Seen as a diversion from Mann's startling use of western landscapes begun with *Border Incident* and continued through the westerns for which he is best known, *Side Street* seems of relatively little interest and Stephen Handzo names it "one of Mann's least interesting films" (5). For Robert Smith, however, it represents the apogee of Mann's earlier noir work (200).

(melo-)dramas, the power-structure – here forces of state justice and genocidal, patriarchal, colonial oppression – is personified. Still, *Devil's Doorway* makes it unusually clear that the violence and denial of human rights is institutional and requires change at that level. It is highly unusual, perhaps uniquely critical, amongst Hollywood films from the studio era in questioning the manifest destiny of the settler-colonialist national enterprise, presenting it explicitly as a means of denying rights to the indigenous population. Additionally, it finally rejects the possibility of redemptive romantic love. Jeff Stafford, in his Turner Movie Classics review written prior to a rare television screening of *Devil's Doorway*, concludes: "*Devil's Doorway* is … unique for its refusal to fall back on the clichés of the genre. There is no romantic subplot to detract from the rising tension in the narrative and no 'happy ending' for our hero either – the movie ends in genocide with the surviving Shoshone women and children being escorted by the cavalry to a reservation" (n. pag). Stephen Handzo similarly argues; "one keeps wondering … at what point the Hollywood cop-out will take place. It never does. … Love plainly cannot conquer in a struggle for hegemony" (11).

Audiences are likely to identify strongly with Lance – who manifests all kinds of heroic, noble qualities: bravery, hospitality, a tenacious hold on traditional values, hard-workingness, a capacity for all kinds of love – despite (or because of?) the (so-called) redfacing. Similarly, lawyer Coolan is a menacing, pompous, smarmy, lying, vicious racist. This, of course, is one means for Hollywood to fix our spectatorial position, one that is apparently problematic; as Katarzyna Marciniak, writing about the discourse of identification with 'others,' argues "it invites "appropriation, consumption, self-indulgence, empty empathy, or sentimental gestures of pity – precisely a denial of difference as difference" (876). The Shoshone are clearly the 'other' in *Devil's Doorway*, their customs and costumes displayed, and to some degree explained,[2] to a putatively white audience; however, because of some of the characteristics I have mentioned, its engagement in this discourse is somewhat less problematic than, say, the much more commercially successful, Oscar-nominated, *Broken Arrow* which was made later but released first. Acclaimed as a new direction in liberal westerns, its success seems to have prompted MGM to release *Devil's Doorway* which had been shelved in favor of Mann's subsequently-made feature, *Winchester 73*, first in the series of so-called psychological westerns with *Broken Arrow* star Jimmy Stewart, in which the Technicolor literally and metaphorically stalls the 'dark' tenor of the redemption-driven narratives. *Devil's Doorway* was neither commercially nor critically successful and Taylor's performance, which a couple of critics have lately re-evalu-

---

2 This nexus of exoticizing, othering, and explaining is perhaps most evident in a sequence in which Orrie witnesses a boy's return to Lance's house after a three-day mission to find an eagle's talons that functions as his initiation into manhood. Jimmy appears hurt and tired but Lance must wait until the boy reaches the porch before helping him. Lance explains to Orrie that the small Shoshone tribe need the self-reliance and bravery of every man in order to survive.

ated, came in for quite a bit of stick.[3] Still, industry circumstances dictated the project needed a star and ex-matinee idol Taylor, who, like Stewart had been compelled to sing for his living by MGM,[4] needing a new *persona*, was it.

If noir is best defined as a discourse, a means of talking about a group of stylistic features and narrative traits apparent in films from a specific time and place, with, 1950, perhaps the year of its greatest achievements, the western, taking place mostly outdoors over sweeping vistas, is a genre that seems not to lend itself to such discourse. Nevertheless, various critics have identified small numbers of noir westerns. James Ursini claims six: *The Ox-Bow Incident* (1943), *Duel in the Sun* (1945), *Pursued* (1947), *Ramrod* (1947), *Blood on the Moon* (1948), and *Devil's Doorway*, "which most clearly evidence this grafting of noir onto the western genre" (247). Jeanine Basinger calls *Devil's Doorway* "an extremely dark film as befits its subject matter" (72), and it follows closely not only MGM's *Border Incident* but also the more typical, indeed archetypical, Alton-Mann noir collaborations *T-Men* (1947) and *He Walked By Night* (1948) for B-movie outlet, Eagle-Lion. So, I ask, to what degree does the shooting at night and in dark interiors that characterize the noir western in general and *Devil's Doorway* in particular, counter the traditional space of the genre, thus challenging, to quote Ella Shohat and Robert Stam, "[a] narrative paradigm … enlisted to serve teleological notions of national progress and manifest destiny"? (118).

As in much noir, the protagonist of *Devil's Doorway* returns from war[5]: here however, it is peace-time settler-colonial society not war-time trauma that sours his outlook on life.[6] Another link is to the oft-remarked upon fascination with the foreign and the exotic, the manifest Orientalism of so many noir classics: *The Big Sleep*, *DOA*, *World for Ransom*, and *Chinatown* are examples that come immediately to mind. Barbara Babcock and Richard Francaviglia, amongst others, have remarked upon a southwestern version of this phenomenon. Babcock writes: "I have … implicated Edward Said's *Orientalism* in my argument because I think that the Southwest *is* America's Orient" (406).[7] And certainly, its notoriously inaccurate, conglomerating, depic-

3 Handzo records that *Variety*, for example, found Taylor "too polished and educated" (9). This opinion, of course reflects its own inflection of racist cultural stereotyping. Still, *Variety* was correct in its assessment that "grossing possibilities do not appear good" (9). Somewhat reassuringly, however, considering the film's interrogation of race, class, and gender within the settler colonial context, *The Daily Worker* made *Devil's Doorway* film of the year.

4 As Handzo points out, Taylor sang in *Broadway Melody of 1936*, Stewart in *Born to Dance* (13).

5 This is also true of Nophaie, protagonist in *The Vanishing American* (1925), who precedes Lance Poole in coming home – from World War One – a hero, and in re-embracing his native identity in the face of prejudice.

6 Indeed, participation in an integrated Union army where he has been honored and obeyed is the primary source of his naïve hopes for the future.

7 Today, this practice is characteristic, for example, of most glossy western magazines.

tion of First Nations' customs and costume is fundamental to the Western. *Broken Arrow*, for instance, inscribes its opening title sequence over assorted Indian hides, paintings, and other cultural objects and presents various dances and ceremonies on the idyllic reservation to the curious viewer.[8] Furthermore, if Debra Paget's depiction of Morning Glory is a Pocahontas stereotype whose death will provide the 'glue' to hold the peace together, Basinger suggests that her body serves another purpose earlier in the narrative of *Broken Arrow*: "the sight of Paget in her beautifully designed suede moccasins and color-coordinated beads is enough to send any white man scampering to the reservation" (75).

I do not have time here to survey critical reaction to the portrayal of American Indian characters and behavior on the Hollywood screen in anything but the most perfunctory way. Still, it may be worth identifying a central thread of such criticism of an industry in which the Western was easily the predominant genre – accounting for close to a quarter of all films made in the U.S. up to 1950 – and the only genre in which American Indians or their representations were visible. These films, it has long been argued, reinforced dominant stereotypes and ideology: the Indians were part of the wilderness to be tamed, closer to animals, whether savage or noble than reasoning human beings. In what little attention it has received, *Devil's Doorway* has been seen as an outlier. Thus, John O'Connor describes it, in a parenthetical comment, as "a film that played up complex moral questions related to race and prejudice … a rare exception to an almost ironclad Hollywood rule" (33). A glance at the contemporary advertising copy for the film, however, reveals nothing to suggest such an inversion, seeming instead indicative of the typical Hollywood approach. The movie poster proclaims: "See the wild Shoshone tribesmen vs the US cavalry! See covered wagons put to the torch. See Taylor as he fights for the land of his wild heritage!" These words could stand parsing; to some extent they represent standard copy – covered wagons do appear in the film, for example, but are hardly a major part of it; rather the use of the phrase stands in for the western conflict, the wagons representative of the settler community, miniature harbingers of civilization, which are destroyed by disrespectful Indians. Especially worthy of note in the context of this essay, however, are two things. First, the repetition of "wild" which is applied to the Shoshone and implicitly both links them to the land and simultaneously denies them the rights to it as uncontrolled/uncontrollable beings, living outside the law and unacknowledged by it. Second, the copy emphasizes visibility: addressed to a non-native audience it promises something worth seeing – in this case, not the sexualized body of the woman but the wild body of the man.[9]

---

8 Indeed, this is much more pervasive than the relatively subtle celebration/reification of African-American experiences in *Out of the Past*, *DOA*, or *Kiss Me Deadly*.

9 The film's trailer emphasizes the love angle almost exclusively, beginning with the title: "A Man and a Woman Meant for each other. They met and loved at "Devil's Doorway," and concluding with one that reads: "A Love story against a background of treachery … AND WILD PASSIONS," as Lance puts his arm around Orrie.

Figure 1: Original movie poster for *Devil's Doorway* (Anthony Mann. Metro-Goldwyn-Mayer, 1950).

But what of a potential indigenous audience? If earlier accounts saw only a tiny minority of westerns, such as *Devil's Doorway* itself, as presenting indigenous representations that were in any sense useful,[10] more recent criticism has somewhat revised this argument. Michelle Raheja, for example, citing Rey Chow's notion of "ethnic spectatorship," argues that first Americans may indeed find the erroneous, stereotypical Hollywood portrayals potentially productive in that they at least signify some degree of native presence in a culture that has largely defined them as absent or inherently separate: better badly-represented than invisible (xi). Native peoples are not "innocent dupes," asserts Raheja (xii): like any other audience they can reinterpret and reuse, whilst a presence in Hollywood, she asserts, allowed access to policy-makers unavailable on the reservation (13). Raheja's argument suggests that films like *Devil's Doorway* that clearly foreground a native character – even one played/appropriated by Taylor, as he "fights for his wild heritage" – offer a possibility of progressive interpreta-

10 For a summary of the argument, cf. Raheja (16).

tion, unavailable in *Broken Arrow* and *Little Big Man* (1970), for example, where the main characters are white and the narratives, however sympathetic, are explicitly presented from their points-of-view. Nevertheless, redfacing, ostensibly 'necessary' because the film industry, like the nation, sought to render the Indian body invisible, mirrors the policies of genocide and necessitates a complex and perverse form of identification. In fact, Lance is not solely idealized as wild and noble: he reveals gender and class prejudices against female lawyers and sheep-men and, showing good potential as a capitalist landowner in the making, is made happy by money or at least by the respect that it lends him – thus opening up some space to question stereotypes alongside the critique of the settler-colonial society's denial of human rights through its assertion of racialized property rights.

In any case, it is the striking visuals of *Devil's Doorway* that most prominently mark it as noir and inscribe a comparison between post-war societies. Just as, in the original bar scene, when Lance Poole returns to Medicine Bow at the film's beginning, his presence is overseen by the silhouette of Coolan in the foreground, five years on, he is there again. Lance, having raised and sold his cattle in town, and thus now a man of means – but one disillusioned with white society for its treatment of his father – stops in for a drink. In the same extreme depth of field, we see Coolan again in the foreground which he shares with his henchman, Ike, as if squeezing Lance out, even though he occupies the middle of the frame, his dark shape counterpointed by a brightly-lit sign behind the bar: "No liquor for Indians." The public space is no longer open to Lance as an American: the bar has become a symbolic place to express communal rejection. This liminal social space is being settled, just as is the land outside its doors. Ike, acting as stalking horse for Coolan, issues a threat all the more chilling for its mock compliment: "Nice head of hair, you've got there Redskin. … It would look fine hanging from my belt." What follows is a bar fist-fight – Lance's companion, Red Rocks, disarms Coolan when he pulls out a pistol – using text-book noir cinematography: chiaroscuro; choker close-ups; bizarre, low-angle compositions; objects close to camera. Occasional flashes of light are diegetically justified by a lightning storm supposed to have sprung up outside which also provides background sound as expressive as any music. "Rarely has the struggle between good and evil been visualized on screen in such potent, primeval terms" (n. pag.)[11] asserts Jeff Stafford. But I think it is more specific than this. The scene demonstrates Mann's ability to develop character and story with composition and light in a purely visual manner. Alton's camera work[12]

11 Stafford's words reflect the reputation that Mann earned for depicting the infliction of pain on his characters, although *Devil's Doorway* is less marked in this regard than *Border Incident* which perhaps remains best known for the torture, and then brutal, drawn-out killing of the Anglo hero, Jack (George Murphy).

12 Alton's cinematography has long been seen as archetypical of film noir in its visualization of alienation and the dark side of human nature. His work with Mann in *He Walked by Night*, *Border Incident*, and *Devil's Doorway* epitomizes this aesthetic, one explained in his book, *Painting with Light*, published the same year (1949) as he shot *Devil's Doorway*.

clearly establishes the sides and those who refuse to take sides. As Lance enters the room, the bar lies on a diagonal, dividing the image in two, predicting the conflict. As the fight develops, Lance and Ike pounding at each other, the space seems increasingly crowded. As shocking as Mann's habitual brutality is the chilling passivity of the onlookers, under-lit and shot close with a wide lens that distorts their features.[13] Thus, Lance faces a range of settler racism: vicious, violent hatred; cool, calculating contempt; uncaring indifference, with only the barman – an old acquaintance, but the weakest man in the room, already enlisted to work beneath the "No Liquor for Indians" sign – showing any kind of sympathy.

Figure 2: Bar fight scene from *Devil's Doorway* (Anthony Mann. Metro-Goldwyn-Mayer, 1950).

13 For a somewhat more detailed – and highly appreciative – analysis of this scene, cf. Basinger (72–73).

Figure 3: Bar fight spectators, *Devil's Doorway* (Anthony Mann. Metro-Goldwyn-Mayer, 1950).

These crowded frames inevitably contrast with outdoor scenes. At the beginning of *Devil's Doorway*, typical of a Western, we see a wide, empty landscape. We look down on a huge valley – at Sweet Meadows, the ancestral Shoshone grazing land accessible through the rocky pass called the Devil's doorway. A rider on horseback comes into frame, a speck on the landscape: Lance, returning home from war. The removal of the remaining Shoshone from that land to the reservation is the central subject of the film. While Orrie explains that the Shoshone want "to speak their own language, worship their own God," Lance, voicing traditional indigenous attitudes, eloquently asserts his ties to Sweet Meadows: his desire to remain on, to be connected to, ancestral lands. Thus, attention to cultural and geographic roots – in contrast to routes[14] – is central to the effectiveness of *Devil's Doorway*'s critique of American settler society's reservation policy as well as to the subsequent jettisoning of federal responsibility for native lands via tribal terminations officially pursued by Congress from 1953 – and violently foreshadowed here. Indeed, whilst *Broken Arrow* minimizes the significance of the land Cochise must bargain away to achieve peace, *Devil's Doorway* emphasizes it. Lance explains to Orrie that the land is: "the pumping of our blood, it's the love we've got to have. … I was raised in this valley, now I am part of it like the mountains and the hills, the deer, the pine-trees and the wind. Deep in my heart I know I belong." These words not only stress the role of the land in Lance's individual identity but also anthropomorphize the relationship and indicate its communal nature, something antithetical to the settler society intent on home-steading and the

14 By routes, I mean the the claims of the traveler, colonizer or settler.

taking of property rights. When Lance finally dies, defeated, in front of the U.S. cavalry, he topples like a tree, a part of the landscape, thus dying symbolically rather than obeying the usual tenets of Hollywood realism. Classic noirs, most famously perhaps *Out of the Past* (1947), have set scenes in the western landscape, crisply-lit, to contrast the dark entrapping spaces of the mansion, the apartment, or the city street. This is the way Sweet Meadows is shot, with a nod to Ansel Adams, early in *Devil's Doorway*, but as the film progresses and Lance's options and identity are restricted, more and more scenes take place in shadow, at dusk, or fully at night.

Several scenes are set in Lance's cabin at Sweet Meadows or outside on the porch. When Lance returns from the war, he is at first able to brush off Coolan's antipathy in the bar but, having expressed his desire to establish a welcoming space of racial equality on his land, his first doubts are planted at home by his dying father who reminds him: "You are home. You are again an Indian." In the *normal* course of things, it is not Lance or the Shoshone who can define the home. Thus is home given a threatened valence in the film that is reflected in the way it is shot: inside and out, Lance's cabin is lit dark, with inanimate objects close to the camera – on the porch, as he attempts to make Orrie understand his connection to the land, it is Lance who is silhouetted, a black shape in the foreground, right side of the frame.[15] Inside, before the final stand-off with white society, the camera draws unusual attention to ordinary utilitarian objects: curtains, corn-cobs, bread, baskets, jars, and the silhouettes of a mincer and bowl that dominate the foreground just before the domesticity they represent is to be destroyed, the bigger home of the United States having subsumed the domestic space of the individual Indian as well as the various tribes. As Shohat and Stam have remarked: "rarely do westerns show Native Americans as simply inhabiting the domestic space of their unthreatening daily lives, although it was their lives and habits that were brutally disrupted by western expansion" (119). Here we do explicitly see exactly that. Indeed, the script specifies the pump and food provisions as being visible, and that Lance is seen to be "feasting his eyes on the familiar objects that made his home" (Trosper, *Devil's Doorway* 107).

15 There are, however, a couple of soft-focus close-ups of Paula Raymond inserted at this point in the narrative, presumably to indicate the desirability of a possible union between Orrie and Lance. Handzo remarks that these are "sufficiently out of keeping to suggest the intrusion of MGM's notoriously glamor-conscious front-office" (9).

Figure 4: Domesticity about to be destroyed as Broken Lance's living quarters come under attack in *Devil's Doorway* (Anthony Mann. Metro-Goldwyn-Mayer, 1950).

The name Lance Poole comes straight from Guy Trosper's original story, "The Drifter," written for MGM in 1946. At this point – and indeed for a couple more years, as the story was adapted by studio writers – Lance remained an Anglo character, the drifter of the title, though not the main character by most measures (first appearing only on page 17 of 28). By the time the film was made, he had become a character diametrically opposed to his origin, one with fiercely important ties to home and the land rather than a drifter who, we learn when he first appears "comes and goes, as he has no home, doesn't want one. He's a saddle bum, hiring out as a cow hand when the mood strikes" (18). In *Devil's Doorway*, however, just as Lance's allegiances, feelings, manner, and costume shift as he becomes more disillusioned and consequently more Indian, so does his name. He returns to Medicine Bow Lance Poole, but dies, in Sweet Meadows, as Broken Lance, the adjective a clear indication of his lack of power. The phallic reference unavoidable; he falls like a tree but also a lance more metaphorically uprooted from the ground, as the last act in a betrayal of his manhood as well as his race. This symbolic power is largely missing from *Broken Arrow*, where a similar disempowering of the Indian occurs but the title refers to the situation in the abstract only, the imagery never being specifically tied to Cochise. Indeed as Jeff Stafford notes "seen today, *Broken Arrow* seems preachy and patronizing whereas *Devil's Doorway* … stands out as a much more realistic and grim depiction of how the west was really won."[16] *Devil's Doorway*, indeed, offers an unusual mix of the interrogation of social identities with noir themes of determinism, the latter epitomized by a reference to the former in Lance's father's prediction of the inevitable and inexorable destruction of his son's optimistic vision of a future where he owns the land but welcomes men of every color: "You are home. You are once again an Indian."

The thematic emphasis in "The Drifter," through the 1949 script, to the final script, all by Trosper, shifts from the rights and strengths of women towards those of native Americans. Despite the complete lack of Indian characters in the original story treatment, the one-page synopsis of the plot provided by Marjorie Dudley at MGM on November 18, 1948 picks up on the single reference to them: "[a]fter the wedding she refuses to go back to Wyoming among the Indians with him." Both the "she" and the "him," Barney Walton and Letha, along with the villain, Ira Coffee, and Charlotte Carmody, leader of the independents who challenge Walton's land monopoly, are gone from the final film – although aspects of Coffee may remain in the character of Coolan's henchman, similarly named Ike. Elements of the independent woman certainly remain in the character of Orrie, but references to her coming to Wyoming because the state had given women the right to vote which occur in the earlier script version are absent.[17]

The land itself is represented in gendered terms throughout *Devil's Doorway*. In addition to Lance's description to Orrie of how it functions as a nurturing, domestic, motherly space, Sweet Meadows is given a different valence by Coolan, who advertises its beauty and fecundity by describing it as being "like the lap of a beautiful woman." It is worth noting the differences in the depiction of land and land rights in Mann's *The Furies*, which was released later in 1950. Indeed, some traces of Trosper's "The Drifter," are evident here, although he seemingly had no role in scripting this time. John Alton's work with Mann had also ended but nevertheless, the West is again shot as a noir landscape, and the camerawork reflects strategies from *Border Incident* and *Devil's Doorway*.[18] The heroine, Vance (Barbara Stanwyck), is determined to take

16 Basinger, deploring *Broken Arrow*'s greater acclaim, calls *Devil's Doorway* a "far superior film" (74). She also records Mann's own assessment that his film was "more powerful than *Broken Arrow*, more dramatic too" (71).

17 In the original story, Trosper includes the following parenthetical aside: "A bit of Wyoming history is not amiss at this point. One of the weird contradictions in the history of the frontier west, where a woman was only at home in a kitchen or a brothel, is that the territory of Wyoming, in 1869, was the first place on earth to give a woman the vote. A few years later, this precedent shattering event was followed by one equally sensational: a woman was elected justice of the peace in South Pass, Wyoming. Again, Wyoming leads the world. How this happened in a culture dominated exclusively by males, where a man wouldn't even dream of having an ordinary friendship with an ordinary woman, is one of America's yet unexplained mysteries. In our story, however, we will capitalize on this brace of historical facts, and explain them in terms of characterization" (10). Cf. Rea.

18 The inside of the big Furies ranch house features a sweeping staircase that facilitates some archetypical use of de-centered and blocked characters, extreme angles, deep

over the vast ranch owned by her father, TC and, like him, rides back and forth across the land with all the confidence of ownership. The story turns on her double-crossing of her brutal father with the help of a local gambler, Darrow, whose father TC has killed, thus acquiring the most valuable land on the Furies ranch, which Vance must pledge to give up in order to enlist Darrow's help. However, it is the presence of "squatters" on the land that threatens TC's ability to raise money against his assets, and a key part of the story concerns the rights of these long-established Latinx families, pushed off the land by ever-vaster property consolidations in 1870s New Mexico. They "constitute a cloud on the titles of the Furies," we are told. Vance protects the Herrera family not because she acknowledges their rights to live there but because she is in love with Juan, who is eventually sacrificed for the story, dying stoically, hung by the violent patriarch TC. A single-limbed Saguaro cuts through the frame as TC talks of the rights *he* has – property rights that allow him to be the controlling patriarch of the land, long utilized by the Herreras. Indeed, all four main characters value land over love. The film's narrative gives TC a lot of leeway, suggesting that despite his brutal assertion of settler colonialist power, we – a putatively white audience – admire his manly resolve.[19] Visually, however, the film fractures this identification, implicitly denying him the rights he asserts, revisualizing the mestizo presence, a cloud that cannot be blown away.

Whilst *Devil's Doorway* might certainly be faulted for its history, its use of melodrama and the denial of difference implicit in its identificatory strategies with a white actor, it does, I believe, provide a fascinating and surprisingly little noted companion piece for Mann and Alton's first attempt to tie noir aesthetics to both the west and to national policy in *Border Incident*. Just as that film exposes the abuse of the *braceros* and Farm Labor Program, *Devil's Doorway* describes the consequences of economic and political decisions in Washington on another nation as depicted in a series of liminal border spaces – only here the very border itself is contingent, to be moved rather than circumnavigated – and it proves impossible to forge even an uncomfortable resolution.

Such resolutions to Indian land and water rights claims, are still highly-charged today. U.S. settler colonialism is an ongoing proposition, whilst anti-Native propagan-

---

shadows, and depth of field cinematography. Choker close-ups characterize the many scenes of confrontation.

19 Indeed, the politically-progressive elements inherent in many aspects of *Devil's Doorway* are much more muddled in *The Furies*. Whereas Vance, the epitome of an independent woman, seemingly agrees to Darrow's patriarchal view of domestic happiness at the end of the film, TC is presented, even celebrated, as a man who understands the land, always ready to get his hands dirty – in contrast to his effeminate son – and thus a worthy owner for it. A song, created by his ranch-hands to commemorate a final cattle-drive, includes the line: "he swings his boot, and squatters scoot." Although the film hardly draws attention to these words so that many audiences may not pay them much attention, they include a chilling irony, since it is with the swing of a rope not a boot that TC has disposed of Juan.

da continues in, for example the work of the Citizens for Equal Rights Alliance (CERA), which advocates for the abrogation of native land and water rights[20] – and is currently being considered by the Southern Poverty Law Center Action Committee for inclusion on its list of hate groups.[21] Static notions of indigenous culture continue to position Native Americans in the past, as opponents of a "progress," that may not today be literal but still frequently involves the taking of land and water. The fight to control river flows persists, for example, and in September 2015 the confederated Salish and Kootenai Tribes of the Flathead Nation in Montana became the first tribe to manage a hydro-electric dam, acquiring the Kerr Dam on Flathead Lake and renaming it the Seliš Ksanka Qlispe' Dam. The fight of the Standing Rock Sioux and their supporters against the Keystone pipeline inspired a large and disparate support movement which, it may be argued, energized progressive movements throughout the United States. Pressure to drill for oil under the Trump administration threatens native land in many places, notably in its encroachment on the greater Chaco region of northern New Mexico. In Utah, President Obama created a new National Monument upon leaving office. In the past, similar decrees have often raised the ire of rural white Utahans, and such was the case again this time. Distinctively, however, the push for protection of The Bears Ears in San Juan County in the south-east of the state came specifically from native peoples.[22] Indeed, the visibility and rights of American Indians to protect land and heritage outside the reservation has become central here as Utah legislators try to make the case that tribal support for the idea was in fact drummed up by environmental organizations led by the Southern Utah Wilderness Alliance, whilst the Alliance itself emphasizes that the impetus came from first Americans: an inter-tribal coalition founded by Hopi, Navajo, Ute Mountain, Pueblo of Zuni and Ute Indian nations with support from 21 other tribes. In April 2017, Donald Trump and his Minister of the Interior, Montanan Ryan Zinke, ordered a review of the Monument designation, and in

20 Many tribes hold water rights that pre-date and thus legally take priority over water rights negotiated by settlers. Efforts to codify such rights through congressionally-approved settlements with the federal government are continuing on a case-by-case basis.

21 If a group like CERA can be seen as a contemporary reflection of Coolan the establishment lawyer, a more casual, less informed, racism somewhat akin to Mann's passive by-standers also persists today, reflecting perhaps a preference for European-originating social norms and values. Consider, for example, the April 30, 2018 episode at Colorado State University when two native prospective students were pulled off a campus tour after the mother of another potential student called campus security, apparently because they were too quiet, thus "creepy," and would not answer her questions (cf. Levin).

22 One of the factors that had prompted the Navajo nation and other native peoples to push for the Monument designation, had been the rampant stealing and selling of ancient artifacts from around the many ancestral dwellings in the area. San Juan county in which the Monument and the Utah section of the Navajo reservation reside has been gerrymandered to reduce native representation on the county commission. Federal orders to redistrict promises to give the substantial Navajo population more say in how the county is run, including in land use debates.

December 2017 ordered its reduction in size by 85%, with the new boundaries drawn to exclude areas with any potential for oil, gas or uranium, leaving two small non-contiguous areas – but one instance of how the negotiation of borders and the visibility of First Nations people in the United States remains highly contested today.[23]

Works cited

Alton, John. *Painting with Light*. 1949. Berkeley: U of California P, 1995. Print.

Babcock, Barbara. "'A New Mexican Rebecca': Imaging Pueblo Women." *Journal of the Southwest* 32.4 (Winter 1990): 400–437. Print.

Basinger, Jeanine. *Anthony Mann*. 1979. Middletown, CT: Wesleyan UP, 2007. Print.

Dudley, Marjorie. Synopsis of "The Drifter" (1 page). Collection of the Margaret Herrick Library at the Academy of Motion Picture Arts and Sciences, Los Angeles, 18 Nov. 1948. Print.

Francaviglia, Richard V. *Go East, Young Man: Imagining the American West as the Orient*. Logan: Utah State UP, 2011. Print.

Handzo, Stephen. "Going Through the Devil's Doorway: The Early Westerns of Anthony Mann." *Bright Lights* 1.4 (Summer 1976): 4–15. Print.

Levin, Sam. "They Don't Belong. Police Called on Native American Teens on College Tour." *Guardian*. 4 May 2018. Web. http://www.theguardian.com/us-news/2018/may/04/native-american-students-colorado-state-college-tour-police.

Marciniak, Katarzyna. "Pedagogy of Anxiety." *Signs: Journal of Women in Culture and Society* 35.4 (Summer 2010): 869–892. Print.

O'Connor, John. "The White Man's Indian: An Institutional Approach." *Hollywood's Indian: The Portrayal of the Native American in Film*. Ed. Peter Rollins and John O'Connor. Lexington: U of Kentucky P, 2003. 27–38. Print.

Raheja, Michelle. *Reservation Reelism: Redfacing, Visual Sovereignty, and Representations of Native Americans in Film*. Lincoln: U of Nebraska P, 2010. Print.

Rea, Tom. "Right choice, Wrong Reasons: Wyoming Women Win the Right to Vote." 8 Nov. 2014. Web. www.wyohistory.org/encyclopedia/right-choice-wrong-reasons-wyoming-women-win-right-vote.

Said, Edward. *Orientalism*. New York: Pantheon Books, 1978. Print.

Shohat, Ella, and Robert Stam. *Unthinking Eurocentrism: Multiculturalism and the Media*. 2nd ed. New York: Routledge, 2014 (1994). Print.

Smith, Robert. "Mann in the Dark." *Film Noir Reader*. Ed. Alain Silver and James Ursini. New York: Limelight, 1996. 188–201.

Stafford, Jeff. "Devil's Doorway." TCM Film Article. www.tcm.com/this-month/article/135957|0/Devils-Doorway.html.

23 Acknowledgments: My thanks to the Margaret Herrick Library at the Academy of motion Picture Arts and Sciences in Los Angeles; also, to students at the University of Utah with whom I have discussed *Devil's Doorway*, particularly Brent Rowland and Jordan Boge.

Trosper, Guy. "The Drifter" (short story, 28 pages). Collection of the Margaret Herrick Library at the Academy of Motion Picture Arts and Sciences. Los Angeles, 3 Sept. 1946. Print.

———. *Devil's Doorway* (script, 67 pages). Collection of the Margaret Herrick Library at the Academy of Motion Picture Arts and Sciences. Los Angeles, 20 May 1948. Print.

———. *Devil's Doorway* (complete OK script, 109 pages). Collection of the Margaret Herrick Library at the Academy of Motion Picture Arts and Sciences. Los Angeles, 18 Jul. 1949. Print.

Ursini, James. "Noir Westerns." *Film Noir Reader* 4. Ed. Alain Silver and James Ursini. New York: Limelight, 2004. 246–259. Print.

Filmography

Blood on the Moon. Directed by Robert Wise, RKO Radio Pictures,1948.

Border Incident. Directed by Anthony Mann. Metro-Goldwyn-Mayer, 1949.

Born to Dance. Directed by Roy Del Ruth. Metro-Goldwyn-Mayer, 1936.

Broadway Melody of 1936. Directed by Roy Del Ruth. Metro-Goldwyn-Mayer, 1936.

Broken Arrow. Directed by Delmer Daves. Twentieth Century Fox, 1950.

Chinatown. Directed by Roman Polanski. Paramount Pictures, 1974.

Devil's Doorway. Directed by Anthony Mann. Metro-Goldwyn-Mayer, 1950.

DOA. Directed by Rudolph Maté. United Artists, 1949.

Duel in the Sun. Directed by King Vidor. Selznick International Pictures, 1945.

He Walked by Night. Directed by Alfred L. Werker, Anthony Mann (uncredited). Eagle-Lion, 1948.

Kiss Me Deadly. Directed by Robert Aldrich. United Artists, 1955.

Little Big Man. Directed by Arthur Penn. Cinema Center Films, 1970.

Out of the Past. Directed by Jacques Tourneur. RKO Radio Pictures, 1947.

Pursued. Directed by Raoul Walsh. Warner Brothers, 1947.

Ramrod. Directed by André de Toth. United Artists, 1947.

Side Street. Directed by Anthony Mann. Metro-Goldwyn-Mayer, 1950.

The Big Sleep. Directed by Howard Hawkes. Warner Brothers, 1946.

The Furies. Directed by Anthony Mann. Metro-Goldwyn-Mayer, 1950.

The Ox-Bow Incident. Directed by William Wellman, Twentieth Century Fox,1943.

The Vanishing American. Directed by George B. Seitz. Paramount Pictures, 1925.

T-Men. Directed by Anthony Mann. Eagle-Lion, 1947.

World for Ransom. Directed by Robert Aldrich. Allied Artists Pictures, 1954.

Winchester 73. Directed by Anthony Mann. Universal Pictures, 1950.

Border Crossings, Memory, and Performativity in Juan Carlos Zaldívar's *90 Miles* (2001)[1]

ANNETTE L. RUKWIED

> "Memory and identity, memory and modernity. For us, exile is among our most painful, most degradative, self-consuming, and tragic expressions of the labyrinth we inhabit."
>
> – Ilan Stavans, *The Hispanic Condition* (1995)

The year 2019 saw the 60th anniversary of the Cuban Revolution. Celebrated by many, drawing the ire of others, Fidel Castro's *coup d'état* marked the beginning of a new era regarding the relationship between two nations which, obviously, could not be more different – the crocodile-shaped Caribbean island on the one hand, the North American world power on the other – a relationship which has been fraught with ambivalence to this day. Echoing a pronouncement by one of Cuba's most famous one-time exiles to the U.S., writer and freedom fighter José Martí,[2] Ilan Stavans astutely describes this conflicted relationship: "In exile in the belly of the beast, the Anglo's friendly hand ..., simultaneously opens a cozy shelter and subjugates as a victimizer" (59).

Historically, it was the revolution of 1959 that triggered the first large wave of immigration to the U.S. Although there had always been a presence of Cubans in the United States, it was this major exodus that led to the emergence of the hyphenated *Cuban-American* as a representative of a small but influential minority.[3] Juan Carlos

1 This article is based on a paper presented at the symposium "Beyond Borders: Reconceptualizing Fine Lines, Fences, and Frontiers in the Americas," at the Center for Interdisciplinary Studies (ZiF), Bielefeld University, June 2009. I am indebted to the convenors, Prof. Dr. María Herrera-Sobek and the late Prof. Dr. Josef Raab, for offering me a platform to share my thoughts. I also owe many thanks to Juan Carlos Zaldívar for granting Sandy Waters Milord and myself an interview at the sidelines of the 2009 Flaherty Seminar. Lastly, I wish to thank Dr. Astrid Haas, Beate Kaebel, Corinna Kaebel, Dr. Daniela Noll-Opitz, and Mirta María Peralta Abad for their graceful critique of this paper.

2 "I have lived in the monster and I know its entrails," from his unfinished letter to Manuel Mercado, May 18, 1895.

3 According to a study conducted by the Pew Research Center (2017), "Cubans are the third-largest population (tied with Salvadorans) of Hispanic origin living in the United States, accounting for 4% of the U.S. Hispanic population in 2017. Since 2000, the Cuban-origin population has increased 84%, growing from 1.2 million to 2.3 million over the period. At the same time, the Cuban foreign-born population living in the U.S. grew

Zaldívar's award-winning personal documentary from 2001, *90 Miles* (its title drawing attention to the proximity between Cuba and Florida), takes off with yet another such decisive wave of immigration: the so-called Mariel boatlift of 1980, with numbers of up to about 125,000 people leaving the country.[4] It so happens that Zaldívar's film, having started out as a project based on interviews between the director and his family, which revolve around their decision to leave Cuba for the U.S., was to turn into a large-scale meditation on the manifold entanglements of official historiography and memories, both individual and collective, in the course of the five years of its making and against the backdrop of a fast-changing, "accelerated" history (Halévy).

Accordingly, I argue that *90 Miles*' overall objective is to bridge difference, both by establishing what Michel Foucault has called "counter-memory"[5] and by means of its performativity. There are the seemingly insurmountable differences – most prominently, of a geographical, generational, and ideological nature, but also of sexual orientation – that separate the family members from one another and from their friends and kin in Cuba. Thus, the film engages in negotiating what I will call a "site of communion" or "reconciliation," where the different family members can come to terms both with the circumstances surrounding their departure from Cuba as well as with its impact on their lives. Remembering turns into a source of empowerment as *90 Miles* metaphorically crosses the borders of past and present, re-examining the past through the lens of individual and collective memories, thus granting a voice to those who were hitherto silenced. Centering on how the conflicted relationship between the two states has impacted individual biographies, with the director's family serving as a paradigmatic case in point, the film, in a truly polyphonic fashion, taps both "official" public and private discourses. Accordingly, *90 Miles* not only mines material from U.S. and Cuban television and film archives,[6] but also draws on a wealth of private

---

by 50%, from 853,000 in 2000 to 1.3 million in 2017. By comparison, Mexicans, the nation's largest Hispanic origin group, constituted 36.6 million, or 62%, of the Hispanic population in 2017." (Noe-Bustamante, Flores, and Shah). Florida's Miami-Dade district, where the filmmaker's family relocated after their move to the U.S., is a traditional Cuban-American hub.

4 Cf. Stavans (55). Among these, many were criminals and people imprisoned for their political views or gay sexual orientation.

5 This essay draws on Aronowitz's and Giroux's adaptation of the term in conjunction with what they call "border pedagogy." Their take on counter-memory actually not only references Foucault's seminal writings on "counter memory as … philosophy of difference" (Aronowitz and Giroux 111), but also Teresa de Lauretis's *The Technology of Gender*: "Counter-memory refuses to treat democracy as merely inherited knowledge; it attempts, instead, to link democracy to notions of public life that 'afford both agency and sources of power to empowering investments'" (de Lauretis 25, qtd. in Aronowitz and Giroux 111).

6 The stock footage was provided by, among others, the Media History Center (Miami), private persons, the Miami based television broadcast company WLRN-CH 17 as well as two Cuban sources, ICAIC Archives and ICRT. The fiscal sponsor was the Film Video Art, New York City. The film received major funding by: The Jerome Founda-

sources from Zaldívar's family, old photographs, and home movies as well as more recent interviews the director conducted with family and friends. Last but not least, there is additional footage produced for the film in cases where, as film scholar Amy Villarejo succinctly put it, "memories [are] in search of images" (83). Among these voices, and in addition to that of the director's own, the most important ones belong to his family. His father cannot deal with his perceived failure in two political systems, in terms of ideology in revolutionary Cuba, and economic failure in the U.S., and his strained relationship with his son serves as one of the film's focal points. The director's mother, conversely, seems to have successfully accustomed herself to living in the U.S. but must cope with her husband's bitterness ("his menopause," as she calls it). Then, there are also the director's sisters, who have to build their own lives as hyphenated Americans: while Juan Carlos's younger sister, Annie, came to the U.S. as an infant and only remembers Cuba through the memories of her grandparents, the two older siblings, a sister, Nilvi, and Juan Carlos himself, belong to the generation of "one-and-a-halfers." This term, coined by sociologist Rubén G. Rumbaut, is referenced in cultural critic Gustavo Pérez-Firmat's seminal work on the Cuban American condition, *Life on the Hyphen* (1994), in order to describe the dual obligation of fashioning one's identity *vis-à-vis* adolescence and acculturation all at the same time as experienced by teenage immigrants to the U.S.[7] In addition, the Miami relatives on the paternal side tell their own story of their exit in 1959; and finally, in Holguín, Cuba, Zaldívar talks to maternal relatives and with friends. Accordingly, his perspective is that of a "Cuban border crosser," someone who "allows[s] ethnic, kinship, and emotional ties to override ideological differences; [someone] whose intellectual and political perspective is less nationalist and less invested in fictions of separate development" (Fusco 3).

Moreover, it is important to take considerations of genre into account. As a documentary, *90 Miles* belongs to a filmic tradition fraught with expectations of objectivity and authenticity. But it also corresponds to some of the criteria film scholar Bill Nichols (2001) cites for the personal portrait documentary, such as its emphasis on subjectivity and experience and the impact of the filmmaker's relationship with his subjects, who in turn may "speak for themselves" (166). However, while it is one of *90 Miles*' key concerns to reconstruct the family history through individual voices, it is obvious that they are actually being orchestrated by Zaldívar, which results in the film's highly self-

tion; The Lucius & Eva Eastman Foundation; the New York Foundation of the Arts; The New York State Council on the Arts; The Cuban Artistic Funds; private persons. Juan Carlos Zaldívar stated that making the film would have been much easier had he accepted funding by Cuban American conservative sponsors, which he chose not to (Interview with Sandy Waters and myself, June 2009).

7 "One and a halfers," with reference to Cuban sociologist Rubán Rumbaut, are "[c]hildren who were born abroad but are being educated and come of age in the U.S., … who must cope with two crisis-producing and identity-defying transitions: (1) adolescence and the task of managing the transition from childhood to adulthood, and (2) acculturation and the task of managing the transition from one sociocultural environment to another" (Rumbaut 61, qtd. in Pérez-Firmat 4).

reflexive tone. In addition, there is a second strategy at work to bridge these many differences, namely, the documentary's potential for performativity. I am drawing on the terminology originally developed by John Austin in his theory of speech acts (1955) as it has been appropriated more recently in film studies by Stella Bruzzi (2006) and others. As I will show, performativity provides the subjects in front of the camera – as well as the filmmaker himself – with a symbolic arena where to revisit and re-enact, and potentially revise, past events. I will look at the ways performativity, performance, and memory all intersect in *90 Miles* to the extent that "memory as restoration is a simulacrum, a belated performance, purporting to bring back what is lost" (Kunow and Raussert 11). Accordingly, I will consider performance studies scholar Diana Taylor's (2003) investigations on performance as a way to address trauma, and Victor Turner's (1988) socio-anthropological concept of "performative reflexivity" in order to show how the film's subjects use performative strategies to respond to and find ways to counter social crisis – in this case, when facing the dislocation and identity crisis brought on by living in the diaspora. Doing so enables them to critically revise past actions, as these "belated performances" assume the dimension of an alternative ritual and thus function as a counter-stance against all totalizing efforts to submerge the individual's place and voice in history, instead foregrounding its potential for agency. Accordingly, on the one hand, *90 Miles* criticizes Cuba's totalitarian system which, in order to implement its own political agenda, invades all structures of kinship, such as family, friendship, love relationships, et cetera, and ostracizes "aberrant" subjects. Here, the film in particular targets the practice of superimposed "acts of hate" or "acts of repudiation"[8] [actos de repugno; actos de repudio]. On the other hand, the film exposes the questionable stance of a political super-power enforcing an embargo on a small island state harming not those in power but a people facing the effects of an already weakened economy – all the while kindling the hopes of a small but politically influential élite of right-wing Cuban Americans subsisting on an unhealthy diet of nostalgia and revanchism.

In a nutshell, the film makes a case for both remembering as counter-memory and performativity as a means of re-enacting and conquering the multiple traumas suffered by individuals subjected to separation and alienation in and by two warring political systems. This dual strategy enables the director as well as his subjects to address and thus at least temporarily surmount multiple psychological and physical borders and to reach out to family and friends instead. This bridging thus connects, and gives new meaning/s to, past and present via remembrance, while eschewing both the stasis of nostalgia and the easy solutions and explanations in terms of "predetermined endings" that much of written history would have us buy into. It follows that the film negotiates a however precarious site of reconciliation that offers a space to communicate

---

8 Throughout the film, these ritualized acts of ostracization are referred to as "acts of hate" [actos de repugno]. However, the term "acts of repudiation" [actos de repudio] is in more common usage. Despite their slightly different meanings, in the context of this essay, both terms will be used interchangeably.

and, possibly, heal in, very much in the sense of Diana Taylor's observations. She points at the way performance can be used to enact traumatic memory, turning it both into social protest and a coping strategy (165). In this light, *90 Miles*' appeal to a wide range of audiences is further evidence as audiences are bound to engage with the film's performativity as well. It does not come as a surprise that the film was awarded the first prize in the documentary category both at New York City's Latino Film Festival in 2001 and at the Havana Film Festival of the same year, and it is precisely the point I hope to substantiate in my essay that (apart from considerations guided by a certain political pragmatism) the respective juries, too, responded to the film's reconciliatory nature.

Synopsis

To frame the film in a short synopsis, *90 Miles* takes off with the Mariel boatlift in May 1980 as a turning point in the lives of all family members. The parents and older sister relate what it took for them to leave, which includes the kidnapping of young Juan Carlos from his boarding school. This is followed by a reunion with their Miami-based relatives, an account of the family's many adjustments to U.S. culture, and, subsequently, Juan Carlos's going off to college in New York City, where he embraces his gay identity. The topic of (national) identity that runs through the film is further highlighted when we witness the birth of his niece as "the first family member who is not Cuban," the parents becoming naturalized U.S. citizens, and Juan Carlos's decision in 1997 to visit his relatives in Holguín. We see his second visit one year later when Zaldívar follows an official invitation to participate in the Havana Film Festival. Finally, various episodes in Miami touch on the meaning of story-telling and belonging, such as the parents' eventual purchase of the house they had been living in ever since they came to the U.S.

Diaspora and memory

I would like to begin my analysis by briefly outlining different critical perspectives on diaspora, since this is what the film addresses as the Cuban American émigré community's main dilemma, and use them as a point of departure to investigate how remembering is foregrounded by the film as a coping strategy for this traumatic experience.

First-wave (post-revolution) exile Coco Fusco gives us a taste of a specifically diasporic sensibility, a longing for the intangible, when she refers to her Cuban American childhood home as "living with the presence of an imaginary country," replete with "another language, … stories, rhymes, and prayers" (4). Andrew Smith (2004), who analyzes diaspora within a framework of postcolonial, post-empire cultural production, alerts us to the concept's inherent paradox, since it is "intimately linked to a sense of territory, to the lost homeland and the once-and-future nation. Yet at the same time, because diaspora formations cross national borders, they reveal precisely the fact that cultural practices are *not tied to place*. They show culture … as *deterritorialized*" (256, emphasis in the original).

But while Fusco, New York born and raised, expresses what constitutes the dilemma for many exiles, namely that "unlike other immigrants who could return and replenish their repertoire of cultural references, we could not" (4), Zaldívar's case seems to be entirely different – at least at first glance, since Cuban culture is very visible and in fact thrives in the family's new home in Miami-Dade county. And the film indeed makes a strong case in favor of Cuban Americans in touch with their culture, presenting us with a community taking pride in their traditions, be they the usage of Spanish, Christmas celebrations complete with salsa [music] and *lechón* [pork roast], or a pronounced sense of connectedness, solidarity, and affection that spells out as *familia*. But *90 Miles* also uncovers the limitations of such deterritorialized cultural practices that privilege not only the preservation but also the uncritical appreciation of everything Cuban over the necessity to acknowledge one's "life on the hyphen" (Pérez-Firmat), and with it, the emergence of a new cultural identity. An alternative view might for instance draw on Stuart Hall's observation that identity is in constant flux and positioned and negotiated rather than essentialized (qtd. in Smith 256). Thus, in his highly personal film, the director's own negotiations of his identity and belonging, and his determination to bridge rather than choose sides, inevitably bring him into conflict with the stasis of Miami's Cuban émigré enclave exposed by such powerful images as those of right-wing extremists on horseback calling to arms in the fight against Castro's Cuba, leading Zaldívar to pronouncements such as "[s]ometimes I wish we had moved further away from Cuba." In *90 Miles*' characteristic fusion of the political and the private, this image is complemented by Zaldívar's comment that as a young adult, he needed to break free and move to New York City to live his queer identity, something, we infer, would have been unthinkable for him in the ultra-conservative and often homophobic climate of 1990s Miami.[9]

Accordingly, while the film champions remembering as a strategy serving to empower the diasporic subject, it by and large eschews nostalgia, "the emotional investment in a specific space" (Smith 256) even while it reflects "the exile's need to substitute remembrance for reality, words for things" (Pérez-Firmat 179). In fact, the film celebrates memory as a strategy to compensate for the loss of orientation and identity felt by those who experience the dislocation of diaspora. This tendency corresponds with the "world-wide upsurge in memory" (Nora) as part of more encompassing decol-

9 Ilan Stavans cites the case of Cuban writer Reinaldo Arenas, another Mariel refugee, as one prime example of the homophobia not only prevalent in Cuba and Miami's Cuban American enclave (55) but also in U.S. Latino culture at large, calling this phenomenon "another repressed ghost in our closet" (107). As to *90 Miles*' sparse discussion of the director's own identity-formation as a gay man, I agree with Amy Villarejo's observation, according to which Zaldívar chose to focus on his own biography precisely to the extent as it unfolds in relation to his family in Miami and the friends left in Cuba, and "to the ways in which the past seems to etch itself on his own present" (89).

onization trends, with subaltern groups all over the world – among them ethnic and other minorities as well as peoples in formerly totalitarian states – striving to have their collective and individual (his)stories acknowledged and validated. In the same vein, *90 Miles* draws on a dialectics of official history and personal experiences which complement, challenge, and redefine what we perceive as history.[10] In their writings on border pedagogy, Stanley Aronowitz and Henry Giroux, too, point to the relevance of remembering, referencing Foucault's usage of counter-memory, which, in their interpretation, translates into "a vision of public life that resurrects the ongoing struggle for difference, and situates difference within that broader struggle for cultural and social justice" (127). At the same time, they speak out against any sort of monocausal view on history (in their words, "custom"), as it tends to "construct subjects within a discourse of continuity in which knowledge and practice are viewed as a matter of inheritance and transmission … [and] the ideological basis for forms of knowledge … that refuse[s] to interrogate public forms and that den[ies] difference as a fundamental referent for a democratic society" (123).

In order to give one example as to how *90 Miles* deals with difference and draws attention to remembering as a means of empowerment, I will attempt a brief close reading of the film's very first minutes which illustrate the particular aesthetic and narrative techniques at work there, namely, the director's *bricolage* by way of assembling, layering and juxtaposing images and voices in a constant flux (a process that is, however, tightly controlled by Zaldívar's voiceover).

90 Miles takes off with a pivotal time in Cuban history that has become part of the collective Cuban and Cuban American memory: the occurrences that led to the so-called Mariel boatlift of 1980 as the second great exodus in the history of postrevolutionary Cuba. But first, there is a flashback to footage showing the late Fidel Castro engaged in one of his famous speeches of the early revolutionary days of 1959, during which a white dove landed on his shoulder, an incident that, ironically, was bound to invest him with "messianic" attributes in the eyes of the then predominantly Catholic Cuban people. This irony is accentuated by Zaldívar's voiceover: "The revolution was the biggest thing in my life. Bigger than anything else." There is a cut and a leap to 1980, film material showing an elderly, bespectacled Castro, pronouncing the political dissenters who are crowding the embassies of Perú and Venezuela "parasites to the revolution" and granting them the right to leave the country. We witness jeering demonstrators in the streets of Havana, denouncing the "traitors," and we see the impossibly packed properties of the two embassies. All of the above would by and large neatly fit in with regular social commentary documentary, if it were not for the director's intensely personal voiceover. In fact, the very first sentence we hear is "In 1980, *I* was a thirteen-year-old schoolboy…." By privileging the "I," the director politically

10 And while we are constantly made aware of the film's inherent self-reflexivity as the filmmaker's control over the unfolding narrative is permanently foregrounded, paradoxically, this also further underlines the validity of these testimonies, as I will show later in my discussion of the film's performative aspects.

situates himself among the enraged Communist demonstrators. It is only immediately before we are introduced to the film's title that we learn that he and his family, too, were to join the dissenters. The only private glimpse we get is a photo collage showing young Juan Carlos, reduced to a pair of eyes peeking at the observer, a signature appearance only seemingly self-effacing. For one, the director not only prepares us for his alternative (re)vision of these historical events depicted, but he also communicates an underlying ambivalence that results from the tension between his thirteen-year-old self and his present situation, a tension this film seeks to contain rather than solve – for the sake of sharing it with the audience.

And it is this very ambivalence that is amplified by means of how, in the subsequent sequences, the film juxtaposes the historical, "official," material to the private accounts of the complicated circumstances surrounding the family's flight, this time drawing on interviews and photographs. The latter material is complemented by footage from archives as well as material shot later and integrated into the narrative of the film, thus artfully "reconstructing" memory. We learn that the Miami relatives sent a boat to get the family out of Cuba, making it mandatory, however, that either all or none go. The adult members of the family then decreed that this decision was for the two older children, Juan Carlos and Nilvi, to make. After his sister gave her consent to leave Cuba, everything depended on Juan Carlos, who at the time was enrolled at a boarding school for gifted children and already studying film-making. Very probably to some extent in response to the pressure of the rest of the family, he, too, finally decided in favor of leaving, which meant no less than betraying his loyalty to a country whose ideology he had heretofore never questioned. This early episode in the film is so important because it makes a statement that will emerge as one of the film's recurring themes, namely, how remembering is presented as a process of negotiating many different accounts of the past and how one can never retrieve the past but has to reinvent it through stories, and that "truth" and "authenticity" are but contested claims. This in turn will prove important in regard to performativity, when it also becomes clear to which extent these re-told events are subject to manipulation, intentionally or subconsciously, an aspect I will address next.

Performativity

An investigation of *90 Miles*' performative aspects necessitates a brief return to considerations of genre. Earlier on in this essay, I situated *90 Miles* among films falling into the category of "personal portrait documentary" (Nichols 166). As such, this work is highly reliant on interaction and on a permanent negotiation of relationships between the filmmaker and his subjects (166). Accordingly, much of the film's dynamics depends on the director's interventions, that is, an ongoing crossing of boundaries between his dual role both as the director behind the camera and a subject (son, brother, friend) in front of it. Interestingly, these interactions appear to be very natural. This may be due to a number of factors. For one, the cast consists for the most part of the director's own family, which presupposes a higher degree of trust and cooperation and also results in their relative ease at being interviewed. Then, according to Zaldívar, it was also the camera's presence which made it much easier to get answers that in other contexts would have been more difficult to obtain (Villarejo 83). However, the family's surprising compliance and ease should not make us forget that their situation is in fact quite artificial and part of this documentary's performative agenda.

In the context of this paper, I will use the term performative in the sense of how it has been applied in recent film studies. However, the concept of course goes back to language philosopher John L. Austin's coinage, which, simply put, centers on the assumption that contrary to so-called constative verbs – which tell us something about the world out there – so-called performative verbs not only make a statement about the world but actually *perform* an action, such as in a wedding or baptism ceremony. Performativity is thus connected to agency. Ethnographer-filmmakers Ilisa Barbash and Julien Taylor argue along these same lines when they allude to certain "ambiguities about the camera's relationship to what it records" (16) as a defining feature that has been with film-making from its inception in the mid-nineteenth century.[11] However, the documentary's purported performativity has long been a contested topic, in particular in light of its claim to authenticity. Film scholar Stella Bruzzi is among those who have argued against this more traditional stance and in favor of the genre's performative potential. In fact, Bruzzi even takes the argument one step further by calling attention to the documentary's overall "inherent instability" (187), putting forth the rhetorical question as to "what else is a documentary but a dialogue between a filmmaker, a crew, and situation that, although in existence prior to their arrival, has irrevocably been changed by that arrival?" (198). Bruzzi goes on to argue that

> what author-performed-based documentaries reiterate are the twin notions that a documentary is its own document and that the interventionist documentary filmmaker is a fluid entity defined and redefined by every context in which he or she appears. The author-performer is thereby one constituent of a film's ongoing dialectical analysis. (198)

90 Miles, then, pursues a double strategy: in addition to establishing remembering and counter-memory, the film's performativity and self-reflexivity carry the demasking of seemingly straightforward truths to yet another level by emphasizing how, when viewing a film, our notions of reality and artifice are subjected to constant negotiation – to dialogic process rather than monolithic fact. Accordingly, in *90 Miles*, these negotiations serve to establish a highly precarious contact zone based on communication and mutual trust as the basis of all human affiliation, as I will show by means of the following examples.

Early on in the film, there is one such performative moment which actually has the director move in front of the camera for the first time. The scene shows him trying

---

11 Barbash and Taylor ask: "Should they acknowledge it [i.e., the camera], or should they ignore it? Soon enough, people affecting to ignore it were doing so with a concentration of the mind that rivaled that of the people approaching and gesticulating self-consciously, or posing as if for a still photograph" (16).

on various pieces of clothing he took with him as a thirteen-year-old immigrant to the U.S. We see Zaldívar somewhat self-consciously gesturing to the camera and thus addressing the audience directly, his arms in the sleeves of a shirt obviously too small for him. By crossing the boundary between director and subject, and, albeit symbolically, by obliterating the fourth wall between film and audience, his performative move enables him to reenact, while making light of, the no doubt disturbing experience of his arrival when everybody had to give up their clothes. Thus, he personalizes the televised material from 1980 immediately preceding this scene, showing the Cuban fugitives in a crowded internment camp next to a pile of clothes. I want to discuss Zaldívar's performance of the diasporic body on the basis of Diana Taylor's observations on the connection between traumatic memory and the performance of protest.[12] An example Taylor draws on are the performances staged by H.I.J.O.S., children of the "disappeared" political victims of Argentina's military dictatorship of the 1970s–1980s. The protesters' so-called *escraches* (public denunciations) are directed against the perpetrators of these crimes. Taylor describes these performances as "acts of transfer" (165) between children and parents, and by extension, between the protesters and their audiences. There are certain similarities between both types of performance(s).[13] First, just as the *escraches* by young Argentineans who use their bodies as stand-ins for those of their disappeared parents, Zaldívar's reenactment of diasporic trauma invokes its political dimension and becomes a coping strategy. Second, as Taylor argues, traumata as well as performances share a repetitive aspect. Accordingly, Zaldívar not only revisits his younger self; it may be equally important to recall the truism that everything recorded on film is potentially endlessly repetitive by virtue of its distribution and of present-day technical possibilities. Here it is Zaldívar's triumphant gesture of actually having salvaged a personal item connecting him to his Cuban identity, an item he performatively reappropriates. Third, in the case of H.I.J.O.S. as well as in regard to *90 Miles*, the reenactment of traumatic memory always takes place "in situ" and "make[s] itself felt viscerally [or, in the flesh] in the present" (165). Both, the protesters and Zaldívar, put their own bodies center stage. Lastly, the idea of the witness is central in both cases. However, while Taylor argues that "the transmission of traumatic memory from victim to witness involves the shared and participatory act of telling and listening associated with live performance" (167), in the case of *90 Miles*, Zaldívar's performance, as recorded on film, transforms his audiences into witnesses. In both

12 While Diana Taylor's findings are a very helpful point of reference for my analysis, by no means would I attempt to compare the respective socio-political situations of Argentina, Cuba, and the U.S.

13 I am grateful to Daniela Noll-Opitz who reminded me of some important structural differences. *Escraches* are mass manifestations which are staged in the public sphere and rely on the public's becoming involved, while *90 Miles*' performative acts take place for the most part in private, and involve a smaller number of persons (or just one), and involvement happens by means of a breaking through of the "fourth wall," that is, the audience's engaging with the actions onscreen.

cases we can again concur with Taylor, who refers to Felman and Laub's observation that audiences may "come to be … participant[s] and … co-owner[s] of the traumatic event" (57). Lastly, all this is also consistent with Roxana Waterson's findings on the relationship between testimonies and the transmission of memory in certain documentary films, or how memories become, as she calls it, "social (53)." Waterson maintains that "testimony necessarily involves a performative aspect," and she calls attention to the "need for an audience" and "the dialogical relationship" providing the basis for our understanding of these films (53).

Lastly, and again tying in a personal recollection with an experience shared by an entire generation, the above episode sheds light on the one immediately following, which may very well be ranking among the most unsettling sequences of the film. There is a cut to a television program from 1980 showing some of the newly arrived *Marielito* children at a Miami-Dade high school, having been asked to paint self-portraits. To the journalist's surprise – and, presumably, also to the audience – the children, regardless of gender, invariably come up with bearded men in military gear smoking a cigar, unmistakably Fidel Castro avatars. This incident highlights the identity crisis that all immigrants, in particular young ones, caught between two competing narratives face.

In another episode of *90 Miles*, performativity can be seen to bridge difference(s) caused by competing discourses on gender, in particular by notions of masculinity, and homophobia. We are witnesses to Juan Carlos's "coming out" to Pachuco, his father. While we actually do not hear the son say the very words, his voiceover prepares us for the father's reaction. As it turns out, his father confirms his unconditional acceptance of his son's homosexuality: "It's better to know things sooner … so we can mature together."[14] As the son emerges from behind the camera to embrace his father, the camera, resting on a tripod, goes on recording, capturing the father's face. Of course, one might argue that Pachuco has been put on the spot, for which his glance towards the camera could be taken as further evidence. One could also suspect that this scene had been pre-staged, which – alas – is indeed the case.[15] However, any considerations of authenticity are beside the point. Here, Jonathan Culler's observation regarding the truth value of televised events is equally valid for documentaries as well, namely, "[w]hether the image corresponds to a reality or not, the mediatic event is a genuine event to be reckoned with" (107). As such, the father's speech act, his pronouncement of his unfaltering support of the son, becomes a fact in the world out there. The father's positive response, and his son's acceptance thereof, mark a watershed moment in their relationship, as it establishes a common ground from which to renegotiate their relationship.

---

14 I am referring to the subtitled version of the father's words, since his answer is in Spanish, which is the language Juan Carlos tends to use with family members of his parents' generation, while he speaks English with his sisters.

15 In our interview, Juan Carlos Zaldívar revealed that this confrontation had in fact been rehearsed (June 2009).

As I mentioned before, the father-son relationship occupies a central position in Juan Carlos Zaldívar's film about the power of remembering and revisiting his family's past. As we have seen, both remembering and performativity may serve to illustrate issues of truth and authenticity. In the following example, they may be taken as a strategy to shed light on internalized attitudes and behaviors that have their origins in the past and that impact the present relationship. One key conflict the film addresses is the question as to how the father's obvious unhappiness relates to family's having left Cuba – which seems to elicit a diffuse sense of guilt on the son's part. As Zaldívar probes deeper into the family's past, there is a moment when he apparently decides to meet the father's accusations head-on. In this episode, we see the father shaving in the bathroom, and quite defenseless, when Juan Carlos asks him the question he appears to have asked himself countless times before: "Why did you always tell me that I abandoned you?" The father's reaction: tears, defeat, and the plea towards the son to go away – in English, this probably in reaction to the camera. Staging this confrontation – a trial, almost – is a brave move indeed, for Zaldívar risks alienating his audience with an act that could be perceived as a selfish quest for some ephemeral truth or venting his pent-up grievance going back to a traumatic experience, with the adult putting himself in the place of the young boy that was once just as defenseless. In addition, the director does not provide us with a reconciliatory closure, as we leave the scene with the unsettling image of his helpless father in mind.

In the course of the film, however, it becomes evident that the idea of abandonment looms much larger than indicated in this scene. What *90 Miles* reiterates is the old story that is the flip side of the promise of a, hopefully brighter, future that the diasporic experience holds in stall: the right to an unconditional loyalty that children of immigrants presumably owe their parents, in exchange for what is no doubt one of the greatest sacrifices one can make by giving up one's home, community, and status. Juan Carlos's performative assault is the culmination of a presumed breach of loyalty, which also includes the son's venturing both out of the family's sphere and the Miami community to live according to his calling and to embrace his homosexuality, as well as his indiscretions, his "telling it all" via filmmaking. But we can also view the episode as being part of his greater agenda to negotiate a common ground by trying to set the record straight and creating an understanding not only of his own but also of his father's situation. Accordingly, in the course of the film, the father's image is rehabilitated as we get to know him as a once proud young revolutionary who, after his beliefs were shattered, directed his energies to the welfare of his family. To him, this meant keeping them together at all costs, a determination that, still back in Cuba, would lead him to secretly building a house and thus provide even for the next generation. That same determination to keep the family together would lead Pachuco to disapprove of his son's stay at a boarding school as well as Juan Carlos's going away to college in New York City later on.

We have seen that the performative strategy allows Juan Carlos Zaldívar to bridge his own position as director-subject behind the camera and object in front of it, although an ambivalence surrounding authorship and control remains. Contrary to most of the episodes taking place in the U.S., during his first return to Cuba to reconnect with relatives and friends in 1998, he is mostly seen in front of the camera, directly engaging in conversations with his subjects – for several reasons. For one, there is a relationship of mutual trust that was a given back with his family in Florida, something he first must negotiate in his native Holguín with his subjects, all of whom he has not seen since the family's departure in 1980. As a result, he gives up his privileged but alienating position behind the camera.[16] However, most importantly, what happens in Cuba is that several persons respond to the superimposed *actos de repudio* [acts of repudiation]. These ritualized acts serving to ostracize political dissenters also figure prominently earlier in the film when Juan Carlos talks about his political commitment to Castro's Cuba as a high school student and his own involvement in these acts. If the performance of traumatic memory by H.I.J.O.S. was used both as a ritual and a strategy to "reappear the disappeared," in *90 Miles*, we witness a revisiting of these traumatic events that served to divide friends and families. This happens in terms of a reversal of the same "acts of repudiation," serving the end of reconciliation. Interestingly, contrary to Juan Carlos, who at times speaks to the camera as a stand-in for the audience, or his parents and sisters, who address their son/brother through it, the mother's cousin, Lilia, and her husband, Otero, use the camera as a means to communicate with Juan Carlos's parents. To reiterate Bruzzi, the documentary thus becomes a "document" (198) that communicates their friendship and unfailing closeness despite the multiple borders separating them from Zaldívar's family. The potential of film to bridge separation becomes evident when Lilia and Otero turn from talking to Juan Carlos and about his parents in the third person to directly asking Pachuco, Zaldívar's father, whether he still likes firewater, seemingly an insider's joke that makes their intimacy felt. Conversely, in another scene, Aguirre, the father's friend, directly turns to Juan Carlos as a representative of his family. Like Lilia and Otero, he addresses the dilemma of those left behind, namely, their being summoned to denounce Zaldívar's family after their departure. Contrary to the relatives, who voice their disgust both with this practice as well as with those who participated in it, Aguirre admits to having been at one of those gatherings, but says that "there was no hate in this meeting." Again, the credibility of his words is not what the film targets. As it were, it is the film's performativity which offers the subjects in front of the camera an alternative strategy to deal with these superimposed rituals. Victor Turner's observations on performance as a social ritual, and as a means of a society's self-reflection, may be useful here. He argues:

> Performative reflexivity is a condition in which a sociocultural group, or its most perceptive members acting representatively, turn, bend or reflect back upon themselves, upon the relations, actions, symbols, meanings, codes, roles, statuses, social structures, ethical and legal rules, and other sociocultural components which make up their public "selves." (24)

---

16 Furthermore, Zaldívar acts as a translator for the person behind the camera, his co-producer, and also for those in the audience who do not speak Spanish.

Accordingly, the truth value of these assertions is of lesser importance than the speaking subject's embracing the chance to revisit these past events and to set the record straight by reaching out to family and friends.

That said, the film also points to the limitations of this platform for negotiating a reconciliatory space. It is here that we, as the audience, are made to engage with the director's frustration of not belonging and the overall ambivalence of the "the familiar stranger," as he calls himself elsewhere in the film. This happens when the film shows Juan Carlos Zaldívar's second return to Cuba, this time in response to an official invitation to participate in the prestigious Havana film festival. First, there is an incident that leaves him irritated, that is when he is not being recognized as a fellow Cuban by a stranger on Havana's Malecón sea promenade. On a later occasion, he observes demonstrations on behalf of the world-famous case of young Elián Gonzáles. These demonstrations obviously summon disturbing memories of all too familiar rituals, featuring a group of functionaries cheering on young pioneers who, in turn, chant slogans demanding the boy's return to Cuba, and with it the routine anti-U.S. propaganda, including absurdities such as denouncing them a drug paradise where children's organs are sold. As Zaldívar muses about the very high probability of his own involvement in such demonstrations had he remained in Cuba, he gives in to the sort of ambivalent feelings that communicate to us the split he feels between his younger and his adult selves described earlier on. In fact, it stands to reason that it is only because of Zaldívar's having left Cuba for the U.S. twenty years earlier that his memories enable him to be in a position "in two places in one time" (Kunow and Raussert 10) where he can weigh past and present against one another. Again, what emerges is a psychological common ground, a space of sympathy and understanding, which may serve as point of departure for change, and it is this, last but not least, which he shares with us as viewers and witnesses. As his outsider status makes itself painfully felt, Zaldívar laments his being forced to take sides, rather than bridge, once more after all these years. However, the more effectively he communicates his feelings, the more effective the act of their transmission to the audience becomes. This is also substantiated by the enthusiastic responses the film enjoyed among very different audiences. Accordingly, on the film's website, Juan Carlos Zaldívar shares with readers some of the reactions of the various audiences and juries, including the personal triumph of a sold-out house when screening *90 Miles* in the director's childhood town of Holguín.[17]

17 "[S]ome [more] of the highlights include a tearful Q & A in Cuba, winning the Black Coral Award for Best Documentary in Cuba, a passionate discussion of generational differences in our attitudes towards Cuba in Miami, and the audience breaking into applause at the San Francisco Gay and Lesbian International Film Festival when I come out to my father on camera and he accepts my news in stride. A sold-out show at Lincoln Center during our New York premiere at the International Human Rights Watch Festival in 2001 was also followed by a fervent discussion attended by many Cuban media makers. The effects of that screening continue to echo in the Cuban and Cuban American zeitgeist today and are just now opening doors for me to go on the Cuban radio stations here in Miami" ("*90 Miles*").

Conclusion

"What could you possibly bring me from Cuba?"
– Pachuco Martínez, the filmmaker's father.
Juan Carlos Zaldívar, *90 Miles* (2001)

90 Miles, Juan Carlos Zaldívar's personal documentary about his family, manages to convey to its audiences an impression of the experience of the two generations of Cubans and Cuban Americans who at first hand witnessed one or both great waves of emigration from the island state. For one, the film summons the power of remembering by pitting individual stories, and in particular the specific history of the director's family, against official history. Furthermore, *90 Miles*, as a personal documentary with a strong reliance on testimonial elements, resorts to the performative formulation and re-enactment of pivotal and often traumatic incidents involving the director's relationship to his family and/or the family's shared history. All of this serves the end of providing a third space of reconciliation and healing whenever possible, and at the level of reception, viewers are able to share in this experience as well, which, as I argued above, may well account for the film's success with its very diverse audiences.

Accordingly, in the end Zaldívar's film seems to provide one such arena as we learn that his father has eventually bought the family's house. The film shows Pachuco giving their home a new paintjob, seemingly coming to terms with the fact that he is there to stay. I agree with Amy Villarejo's observation that *90 Miles* is indeed the gay, "wayward" son's gift to his father, a key to "produc[ing] home as a gift for self-understanding" (89), but I also share some of her reservations as to a final resolution of their conflicted yet loving relationship. That the director may be on the brink of giving in to the temptation of (narrative, at least) closure towards the end of his film can be understood in this context, but the insights we have been hitherto granted remind us that their relationship, just as the relationship between the exile and his (or her) cultural affiliations, remains one that must be continuously re-negotiated.

Remembrance, performative repetition, all these are coping strategies, as is the telling of stories. During the concluding episode, we witness Annie, Juan Carlos's younger sister, who for the first time has come to the Miami cemetery where her paternal grandparents lie buried. She has brought along her infant daughter, presumably wishing to share with her child the experience of connecting to these kin whom she only remembers through narrative recollections and photographs since she was too young to get to know them when they were alive. Accordingly, her visit, too, becomes a performative act and part of the film's agenda. While Zaldívar's voiceover commentary further makes us aware of the importance of story-telling, we cannot help but think of the many biographies obliterated and forgotten in the course of the displacement that is part of the diasporic experience, stories, and lives that were not given the loving attention that this film holds in stall for its subjects. Moreover, we are also reminded of the film's exposure of the at best ambiguous truth value of testimonies, recalling Aronowitz's and Giroux's observation that "remembrance as a counter-memory opens up the past not as nostalgia but as the *invention* of stories" (127, emphasis added). It is thus the dialogic, often contradictive, and processual nature of these narratives the film seeks to underline. Thus, rather than providing us with comfortable semi-truths, *90 Miles* remains true to itself.

Works cited

Aronowitz, Stanley, and Henry A. Giroux. *Postmodern Education: Politics, Culture, and Social Criticism*. Minneapolis: U of Minnesota P, 1997. Print.

Austin, John L. *How to Do Things with Words.* Oxford: Clarendon P, 1963. Print.

Barbash, Ilisa, and Lucien Taylor. *Cross-Cultural Filmmaking: A Handbook for Making Documentary and Ethnographic Films and Videos*. Berkeley: U of California P, 2001. Print.

Bruzzi, Stella. *New Documentary*. London: Routledge, 2006. Print.

Culler, Jonathan. *Literary Theory: A Very Short Introduction*. Oxford, UK: Oxford UP, 2000. Print.

Felman, Shoshana, and Dori Laub. *Testimony: Crisis of Witnessing in Literature, Psychoanalysis, and History*. New York: Routledge, 1992. Print.

Foucault, Michel. *Language, Counter-Memory, Practice*. Ithaca: Cornell Press, 1980. Print.

Fusco, Coco. *English Is Broken Here. Notes on Cultural Fusion in the Americas*. New York: New Press, 1995. Print.

Halévy, Daniel. *Essai sur l'accélération de l'histoire*. Paris: Self, 1948. Print.

Hall, Stuart. "The New Ethnicities." *Ethnicity*. Ed. John Hutchinson and Anthony D. Smith. Oxford, UK/New York: Oxford UP, 1996. 161–163. Print.

Kunow, Rüdiger, and Wilfried Raussert. "Introduction." *Cultural Memory and Multiple Identities*. Ed. Rüdiger Kunow and Wilfried Raussert. Münster, Berlin: LIT Verlag, 2008. 7–17. Print.

Lazarus, Neil, ed. *The Cambridge Companion to Postcolonial Literary Studies*. Cambridge, UK: Cambridge UP, 2004. Print.

Martí, José. "Letter to Manuel Mercado." Dos Rios Camp. 18 May 1895. Web. http://www.historyofcuba.com/history/marti/mercado.htm.

Nichols, Bill. *Introduction to Documentary*. Bloomington: Indiana UP, 2001. Print.

Noe-Bustamante, Luis, Antonio Flores and Sono Shaha. "Facts on Hispanics of Cuban Origin in the United States, 2017." *Pew Research Center*. 16 Sep. 2019. Web. https://www.pewresearch.org/hispanic/fact-sheet/u-s-hispanics-facts-on-cuban-origin-latinos/.

Nora, Pierre. "The Reasons for the Current Upsurge in Memory." *Tr@nsit Online*. 19 Apr. 2002. Web. https://www.eurozine.com/reasons-for-the-current-upsurge-in-memory/.

Pérez-Firmat, Gustavo. *Life on the Hyphen: The Cuban-American Way*. Austin: U of Texas P, 1994. Print.

Rukwied, Annette, and Sandy Waters Milord. "Interview with Juan Carlos Zaldívar." Colgate University, Hamilton, New York (Flaherty Seminar: "Witnesses, Monuments, Ruins."). 24 Jun. 2009.

Smith, Andrew. "Migrancy, Hybridity, and Postcolonial Literary Studies." *The Cambridge Companion to Postcolonial Literary Studies*. Ed. Neil Lazarus. Cambridge, UK: Cambridge UP, 2004. 241–261. Print.

Stavans, Ilan. *The Hispanic Condition: Reflections on Culture and Identity in America*. New York: Harper Perennial, 2001. Print.

Taylor, Diana. *The Archive and the Repertoire: Performing Cultural Memory in the Americas*. Durham: Duke UP, 2003. Print.

Turner, Victor. *The Anthropology of Performance.* Edited by Richard Schechner. New York City: PAJ Publications, 1988.

Villarejo, Amy. "*90 Miles*: The Politics and Aesthetics of Personal Documentary." *Mining the Home Movie*: *Excavations in Histories and Memories*. Ed. Karen L. Ishizuka and Patricia Rodden Zimmermann. Berkeley: U of California P, 2008. 78–91. Print.

Waterson, Roxana. "Trajectories of Memory: Documentary Film and the Transmission of Testimony." *History and Anthropology* 1.18 (2007): 51–73. Print.

Filmography

90 Miles. Directed and written by Juan Carlos Zaldívar, 2001.

"*90 Miles*." PBS: Documentaries with a Point of View. www.pbs.org/pov/90miles/.

Latinos on U.S. Primetime Entertainment Television

CLARA E. RODRÍGUEZ

Latinos and U.S. primetime television[1]

With the steadily growing presence and influence of Latinos in all parts of U.S. society, one might expect to find more Latino characters on television than has been the case in the past. Are (or were) the highly visible Latinos characters in such hit shows as *Ugly Betty* and *Dora, the Explorer* representative of greater Latinidad across the primetime programming board? This paper investigates that issue. It reviews the settings and the opening casts of the most watched (according to Nielsen ratings) primetime dramatic programs during the spring 2006 and spring 2007 seasons. Despite some notable improvements, it finds that Latinos continue to be under-represented in lead roles and in shows set in cities and areas where Latinos make up substantial proportions of the populations. It also notes Latino actors and characters tend to be concentrated in certain programs, with other programs having no Latinos in lead or supporting roles. Finally, it finds a number of ambiguously drawn Latina/o characters.

Does the high visibility of some Latina/o performers – in the case of Jennifer Lopez it was referred to as over-exposure – further obscure the relative *invisibility* of Latinos as a whole on primetime television? The fact that there are now some highly visible Latinos could suggest that the issues of Latina/o representation raised in the past are behind us. For example, we now have *Ugly Betty*, which has a strong Latina lead, several Latina/o characters and actors, and has received numerous awards. We also have *Dora, the Explorer* for the youngest set, which is a huge hit with all audiences.[2] So, since we are now in the twenty-first century and Latinos have become the largest minority group in the U.S. – 15% of the total population and projected to grow rapidly –, have the number of Latina/o actors and characters on primetime television grown accordingly? Or, are these exceptions?[3]

Reviewing the settings and the opening casts of the most watched (according to Nielsen ratings) primetime dramatic programs during the spring 2006 and spring 2007

1 There are a number of generic terms that are used to refer to the Latino population in the United States. They include Hispanics, Latina/os, and Latinx. In the interest of consistency, I use the term Latinos.

2 In the interest of full disclosure, I served as a cultural consultant for the development of the *Dora, the Explorer* show.

3 "U.S. Hispanic Population Surpasses 45 Million Now 15 Percent of Total." U.S. Census Bureau News 1 May 2008 (http://www.census.gov/Press-Release/www/releases/archives/population/011910.html). If we add the 3.9 million Puerto Ricans residing in Puerto Rico in 2000, the figure is actually 48.9 million.

seasons, we find that, despite some notable improvements, Latinos are still under-represented relative to their size in the population. These findings confirm the results of earlier studies which found Latina/o under-representation to be especially evident in "lead" roles and in shows set in cities or areas where Latinos make up substantial proportions of the populations (Mastro and Behm-Morawitz, "Latino Representation"; Hoffman and Noriega; Children Now, *Fall Colors*). My examination found that Latinos were highly concentrated in a small subset of these shows. This analysis also found that the "Latino-ness" of a number of Latina/o characters was ambiguous. These findings raise important questions about whether all groups are equally represented in the media and the consequences of this lack of equal representation to those who view U.S. media both within the U.S. and elsewhere. These findings also raise questions about whether depictions of Latinos (or other groups) should accentuate their Latino-ness (or ethnic/racial difference) or present more assimilated, perhaps less stereotyped representations of Latinos.

Why is this issue important? Underlying this analysis of Latinos is the question of why is it important to examine racial/ethnic representation on the shows that *more* people watch, i.e., the primetime offerings on the major networks. There are a number of reasons. It is easy to be lulled into viewing and enjoying shows that have little, if any, representation of groups other than what appear to be mainstream, middle class, and WASP individuals. These shows reinforce what is perceived or understood as normative. Viewers watch these shows and never notice that they leave out groups and individuals that are important parts of the scenes and stories they tell. Long-running hit shows like *Friends* (1994–2004) were set in NYC in the enlightened nineties – yet, these friends seldom encountered or had as "friends" any of the African Americans, Asians, or Latinos who constituted the majority of the city's population by 1999. This type of monocultural, middle class privileging of one group, impacts on our collective expectations of (a) what NYC was then and (b) who viewers' "friends" were or should be. Indeed, when Census 2000 announced that New York City had become a majority minority city, joining the ranks of several other major U.S. cities, this came as a surprise because of the way that the city tended to be projected on primetime network television.

We also lose the opportunity to have those who are not included in the major story lines tell their stories, which might have been just as – if not more – dramatic, compelling, and contrasting. Finally, since the media seldom covers its own coverage of particularly race/ethnic issues, few viewers are even aware of this as an issue to be addressed in terms of fair and just representation. Add to this the extent to which these U.S. shows are picked up abroad and we can see how much such representation influences the views that those in other countries have of the U.S.

Perspectives in the literature on Latinos in the media

The literature on media depictions and the representation of ethnic minorities is extensive and insightful. Some earlier works examined "unspeakable images" (Friedman) and within this had a minor focus on Latinos. Others began to address questions of how diverse our media was (Wilson and Gutiérrez). Still other classic works asked about the degree to which our media projected a Eurocentric view of the world (Shohat and Stam), and how the white eye or white gaze influences how we see the world (Hall).

More specific to Latinos has been the work of Valdivia and Perez who explored the notions of "symbolic annihilation" with regard to the treatment of Latinos in film. Ramírez Berg's extensive work on narrative approaches to stereotyping presented a clearer understanding of the concept and process of stereotyping, as well as the existence of Latino stereotypes in films. More recently, Mendible and her colleagues have explored the role of the Latina body in media. The title of her edited collection, *From Bananas to Buttocks: The Latina Body in Popular Film and Culture* suggests how Latina bodies in the media have changed in some ways but not in others. With greater distribution in international markets, authors have begun to focus on how hybrid products (with more multi ethnic casts and stylized urban settings) subtly reinforce notions of white centrism (Beltrán, "'New Hollywood Racelessness'") or contribute to erasing local differences in order to attract greater audiences (Valle).

Post-modernist approaches examining authenticity and audience reception have also investigated how "real" or recognizable the characters, settings and themes were to audience members from the group (or the locale) being portrayed on the screen (Valdivia; Sandoval-Sánchez). While other authors (Kotz; Jimenez; Williams) sought to illustrate how, when "the others" (e.g. Latinos) created and presented themselves and developed alternative images, (e.g. by directing and producing their own films), the products had greater authenticity and, in some cases, greater success (Nieves and Algarin). Still others focused on Latino subversion and resistance (Ramírez Berg, *Latino Images*), intertextuality, gendered subjectivity, and deconstructionist approaches (Fregoso).[4]

Some authors have examined media images from a post-Civil Rights perspective in the U.S. They find that a new race paradigm has developed, which is variously referred to as modern racism, enlightened racism, inferential racism (Hall; Entman) or color-blind racism (Bonilla-Silva). Within this view, explicit racial differences are down-played and racism is often denied or explained as existing in the past. Within this perspective, racism is seen as subtle and implicit and "produced and reproduced in the media without the conscious acknowledgement of the media producers or several sectors of the audience" (Valle 6; Entman). As Hall notes, one becomes aware of this

4 More historical approaches include: Cortes ("Chicanas in Film"); Garcia Berumen; Lichter and Amundson, *Distorted Reality*; Navarrete and Kamasaki; Subervi-Vélez et al.; Montalvo and Torres; Noriega ("'Citizen Chicano'"; *Chicanos and Film*); Noriega and López.

inferential racism by examining the silences and the absences. Still others focus on the amount of money, time, and attention given to the products and the role of corporations in creating and influencing racial/ethnic images (Dávila); or, on the historical and political-economic contexts influencing media images (Lopez; Gandy; Mendible; Ramírez Berg; C. E. Rodríguez, *Heroes, Lovers, and Others*; I. Rodríguez; Sandoval-Sánchez, *José, Can You See?*; Shohat and Stam; Valdivia) and political messages (Subervi-Vélez, *Mass Media*). These authors draw attention to how public statements and media representations can racially essentialize others without discussing the role of state or corporate interests (Valle). Within this literature, attention is paid to how the media projects and reinforces – as normative – a social structure that has underlying racial, ethnic, gender, and age inequalities, to cite just a few dimensions (Chito Childs).

The work presented here extends this last tradition because it examines the absence and presence of Latinos in primetime opening casts. Empirically based research that has focused on Latinos on television, has found a fairly persistent pattern of Latina/o under-representation. The Kerner Commission report in 1968, which arose out of the urban riots of disenfranchised African Americans and other minorities, brought this under-representation to the nation's attention (United States Kerner Commission 1968).[5] Subsequent studies continued to find substantial under-representation of Latinos as actors and as characters on television (Lichter and Amundson, *Distorted Reality*; Children Now, *Fall Colors*; Mastro and Behm-Morawitz; Montalvo and Torres). Indeed, in 2004, a Joint House Task Force held hearings on just this issue (C. E. Rodríguez, *Heroes, Lovers, and Others*). Researchers have concluded that Latino characters have tended to be associated with violence and crime and to be drawn stereotypically (Ramírez Berg; C. E. Rodríguez, *Latin Looks*). An extensive examination of the portrayal of Hispanic characters on network television from 1955–1986 and during the fall 1992 season concluded that Hispanic characters were portrayed more negatively than others (*Latin Looks*). Common stereotypes were: lazy & lower class, failures, poor, criminals, and "not to be taken seriously" or devious and "untrustworthy" (Lichter and Amundson, "Distorted Reality").[6] Hispanic characters were twice as likely as White, and three times as likely as Black characters to commit a television crime. As Navarrete and Kamasaki noted, even the "token Hispanic characters that did appear tended to be 'stick figures' in secondary or stereotypical roles, with few lines, or with minimal contribution to the story plots" (6–7).

More recently, Mastro and Behm-Morawitz ("Latino Representation") conducted a two-week viewing of the 2002 primetime television season and analyzed 67 programs and 1,488 characters. Although they concluded that there had been some advances in the quality of depictions of Latinos, they also found that many images remained tied to longstanding media stereotypes. They also discovered that the rate at which Latinos

5 The Kerner Commission refers to the report by the National Advisory Commission on Civil Disorders which examined television characters during the 1960s.

6 This study also included samples from reality-based series, and first-run syndicated fictional programming.

were portrayed was dramatically below that of their proportion in the population. In effect, non-Hispanic Whites were over-represented, constituting 80.4% of all characters observed (in contrast to the 69.1% that they comprised of the total U.S. population then). Latinos, however, made up only 3.9% of the characters observed and yet constituted 12.5% of the population then (African Americans were slightly overrepresented; they were 13.8% of all characters and 12.3% of the population in 2002 [2004]).[7]

Children Now, a non-profit organization that conducted regular studies of television, found, in their review of the 2003–2004 primetime series offered on the six major broadcast networks for the season, that there was a slight increase in the number of Latino characters, i.e., from 4% in 2001 to 6% in 2003 (Children Now, *Fall Colors*). However, this is still well below the 12.5% that Latinos comprised of the U.S. population. Moreover, they noted that the increase in the number of Latino characters "is tempered by the fact that Latino characters were more likely to appear on real life shows such as *Cops* and *America's Most Wanted*, often as criminals, than on situation comedies" (14). In addition, Latino youth were even less represented – even though they represent a larger proportion of the youth population in the U.S. (U.S. Census Bureau 2007). In addition, they found that Latino characters "were also more likely to hold low-status jobs than were members of other racial groups" (14). As they observe, "Latinos continue to be cast as characters with low-status occupations," with Latino characters being "four times more likely to portray domestic workers than" other groups (6).

In a novel approach, Hoffman and Noriega examined the web pages of ABC, CBS, FOX, NBC, UPN, and WB for recurring Latino characters on each primetime series during the July–Sept. 2004 period. They also compared their results with previous analyses they had made, beginning in 2002. They found that the appearance of Latina/o regular characters (LRC) on network primetime TV had "steadily decreased over the last three years" (1). In essence, most series excluded Latinos among their regular characters. They also found that the imbalance was even starker when they examined the settings. For example, Los Angeles County, the setting for eight series, was 45% Latino and 12% Asian at the time. Yet, Latino regular characters appeared in just *one* of the eight series set in LA County. Of the 16 series set in NYC – which at the time was 27% Latino – only 8% had Latino regular characters. Like the case of the earlier *Friends* show, which was set in a majority-minority city, few people initially noted the general absence of minorities (3). In addition, a number of popular and some award-winning shows had no recurring Latina/o characters, e.g., *Everybody Loves Raymond* (Long Island, NY), *Joey* (L.A.), *Boston Legal*, *The O.C* (Greater L.A.), and *Still Standing* (Chicago). They concluded that Latino recurring characters were "virtually absent from three of the networks, FOX, WB, UPN" and that they had "decreased slightly" and were "perhaps more marginal than past years" (3) being sidekicks, supporting characters, and ensemble players on white and black- themed series.

---

7 As is consistent with the portrayal of gender on television, Latino male characters – at 58.6% of Latino characters – outnumbered Latina characters (Mastro and Behm-Morawitz, "Latino Representation").

Does this under-representation and misrepresentation of Latinos impact the attitudes of the average American?[8] Entman examined the 2000 National Opinion Research Center (NORC) General Social Survey and found that respondents had a racial/ethnic hierarchy with regard to whether members of particular groups tended to be violence-prone, hardworking, or intelligent.[9] At the bottom of the hierarchy were Blacks, followed by Hispanics, and Asians equaled or surpassed Whites at the top. The figures are striking: 37.4% of those sampled said Latinos were violence prone; 23.9% said they were unintelligent, and 21.9% said they were lazy. Entman adds that, "given the tendency of people to not reveal their racial/ethnic biases, the prevalence of negative stereotyping is almost certainly greater than suggested in the table" (7). This is what the average American thinks, but what about the children? Studies by both Children Now (*A Different World*) and Cortés (*The Children*) have expressed alarm at the impact of TV viewing on children and the lack of diversity to be found in programming. They maintain that this influences the expectations that children have of themselves and that others have of children of different racial and ethnic groups.

Method: Utilizing a critical viewing form developed by Clara Rodríguez (*Latin Looks*), I analyzed the opening casts and settings of Nielsen's top-rated, hour-long dramatic programs during the spring 2006 and spring 2007 seasons and determined whether the actors and characters were Latino. I chose to review primetime programming on the major networks because as a recent ABC television ad proclaimed "No medium reaches more viewers than network television."[10] Also, they are viewed and project themselves to be what mainstream America tunes into, i.e., the "big tents" that address and represent everyone. Consequently, if they represent everyone, are they adequately representing Latinos and the U.S. as a whole?

8 Estimates on the amount of television that the average American child, youth, and person spends watching varies from 3.5 to 4.5 hours a day, depending on the age group.

9 The General Social Survey is conducted by the University of Chicago's NORC center and is taken every two years. It strives to include a representative sample of the total U.S. population, so the responses represent all groups.

10 Viewed on ABC, 3 May 2009, 7:20 EST.

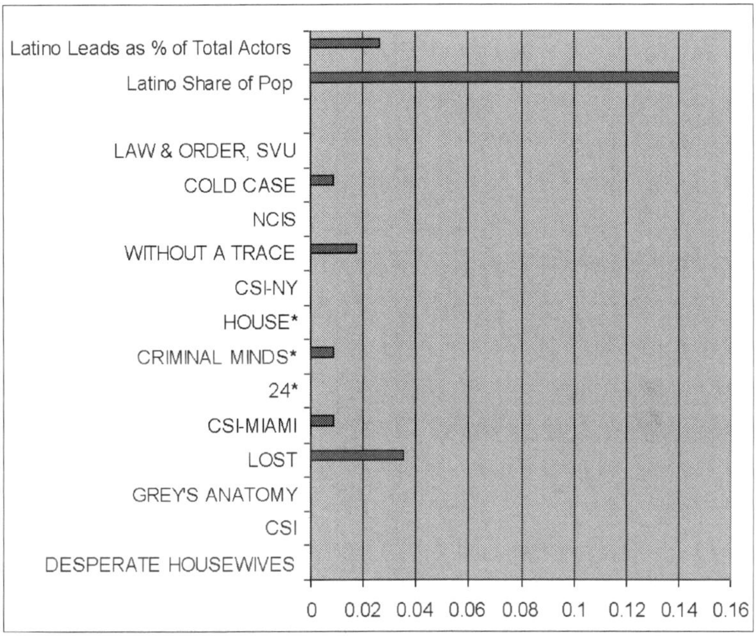

Figure 1: Latino characters as a percent of the opening cast.

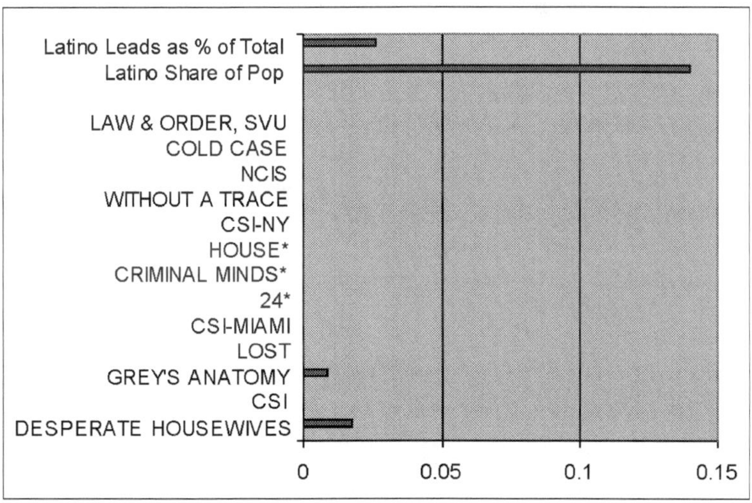

Figure 2: Latino leads as a percent of opening casts.

I focused on the opening casts and on leading roles because "audiences often identify and connect most with series' regular characters" (Hoffman and Noriega 3). Moreover, it is the lead characters that are the stars; and, stardom operates on a national and increasingly global scale as a powerful social force. Stars – or the lack of stars – from particular groups in a society "teach" notions of identity and leadership to citizens from all walks of life. These include lessons regarding the meaning of gender, class, race, and ethnicity in a particular time and place (Beltrán, *Hollywood Latinidad*). In the process, they also convey or reinforce notions about social relations, i.e., which groups are dominant (both numerically and with regard to political, economic, or social power), and which are more moral, trustworthy, etc. Stars' public images have long assisted in the reification and reinforcement of U.S. racial categories, such as "whiteness" and "blackness" and particularly in the construction and celebration of whiteness.

In order to determine the "Latinidad" of a character and whether the actor was Latino, I used a variety of criteria and methods. I considered names and researched the actors' bios and the description of the characters on network web sites; I also paid close attention in the shows to references about being Latina/o, to the use of Spanish by the characters/actors, and to whether they conformed to the standard "Latin look" (C. E. Rodríguez, *Latin Looks*). To determine the most watched shows, I consulted the Nielsen rankings for the top programs on primetime network television for these seasons.[11] For the sake of analyzing a consistent category, I selected the genre that dominated the rankings.

These were the one-hour dramatic shows. I excluded reality shows, sports shows (e.g. Monday Night Football), the news magazine show, *60 Minutes*, and one *half-hour* situation comedy show, entitled, *Two and a Half Men*. Figures 1 and 2 show the ranking of the top ten shows that I examined during spring 2006 and spring 2007, as well as the proportion of supporting characters and lead figures in the shows. There are actually 13 shows listed in the figures, as three new shows joined the top ten list in spring 2007; these were *24* and *House* (both programs on Rupert Murdoch's Fox network) and *Criminal Minds* (on CBS). *NCIS* moved down to #11, *Cold Case* to #12 and *Law & Order, SVU* moved way down to number 17.[12] However, in general, the shows in the top 10 shifted only slightly during this period. Consequently, I reviewed a total of 13 programs and their casts for a period of five weeks in spring 2006 and spring 2007. All of these programs aired on the major networks, ABC, CBS, NBC, and Fox.

11 The sources originally accessed were the Nielsen "Top 20 Network Primetime Series – Total Households, 2006–2007 Season Through 1/21/07" and the "Top Ten Primetime Broadcast TV Programs (by Total Households) for the 2005–2006 Season Through 2/12/06." But the programs are also listed in the following: https://en.wikipedia.org/wiki/Top-rated_United_States_television_programs_by_season.

12 The exact ranking on the list is apparently not as significant as we might think. In other words, there may be little statistical significance between the number one program and the number three program (Calame).

In my analysis, I recorded (a) whether the characters and actors were in lead or supporting roles; (b) how much time screen time they had; (c) the settings of the programs; and, (d) the genres of each of the programs. In order to determine the numbers and proportion of Latino residents in different settings, I used census reports as my major source.

Clearly, there are some limitations to this study. For one, although a great deal of care was taken to carefully record characters and actors, the identification of a "Latina/o" is not an exact science. Also, the analysis was limited to two particular time periods; other periods may have yielded other results. In addition, it is possible that some of the excluded programs, e.g., the reality and sports shows, may have greater and better representation of Latinos. But that is clearly a topic for another research project. However, this analysis draws attention to what the *largest* audiences saw – or did not see – on these programs during these particular time periods. In so doing, it examines the place that Latinos occupied within the early twenty-first century narrative of popular culture and within one dimension of the highly profitable world of media conglomerates, i.e., primetime TV.

Findings

The shows and their settings: As figures 1 and 2 show, the top shows that most people were watching were about crimes, investigations, and forensics work. There were the three *CSI* shows, all of which follow teams of forensic scientists as they investigate crimes. The first *CSI*, set in Las Vegas, spawned the other two which are set in Miami and New York City.

Similarly, the earlier primetime giant, *Law and Order*, spun off *Law and Order, SVU* which also involves crime solving, but focuses on sexual crimes, often against minors.[13] The shows *24* and *NCIS* also involve crimes, although these shows emphasize the federal government's roles in combating political espionage and naval crimes. The prevalence of crime shows and the existence of the two political-military shows are not surprising when one reflects on the fact that the U.S. now has the highest incarceration rate in the world, that it experienced the events of 9/11, and that it has been engaged in military activities in Iraq and Afghanistan. As usual, popular culture reflects the times.[14] Also on the list were shows with medical settings. There is *Grey's Anatomy*, which follows the sexual intrigues and dilemmas between interns and residents. There is also *House*, which explores the medical mysteries encountered by an irascible, but brilliant MD. Lastly, there are the shows that are set in imaginary places, i.e., *Desperate Housewives* in Suburbia, U.S.A. and *Lost* on an undiscovered island. In

13 The *Law and Order* franchise is huge, as earlier *Law and Order* episodes can also be seen on cable.

14 All but one of the shows in figures 1 and 2 was introduced after 2000. *Law and Order, SVU* is the exception and this was a spin-off of the older *Law and Order* series, which was begun in the early nineties and has been a mainstay on primetime.

sum, we had in the top slots of primetime viewing, investigations into general crime, naval and military crimes, sexually offensive crimes, medical mysteries, and more mysteries and crimes on an unidentified island.

Some continuing patterns and some surprises

Results were sadly familiar in some ways; in other ways, they were surprising and encouraging. As figures 1 and 2 indicate, only 2 of the 13 shows had both Latino characters and actors in *lead* roles. These 13 top shows had a total of 97 characters in their opening casts. However, only 3 (or 3.09%) had Latino lead characters and actors. These were Mr. & Mrs. Solis (played by Ricardo Chavira and Eva Longoria), who are still part of the ensemble cast on *Desperate Housewives* and Dr. Callie Torres (played by Sara Ramírez) on *Grey's Anatomy*. This lack of Latino leads was especially evident in the numerous crime shows on primetime, many of which were set in cities or areas with high proportions of Latinos. These findings are consistent with the research reviewed earlier, which found few Latino actors in lead roles.[15] On a more positive note, there were *supporting* Latino characters and actors in 7 of the 13 shows. However, the remainder (6 of the 13 shows) had *no* recurring Latina/o characters in either supporting or lead roles.

Consequently, despite an increase in supporting roles, Latinos continue to be under-represented, especially in lead roles, concentrated in particular shows, and totally absent from the opening casts of other shows. Accentuating the general absence of Latinos was the fact that the settings of the shows were in areas with large numbers of Latinos. For example, *CSI-NY* and *Law and Order, SVU* are/were both set in New York City, which in the last 2000 census had a population that was 27% Latino.[16] In *CSI-NY*, there were *no* Latinos in lead or recurring roles, but there were smaller characters in stereotyped roles or in stereotyped occupations. In *Law & Order SVU*, which accentuates its NYC setting and has been in existence since 1999, there were *no* Latinos in lead roles. There were some in the background, but not the foreground.

Only in *Without a Trace* (2002), which is also set in New York City, was there some representation of Latinos, i.e., Agent Elena Delgado (played by Roslyn Sanchez) and Danny Taylor (played by Enrique Murciano). But then again, despite the general diversity with regard to background of the ensemble cast, the lead characters and bosses in the show were cast as white Americans. This show focuses on a special unit of the FBI that finds missing persons. In general, during the period viewed, to the extent that ethnicity was a part of the show, it was related to the person who had disappeared

15 This pattern of few Latina/o actors in lead roles was not a pattern in the early film period. For more on this, cf. C. E. Rodríguez (*Heroes, Lovers, and Others* chapters 1–2).

16 The figures cited in this text are from the 2000 decennial census of the U.S., unless otherwise indicated. These figures tend to underestimate the actual count of Latinos, are seven years old, and the Latino population has been increasing rapidly during this period in all the cities discussed.

and if, they happened to be, for example, Chinese, then this took the investigators to that part of the city where more Asians were then seen on screen.

The CSI shows are set in different cities, but they all involve elite teams of police forensic experts. *CSI, Miami* is set in a city that is heavily Latino – 57.3% Latino in the last decennial census. Here, there were a few more Latinos but fewer than 57%. In terms of major leading roles, Adam Rodríguez plays Eric Delko, a forensics specialist.[17] Although he is a full time series regular, he is very clearly a supporting character. Another possible Latina character is Natalia Boa Vista played by Eva la Rue, who is of Puerto Rican, French, Dutch, and Scottish ancestry. However, the ethnic origins/dimensions of these characters were not observed during the episodes viewed. One more clearly delineated Latina character is Anna, who is not a member of the forensics team, but returned in more than one episode during the Spring 2007 season. She was a stripper and a prostitute who was periodically saved by the series' hero, the traditional Anglo/White savior, Lt. Horatio Caine (played by David Caruso). Philadelphia, where 8.5% of the population was Latino in the year 2000, is the backdrop for *Cold Case* (2003). The show features a team that reopens and solves cases of dormant, unsolved homicides that occurred years ago. The cast had one possible Latino character; this was Det. Scotty Valens (played by Danny Pino), who plays a supporting role.

The show that advertised itself on TV as "the most watched show" during this period was CSI, which is set in Las Vegas, where the Latino population constituted almost a quarter of the city's population (or 23.6%) in the 2000 census. During the periods observed, CSI had no Latino characters or actors in leading roles.

What about the shows in medical settings? *House* (2004) focuses a brilliant doctor who specializes in diagnostic medicine and uses all means necessary to solve the puzzling cases that come his way. It was unclear during my viewing where the show was set, other than in a large general hospital. In any case, there were no Latinos in leading or supporting roles seen. In contrast, the very popular *Grey's Anatomy*, set in Seattle General Hospital, did introduce a Latina character into their rather diverse medical setting in 2006. This was Dr. Callie Torres, who is a surgeon and is played by Sara Ramírez. According to the 2000 census, Latinos made up 5% of the Seattle population (where the show is set) and 9.1% of the Washington state population. With the introduction of Dr. Callie Torres (Sarah Ramírez), there was one continuing Latino character in the cast. During the periods observed, the character of Dr. Torres appeared to be very otherized, i.e., she was often depicted as outside of the primary cast, i.e., the in-group of interns; she had very little on air time and most of it revolved around her attempts to pursue the young male intern.[18]

Given that the proportion of Latinos in the armed services is and has been disproportionately high, do we find Latinos in shows with military settings (cf. Barroso)? In

---

17 It is important to note that Khandi Alexander, an African American, also has a strong lead role as the Chief Medical Examiner, Dr. Alexx Woods, in this series.

18 Even though an Emmy was received by Sandra Oh (who plays Dr. Christina Yang), the Asian population was also under-represented relative to its proportion in this city.

the *NCIS* show, there were no Latino characters in lead roles and the few minor Latino characters that appeared had minimal air time and speaking roles. NCIS stands for Naval Criminal Investigative Service. The show focuses on a team that operates outside of the military chain of command to investigate all crimes associated with the Navy or the Marine Corps.[19] Are Latino characters to be found in counter terrorism? In the show *24*, each season shows how agents in a Counter Terrorism Unit (CTU) try to thwart terrorist plots against the U.S. It was on the top ten list in 2007 (but not 2006). That season's story line focused on how Middle Eastern terrorists had detonated a nuclear weapon in California and had plans to detonate more in different locations throughout the U.S. Because in this drama the two presidents of the United States that have been featured are both African American, i.e., David Palmer (Dennis Haysbert, 2001–2006) and Wayne Palmer (D. B. Woodside), one would expect that the series would be quite diverse. However, the diversity did not include Latinos as leading characters. To a certain extent, this may have been due to the fact that the focus was on Middle East terrorists. But there were curiously no Latino government officials on any level. With the exception of Nadia Yassir (Marisol Nichols), who was a CTU agent of Middle Eastern descent, all of the CTU employees featured in significant roles would be socially classified as American white.[20]

Criminal Minds, which is set in Quantico, Va., did not include any Latino actors but did have one Latina character played by a non-Latina actress. This program, which began in 2005, was an interesting new entry into the top 10 list in spring 2007. It featured a team of FBI profilers who analyzed the dangerous criminal minds so as to anticipate their next moves before they struck again. In this show, Penelope Garcia is presented as an exceptional computer whiz who can gain entry to any database so that she can assist the investigation. She is played by Kirsten Vangsness, who is not Latina, and is portrayed in the series as a blond, pig-tailed, bespectacled computer expert who assists the team by finding and providing information from her vast computer database and files. Although the show is set in Quantico, Va. and Washington, DC, the team travels to various locations throughout the U.S.A.

There were more Latino characters and actors in the imaginary worlds of a lost island and suburbia and they included some Latino leads and recurring characters. In *Lost*, a show about survivors of an airplane crash on an unknown island, there were two recurring characters who were Latinos and they were played by Latino actors.

19 The issue of the exclusion of Latinos from films and TV programs set within the military context has been a long-standing issue and recently became a major issue in Ken Burns's documentary series on World War II (www.defendthehonor.org).

20 It is possible that there may have been an earlier Latino character, which had been part of the regular cast in previous seasons. This was CTU agent Tony Almeida. His role was played by actor Carlos Bernard (2001–2006), whose mother's family was originally from Spain and whose father is from Poland. However, the Latino ethnicity of his character was oblique and he met the fate of many other Latino characters we viewed – the character was killed off by the spring 2007 series – although he returned in the Spring 2009 season.

They were Ana Lucia (Michelle Rodriguez) and Hugo "Hurley" Reyes (Jorge Garcia). In the imaginary suburb of Fairview, U.S.A, on Wisteria Lane, *Desperate Housewives* actually had the two Latino characters and actors in lead roles noted earlier (Carlos and Gabrielle Solis were played by Ricardo Chavira and Eva Longoria).

In sum, Latinos are still absent or few in many shows set in cities and areas where Latinos make up substantial proportions of the populations. Despite the general dearth of Latina/o actors in lead roles, it was encouraging to see the existence of Latino actors playing substantial Latino characters as part of ensemble casts. For example, in *Lost*, Michelle Rodriguez played Ana Lucia Cortez and in *Desperate Housewives*, both Eva Longoria and Ricardo Chavira play lead roles, as Gabrielle and Carlos Solis and Sara Ramírez played Dr. Callie Torres in *Grey's Anatomy*. However, during the periods viewed, in both *Lost* and in *Grey's Anatomy*, the time these characters had on screen – relative to their respective cast members – was less. This raised the question of how important some of these characters were to the show or the storyline. It also seemed that a number of Latino characters seem to have higher mortality rates during the periods viewed. For example, Ana Lucia (Michelle Rodriguez's character), and two lesser characters (Paolo and Nikki) on *Lost* left or died prematurely on these shows. This raises the question of, if they could so easily be written out, without much consequence to the show, how important were they as characters.

Surprises

There were also some surprising findings, e.g., two Latina actors played non-Latina characters. One was Marisol Nichols, whose mother is of Mexican descent,[21] and who plays Nadia Yassir, a CTU agent of Middle Eastern descent on *24*. The other is Cote de Pablo, who is Chilean, and plays an Israeli (Ziva David) on *NCIS*. The Ziva character was added in the series' fifth season, so she has been a cast member since 2005. All of the other cast members on *NCIS* are white Americans. Ziva and Abby (a Goth-type character) supply the diversity by their dress and foreign-ness. It is interesting to see a Latina actor play a trained assassin and coercion expert, who is highly versed in guerrilla/martial tactics, has a photographic memory and is an expert sniper. It is a bit reminiscent, however, of other Latina actors who have played physically powerful roles but are not always clearly recognized as Latina characters, e.g., Lynda Carter (born Lynda Jean Cordova Carter) as *Wonder Woman* on television's hit TV show (which ran from 1975–1979), and, Jessica Alba in another hit show, *Dark Angel* (2000–2002). Often Latina characters are highly sexualized vamps or submissive, beaten welfare moms, and maids. More recently, when strong female characters are Latinized, they often become "kick-ass Latinas" or tough-chick characters, or as Beltrán notes with regard to

21 According to www.imdb.com, Marisol Nichols is of "Romanian-Hungarian descent on her father's side and of Mexican descent on her mother's side. She never met her father" (http://www.imdb.com/name/nm0629653/bio).

the new Latina action hero, "más macha" ("MÁS MACHA" 188). We can see this characterization in Michelle Rodriguez's various roles, in particular her lead character in *Girlfight* (2000) and her character on *Lost*.

In a reversal of recent patterns, only one *non* Latina played a Latina character. This was Kirsten Vangsness who played Penelope Garcia in *Criminal Minds*. This character, who is often referred to as "Garcia," has an explicit Spanish surname, but she had few of the other traditional markers of Latino ethnicity, e.g., accent, "Latin looks," or references to Latino background (C. E. Rodríguez, *Latin Looks*).

Another unexpected finding was the existence of *ambiguous* Latino characters. Indeed, the Penelope Garcia character described above might fall into this category. These are characters that (whether played by Latino actors or not) had their "latinidad" or references to their Latino origins obscured or seldom addressed. Examples of such characters include those discussed above, Danny Taylor (Enrique Murciano) on *Without a Trace*, Eric Delko (Adam Rodriguez) on *CSI Miami*, and Det. Scotty Valens (Danny Pino) on *Cold Case*. The Danny Taylor character was originally named Danny Alvarez but his name was changed to Danny Taylor. Because he is a Latino actor who has "Latin looks," one might assume the character is also Latino. However, in the shows viewed, his character's ethnicity was unclear. He has been on the show since it began in 2002. In the 2005 season, Roselyn Sanchez was introduced as Agent Elena Delgado. In contrast to the Danny Taylor character, Latino-ness was underscored, e.g., she had an accent, spoke Spanish at times, and there were references to family that suggested a Latino dimension. However, the episodes viewed did not revolve around the one distinctive Latina character in the cast.[22]

Like the character of Danny Taylor in *Without a Trace*, Eric Delko (played by Adam Rodriguez) had a somewhat vague Latino-ness, with little other than his "Latin looks" distinguishing him during the periods observed.[23] In the case of Detective Scotty Valens (played by Danny Pino), the last name "Valens" is ambiguous. Some might remember the singer Ricky Valens of "La Bamba" musical and film fame and they might recall that he changed his name from Valenzuela to Valens. However, it is not clearly a Spanish surname, and "Scotty" does not conjure up images of Latinidad. Some earlier episodes of Scotty growing up and of family members in seasons before the periods under review indicated that he was Latino, but this was not evident in the seasons studied.

Hugo Reyes (played by Jorge Garcia) in *Lost*, is another example of an ambiguous Latino character. We see references to his "Latinidad" but these references belong to his past and not the present. His character is referred to by the others in the cast as

---

22 These characters have, in subsequent seasons, been given more air time, story lines, and Danny's Latino ethnicity has received some attention.

23 However, greater attention has been paid recently to emphasizing this dimension of his character. One episode in the fall of 2007 had him establishing a bond with a young Amish boy who had been barred from returning to Amish country – just as Delko's parents had been unable to return to Cuba.

"Hurley" and very little of his performance invokes images of Latinidad. The presence of ambiguous Latino characters appears to be a new development, but it can also be seen as a newer version of the earlier "invisible" Latinos common in film; for example, Rita Hayworth (who was born Margarita Carmen Cansino) and Anthony Quinn (born Antonio Rudolfo Oaxaca Quinn). These were actors who began as Latin actors, but as their careers advanced, and in part to advance their careers, they came to be identified and projected as non-Latinos (C. E. Rodríguez, *Heroes, Lovers, and Others*). It may also be related to what at least one news reporter termed the ethnic ambiguity that seemed in vogue at the start of the twenty-first century (La Ferla) and to what Beltrán ("'New Hollywood Racelessness'") refers to as the new Hollywood racelessness. In either case, Hugo Reyes's character is drawn so that his ethnic identity is ambiguous in the present and only surfaces in flashbacks.

Conclusion

Thus, despite the high visibility of some Latina/o stars, Latinos in the most watched programs are still relatively invisible, especially as leads. Those that do exist are concentrated in particular programs. Moreover, they are scarce in settings where demographic data might lead you to expect some, e.g., in cities that are 25% or more Latino and in military and health settings. There were Latino actors and characters in supporting roles and as part of ensemble casts in a bare majority (53.8%) of the 13 shows reviewed, however, almost none (2.63%) in *lead* roles. Unexpected findings in the analysis included (a) two Latina actors playing a Middle Eastern and an Israeli character; (b) one non-Latina playing a Spanish-surnamed character; and (c) ambiguous: Latina/o characters in supporting roles, i.e., characters whose Latino-ness was not highlighted or particularly marked by accents, references to their ethnic families, culture or difference.

In conclusion, the emphasis in this research on examining what types of characters occupy the lead roles is important because casting can be used to convey a more inclusive – and perhaps more realistic – view of the U.S. Also, as noted above, national and global audiences connect and identify with recurring characters and the leads/stars, so, it is important to convey diversity at this level. There are also important practical implications. The presence of *continuing* and *substantial* Latino lead characters often opens up the opportunities for other Latino characters to be cast, as relatives for example. In *Lost*, Hurley's mother was played by Lillian Hurst, his father by Cheech Marin.

Limiting any group to supporting or subservient positions is a problem from a number of perspectives. As Mastro and Behm-Morawitz note: "From the theoretical perspectives of cultivation theory and social identity theory, these images may contribute to the development of stereotypes about Latinos and attitudes toward Latinos by out-group members, potentially establishing unwarranted status differences for utilization in intergroup contexts" ("Latino Representation" 125).

From a more practical perspective, this situation [and that of other groups] conveys the persistent and deleterious message that some groups of people are more valued by society and worthy of attention than others.[24] Temporary fix-its are not the solution. On occasion there are constructive, but token, Latino characters. But, how often do they interact with the show leads or with other continuing characters, and does this serve to remove Latinos from cultural inclusion?

The solution is to introduce interesting, diverse, and engaging characters who are Latino; the extremes of, on the one hand, "blind casting" wherein there is minimal or no cultural specificity (perhaps represented by Hurley in *Lost* above) and, on the other hand, stereotypical representations (perhaps represented by Hurley's parents) must be avoided. One obvious way to begin to do this is to hire Latinos and others who can develop valid, three-dimensional characters and story lines about Latinos. Only then can viewers get "the best of the best" for their programming. All viewers miss out if we do not improve our media products by incorporating all people, and making use of the best of all we have.

Works cited

Barroso, Amanda. "The Changing Profile of the U.S. Military: Smaller in Size, More Diverse, More Women in Leadership." *Pew Research Center*. 10 Sep. 2019. Web. https://www.pewresearch.org/fact-tank/2019/09/10/the-changing-profile-of-the-u-s-military/.

Beltrán, Mary. "MÁS MACHA: The New Latina Action Hero." *Action and Adventure Cinema*. Ed. Yvonne Tasker. London: Routledge, 2004. 186–200. Print.

———. "The 'New Hollywood Racelessness.'" *Cinema Journal* 44.2 (Winter 2005): 50–67. Print.

———. *Hollywood Latinidad: Latina/o Stars, Shifting Borders*. Champaign, Ill.: U of Illinois P, 2009. Print.

Bonilla-Silva, Eduardo. *Racism without Racists: Color-Blind Racism and the Persistence of Racial Inequality in the United States*. 2nd edition. London, Boulder, New York, Toronto, Oxford: Rowman & Littlefield Publishers, Inc., 2006. Print.

Calame, Byron. "The Time's Picture of TV Viewing is Fuzzier than it Appears." *New York Times* (8 Apr. 2007): 1. Print.

Children Now. *A Different World: Children's Perceptions of Race and Class in the Media*. Oakland, CA: Children Now, 1998. Print.

———. *Fall Colors, 2003–04 Primetime Diversity Report*. Oakland, CA: Children Now, 2004. Print.

Childs, Erica Chito. *Fade to Black and White*. London: Routledge, 2009. Print.

24 www.childrennow.com.

Cortes, Carlos E. "Chicanas in Film: History of an Image." *Latin Looks: Images of Latinas and Latinos in the U.S. Media*. Ed. Clara E. Rodríguez. Boulder, CO: Westview Press, 1998. 121–141. Print.

———. *The Children are Watching: How the Media Teach About Diversity*. New York: Teachers College Press, 2000. Print.

Dávila, Arlene M. *Latinos, Inc.: The Marketing and Making of a People*. Berkeley, CA: U of California P, 2001. Print.

Entman, Robert M. *Young Men of Color in the Media: Images and Impacts*. Washington, DC: Joint Center for Political and Economic Studies Health Policy Institute, 2006. Print.

Fregoso, Rosa-Linda L. *The Bronze Screen: Chicana and Chicano Film Culture*. Minneapolis: U of Minnesota P, 1993. Print.

Friedman, Lester D. *Unspeakable Images: Ethnicity and the American Cinema*. Urbana: U of Illinois P, 1991. Print.

Gandy, Oscar H. *Communication and Race: A Structural Perspective*, London: Oxford UP, 1998. Print.

Garcia Berumen, Frank J. *The Chicano/Hispanic Image in American Film*. 1st ed. New York: Vantage Press, 1995. Print.

Hall, Stuart. "The Whites of Their Eyes: Racist Ideologies and the Media." *Gender, Race, and Class in Media: A Text-Reader*. Ed. Gail Dines and Jean M. Humez. 2nd edition. Thousand Oakes: Sage, 2003. 89–93. Print.

Hoffman, Allison R., and Chon A. Noriega. *Looking for Latino Regulars on Primetime Television: The Fall 2004 Season*. Los Angeles: University of California, Chicano Studies Research Center, 2004. Print.

Jimenez, Lillian. "From the Margin to the Center: Puerto Rican Cinema in the United States." *Latin Looks: Images of Latinas and Latinos in the U.S. Media*. Ed. Clara E. Rodríguez. Boulder, CO: Westview Press, 1998. 188–199. Print.

Kotz, Liz. "Unofficial Stories: Documentaries by Latinas and Latin American Women." *Latin Looks: Images of Latinas and Latinos in the U.S.* Media. Ed. Clara E. Rodríguez. Boulder, CO: Westview Press, 1998. 200–213. Print.

La Ferla, Ruth. "Generation E.A.: Ethnically Ambiguous." *New York Times*, sec. 9 (28 Dec. 2003): n. pag. Print.

Lichter, Robert, and Daniel R. Amundson. *Distorted Reality: Hispanic Characters in TV Entertainment.* Washington, DC: Center for Media and Public Affairs, 1994. Print.

———. "Distorted Reality: Hispanic Characters in TV Entertainment." *Latin Looks: Images of Latinas and Latinos in the U.S. Media*. Ed. Clara E. Rodríguez. Boulder, CO: Westview Press, 1998. 57–72. Print.

Lopez, Ana M. "Are All Latins from Manhattan? Hollywood, Ethnography, and Cultural Colonialism." *Unspeakable Images: Ethnicity and the American Cinema*. Ed. Lester D. Friedman. Urbana: U of Illinois P, 1991. 425–440. Print.

Mastro, Dana E., and Elizabeth Behm-Morawitz. "Latino Representation on Primetime Television." *Journalism and Mass Communication Quarterly* 82.1 (2005): 110–131. Print.

Mendible, Myra E., ed. *From Bananas to Buttocks: The Latina Body in Popular Film and Culture*. Austin, TX: U of Texas P, 2007. Print.

Montalvo, Daniela A., and Joseph Torres. *Network Brownout Report 2006.* Washington, DC: National Association of Hispanic Journalists, 2006. Print.

Navarrete, Lisa, and Charles Kamasaki. *Out of the Picture, Hispanics in the Media.* Washington, DC: Policy Analysis Center, Office of Research Advocacy and Legislation, National Council of La Raza, 1994. Print.

Nieves, Santiago, and Frank Algarin. "A Review of 'Mi Familia/My Family' and The Perez Family." *Latin Looks: Images of Latinas and Latinos in the U.S. Media.* Ed. Clara E. Rodríguez. Boulder, CO.: Westview Press, 1998. 221–224. Print.

Noriega, Chon A. *Chicanos and Film: Essays on Chicano Representation and Resistance.* New York: Garland, 1992. Print.

———, and Ana M. Lopez, eds. *The Ethnic Eye: Latino Media Arts.* Minneapolis, Minn.: U of Minnesota P, 1996. Print.

———. "'Citizen Chicano.' The Trials and Titillations of Ethnicity in the American Cinema, 1935–1962." *Latin Looks: Images of Latinas and Latinos in the U.S. Media.* Ed. Clara E. Rodríguez. Boulder, CO: Westview Press, 1998. 85–103. Print.

Pérez, Richie. "From Assimilation to Annihilation: Puerto Rican Images in U.S. Films." *Latin Looks: Images of Latinas and Latinos in the U.S. Media.* Ed. Clara E. Rodriguez. Boulder, CO: Westview Press, 1998. 142–163. Print.

Ramírez Berg, Charles. "Stereotyping in Films in General and of the Hispanic in Particular." *Latin Looks: Images of Latinas and Latinos in the U.S. Media.* Clara E. Rodríguez. Boulder, CO: Westview Press, 1998. 104–120. Print.

———. *Latino Images in Film: Stereotypes, Subversion, and Resistance.* U of Texas P, 2002. Print.

Rodríguez, Clara E., ed. *Latin Looks: Images of Latinas and Latino in the U.S. Media.* Boulder, CO: Westview Press, 1998. Print.

———. *Congressional Testimony.* U.S. House of Representatives Report, Joint Task Force Forum, 8 Sep. 2004. Print.

———. *Heroes, Lovers, and Others: The Story of Latinos in Hollywood.* Washington, DC: Smithsonian Books, Oxford UP, 2008. Print.

Rodríguez, Ilia. "Telling Stories of Latino Population Growth in the United States." *Journalism* 8.5 (2007): 573–590. Print.

Sandoval-Sánchez, Alberto. "*West Side Story*: A Puerto Rican Reading of 'America.'" *Latin Looks: Images of Latinas and Latinos in the U.S. Media.* Ed. Clara E. Rodríguez. Boulder, CO: Westview Press, 1998. 164–179. Print.

———. *José, Can You See? Latinos on and off Broadway*. Madison: The U of Wisconsin P, 1999. Print.

Shohat, Ella, and Robert Stam. *Unthinking Eurocentrism: Multiculturalism and the Media*. London/New York: Routledge, 1994. Print.

Subervi-Vélez, Federico A. *The Mass Media and Latino Politics: Studies of U.S. Media Content, Campaign Strategies and Survey Research: 1984–2004*. New York: Routledge, 2008. Print.

———, Charles Ramírez Berg, Patricia Constanakis-Valdes, Chon Noriega, Diana I. Rios, and Kent T. Wilkinson. "Hispanic Oriented Media." *Latin Looks: Images of Latinas and Latinos in the U.S. Media.* Ed. Clara E. Rodríguez, Boulder, CO: Westview Press, 1998. 225–237. Print.

U.S. Census Bureau. *Current Population Survey, Annual Social and Economic Supplement, 2006.* Ethnicity and Ancestry Statistics Branch. www.census.gov., 2007. Print.

United States Kerner Commission. *Report of the National Advisory Commission on Civil Disorders.* New York: Bantam Books, 1968. Print.

Valdivia, Angharad N. *A Latina in the Land of Hollywood and Other Essays on Media Culture*. Tucson: U of Arizona P, 2000. Print.

Valle, Trinidad. *Methodological Approaches in Media Studies Examining Race and Ethnicity*. Fordham University. Unpublished Ms., 2008. Print.

Williams, Linda. "Type and Stereotype." *Latin Looks: Images of Latinas and Latinos in the U.S. Media*. Ed. Clara E. Rodríguez. Boulder, CO.: Westview Press, 1998. 214–220. Print.

Wilson, Clint C., and Gutiérrez, Felix. *Minorities and Media: Diversity and the End of Mass Communication*. Newbury Park, CA: Sage Publications, 1985. Print.

———. *Race, Multiculturalism, and the Media: From Mass to Class Communication* (2nd Ed.). Thousand Oaks, CA: Sage Publications, 1995. Print.

Filmography[25]

Boston Legal – Comedy. ABC (American Broadcasting Corporation), 2004–2008.

Cold Case – Drama. CBS (Columbia Broadcasting System), 2003–2010.

Criminal Minds – Drama. CBS (Columbia Broadcasting System), 2005–2020.

CSI, Miami – Drama. CBS (Columbia Broadcasting System), 2002–2012.

Dark Angel – Action. Fox Broadcasting Company, 2000–2002.

Desperate Housewives – Romance. CBS (Columbia Broadcasting System), 2004–2012.

Dora, the Explorer – Education. Children's Adventure, Nickelodeon Jr., 2000–2019.

Everybody loves Raymond – Comedy. CBS (Columbia Broadcasting System), 1996–2005.

Friends – Situation Comedy. NBC (National Broadcasting Company), 1994–2004.

25 Many of the programs that were discontinued on their original networks are still available on cable networks, or via Netflix, Amazon Prime Video, iTunes, and YouTube.

Girlfight – Sport Drama. Directed by Karyn Kusama, produced by John Sayles and the Independent Film Channel, 2000.

Grey's Anatomy – American Medical Drama. ABC (American Broadcasting Corporation), 2005 first episode, renewed for a 17th season.

House – American Medical Drama. Fox Broadcasting Company, 2004–2012.

Law and Order – Crime Drama, Television Series. NBC (National Broadcasting Company), 1990–2010.

Law & Order, SVU – Crime Drama. Television Series. NBC (National Broadcasting Company), 1990–2010.

Lost – Drama. ABC (American Broadcasting Corporation), 2004–2010.

NCIS (Naval Criminal Investigative Service), Military Drama. CBS (Columbia Broadcasting System), 2003–present.

60 Minutes – News Magazine. CBS (Columbia Broadcasting System), 1968–present.

Still Standing – Comedy. CBS (Columbia Broadcasting System), 2002–2006.

24 – A Serial Drama. Fox Broadcasting Company, 2001–2010.

Two and a Half Men – Comedy. CBS (Columbia Broadcasting System), 2003–2015.

Ugly Betty – Comedy-Drama. ABC (American Broadcasting Corporation), 2006-2010.

Without a Trace – Drama, CBS (Columbia Broadcasting System), 2003–2009.

Wonder Woman – Action Drama. CBS (Columbia Broadcasting System), 1975–1979.

Prickly Politics in Borderlands Art: Aesthetic Activism and the Barbed Wire Motif in Consuelo Jimenez Underwood's Artwork[1]

MARÍA HERRERA-SOBEK

> Barbed wire I see as the futile attempt of man to control life, so there are two powerful forces: the flowers and the barbed wire. And they are always battling against each other. Maybe in the next generation or two those two will come to be at peace. But right now I am the one that is bringing these two together.
> Consuelo Jimenez Underwood ("An interview" n. pag.)

Consuelo Jimenez Underwood articulated the above sentiments in an interview undertaken in December 5, 2012, regarding the incorporation of barbed wire in her artwork and how this icon functioned. Indeed, this Chicana/Indigenous, activist artist, or artivist, brings two disparate entities, barbed wire and flowers, together in a dialogic conversation of opposites but that in time will reunite as one.[2] Eventually, Mother Earth will reclaim both of them – time will disintegrate each discreet object and both will be transformed into dust. For the here and now, the dangerously constructed barbed wire will serve artists, such as Jimenez Underwood, as a perfect metaphor for "man's inhumanity to man"; it is a simple but searing multivalent sign for the dehumanization of people. I use the terms Chicana and Chicano to designate people of Mexican descent who were born or raised in the United States and self-identify with those terms due to, in most cases, a raised political consciousness and a keen awareness of their indigenous roots as well as their political, social, economic, and racial oppression in the United States.

Predating the conflated term "artivist" (artist activist) to describe artists who incorporated themes of social justice in their works, I use the term "aesthetic activism"

---

1 I am very grateful to Professor Laura Pérez from UC Berkeley who carefully edited my essay. Any errors are of course my own.

I want to express my gratitude to artist Professor Consuelo Jimenez Underwood for her gracious permission to use the beautiful images that encompass barbed wire in different reiterations with respect to La Frontera, i.e., border issues. I am also grateful to Alyssa Erickson for her outstanding assistance in identifying excellent copies of the art images.

2 The definition of the term "artivist" by *YourDictionary* is given as: "A person who engages in artivism. Origin [is] Blend of art and activist" (www.yourdictionary.com). The *Urban Dictionary* defines the term as: "An activist who incorporates creativity into his or her schtick without losing credibility or street cred" (https://urbandictionary.com/). Even if he or she does lose a little of those two things, the art usually makes up for the loss, rendering the person more soulful and/or funky, or at the very least rejuvinated for more activism – sort of like what happens with religion, but less complicated, depending on the scope of the artivistic endeavor (cf. Asante; Sandoval and Latorre).

(Herrera-Sobek, "Border Aesthetics").[3] The term artivism appears later in 2007, in an article by Chela Sandoval and Guisela La Torre titled "Chicana/o Artivism: Judy Baca's Digital Work with Youth of Color" (2007). My term seeks to address not only the works of visual artists but a wider scope of artistic production such as literary works, sculpture, artistic installations, music, film, photography, comic strips, textile weavings, as well as other types of artistic expressions. The border has generated a substantial work of artistic production due to the suffering and deaths of immigrants trying to cross the U.S.-Mexican border. The political climate extant in the United States continues to elicit anti-immigrant discourse and policies; these factors in turn motivate artists to articulate their aesthetic activism through their works. As I elucidated in my 2006 essay:

> Aesthetic activism is that process by which the "bellas artes" or fine arts and letters are used to seek, promote, and advance social justice. In aesthetic activism the artist becomes politically engaged and uses aesthetic strategies in order to disrupt master narratives of oppression. Aesthetic activism is used to promote social change, to alter institutionalized racism, and disrupt social relations of exploitation which are rooted in what Carl Gutiérrez-Jones explains in his book *Rethinking the Borderlands: Between Chicano Culture and Legal Discourse* (1995) as "class, gender, sexuality, race, and ethnic hierarchies." The *comprometido* or committed artist uses aesthetic activism as a strategy to convey his/her message and alter the political consciousness of the viewer. It is a methodology of the oppressed (Chela Sandoval's theory, see 2000) that is used to transform society. Guerrilla art Gutiérrez-Jones argues "disrupts the stability" and the "conventional rhetorical configuration by placing it in a different cognitive framework ...." ("Border Aesthetics" 61–62)

Visual artists have incorporated the icon of barbed wire or the Devil's Rope, as it is also known in popular usage, to convey an image representing extreme pain and suffering. The Devil's Rope was invented in the second half of the nineteenth century as a near perfect barrier for keeping cattle out of Midwestern farmers' agricultural fields (Krell). However, it was soon converted into a killer weapon during the First World War (1914–1918). Soldiers coming into contact with it quickly learned to avoid its sharp, wounding spikes. From the battle fields of World War I to the concentration camps of World War II, barbed wire served to enclose and limit the mobility of those incarcerated in the numerous prisons that sprouted throughout Europe, especially Germany, during that particularly bloody warfare. It served to keep some people in and to keep others out. Barbed wire is still a common element in the construction of

3 I first presented my theory on aesthetic activism in a scholarly paper titled "Border Aesthetics: The Politics of Mexican Immigration in Film and Art," at the Annual Conference of the Western Humanities Alliance that took place at the University of Arizona in October 2005. This essay was published a year later in *WHR Western Humanities Review*. I have continued exploring the concept of "aesthetic activism" in other forms of cultural production such as literature. Cf. – among others – Herrera-Sobek ("Estética activista").

prisons as well as to demarcate national geographic boundaries. In addition, farmers continue to find it useful in their agricultural fields and to keep animals enclosed.

In this study, I focus on Consuelo Jimenez Underwood's incorporation of barbed wire both as a material element integrated in her weavings and as a salient image in her artistic corpus of installations, weavings, and paintings.[4] I am positing that she employs the barbed wire motif as a powerful symbol in the construction of her aesthetic activism. Jimenez Underwood juxtaposes beauty (of color, flowers, yarn, textiles, jewelry, and so forth) and the pain inflicted by an unjust society on other human beings as represented by the sharp, blood-spurting, points of the barbed wire.

Although my central theoretical focus is on Jimenez Underwood's incorporation of aesthetic activism in the production of her *oeuvre*, I also find other critical theories valuable as they relate to a deeper understanding in the analysis of her work. Principal among these are critical race theories since Consuelo Jimenez Underwood's work is very much focused on the representation of the Chicano-a/Latina-o experience and the critiques leveled against immigrants. Equally effective in analyzing Chicano/a cultural production are Américo Paredes's theories on the clash of cultures as a significant and inspiring factor (Paredes, *Uncle Remus*, *"With a Pistol"*; Bauman). Chela Sandoval's theory of oppositional consciousness confirms Paredes's early theoretical elucidations (Sandoval). The persistent critique of American society within art and literature can also be comprehended through within Emma Pérez's thesis of Chicanos/as' drive to achieve a de-colonial imaginary that is freedom from colonial European encounters and the subjugation, both mental and physical (Pérez). Consuelo Jimenez Underwood's creative artistic production challenges the hegemonic conceptualization of Mexican immigrants and immigration.

Jimenez Underwood chose the art of weaving as a means of conveying her thoughts, documenting events, and critiquing society. As an artist, she has selected what she calls her "personal thread" that is the material that best articulates her political, socio-historical, and personal history.[5] A person's "personal thread" is one that fits their personality, their political ideology, as well as their cultural belief system. In Jimenez Underwood's case, she perceives herself as a "tough" human being. Thus, one of her "personal threads" is the barbed wire that in her artwork becomes an iconic sign for the border, for being tough, and being a survivor. Barbed wire, then, is used repeatedly in her creative works.

Barbed wire: historical context

The history of barbed wire is politically interesting. Invented by Joseph F. Glidden, a farmer from De Kalbe, Illinois in 1874, it became a transformative agent in three im-

4 Laura Pérez notes the importance of barbed wire in Jimenez Underwood's work: "But perhaps Underwood's most unforgettable signature has been the visually stunning and weaving of barbed and other wire …" (164).

5 *Craft in America* 2013. https://www.craftinamerica.org/artist/consuelo-jimenez-underwood.

portant areas of world history. Olivier Razac, in *Barbed Wire: A Political History* (2000), highlights the three areas where barbed wire served as a powerful tool and that had a "direct political impact in three disasters" (Razac 4): (1) the physical elimination and then the ethnocide of the North American Indians; (2) the bloodbath of modern war; and (3) totalitarian catastrophe [of] concentration camps and the Jewish and Gypsy genocides. For Razac, barbed wire is a tool of power and domination. He describes how barbed wire was constructed: "[Barbed wire] consisted of two iron wires with a series of barbs (pieces of twisted iron whose two ends are beveled and thus sharpened). [Glidden reinforced it] by rolling a second wire around the first and its barbs" (5–6). The second wire served to fasten the barbs that had been inserted in the first wire at specific intervals and in this manner secured them and prevented them from slipping and moving around.

The Devil's Rope was first invented to enclose agricultural lands and to restrain cattle from trampling farmers' crops. It also prevented the North American Indian populations from roaming freely in the Great Prairies hunting for their sustenance, bison, and this delimitation of space eventually spelled the demise of large numbers of their population. It was highly instrumental in the conquest of the West, as Razac and other scholars have underscored in their writings. Two of these historians include Joanne S. Liu (2009) and Alan Krell (2002).

Barbed wire's incorporation as a war tool in World War I and the carnage that its introduction brought forth in the trenches and battle fields sealed its fate as a semiotic sign for cruelty and suffering. Later, in the 1940s, the ubiquitous barbed wire fences in Nazi concentration camps further transformed it into a symbol of oppression. Razac comments that its appearance in concentrations campus "sums up the various barbarities and tyrannies with which it is associated" (106). Since the second half of the twentieth century, barbed wire has been used continuously to keep people enclosed, for example in Hungary during the reign of the Soviet Union or to keep people out as the fence/wall between the United States and Mexico.

Because Jimenez Underwood lived close to the U.S.-Mexico border and crossed the checkpoints frequently, she became acutely aware that barbed wire could be used as a symbol that visually articulated the suffering and humiliation of her people. Barbed wire is incorporated as a striking and important element in five categories within her work: 1. The CAUTION sign in Southern California's Interstate 5 Freeway and Barbed Wire (*La Virgen de los Caminos*, *The Sacred, Jump*; *Run, Jane Run!*); 2. The Virgin of Guadalupe and Barbed Wire (*Virgen de la Frontera*; *Virgen de los Nopales*); 3. The American Flag Series (*Frontera Flag 1*; *Revolution*; *Home of the Brave*; *One Nation Underground*); 4. Cartographies, Flowers, Barbed Wire, and the Border (*Mi Oro, Tu Amor*; *Undocumented Border X-ings, Xewa (Flower) Time*); (5) Undocumented Tortilla Happening (performance at the border, installations).

The CAUTION sign in southern California's Interstate 5 Freeway and barbed wire

Figure 1: Consuelo Jimenez Underwood, *Virgen de los Caminos* (1994).[6]

Jimenez Underwood's awakening to the political issues of undocumented immigrants came to her almost as a mythic experience. Joseph Campbell in his book, *A Hero with a Thousand Faces* (1973), describes the awaking of the hero to embrace a new path in life as a mythic experience; a sudden awakening that will bring the person to seek higher forms of knowledge and impart them to his/her people.

6 Cotton, silk, metallic thread, 5 ft. x 3 ft. Collection of the Renwick Gallery, Smithsonian American Art Museum, Washington, DC. https://americanart.si.edu/artwork/virgen-de-los-caminos-35365.

Consuelo states that she was becoming bored and frustrated with the themes and type of artistic work she was creating. She describes the exact moment of her transformation; of her awakening to the beginning of what was to be a new inspiration in her artistic production[7]:

> I have almost gone full circle. When I first began to work as an artist the impetus was the form; the needle and thread. How can I make weaving brighter, cutting edge artwork? But I was getting to the point where I felt that the artwork that I was doing was becoming predictable. I had the form; I had my issues; I had my methodology all down twenty years of it. It becomes like a formula. I don't want this anymore. I do not want a formula. I wanted to make a new kind of art. ("An interview" n. pag)

Jimenez Underwood describes the emotional reactions she had while driving on the freeway [Interstate 5] and seeing the "CAUTION" sign:

> I thought, "Oh my God, they are thinking about animals now!" because you would always see these freeway crossings for animals. Then it hit [me] so hard that that I can't shake it. I decided to make the quilt for them; for those young ladies or little girls that perished traveling that freeway. I acquired the cloth and it was a beautiful cloth that needed embroidery. Halfway through the embroidery I saw the *Virgen*. I saw her in there and she was dead. And right after that, barbed wires, barbed wires. Then I saw the CAUTION sign that needed to be quilted in. That is how the *Virgen de los Caminos* [The Virgin of the Roads] was born in 1994. [My transcription of the video tape.]

The "CAUTION" sign was commissioned by the Caltrans (California Transportations System) to warn drivers about possible immigrants darting from the northern bound side of the Interstate 5 Freeway to the southbound side in order to avoid the border patrol check point at San Clemente, California. More than 100 people had died crossing the Interstate 5 Freeway. The check point is about 50 miles north of the U.S.-Mexico border. The graphic artist, John Hood, drew the three figures: father, mother, and young girl with pigtails flying. The signs were erected along the Interstate 5 Freeway on September 1990.[8]

The artist mythically awakens to a new world of aesthetic activism, i.e., using the beauty of her art to denounce immigration policies that forced people into undertaking dangerous journeys due to dire economic or political circumstances. Poor people risked their lives and those of their loved ones in order to cross the border unauthorized and to dash across a major California freeway and running away from the border patrol, *la migra*, when they feared being apprehended and deported. The Mexican people who exposed themselves to being crushed by automobiles speeding at 65 to 70 miles per hour are generally from rural areas in Mexico or Central America and may not be aware of the high speed automobiles and their drivers inhabiting the freeway systems in the United States are.

The quilt artwork titled *La Virgen de los Caminos* honors and memorializes the numerous deaths of people accidently hit by cars on the freeway while fleeing the bor-

---

7 https://www.youtube.com/watch?v=j25Z8jzqWo0.

8 "Immigrant Sign," Wikipedia (https://en.wikipedia.org/wiki/Immigration_sign).

der patrol. As cited earlier, Consuelo Jimenez Underwood was emotionally impacted by the freeway sign that warned motorists to watch out for possible humans running across the freeway. The impact of viewing the freeway sign with the words "CAUTION" boldly imprinted in big, black letters against a yellow background and with three figures running, a father, a mother, and a little girl, inspired her to immortalize those immigrants who died on the freeway in search of the American dream. The artwork is a rectangular piece 58" x 36" with the Virgin of Guadalupe, Patron Saint of Mexico, and the protector of the oppressed, delicately embroidered at the center. Surrounding the Virgin is a mandorla embroidered with roses at the top, bottom, and each side of the image. The rectangular quilt is divided by three barbed wires stretched across its width at uneven intervals. These wires symbolically signify the division between the United States and Mexico, i.e., they represent the fence/wall that divides the two countries. Additionally, it also represents the danger and suffering the people who are being kept out endure.

The Virgin of Guadalupe is an iconic symbol of the Mexican people, especially the Mexican indigenous population. According to legend, she appeared as a beautiful lady in 1531 at the Cerro del Tepeyac to a Mexica (Aztec) Indian by the name of Juan Diego. She informed him that she had chosen him to deliver a message to the then Archbishop of Mexico, Juan de Zumárraga (1468–1548). The message consisted of the Virgin's wish to have a church built at El Cerro del Tepeyac located in the outskirts of Mexico City in her honor. He obeys the instructions given and gathers the roses which he delivers to the Archbishop. As Juan Diego unfolds his cloak where he was carrying the flowers, they fall to the floor and expose the image of the Virgin of Guadalupe imprinted on the *tilma* or cloak. This image continues to be available for viewing to the public at the Basílica of the Virgin of Guadalupe at the Villa de Guadalupe in Mexico City. The roses have become a symbol of the Virgin and are associated with the miracle of her apparition dated December 12, 1531 (Leal 123–130). This sacred female deity is perceived to be the mother of all Mexicans and one who protects them. The barbed wire associated with the Miracle of the Roses bears witness to the fact that although there is suffering, the Virgin of Guadalupe will never forget her chosen people. She is a symbol of hope and optimism for a better future for the Mexican people.

The white quilt where the Virgin appears center stage also has finely embroidered figures of the running family: the father, mother, and child and the accompanying "CAUTION" sign. They are embroidered in white thread which makes it very difficult to see and identify the three running figures and the freeway sign. However, on another website the description of the nearly invisible freeway sign and figures is given thusly: "The word 'caution' and image of a fleeing family are taken from road signs in Southern California. Executed in white on white they reflect Underwood's belief that immigrants become indistinguishable from other members of American society. I agree with Yorba's interpretation and with Jimenez Underwood that the images are almost invisible because they are dead; they are ghosts haunting our conscious because of what an uncaring society has inflicted on them. This is her aesthetic activism underscoring the maiming and killing of innocent lives and hopefully motivating the public to take action.

Figure 2: Consuelo Jimenez Underwood, *Sacred Jump*, 1994.[9]

The second artwork featuring the "CAUTION" sign and the three family members running for their lives is titled *The Sacred Jump*, dating from 1994 (Figure 2).

The hanging art exhibited on a wall is an 83" x 38" woven fabric and encompasses several components, among them are two silk-screen stamped with the CAUTION sign of the three running figures; one is in red ink and one in black. Although small images, they vividly evoke the danger that the family finds itself. There are two large, red X X's to the left of the black version of fleeing figures from the viewer's perspective. The two XX's are positioned one on top of the other. They are reminiscent of railroad crossing signs but in this instance the family seems unaware of both the CAUTION sign above them and the XX's they are running toward. Furthermore, the CAUTION sign with the family enclosed within its frame are viewed behind a grid of small squares formed by the golden thread and barbed wire layered on and framing the work. The grid formed by the golden thread and barbed wire symbolically imply the family is imprisoned within both the square CAUTION sign as well as the landscape through which they are running to nowhere. The three family members resemble hamsters enclosed in a spinning wheel forever destined to run.

9 Woven, silkscreened, embroidered, silk threads, barbed wire, and gold wire, 83 in. x 38 in. Photography by Curt Fukuda. Collection of the Artist. http://www.consuelojunderwood.com/sacred-jump.html.

Figure 3: Consuelo Jimenez Underwood, *Run, Jane Run!*, 2004.[10]

The CAUTION sign appears in a 2004 wall tapestry titled, *Run, Jane Run!* and prominently features the fleeing threesome family members: father, mother, and daughter (figure 3). It is a 10' x 6' bright yellow and black weaving made with woven cotton and linen fabric, barbed wire, and CAUTION tape.

The title *Run, Jane Run!* is a caustic, bitter play on the Dick and Jane elementary school readers written by William S. Gray and Zerna Sharp. These readers were most popular during the decades of the1940s and 1950s.[11] They were characterized by simple sentences such as "See Spot run." The characters depicted in this reading series were happy, blond, middle class, Euro-American youngsters far removed from experi-

10 Woven cotton, linen, fabric, barbed wire, and CAUTION tape, 10 ft. x 6 ft. Photography by Rueben Diaz. Collection of the Artist. http://www.consuelojunderwood.com/run-jane-run.html.

11 "Dick and Jane." Wikipedia (https:en.wikipedia.org/wiki/Dick_and_Jane).

encing the hard life of poor children or the life of racialized minorities. Mexican and Mexican American people, on the other hand, were being subjected to deportation drives such as those of the 1930s under the Great Depression. In the 1950s, at the directive of President Dwight D. Eisenhower what was unabashedly called "Operation Wetback" deported 1.3 million Mexicans and Mexican American citizens, mostly children that had to leave with their parents when they were deported (García). In Texas, men, women, grandmothers, pregnant women, and American-born children were sent to Mexico, most just dumped across the U.S.-Mexico border. The small agricultural border town of Rio Hondo, Texas, for example, became a ghost town soon thereafter and never recovered.

In the 1990s, a new wave of anti-immigrant feelings descended upon California and Proposition 187 was passed. This Proposition prohibited access to education K-12 to the children of undocumented workers. In addition, it tried to deny health services and public social services to these workers. Although Proposition 187 was later declared unconstitutional, the border became more difficult to cross.

Jimenez Underwood describes her own personal experience with the CAUTION sign that led her to create another hanging artwork, *C. Jane Run* (2005) (figure 4).

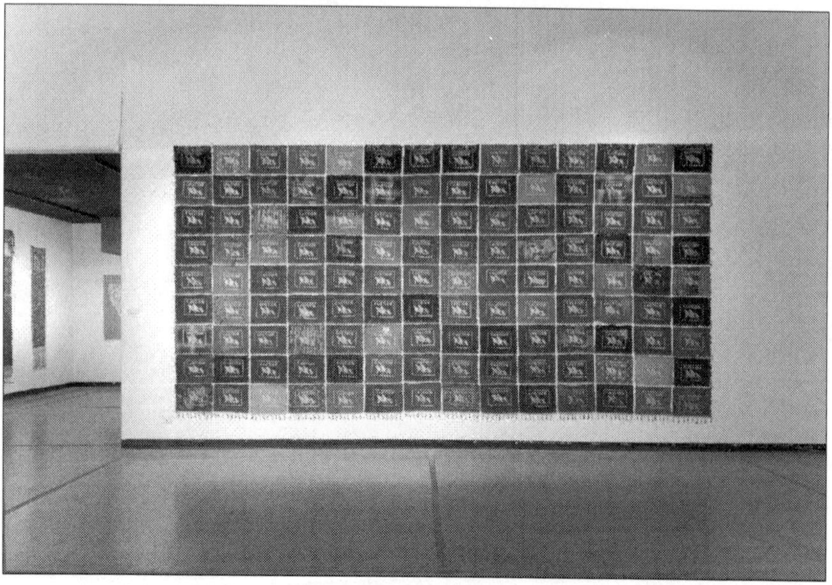

Figure 4: Consuelo Jimenez Underwood, *C. Jane Run*, 2005.[12]

---

12 Silkscreened and pinned fabric, 10 ft. x 17 ft. Photography by Ron Bolander. Collection of the Artist. http://www.consuelojunderwood.com/c-jane-run.html.

Jimenez Underwood further elaborates on the comments cited earlier:

> When I first zipped past the sign at 75 mph, on my way from San Diego to LA, way back in the early eighties, I almost braked. I was appalled, angry and shocked that the citizens of our nation were asked to accept this image of a running family crossing the 405 Freeway [sic, it was the Interstate 5 Freeway]. Plus, I totally identified with the little girl. When I found out that when a person is hit by a car at full speed, nothing recognizable is left, except small fragments of clothing, I felt the need to construct a memorial quilt of sort, a large-scale textile created to honor the anonymous dead who died when crossing the freeway.[13]

The hanging weaving, C. *Jane Run!*, memorializes the running family and captures them fleeing, running forever. The barbed wire present in the wooden rods hanging the woven fabric underscores the suffering of the migrant family. The indigenous style of the hanging wall artwork encodes an ironic statement given that most Mexicans are mestizos or mixed race people with Indian and Spanish genes. Even though of various Indian heritage and native to the American continent, including the U.S.A., they are now perceived as foreigners in their own land. The wall hanging inscribes this painful truth.

The Virgin of Guadalupe and barbed wire

In this second category of Jimenez Underwood artwork, I have identified two artistic renditions where the Virgin of Guadalupe appears with the barbed wire icon. (1) Virgen de la Frontera and (2) Virgen de los Nopales. Virgen de la Frontera (1991) depicts a ghostly image of the Virgin of Guadalupe as a ghostly figure in the composition. It consists of eight strands of wire stretch across the 5' width of the fabric (figure 5). The woven cloth is described as "Dyed and silkscreened linen and synthetic threads, barbed wire." Jimenez Underwood offers the following comments on this work: "My first woven Virgin de Guadalupe. It was the first time I wove barbed wire (5' length) into a woven work. It was the late 80s early 90s and pretty much the first time ever that anyone wove barbed wire. Please note, the Lupe image is resist dyed and kind of spooky – she ain't too happy!!!"[14]

13 http://www.consuelojunderwood.com/c-jane-run.html.

14 http://www.consuelojunderwood.com/virgen-de-la-frontera.html.

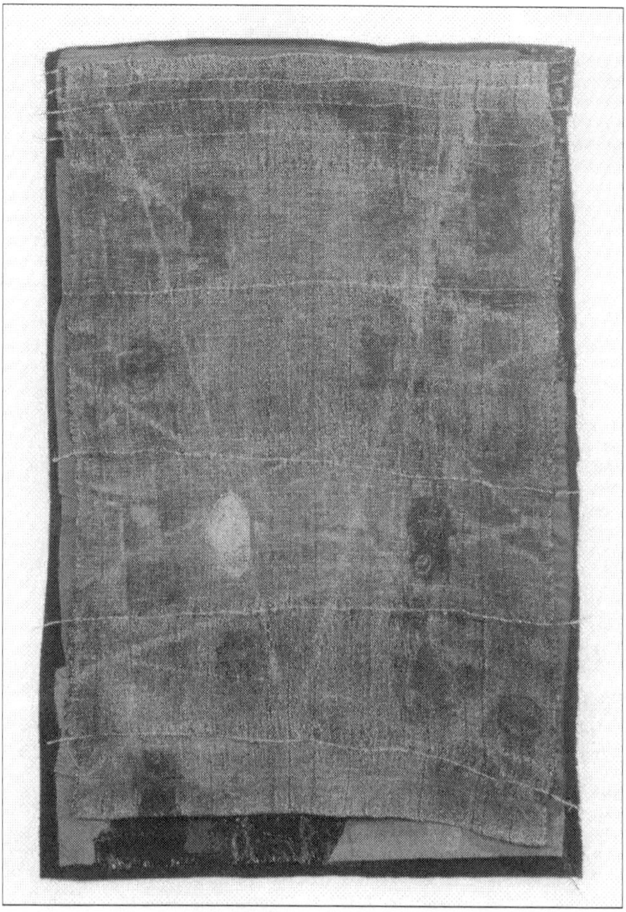

Figure 5: Consuelo Jimenez Underwood, *Virgen de la Frontera*, 1991.[15]

The artwork titled *La Virgen de los Nopales* (2005) is a silkscreen stitched print paper 20'x 26" (figure 6).

15 Dyed and silkscreened linen and synthetic threads, barbed wire, 7 ft. x 5 ft. Photography by Curt Fukuda. Collection of the Artist. http://www.consuelojunderwood.com/virgen-de-la-frontera.html.

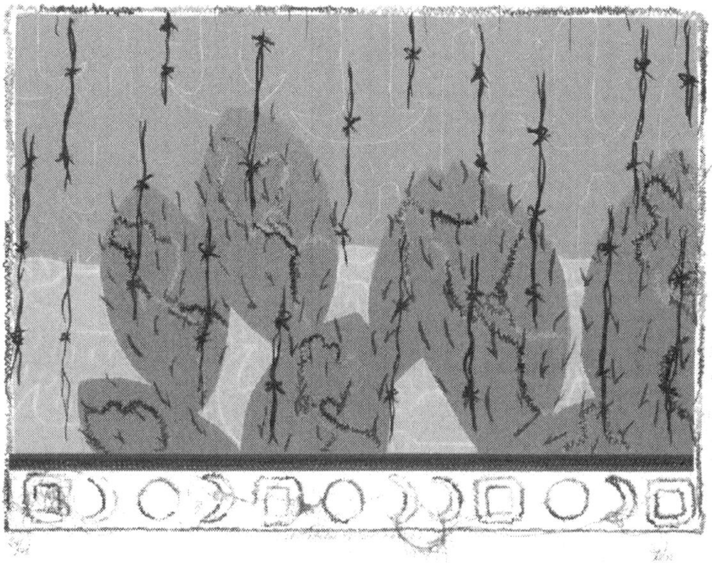

Figure 6: Consuelo Jimenez Underwood, *Virgen de los Nopales*, 2005.[16]

The composition features beautiful, green cactus leaves emanating from desert sands in the foreground; on the background is an aqua-blue sky. Depicted in the background are a series of fine, barely visible white outlines of the Guadalupe image. Some of the Guadalupe images are visible from the waist down, while others only show the lower part of the Sacred Deity as they "rain" from the sky; that is pour down, descend from the sky. In contrast, jet-black barbed wire images rain down from the sky in strands of three to eight inches. The red machine sewn on the cacti seem to denote blood spurting from the cacti. Jimenez Underwood has sewn a border around the silkscreen. At the bottom of the artwork the artist embroidered, the rectangle that serves as a border or platform repeats images of a square within a square, the sun, and the moon. These cosmic entities witness the scene unfolding in the main "stage" of the artwork. The sun and the moon underscore the more transitory nature of human history: the banality of political posturing regarding immigration policies. Jimenez Underwood describes the artwork in this manner:

16 Stitched print on paper, 20 in. x 26 in. Photography by James Dewrance. Collection of the Artist. http://www.consuelojunderwood.com/virgen-de-los-nopales.html.

> Nopales with the Americas are under an intense barbed wire rain. The virgins are watching. America is represented by the nopal. The continent is under attack. The barbed wire that cut up our land are [is] still raining upon us. The *virgen* watches. The sun, moon, and flower below are uncertain and uncomfortable with the situation. (May 18–23, 2003, UCSB CEMA COLLECTION)

The policies that the state of California instituted in the decades of the 1980s and 1990s to stem the flow of undocumented migrants streaming into the state forced people to seek other points of entrance to the U.S.A. The increased reinforcement of border patrol agents forced undocumented immigrants to travel east to the state of Arizona. They began moving from the California border to the harsh mountainous terrain and deserts of Arizona. Hundreds of people have perished in the mercilessly, inferno-like desert heat. Migrants get lost, confused, disoriented due to the intense heat and they perish in the searing temperatures of the desert. Many die of heat exhaustion; others lose their lives from dehydration and thirst since they are without water to last them through the entire hazardous journey. In the artwork, the Virgin of Guadalupe is there to protect the migrants but unfortunately even the *Virgin* is unable to help and save some of these unfortunate migrants.

The Virgin of Guadalupe and the streaming barbed wires are two competing images in the unforgiving desert scape. The barbed wires represent the death and suffering of the men, women, and children who tried to cross the mountains and desert, and died on their perilous journey to the Promised Land. The Virgin is a ghostly figure in the background. Nevertheless, she represents hope and is a reassuring figure for the migrants.

Jimenez Underwood does provide a strong sense of optimism through the green of the sturdy, tough cactus plants which dominate the foreground of the painting. The huge, spectacularly green cactus paddles basically covering the lower half of the foreground of the artwork are a metaphor for the tenacity of life even under the most adverse conditions. While "evil," signified by the menacing barbed wire strands falling upon the cactus, the desert plants seem to almost absorb them and in this manner confirm that life conquers all. The cactus might also be seen as representing the heads and upper torso of human beings crossing the desert. The heads and arms seem to provide some type of support and emotional (heads together) sustenance to the migrants crossing the desert.

The American flag and barbed wire series

Figure 7: Consuelo Jimenez Underwood, *Frontera Flag #1, Revolution*, 1993.[17]

In 1993, Jimenez Underwood produced her first "flag merger," *Frontera Flag #1, Revolution*, a work of art incorporating fiber, fabric, barbed wire, and threads. It measured 4' x 6' x 3" (figure 7). It is presently in the Museum of Art and Design in New York City. On the website featuring her work the artist offers insight regarding her creation:

> This was my first flag merger. I thought of myself as the X's stuck between the wire woven fence and the flags as one. Emiliano Zapata heroically blazed the way through this mire and Guadalupe kept shining on. The eagle seems feminine, maternal, the way the land spirit feels. Once borders are crossed, notions of nation are re-evaluated and reset.[18]

The multimedia piece merges the Mexican and U.S.A. flags like a jigsaw puzzle with the different pieces intersecting one another. Each flag has been cut into sections and when assembled they do not offer separate images of each flag, but a totally new flag made from the various fragments. Salient in the composition of *Frontera Flag #1* are the barbed wires across the entire weaving. The barbed wires shapes three large X's running from one side of the reconfigured flag to the opposite side as well as from top to bottom. The barbed wires symbolically encode the rejection of Mexican Americans

17 Fiber, fabric, wire, threads, 4 ft. x 6 ft. x 3 in. Collection of the Museum of Art & Design, New York, NY. http://www.consuelojunderwood.com/frontera-flag-1.html.

18 http://www.consuelojunderwood.com/frontera-flag-1.html.

from both countries and their pain and suffering. In Mexico Chican@s are perceived as no longer Mexican at best, and at times, such as in the 1910–1920s period, traitors for leaving the country (cf. Herrera-Sobek, *Northward Bound*). In the United States, the racial animosity towards "Mexicans" categorizes them as not 100% Americans; as forever aliens, foreigners. Poet Pat Mora eloquently captures these sentiments in her poem, "Legal Alien," "An American to Mexicans/A Mexican to Americans" (Mora 52). The barbed wire depicted as huge X's crosses out, deletes the Mexican American from both countries.

Jimenez Underwood underscores the Chicanos' indigenous roots via the Aztec symbol inscribed in the Mexican flag; that is the serpent devouring the eagle the sign given to the Aztecs to found an empire, as well as the portrayal of the Virgin of Guadalupe, the Mother and Protector of all Mexicans, whether on Mexican soil or not. The eagle devouring a serpent represents the merging of earth (the snake) and sky (the eagle). This was the sign given to the Mexica-Colhua (Aztecs) from their God Huitzilopochtli that in their migration from the North (supposedly the southwestern area of the United States) to the South they were to found a great empire where they spotted an eagle posed on a cactus devouring a serpent. The Aztecs saw the eagle eating the serpent on Lake Texcoco and founded their empire in 1325 A.D. in what later became Tenochtitlán (today Mexico City). The artist does not negate her American heritage and through the American flag prominently displayed in the merging of the two flags she asserts it.

Figure 8: Consuelo Jimenez Underwood, *Home of the Brave* (2013).[19]

19 Fiber, mixed media. Wire, silk, fabric, safety pins, 72 in. x 99 in. Collection of the Artist. http://www.consuelojunderwood.com/home-of-the-brave.html.

Home of the Brave is an ironic title for another of Consuelo Jimenez Underwood's flag merger (figure 8). The weaving features a portion of an American flag to the left. The red and white horizontal bars are woven in bright red and sparkling white threads. On top of the bars is a blue field but the stars are missing. Instead, there is a sprinkling of beautiful small flowers. In the center of the flag is a white vertical section like the white portion of the Mexican flag. The Aztec symbol depicting the migration legend and founding of the Mexica-Colhua Empire is missing. In its place is a circle constructed with barbed wire. Small flowers are dispersed through the white field. On the top right side is a red block representing both the colors of the Mexican and the American flag; it is also representative of the Aztecs. At the bottom right hand corner is a black block representing the Aztec sacred colors of red and black. At the bottom of the flag there are three different indigenous pieces of cloth making the Native American population visibly present in a beautiful manner.

The title, *Home of the Brave*, emanates from the last line of the United States national anthem which ends with the stanza: "In the land of the free/And the home of the brave." The title is ironic because slavery was very much a part of American history, therefore some people were not free at all and the popular perspective towards the "Indians" in the nineteenth century was encapsulated in the saying: "The only good Indian is a dead Indian."[20] Great injustices have been committed against Native Americans and Japanese Americans to name two groups; for example, Japanese Americans were removed from their homes and incarcerated in concentration camps during World War II. With regards to the Mexican people, many believe the War against Mexico in 1846–1848 was an unjust war. The European American population coveted the territory west of the Mississippi River and since Mexico refused to sell the land, war was inevitable. The U.S.A. obtained about one third of Mexican territory including Texas, California, Colorado, Arizona, Utah, New Mexico, Nevada, and parts of Oregon via the terms of the Treaty of Guadalupe Hidalgo in 1848. The flag *Home of the Brave* references the establishment of a border between the U.S.A. and Mexico after the U.S.-Mexico War. The new border is established with a barbed wire that runs from left to right across the woven cloth. The flowers are also divided by the new border but continue to flower and display their beauty in full splendor unimpeded.

20 Cf. Mieder (38–60). Racist saying attributed to General Philip Sheridan (1831–1888).

One Nation Underground

Figure 9: Consuelo Jimenez Underwood, *One Nation Underground* (2013). Fiber, fabric, leather, threads (56" X 90").[21]

The flag from the flag series that bears title *One Nation Underground* (2013) (figure 9). The phrase is taken from the United States' "Pledge of Allegiance" which states toward the end: "One nation under God...." Jimenez Underwood appropriated the phrase and subverted it by changing the ending to read: "One nation underground." Once again, the artist merges both the American flag and the Mexican flag. The American flag is superimposed on the Mexican flag and thus the word "underground" refers to the Chicano population which for many decades was practically invisible or not acknowledged by the hegemonic population. In Jimenez Underwood's flag, the eagle and the serpent are clearly visible through the fabric of the American flag. Running across the American flag is a blue yarn that has been stitched to resemble barbed wire. The "barbed wire" is a representation of the border; it demarcates the divided land – the U.S.A. and Mexico and the new border established in 1848.

Cartography, flowers, barbed wire, and the border

The fourth category of Jimenez Underwood's artwork that I have identified and titled "Cartography, flowers, barbed wire and the border" encompasses a series of maps related to the U.S.-Mexico border and which displays quite prominently the barbed wire icon together with flowers.

21 Fiber, fabric, leather, threads, 56 in. X 90 in. Photography by Bill Apton. Collection of the Artist. http://www.consuelojunderwood.com/one-nation-underground.html.

Figure 10: Consuelo Jimenez Underwood, *Mi Oro, Tu Amor* (1994).[22]

In the artwork titled *Mi Oro, Tu Amor* [My Gold, Your Love] dating from 1994, a representation of an early colonial map of Mexico is rendered in white cotton (figure 10). Numerous strands of barbed wire wrapped in gold fall like an iron curtain from top to bottom. The artwork measures 48" x 51" and the map of a New Spain is rendered in a rich, dark, brown color, the color of chocolate; it symbolically references the dark complexion of the Indigenous and African peoples and stands out clearly behind the barbed wire. New Spain/Mexico and its population are imprisoned behind the bars of the prickly wire. The composition is striking due to the barbed wire that covers the entire rectangle with the barbs sticking out as if they were longitudinal lines. The title articulates the nefarious intentions of the conquering Spaniards in their quest for gold. It is a sad indicator of the uneven relationship between the Indigenous people. *Mi Oro, Tu Amor* perhaps refers to Mexico, a country who "gave" its gold to the Spaniards under threat of death. The title is ambiguous as to its meaning since it could mean "My gold is your love." That is to say, you love my gold. Or it could mean, "I give you my

22 Cotton, barbed wire, gold wire, paint, corn, 48 in. X 51 in. Photography by Curt Fukuda. Collection of the Artist. http://www.consuelojunderwood.com/mi-oro-tu-amor.html.

gold for your love." However, to complicate matters, more beans and corn kernels are present in the weaving and these, in the final analysis, are more valuable than gold since they represent life-giving sustenance. The extraordinary cornucopia of new food products available and indigenous to the new (for the Spaniards and other Europeans) continent, such as potatoes, tomatoes, chocolate, maize, bananas, avocados, and numerous fruits and vegetable is truly astounding.

The barbed wire here is emblematic of the catastrophe the European Conquest brought to the Indians. Furthermore, in resurrecting a map featuring New Spain, it encodes a reminder of the huge territory Mexico lost to the United States after the U.S-Mexico War of 1846–1848. Jimenez Underwood, by using her artistic and creative talent, is able to articulate her message of Indigenous exploitation.

Figure 11: Consuelo Jimenez Underwood, *Undocumented Border X-ings. Xewa (Flower) Time* (2016).[23]

An exhibit at the Textile Museum at George Washington University, in Washington, D.C. that took place April 16, 2016–September 4, 2017, titled "Stories of migration: contemporary artists interpret diaspora"[24] featured 44 textile artists. Among those se-

23 Mixed media wall installation, 27 ft. x 27 ft. x 5 in. The Textile Museum, George Washington University, Washington, DC. http://www.consuelojunderwood.com/undocumented-border-x-ings-xewa-time.html.

24 https://museum.gwu.edu/diaspora.

lected was Jimenez Underwood who designed an installation titled *Undocumented Border X-ings. Xewa (Flower) Time* (2016) (figure 11). The website describes Consuelo Jimenez Underwood's installation in this manner:

> The American Beauty [official flower of D.C.] is hosting her state flower cousins from the borderlands: California poppy, Arizona saguaro, New Mexico yucca, and the Texas bluebonnet. The visiting state flowers have come to Washington, DC, hoping the American Beauty can influence the policy makers that reside in her region. The flowers live on both sides of the U.S./MX border wall. All are undocumented, and are referred to as "illegal aliens." Worse yet, their homelands are becoming wasteland.[25]

The American Beauty rose is the official flower of the District of Columbia according to the website cited above. In Jimenez's Underwood's installation, the beautiful rose covers the entire background of the artistic composition. Surrounding the magnificent rose are the representative flowers from other states: California poppy, Arizona saguaro, New Mexico yucca, and Texas bluebonnet (see website cited above). The flowers are scattered throughout the composition. They seem almost to be bridesmaids paying homage to the central rose dominating the whole installation. The beauty of the flowers contrasts sharply with the barbed wire encircling the installation. In addition, reminiscent of the U.S.-Mexico border are the green rivers, the Potomac and Anacostia traversing the artistic rendering from left to right. This was not done by accident or serendipity but with obvious intentionality given that at the top, above the rivers almost in imperceptible letterings is the 405 San Diego Freeway's CAUTION sign. And also, like ghostly figures, the silhouettes of the three family members featured in the CAUTION sign are barely visible, but definitely there: the father, mother, and the little girl, pigtails flying in the air in their endless pursuit of the elusive American dream. The family is running in a row with the father in front leading his charges from right to left. They are difficult to see but their outlines are done in light green matching the CAUTION sign.

The Indigenous presence is also there since written in very light, almost invisible letters are the languages spoken in the Washington, D.C. area but as the almost invisible letterings indicate, they are a ghostly evidence of their having lived and thrived there before the Europeans appropriated their lands.

Jimenez Underwood makes her point with the ironic title of Undocumented Borders. The flowers as well as animals represented here by the sturgeons which migrate across human borders that are meaningless to the flora and the fauna living there. Nevertheless, walls, fences, and other obstructions dividing the border bring ecological destruction to the natural world of animals and plants that have lived there on eons of years. With the building of a wall, natural habitats are destroyed and the plants and animals succumb to the loss of their environment.

25 http://www.consuelojunderwood.com/undocumented-border-x-ings-xewa-time.html.

Figure 12: Consuelo Jimenez Underwood, *Undocumented Border Flowers: Dia* (2011).[26]

The artist has exhibited other installations with a similar theme. The installation, *Undocumented Border Flowers: Dia*, was featured in a 2011 exhibition, at the Conley Art Gallery, at California State University, Fresno (figure 12). Julia Bradshaw, the curator, wrote in her press release dated August 9, 2011, regarding Jimenez Underwood's work:

> Created specifically for the Conley Art Gallery, the installation *Undocumented Border Flowers: Dia*, is a representation of the ten pairs of sister cities of the U.S./Mexican border and the environmental and political struggle along the border. By using textiles, paint, barbed-wires, and nails, Jimenez Underwood captures the tension and the beauty of the land between these two states. "My art is a combination of land, spirit and struggle," says Jimenez Underwood, "and by weaving historical, social and personal references into my artwork I am representing cultural resistance and spirituality."[27]

In 2005, Jimenez Underwood became interested in doing a performance at the Tijuana-San Isidro Mexican-U.S. border. She elucidates regarding her idea.

26 Mixed media wall installation, 17 ft. x 28 ft. x 6 in. Conley Art Gallery, California State University, Fresno, Fresno, CA. Photography by Julia Bradshaw. http://www.consuelojunderwood.com/undocumented-borderflowersdia.html.

27 http://www.juliabradshaw.com/Consuelo.html.

Figure 13: Consuelo Jimenez Underwood, *Undocumented Tortilla Happening* (2009).[28]

> The "new" border was being referred to as the Tortilla Wall (that lasted only a couple of years). I needed to create a giant tortilla de maize and present it to the border and then offer it to the Mother Ocean as a token of love and mucho respect. On the one hand, I get very angry lamenting the fact that our species (humans) are building such atrocities like this wall, and at the same time I realize with amazement, these are insignificant gestures, the world will last forever.[29]

Jimenez Underwood continued her interest in the tortilla as an icon representative of the indigenous population as well as the Mexican people. In 2009, she constructed an installation titled *Undocumented Tortilla Happening*, incorporating the two icons she has been using in her work: the tortilla and the barbed wire. Jimenez Underwood constructed a beautiful basket made with barbed wire (figure 13). She set the basket on top of a table with an attractive oilcloth fabric tablecloth that is commonly used in working class Mexican restaurants and homes. The "happening" consisted of white "flying" tortillas, as if they were flying saucers and landing on the barbed wire basket. Calling the installation Undocumented Tortilla Happening, the artist cleverly connects flying saucers with the undocumented migrants who are frequently called "illegal aliens." In

28 Mixed media installation, 12 ft. x 7 ft. x 8 ft. 516 Arts, Albuquerque, NM. Photography by Margot Geist. http://www.consuelojunderwood.com/undoc-tort-happening.html.

29 http://www.consuelojunderwood.com/tortilla-meets-tortilla-wall.html.

this case, they are "undocumented" tortillas flying to earth as "aliens." Jimenez Underwood has a biting humor and, together with her artistic sensibilities, make her especially skillful at constructing stunning artwork in her quest for social justice.

Conclusion

Consuelo Jimenez Underwood and her use of barbed wire motif is deployed widely in her work to symbolically express what I call her aesthetic activism regarding the U.S.-Mexico border. Social injustice and inhumane border deportations and other policies have a long historical trajectory in post-1965 Chicana/o art. Rupert García, an artist from California, possibly depicted the first barbed wire artwork in 1972. The art bore the titled *¡Cesen Deportaciones!* [Cease Deportations!] and featured a bloody red background with three strands of large barbed wire strands colored a jet black strung across the canvas (Keller). Other examples abound. In 1981, Malaquías Montoya painted a human being painfully ensnared in the sharp barbs of multiple strands (six) of barbed wire. Written across the canvas from left to right is a single word: "UN-DOCUMENTED" (Keller). Montoya has several works prominently featuring the barbed wire motif: *Abajo con la Migra* (1981), *The Oppressor* (1989), *Christo Campesino* (1990), *Virgen Campesina* (2001), *Migration* (2002), *An Immigrant's Dream, The American Response* (2003), *Tierra Nuestra* (2004).[30]

Other artists that use the barbed wire motif include Adriana Yadira Gallego, *Con Piedras en los Pies, Cruzó* (1998); Daniel Márquez, *Travesía – El Reptil* (1994) and *Travesía con Picos* (1994); Raoul De la Sota, *Solitario* (1999); Luis Jimenez, *Flirting with Death* (1986); and Francisco Delgado, *Libertad* (1998) (cf. Keller).

These artists have incorporated the barbed wire icon within their artistic renditions to express their social protest against unjust immigration policies. Jimenez Underwood falls within this tradition but she has added a new artistic dimension, i.e. weaving barbed wire into her wall hangings as well as incorporating barbed wire within everyday kitchen utensils (the barbed wire tortilla basket).

30 List of some of Malaquías Montoya's artwork featuring the barbed wire icon: "La opresión," Series, 1978; "La Cruzada," silkscreen, 1978; "The Dreamer," Serigraph; "Empujando tinta," poster; "Immigrant's Dream – America's Response". Serigraph, 2004; "Singing my Way to Freedom"; "Abajo con la Migra" ; "Al empezar,"; "Siempre," 1990; "El Mural de Malaquías Montoya en el Colef: "La Historia de Tijuana.; "Remember Chile."

Works cited

Asante M.K., Jr. *It's Bigger than Hip Hop*. New York: St. Martin's Press, 2009. Print.

Bauman, Richard, ed. *Folklore and Culture on the Texas-Mexican Border*. Austin: U of Texas P, 1995. Print.

Campbell, Joseph. *The Hero with a Thousand Faces*. Princeton: Princeton UP, 1973. Print.

García, Juan. *Operation Wetback: The Mass Deportation of Mexican Undocumented Workers*. Westport, Conn.: Praeger Press, 1980. Print.

Herrera-Sobek, María. "Estética activista en la frontera: La narrative de Luis Alberto Urrea y la justicia social en tres obras – *Across the Wire, by the Lake of Sleeping Children, and The Devil's Highway*." *Cruzando fronteras en las Américas: las dinámicas del cambio en la política, la cultura y los medios/Crossing Boundaries in the Américas: Dynamics of Change in Politics,Culture, and Media.* Ed. Lourdes Sofía Mendoza Bohne, Graciela Martínez-Zalce, and Olaf Kaltmeier. Guadalajara: Universidad de Guadalajara, 2015. 252–275. Print.

———. "Border Aesthetics: The Politics of Mexican Immigration in Film and Art." *WHR Western Humanities Review* (Fall 2006): 260–271.

———. *Northward Bound: The Mexican Immigrant Experience in Ballad and Song*. Indiana UP, 1993. Print.

Jimenez Underwood, Consuelo. "An interview with the artist Consuelo Jimenez Underwood." 5 Dec. 2012. Web. https://www.youtube.com/watch?v=j25Z8jzqWo0.

Keller, Gary. *Contemporary Chicano and Chicana Art: Artist, Works, Culture, and Education*. Tempe, Arizona: Bilingual Review Press/Editorial Bilingüe, 2002. Print.

Krell, Alan. *The Devil's Rope. A Cultural History of Barbed Wire*. London, England: Reaktion Books, 2002. Print.

Leal, Luis. *Myths and Legends of Mexico/Mitos y leyendas de México*. Santa Barbara, CA: Chicano Studies Institute, 2002. Print.

Lui, Joanne S. *Barbed Wire: The Fence that Changed the West*. Missoula, MT: Mountain Press, 2009. Print.

Mieder, Wolfgang. "'The Only Good Indian Is a Dead Indian': History and Meaning of a Proverbial Stereotype." *Journal of American Folklore* 106.419 (Winter 1993): 38–60. Print.

Mora, Pat. *Chants*. Houston, TX: Arte Público Press, 1985. Print.

Paredes, Américo. *Uncle Remus: Pero con Chile*. Houston, TX: Arte Público Press. 1993. Print.

———. *"With a Pistol in His Hand:" A Border Ballad and Its Hero*. Austin, TX: U of Texas P, 1958. Print.

Pérez, Laura E. *Chicana Art: The Politics of Spiritual and Aesthetic Altarities*. Durham: Duke UP, 2007. Print.

Razac, Oliver. *Barbed Wire: A Political History*. New York: The New Press, 2000. Print.

Sandoval, Chela. *Methodology of the Oppressed.* Minneapolis, MN: U of Minnesota P, 2000. Print.

Sandoval, Chela, and Guisela Latorre. "Chicana/o Artivism: Judy Baca's Digital Work with Youth of Color." *Learning Race and Ethnicity*. Ed. Dara N. Byrne, Tyrone D. Taborn, Raiford Guins, and Chela Sandoval. Cambridge, MA: MIT Press, 2007. 81–108. Print.

Yorba, Jonathan. *Arte Latino: Treasures from the Smithsonian American Art Museum (Further Treasures from the Smithsonian Museum)*. New York: Watson-Guptill Publications Inc., 2001. Print.

Contributors

Isabel Caldeira is Associate Professor at the Faculty of Letters, Senior Research Fellow of the Center for Social Studies (CES), University of Coimbra, Portugal, and collaborator in the research field "Intersexualities" at the Instituto de Literatura Comparada Margarida Losa (ILCML), University of Porto. She is the president-elect and former member of the Advisory Board of the Inter-American Studies Association; a former President of the Portuguese Association for Anglo-American Studies and former member of the Board of the European Association for American Studies.

Yolanda Minerva Campos García is Research Professor at the University of Guadalajara, México. She teaches in the Social Comunication Department and offers courses on the history of Mexican cinema and on Mexican cinema and literature. Her field of investigation is the history of Mexican cinema, the history of cinema's critical press, and film adaptation. Her current research covers counterculture in Mexico. Since 2009, she has been co-editor of the online journal *fiar: forum for inter-american research.* She is also co-director of *El ojo que piensa. Revista de cine Iberoamericano.*

Juliana Fillies Testa Muñoz majored in Spanish, Portuguese, and Italian at the University of Cologne and has a PhD in Romance Philology. She is currently pursuing a PhD in Spanish (Visual Studies) at Arizona State University. She has worked as a language instructor and has published articles on Brazilian and Cuban literature, identity, representation, and post-colonialism.

Astrid Haas is currently Marie Curie Research Fellow at the Institute of Black Atlantic Research, University of Central Lancashire, UK. Holding a doctorate from the University of Muenster and a postdoctoral degree from Bielefeld University, she taught American Studies at several universities in Germany. Her research covers travel writing, drama, and autobiography, the Black and Latinx Diasporas, Gender and Science Studies. Her current, EU-funded research is entitled "Black Inter-American Mobilities and Autobiography in the Age of Revolutions (1760–1860)."

María Herrera-Sobek is Professor Emerita from the University of California, Santa Barbara where she taught in the Chicana and Chicano Studies Department from 1996–2020. She served as Associate Vice Chancellor for Diversity, Equity, and Inclusion at UCSB from 2002–2020. In addition, she was Visiting Professor at Harvard University and Stanford University. She has received national and international awards and honors throughout her academic career including the Luis Leal Segundo Galardón from HISPA/USA (Spain).

Saskia Hertlein is a post-doctoral researcher and lecturer at the chair of American Literary and Media Studies at the University of Duisburg-Essen, Germany. Her research focuses on critical diversity literacy; literature, culture, and convictions; inter-American perspectives; and literary urban studies.

Olaf Kaltmeier is Professor of Ibero-American History at Bielefeld University and Director of the Maria Sibylla Merian Center for Advanced Latin American Studies (CALAS). He is founding director of the Center for InterAmerican Studies (CIAS) at Bielefeld University. Together with Josef Raab and Sebastian Thies he conducted the ZiF-Research Group "E pluribus unum?." In the context of this research group, he organized the founding conference of the International Association of Inter-American Studies that elected Josef Raab as its president. Furthermore, he organized with Josef Raab and Sebastian Thies the series *Inter-American Studies/Estudios interamericanos* at WVT. He is general editor of the Routledge Handbooks on the Americas, where he edited with Josef Raab the volume *Routledge Handbook on the History and Society of the Americas.*

Luz Angélica Kirschner is Assistant Professor in the School of American and Global Studies at South Dakota State University. She has taught at the University of Wisconsin-Madison, Penn State University, Bielefeld University, Germany, and the University of Guadalajara, Mexico. Her research is located at the intersection of critical race, gender, human rights, and ethnic studies, and focuses on comparative studies from interAmerican and transatlantic perspectives as it explores how identity formation and difference are mediated through literature and aesthetics as well as impacted by contemporary socio-economic manifestations such as neoliberalism and globalization. Her teaching areas include Latina/o Literatures and Studies, Latin American Literatures and Cultures, U.S. Ethnic Literatures, Decolonization, Globalization, Human Rights, Transatlantic Studies, Transnationalism, InterAmerican Studies.

Chris Lippard is Associate Professor and Director of Graduate Studies in the Department of Film and Media Arts at the University of Utah where he teaches Film Studies and writes about migration and border cinemas in the Middle East and the Americas.

Francisco A. Lomelí is Professor Emeritus from the University of California where he worked for over 40 years. Within his two departments (Chicana/o Studies and Spanish & Portuguese), he specialized in Latin American literature (Mexican, Chilean, Central American) and Chicana/o Studies (literature, border studies, theory of the novel, cultural studies, Spanglish). He has published extensively in the two broad areas of study, including translations, film studies, and folklore. He also served as chair of three departments (Chicana/o Studies, Black Studies, and Spanish & Portuguese) plus as director of the Education Abroad Programs (Costa Rica, Chile, and Argentina). He was elected to the North American Academy of the Spanish Language in 2016.

Marietta Messmer is Associate Professor of American Studies at the University of Groningen (The Netherlands). She has published widely on political and cultural relations between the U.S. and Mexico, Mexican and Central American migration to the U.S., violence in the U.S.-Mexican borderlands, as well as theoretical debates on citizenship, integration, and the rights of cultural and ethnic minorities. One of her current research projects focuses on a comparative study of the U.S.'s and the European Union's ways of outsourcing and privatizing immigration control measures and the social, economic, legal, and ethical consequences this has for migrants and refugees as well as for transit countries like Mexico, Libya, and Turkey. A second project explores the negotiation of gendered forms of power by female leaders in the narco business. Messmer is managing editor of the peer-reviewed book series *Interamericana,* devoted to publications on the literatures, cultures, and societies of North, Central, and South America, published by Peter Lang. Messmer served as president of the Netherlands American Studies Association (2011–2014), as Dutch representative on the Board of the European Association for American Studies (2009–2016) and is current vice president of the International American Studies Association (since 2019).

Gabriele Pisarz-Ramirez is Professor of American Studies and Minority Studies at Leipzig University. Her areas of research include the literatures and cultures of U.S. ethnic minorities, early American hemispheric studies, and the study of the U.S. South in a circum-Caribbean context. Currently, she is working within the Collaborative Research Centre *Processes of Spatialization under the Global Condition* at Leipzig University on a project focusing on "Imperialist Geographies: Transpacific and Circum-Caribbean Spaces in U.S. Literature 1880–1940."

Josef Raab was Professor of North American Literary and Media Studies at the University of Duisburg-Essen in Germany. His research focused on literatures of the Americas, film, television, ethnicity, borders, interculturalism, and U.S. Latina/o studies. He was Founding President of the International Association of Inter-American Studies. Josef Raab passed away on November 10, 2019 at the age of 59.

Wilfried Raussert is Professor of North American and InterAmerican Studies at Bielefeld University. He is co-founder of the Center for InterAmerican Studies and the co-founder of the Black Americas Network at Bielefeld University. He is the director of the International Association of Inter-American Studies and general editor of *fiar forum for inter-american research*. He was chair of the Federal Ministry of Education and Research Project Entangled Americas (2013–2019) and representative of the International Committee of the American Studies Association (2015–2018). Since 2019, he has been a member of the Comité Directivo of the Center for Advanced Latin American Studies CALAS Bielefeld-Guadalajara.

Stefan Rinke is Professor of History at the Institute of Latin American Studies and the Friedrich-Meinecke-Institute of Freie Universität Berlin. Since 2009, he has been the director of the first German-Latin American International Research Training Group, a doctoral program with El Colegio de México, UNAM, and CIESAS. In 2017, the Mexican Academy of Sciences and the Consejo Nacional de Ciencias y Tecnología honored him with the Premio Alzate for his lifetime work.

Clara E. Rodríguez is Professor of Sociology at Fordham University's College at Lincoln Center. She is the author of numerous books and articles. She is also the recipient of numerous research and teaching awards, including the American Sociological Association's Award for Distinguished Contributions to Research in the Field of Latina/o Studies, her university's Award for Distinguished Teaching in the Social Sciences, a Centennial Historian of the City of New York, and she was designated a "Distinguished Lecturer" by the Organization of American Historians. She has been visiting professor at Columbia University, MIT, and Yale University, visiting scholar at the Russell Sage Foundation, and senior fellow at the Smithsonian Institution's National Museum of American History. She has also been a consultant to a number of television shows and documentaries, including "Dora, the Explorer" and "Sesame Street."

Annette L. Rukwied's extensive research on Latino/a film festivals in the U.S. and Latino/a cinema included stays as visiting scholar at the University of California-Los Angeles' Chicano Studies Research Center (2009, 2010), the participation at the Flaherty Seminar 2009 (Colgate University), and fieldwork at a number of Latino/a film festivals in California (2009–2012). At Bielefeld University, she was a research fellow for the SFB 584 (2008–2012) and an associated fellow of the interAmerican research group headed by Prof. Dr. Josef Raab, Prof. Dr. Olaf Kaltmeier, and Prof. Dr. Sebastian Thies, at the Center for Interdisciplinary Research (ZiF; 2008/2009). Her PhD thesis, *Protest, Pitching, and Crossover Dreaming: Californian Latino/a Film Festivals and their Promotion of Latinidad*, Bielefeld University 2019, advised by Prof. Dr. Wilfried Raussert, Bielefeld, and Prof. Dr. Sebastian Thies, Tübingen, is currently reviewed for publication. She works as a Lehrkraft für besondere Aufgaben (LfbA) at Bielefeld University's English Department.

Inter-American Studies
Cultures – Societies – History

Estudios Interamericanos
Culturas – Sociedades – Historia

This interdisciplinary series examines national and transnational issues in the cultures, societies, and histories of the Americas. It creates a forum for a critical academic dialogue between North and South, promoting an inter-American paradigm that shifts the scholarly focus from methodological nationalism to the wider context of the Western Hemisphere.

Vol. 1
Raab, Josef, Sebastian Thies, and Daniela Noll-Opitz, eds. *Screening the Americas: Narration of Nation in Documentary Film / Proyectando las Américas: Narración de la nación en el cine documental.* 2011. 470 pp.

WVT Wissenschaftlicher Verlag Trier	ISBN 978-3-86821-331-7	€ 29,50
Bilingual Press / Editorial Bilingüe	ISBN 978-1-931010-83-2	$ 29.50

Vol. 2
Raussert, Wilfried, and Michelle Habell-Pallán, eds. *Cornbread and Cuchifritos: Ethnic Identity Politics, Transnationalization, and Transculturation in American Urban Popular Music.* 2011. 292 pp.

WVT Wissenschaftlicher Verlag Trier	ISBN 978-3-86821-265-5	€ 29,50
Bilingual Press / Editorial Bilingüe	ISBN 978- 1-931010-80-1	$ 29.50

Vol. 3
Butler, Martin, Jens Martin Gurr, and Olaf Kaltmeier, eds. *EthniCities: Metropolitan Cultures and Ethnic Identities in the Americas.* 2011. 268 pp.

WVT Wissenschaftlicher Verlag Trier	ISBN 978-3-86821-310-2	€ 29,50
Bilingual Press / Editorial Bilingüe	ISBN 978-1-931010-81-8	$ 29.50

Vol. 4
Gurr, Jens Martin, and Wilfried Raussert, eds. *Cityscapes in the Americas and Beyond: Representations of Urban Complexity in Literature and Film.* 2011. 300 pp.

WVT Wissenschaftlicher Verlag Trier	ISBN 978-3-86821-324-9	€ 29,50
Bilingual Press / Editorial Bilingüe	ISBN 978-1-931010-82-5	$ 29.50

Vol. 5

Kirschner, Luz Angélica, ed. *Expanding* Latinidad*: An Inter-American Perspective*. 2012. 292 pp.

WVT Wissenschaftlicher Verlag Trier	ISBN 978-3-86821-309-6	€ 29,50
Bilingual Press / Editorial Bilingüe	ISBN 978-1-931010-84-9	$ 29.50

Vol. 6

Raussert, Wilfried, and Graciela Martínez-Zalce, eds. *(Re)Discovering 'America': Road Movies and Other Travel Narratives in North America / (Re)Descubriendo 'América': Road movie y otras narrativas de viaje en América del Norte*. 2012. 252 pp.

WVT Wissenschaftlicher Verlag Trier	ISBN 978-3-86821-384-3	€ 29,50
Bilingual Press / Editorial Bilingüe	ISBN 978-1-931010-91-7	$ 29.50

Vol. 7

Kaltmeier, Olaf, ed. *Transnational Americas: Envisioning Inter-American Area Studies in Globalization Processes*. 2013. 278 pp.

WVT Wissenschaftlicher Verlag Trier	ISBN 978-3-86821-415-4	€ 29,50
Bilingual Press / Editorial Bilingüe	ISBN 978-1-931010-92-4	$ 29.50

Vol. 8

Raab, Josef, and Alexander Greiffenstern, eds. *Interculturalism in North America: Canada, the United States, Mexico, and Beyond*. 2013. 312 pp.

WVT Wissenschaftlicher Verlag Trier	ISBN 978-3-86821-460-4	€ 29,50
Bilingual Press / Editorial Bilingüe	ISBN 978-1-931010-99-3	$ 29.50

Vol. 9

Raab, Josef, ed. *New World Colors: Ethnicity, Belonging, and Difference in the Americas*. 2014. 418 pp.

WVT Wissenschaftlicher Verlag Trier	ISBN 978-3-86821-461-1	€ 29,50
Bilingual Press / Editorial Bilingüe	ISBN 978-1-939743-00-8	$ 39.50

Vol. 10

Roth, Julia. *Occidental Readings, Decolonial Practices: A Selection on Gender, Genre, and Coloniality in the Americas*. 2014. 284 pp.

WVT Wissenschaftlicher Verlag Trier	ISBN 978-3-86821-446-8	€ 26,50
Bilingual Press / Editorial Bilingüe	ISBN 978-1-939743-07-7	$ 32.50

Vol. 11

Thies, Sebastian, Gabriele Pisarz-Ramirez, and Luzelena Gutiérrez de Velasco, eds. *Of Fatherlands and Motherlands: Gender and Nation in the Americas / De Patrias y Matrias: Género y nación en las Américas*. 2015. 344 pp.

WVT Wissenschaftlicher Verlag Trier	ISBN 978-3-86821-528-1	€ 29,50
Bilingual Press / Editorial Bilingüe	ISBN 978-1-939743-08-4	$ 39.50

Vol. 12

Fuchs, Rebecca. *Caribbeanness as a Global Phenomenon: Junot Díaz, Edwidge Danticat, and Cristina García*. 2014. 298 pp.

WVT Wissenschaftlicher Verlag Trier	ISBN 978-3-86821-533-5	€ 26,50
Bilingual Press / Editorial Bilingüe	ISBN 978-1-939743-09-1	$ 32.50

Vol. 13

Andres, Julia. *¡Cuéntame algo! – Chicana Narrative Beyond the Borderlands*. 2015. 202 pp.

WVT Wissenschaftlicher Verlag Trier	ISBN 978-3-86821-569-4	€ 25,00
Bilingual Press / Editorial Bilingüe	ISBN 978-1-939743-11-4	$ 28.50

Vol. 14

Hertlein, Saskia. *Tales of Transformation: Emerging Adulthood, Migration, and Ethnicity in Contemporary American Literature*. 2014. 228 pp.

WVT Wissenschaftlicher Verlag Trier	ISBN 978-3-86821-570-0	€ 25,00
Bilingual Press / Editorial Bilingüe	ISBN 978-1-939743-10-7	$ 31.50

Vol. 15

Raab, Josef, and Saskia Hertlein, eds. *Spaces – Communities – Discourses: Charting Identity and Belonging in the Americas*. 2016. 382 pp.

WVT Wissenschaftlicher Verlag Trier	ISBN 978-3-86821-590-8	€ 29,50
Bilingual Press / Editorial Bilingüe	ISBN 978-1-939743-13-8	$ 39.50

Vol. 16

Mehring, Frank, ed. *The Mexico Diary: Winold Reiss between Vogue Mexico and Harlem Renaissance. An Illustrated Trilingual Edition with Commentary and Musical Interpretation* (includes color plates and audio CD). 2016. 244 pp.

WVT Wissenschaftlicher Verlag Trier	ISBN 978-3-86821-594-6	€ 29,50
Bilingual Press / Editorial Bilingüe	ISBN 978-1-939743-14-5	$ 39.50

Vol. 17

Raussert, Wilfried, Brian Rozema, Yolanda Campos, and Marius Littschwager, eds. *Key Tropes in Inter-American Studies: Perspectives from the* forum for inter-american research (fiar). 2015. 374 pp.

WVT Wissenschaftlicher Verlag Trier	ISBN 978-3-86821-627-1	€ 29,50
Bilingual Press / Editorial Bilingüe	ISBN 978-1-939743-16-9	$ 39.50

Vol. 19

Rehm, Lukas, Jochen Kemner, and Olaf Kaltmeier, eds. *Politics of Entanglement in the Americas: Connecting Transnational Flows and Local Perspectives*. 2017. 226 pp.

WVT Wissenschaftlicher Verlag Trier	ISBN 978-3-86821-675-2	€ 27,50
Bilingual Press / Editorial Bilingüe	ISBN 978-1-939743-17-6	$ 32.50

Vol. 20
Britt Arredondo, Christopher. *Imperial Idiocy: A Reflection on Forced Displacement in the Americas*. 2017. 194 pp.

WVT Wissenschaftlicher Verlag Trier	ISBN 978-3-86821-706-3	€ 26,50
Bilingual Press / Editorial Bilingüe	ISBN 978-1-939743-20-6	$ 30.00

Vol. 21
Schemien, Alexia. *Of Virgins, Curanderas, and Wrestler Saints: Un/Doing Religion in Contemporary Mexican American Literature*. 2018. 218 pp.

WVT Wissenschaftlicher Verlag Trier	ISBN 978-3-86821-724-7	€ 27,50
Bilingual Press / Editorial Bilingüe	ISBN 978-1-939743-22-0	$ 32.50

Vol. 22
Fulger, Maria Diana. *The Cuban Post-Socialist Exotic: Contemporary U.S. American Travel Narratives about Cuba.* 2020. 266 pp.

WVT Wissenschaftlicher Verlag Trier	ISBN 978-3-86821-769-8	€ 32,50
Bilingual Press / Editorial Bilingüe	ISBN 978-1-939743-27-5	$ 36.00

Vol. 24
Kaltmeier, Olaf, Mirko Petersen, Wilfried Raussert, and Julia Roth, eds. *Cherishing the Past, Envisioning the Future. Entangled Practises of Heritage and Utopia in the Americas.* 2021. 176 pp.

WVT Wissenschaftlicher Verlag Trier	ISBN 978-3-86821-804-6	€ 23,50
UNO University of New Orleans Press	ISBN 978-1-60801-206-0	$ 27.50

Vol. 26
Raussert, Wilfried. *'What's Going On': How Music Shapes the Social.* 2021. 224 pp.

WVT Wissenschaftlicher Verlag Trier	ISBN 978-3-86821-811-4	€ 28,50
UNO University of New Orleans Press	ISBN 978-1-60801-199-5	$ 34.00

Vol. 27
Frank-Job, Barbara. *Immigration as a Process: Temporality Concepts in Blogs of Latin American Immigrants to Québec.* 2021. 138 pp.

WVT Wissenschaftlicher Verlag Trier	ISBN 978-3-86821-820-6	€ 20,00
UNO University of New Orleans Press	ISBN 978-1-60801-215-2	$ 24.00

Vol. 28
Roth, Julia. *Can Feminism Trump Populism? Right-Wing Trends and Intersectional Contestations in the Americas.* 2021. 168 pp.

WVT Wissenschaftlicher Verlag Trier	ISBN 978-3-86821-821-3	€ 23,00
UNO University of New Orleans Press	ISBN 978-1-60801-205-3	$ 26.00

Vol. 30
Buitrago Valencia, Clara. *Missionaries: Migrants or Expatriates? Guatemalan Pentecostal Leaders in Los Angeles.* 2021. 236 pp.
WVT Wissenschaftlicher Verlag Trier ISBN 978-3-86821-818-3 € 28,50
UNO University of New Orleans Press ISBN 978-1-60801-210-7 $ 34.50

Vol. 31
Schwabe, Nicole. *De-Centering History Education: Creating Knowledge of Global Entanglements.* 2021. 92 pp.
WVT Wissenschaftlicher Verlag Trier ISBN 978-3-86821-828-2 € 18,00
UNO University of New Orleans Press ISBN 978-1-60801-214-5 $ 21.00

Vol. 32
Manke, Albert. *Coping with Discrimination and Exclusion. Experiences of Free Chinese Migrants in the Americas in a Transregional and Diachronic Perspective.* 2021. 162 pp.
WVT Wissenschaftlicher Verlag Trier ISBN 978-3-86821-829-9 € 23,00
UNO University of New Orleans Press ISBN 978-1-60801-207-7 $ 27.00

Vol. 33
Rohland, Eleonora. *Entangled Histories and the Environment? Socio-Environmental Transformations in the Caribbean, 1492-1800.* 2021. 92 pp.
WVT Wissenschaftlicher Verlag Trier ISBN 978-3-86821-833-6 € 18,00
UNO University of New Orleans Press ISBN 978-1-60801-208-4 $ 21.00

Vol. 34
Kaltmeier, Olaf. *National Parks from North to South. An Entangled History of Conservation and Colonization in Argentina.* 2021. 208 pp.
WVT Wissenschaftlicher Verlag Trier ISBN 978-3-86821-834-3 € 27,50
UNO University of New Orleans Press ISBN 978-1-60801-204-6 $ 32.50

Vol. 35
Raussert, Wilfried. *Off the Grid. Art Practices and Public Space.* 2021. 232 pp.
WVT Wissenschaftlicher Verlag Trier ISBN 978-3-86821-835-0 € 29,50
UNO University of New Orleans Press ISBN 978-1-60801-213-8 $ 34.50

Vol. 36
Ravasio, Paola. *This Train Is Not Bound to Glory. A Study of Literary Trainscapes.* 2021. 114 pp.
WVT Wissenschaftlicher Verlag Trier ISBN 978-3-86821-836-7 € 18,00
UNO University of New Orleans Press ISBN 978-1-60801-216-9 $ 21.00

Vol. 37

Schäfer, Heinrich Wilhelm. *Protestant 'Sects' and the Spirit of (Anti-)Imperialism. Religious Entanglements in the Americas.* 2021. 242 pp.

WVT Wissenschaftlicher Verlag Trier	ISBN 978-3-86821-855-9	€ 29,50
UNO University of New Orleans Press	ISBN 978-1-60801-209-1	$ 34.50